This book is dedicated to my parents,
William and Eileen,
who taught me that everything is possible if you rise to the challenge.

With thanks to Nic for his patience,
Alex for his support,
and Erik for choosing me to give a voice to his artwork.
It's been totally awesome.

About the Author

Kim Huggens has been studying Tarot since the age of nine, and is the co-author of *Sol Invictus: The God Tarot* (Schiffer Publications, 2007) and the in-progress companion deck *Pistis Sophia: The Goddess Tarot*. She lives in Cardiff, Wales, where she works as a veterinary receptionist part-time to fund her university studies in Ancient History. She moved to Cardiff in 2002 for her undergraduate degree in Philosophy, and also graduated with an MA in Religion in Late Antiquity from Cardiff University in 2007. Kim has given numerous talks and workshops on the subject of Tarot, divination, Paganism, and mythology in the UK, and regularly runs Tarot courses. She is a practicing Vodouisante and Thelemite, and a member of the OTO. She lives with her partner and cat, and in her spare time plays Call of Cthulu and Dungeons and Dragons, writes short fiction, goes for walks in graveyards and wishes she could translate Sumerian.

To Write to the Author

If you wish to contact the author or would like more information about this book, please write to the author in care of Llewellyn Worldwide Ltd. and we will forward your request. Both the author and publisher appreciate hearing from you and learning of your enjoyment of this book and how it has helped you. Llewellyn Worldwide Ltd. cannot guarantee that every letter written to the author can be answered, but all will be forwarded. Please write to:

Kim Huggens
℅ Llewellyn Worldwide
2143 Wooddale Drive)
Woodbury, MN 55125-2989
Please enclose a self-addressed stamped envelope for reply,
or $1.00 to cover costs. If outside the U.S.A., enclose
an international postal reply coupon.

Many of Llewellyn's authors have websites with additional information and resources. For more information, please visit our website at http://www.llewellyn.com

The Complete Guide to
Tarot Illuminati

Kim Huggens

Llewellyn Publications
Woodbury, Minnesota

FIRST EDITION
Fourth Printing, 2022

Cover design by Ellen Lawson

Llewellyn is a registered trademark of Llewellyn Worldwide Ltd.

Library of Congress Cataloging-in-Publication Data
ISBN: 9780738738765

Llewellyn Worldwide Ltd. does not participate in, endorse, or have any authority or responsibility concerning private business transactions between our authors and the public.

All mail addressed to the author is forwarded but the publisher cannot, unless specifically instructed by the author, give out an address or phone number.

Any Internet references contained in this work are current at publication time, but the publisher cannot guarantee that a specific location will continue to be maintained. Please refer to the publisher's website for links to authors' websites and other sources.

Llewellyn Publications
Llewellyn Worldwide Ltd.
2143 Wooddale Drive
Woodbury, MN 55125
www.llewellyn.com

Manufactured in the United States of America

Contents

by Pamela Steele

Erik C. Dunne's "Queen of Swords" appeared on Facebook in late autumn 2011, courtesy of one of the tarot groups. Within minutes, the single elegant image had dozens of fans. I was beyond impressed! Then the artist in me simply had to know if this artist was really this good, and if there were more of these amazing tarot images. Following the cyber breadcrumb trail didn't take long. After viewing his online portfolio, I knew it was pure talent and mastery that had created these breathtaking images, and I was witnessing the birth of a star.

Growing up in a home where both parents were accomplished artists afforded Erik, along with his siblings, the incomparable opportunity to learn from masters. Blending dance, theatre, and travel into the mix yielded a solid appreciation for and experience of artistic creativity that allowed Erik to master several art mediums himself. He was working as a freelance illustrator and designer when, a little over three years ago, the time and opportunity presented itself and he began the series of artworks that would become the Tarot Illuminati.

Erik actually began his tarot journey more than twenty-five years ago when he wandered into a small metaphysical shop—supposedly by chance, but we know tarot doesn't work that way. The owner and Erik quickly became good friends. Soon after, Erik was introduced to the cards and encouraged to pursue a higher understanding of them by his new mentor. Studying and reading with the Rider Waite Smith Tarot, the Aquarian, and the Medieval Scapini gave Erik an introduction to the mysteries and unveiled the inner light of tarot. But as an artist, Erik's own visions of truth and illumination were soon being superimposed over the traditional images. Inevitably, his passion and his love of art and tarot merged and inspiration tackled him like a pro wrestler. He began his tarot creation with the Queen of Swords, trusting the process and allowing the queen to lead.

Creating a tarot deck is not unlike giving birth. Each image draws upon the innermost core of the artist and creator. The artist lives each picture with a totality that encompasses his or her entire being. Every hope, dream, desire, hate, love, and fear is laid bare for all the world to see. And although at times part of your psyche would love to run away screaming and hide in a dark secret place, the need to bring the vision into reality is comparable with the need to breathe. You face your fears. You conquer your demons. You pour your very soul into each and every image. When the deck is complete, it takes its first breath and you realize what you have created is now a living entity. From here on, you can nurture, guide, and protect what you've created, but you cannot control it. The spirit of your creation will choose its own destiny. Its purpose is to bring salvation to the damned, light to the darkness, and beauty to the unspeakable. As the artist, you can finally sit back, take a deep breath, and watch that destiny unfold.

Blending cultures, eras, fantasies, and truths, the seventy-eight-card Tarot Illuminati represents the infinite diversity of human and spiritual experience. Those familiar with tarot will see a Rider-Waite-Smith influence, but it would be inaccurate to refer to this deck as merely a clone. As I wrote this preface, I consulted my eighty-eight-card Steele Wizard Tarot for insights. Ironically, the cards that came up were all additions to the traditional seventy-eight-card decks, which tells me this tarot can and will help you access your inner divinity, going beyond the boundaries of duality. Here's what the cards told me:

- The first card is Soul Twins. It speaks of embracing the shadows and denying yourself nothing. Here is where we accept everything about ourselves, leaving no part hidden. We suspend ego and judgment to allow Spirit full partnership in our lives. The Tarot Illuminati is designed to speak to the shadows as well as the light and accepts all parts of self as valid. The road to wholeness includes all. Sometimes it's necessary for our Inner Warrior to protect and defend. Life is not all sweetness and light, so acceptance of our dark side is imperative. How we express ourselves, what actions we choose to take—that is how we define ourselves.

- Next is the Maiden of Wands, who shows the as-yet-unrealized potential. Within and without, the potential for growth and energy is boundless. She shows untried methods and the potential to endow yourself with the true power of attraction. She is telling us this new tarot has untapped resources that are ours for the taking—if we are willing.

- The final card is Truth—but not the truth you were taught nor the one given to you. This card tells us to take everything we thought was true and examine the core of our beliefs. Disassemble the matrix and see beyond the illusion. What we do for ourselves, we do for the whole of creation. The Tarot Illuminati is a gift beyond measure that contains eternal truths. Will we listen?

As with each new creation, it became apparent this one would need a name, which Erik struggled with for quite some time. Although there is nothing wrong with calling it "Erik's Awesome Tarot," it does lack a certain zing, not to mention originality. After considering and discarding several ideas, he came to understand that the name, like the art, would be inspired. And so it was. A middle-of-the-night epiphany sat Erik bolt upright in bed uttering, "Tarot Illuminati," with the full understanding that the name was not about secret societies, decoder rings, or Dan Brown novels. "Illuminati" is the Light of Wisdom that shines throughout in this deck.

As Erik neared completion of the artwork, the author who was to write the companion book suddenly became unavailable. As he experienced understandable panic, he posted his dilemma on Facebook. It was no surprise, to me anyway, when offers to write the companion book began to pour in from a wide variety of talented tarot authors. One of them, Kim Huggens, has an impressive career and her passion for tarot and art is legendary in the tarot community. In short, Kim is the perfect fit. This lovely lady donned her metaphorical armor, saddled her metaphysical charger, and took on the daunting task of writing an entire companion book with a deadline of weeks rather than months. The words that follow in this book come from Kim's wellspring of talent and experience, which I am sure will enlighten and delight all who read them.

To sum it up, I have had the honor and privilege of watching this amazing tarot grow into being. It is my hope and wish to see Erik's Tarot Illuminati take its place in the upper echelon of Great Tarot Decks.

With grace and gratitude,

Pamela Steele

Steele Wizard Tarot www.steelewizard.com

Wizard's Pets Tarot www.wizardspets.com

Introduction

For centuries now, tarot cards have been used for fortune-telling and future-seeking, transmitting occult wisdom and teaching sacred knowledge. Without fail, its use by a sincere seeker results in flashes of realization or awakening, new knowledge gained, or "Aha!" moments. Thus, using the tarot is primarily an act of searching for illumination or revelation—answers from within the self and from outside the self. The Tarot Illuminati aims to reveal the intricate and beautiful layers of symbolism contained within the traditional Rider-Waite-Smith tarot structure so that the reader can more easily understand the cards. Symbolism is found everywhere, and we learn to govern our lives by interpreting it, from the colour red that tells us to stop at a traffic light, to the thumbs-up gesture that informs us everything is okay. Tarot images are filled with such symbolism, and in the Tarot Illuminati every detail is meaningful, each scene a rich and sumptuous tapestry of colour, action, expressions, and nature. The vivid artwork floods the senses with the essence of each card so that the associated meanings or concepts are almost tangible. You are invited to interact with the cards as if they were friends and allies, enemies and strangers, family members and professional associates; these cards represent real-world human emotions, problems, fears, hopes, and actions, and we must therefore be able to relate to them on a personal level. Every card of the Tarot Illuminati speaks to you, as if you have just walked into its world, and offers you its hand to draw you into its mysteries, so that not only might you read the cards, but you also might gain revelation of your self.

Light and the Tarot Illuminati

In essence, the Tarot Illuminati contains within it the light of illumination, realization, and truth, made dynamic and interactive through image and symbolism. Each card is like a stained-glass window in a church, depicting a meaningful tale and passing down age-old wisdom, brought to life by the light of the sun.

Light plays an important role in the card images of the Tarot Illuminati. It represents God, the divine, the light of truth, attainable wisdom or awareness. In spiritual terms, light—particularly sunlight—is a representation of our divine origin as well as the final goal of our spiritual growth: en-light-enment. Whether it is depicted in the form of the sun, the moon, the stars, a lantern, or a fire, you will find that the Tarot Illuminati's symbolism of light tells a story of revelation, illumination, and the journey toward consciousness and understanding.

The Title "Illuminati"

The Tarot Illuminati is not related in any way to the secret society known as the Illuminati, neither its historical Bavarian manifestation nor the modern idea of a clandestine organization that somehow controls the world. It only shares with the Illuminati the idea of illumination and the origin of the name, from the Latin *illuminatus*, meaning "enlightened." The title also conveys the aesthetics of the deck's images, filled as they are with light.

Using This Book

It is likely that you have already read the shorter companion book that is available with the set edition of the Tarot Illuminati. This book is an extension of what is introduced there, with the images and symbolism of each card revealed and explored in an in-depth manner. In the introduction sections to each part of the tarot deck, and in part 4, "Using the Tarot Illuminati," you will find hands-on exercises, practices, and spreads designed to help you learn more about the cards on a personal level, as well as explore their traditional symbolism and associations. These exercises are called "Making Light Work," since they are designed to help convey the more intricate or occult associations of the cards, and to help you integrate an understanding of the cards into your own life.

Use This Book in Conjunction With …

The Tarot Illuminati is a deck that is so full of beauty and symbolism, whilst remaining faithful to traditional tarot imagery, that it lends itself well to in-depth study. You might find that any of the following books form excellent further reading for your studies with the Tarot Illuminati.

Tarot 101: Mastering the Art of Reading the Cards by Kim Huggens (Woodbury, MN: Llewellyn, 2010).

Around the Tarot in 78 Days: A Personal Journey Through the Cards by Marcus Katz and Tali Goodwin (Woodbury, MN: Llewellyn, 2012).

Tarot Face to Face: Using the Cards in Your Everyday Life by Marcus Katz and Tali Goodwin (Woodbury, MN: Llewellyn, 2012).

Tarot Wisdom: Spiritual Teachings and Deeper Meanings by Rachel Pollack (Woodbury, MN: Llewellyn, 2008).

Tarot and the Tree of Life: Finding Everyday Wisdom in the Minor Arcana by Isabel Kliegman (Wheaton, IL: Quest Books, 1997).

The Pictorial Key to the Tarot by Arthur Edward Waite (Mineola, NY: Dover Publications, 2005).

The Tarot: History, Symbolism and Divination by Robert Place (New York: Jeremy P. Tarcher, 2005).

21 Ways to Read a Tarot Card by Mary K. Greer (Woodbury, MN: Llewellyn, 2006).

Tarot and Astrology: Enhance your Readings with the Wisdom of the Zodiac by Corrine Kenner (Woodbury, MN: Llewellyn, 2011).

The Tarot Court Cards: Archetypal Patterns of Relationship in the Minor Arcana by Kate Warwick-Smith (Rochester, VT: Destiny Books, 2003).

Tarot Spreads: Layouts and Techniques to Empower Your Readings by Barbara Moore (Woodbury, MN: Llewellyn, 2012).

The Major Arcana: Emanations of the Light

The twenty-two cards of the major arcana are the most recognizable of the tarot. They deal with the "big" concepts of life, such as love, loss, death and rebirth, self-mastery, life journeys, changes and transition, and more. They are the greater themes of our lives, the major transformations we go through, as well as the spiritual truths that make up the universe. Taken as a set, they can be seen as the soul's journey toward illumination.

Astrology in the Major Arcana

Astrology is one of the main systems of symbolism embedded in the major arcana. You can see it hidden (or not so hidden!) in the images of the Tarot Illuminati as helpful hints, and it is a useful exercise to do some brief research about what the astrological associations represent, and what they mean for any given card. Here is a quick "cheat sheet" for those associations.

The Fool Uranus / **The Alchemist** Mercury / **The High Priestess** The Moon / **The Empress** Venus / **The Emperor** Aries / **The Hierophant** Taurus / **The Lovers** Gemini / **The Chariot** Cancer / **Strength** Leo / **The Hermit** Virgo / **The Wheel of Fortune** Jupiter / **Justice** Libra / **The Hanged Man** Neptune / **Death** Scorpio / **Temperance** Sagittarius / **The Devil** Capricorn / **The Tower** Mars / **The Star** Aquarius / **The Moon** Pisces / **The Sun** The Sun / **Judgement** Pluto / **The World** Saturn

Aries The sign of the ram: the headstrong leader, fiery and masculine, forceful and ambitious.

Taurus The sign of the bull: earthy, stubborn, and practical, who enjoys possessions and stability.

Gemini The sign of the twins: separation and union, intelligence and quick wit, communication.

Cancer The sign of the crab: the home and security, nurturing and caring, protective.

Leo The sign of the lion: power, strength, confidence, creativity, and the self.

Virgo The sign of the prudent virgin: secure and industrious, down-to-earth and wise.

Libra The sign of the scales: equilibrium, fairness, justice, balance, and partnerships.

Scorpio The sign of the scorpion: inner darkness and mystery, sex, death, and transformation.

Sagittarius The sign of the archer: teacher, philosopher, explorer, and trailblazer.

Capricorn The sign of the goat: self-focused, ambitious, moving up above others.

Aquarius The sign of the water-bearer: peace, harmony, healing, and the New Age.

Pisces The sign of the fishes: inner changes, emotional depth, dreams and intuition.

The Sun The planet of happiness, truth, optimism, and spiritual light. Ruler of and associated with Leo.

The Moon The planet of psychic activity, intuition, silence, mystery, and inner wisdom. Ruler of and associated with Cancer.

Mercury The swift planet of the mind, communication, trickery, and messages between heaven and earth. Ruler of and associated with Gemini and Virgo.

Venus The planet of love, beauty, sensuality, womanhood, and fertility; the Roman goddess of love. Ruler of and associated with Taurus and Libra.

Mars The planet of war and destruction, action and aggression; in Roman myth, the god of war. Ruler of and associated with Aries.

Jupiter The planet of mirth, jovial movement, and expansion; in control of fortune and luck. Ruler of and associated with Sagittarius.

Saturn The planet of cycles, endings, and time. Ruler of and associated with Capricorn.

Uranus The planet of chaos and formlessness; in Greek myth, the primal god of the heavens. Ruler of and associated with Aquarius.

Neptune The planet of water and depth, illusion and creativity; in Roman myth, the god of the sea. Ruler of and associated with Pisces.

Pluto The planet of death and rebirth, hidden truths and secrets. Ruler of and associated with Scorpio.

Making Light Work 1

Examine each card of the Tarot Illuminati's major arcana. Using your knowledge of (or research into) the planets and zodiac signs, look for symbols of these astrological associations in the card images and think about what these associations mean in the context of each card. Some associations will have more layers than others, and some may seem puzzling at first. If you like, make notes to use as handy reminders.

Making Light Work 2

Despite the major arcana containing many abstract and lofty principles, you can approach them on a personal level using just a little imagination. Try interacting with the symbols and images on each of the major arcana card by letting not only the figures on the cards speak to you, but also their companion animals, tools and props, and surroundings.

1. Choose a card from the major arcana that you wish to study.
2. Examine all its symbols closely, and focus on a few of the most prominent (or interesting!) ones.
3. Note these symbols down and start considering them in light of what they mean for the card. Why are they there? What do they represent? Do they support other symbols? Do they contradict other symbols?
4. Try to get down to a core meaning of that symbol in the context of that card. For example, the stars on the Star might mean many different things, but for this exercise we might simply say that their core meaning is "hope." Another person performing this exercise might decide that their core meaning is "guidance." This is also correct; find the answers that are true for you.
5. Now ask yourself, based on the core meanings of each of these symbols, what power they give to that card. The stars, representing hope, might give the Star the power to see light even in the darkest of circumstances; as guidance, they might give the Star the power to guide others when they are lost.
6. Form these powers into a sentence for each of the symbols, and let them speak of what they bring to that card: "I am the stars in the Star; I represent hope, and I offer the power to see light even in the darkest of circumstances." Writing these down will give you a personalized list of each card's associations.

CHAPTER 1

The Fool, the Infinite Possibility of Chaos

"Before the beginning was even a seed of an idea in the mind of God, it was my step that trod the virgin paths from the centre of the sun. What did I desire? Nothing. And everything. I am a blank slate waiting to be written upon, a cup waiting to be filled, yet waiting will not do. We cannot wait at our point of origin and hope that illumination will find us; we cannot sit idly while experience bypasses us for lack of trying. We must take the first step, and only then will the path begin to unfold before us. Until then, it is not a path; it is nothing.

I stand at the centre of all possible paths in the universe, yet even I must take the first step. It is that single step that pushes me headlong into life, immerses me in the wonders and trials of the world and all it has to offer, and I take it all gladly and joyfully, because all is experience and none of it may be discounted. Some will tell you to look before you leap and that you must be careful and plan ahead. I say, take the leap, be completely careless and carefree, and plan nothing. Do not limit yourself in such constructs as fear and worry, convention and plans ... There is so much more to life than that. Let me show you. Let me take your hand. We are here together, fellow traveller, on the precipice of the journey, at the edge of reason and the edge of possibility and the edge of nothing. Don't be afraid, have only joy in your heart, and laugh as you feel the cliff edge falling away from you. It is done, and cannot be undone. Welcome, fair fool, to the journey."

Astrology: Uranus

Illumination

Strangely, the first card of the tarot is not numbered 1, but 0. This is not because this card isn't important. If we have nothing—zero—then we have the potential to become anything; we have infinite possibility. The numeral 0 is shaped like an egg, like the cosmic egg that contains the potential for all life. Thus the

Fool, being the first card, shows us the state of potential before the start of the journey toward growth and illumination, as well as the pure, free, and innocent spirit unburdened by trouble and cares.

Although he is called a fool, the young man depicted on the card is dressed in an outfit that would be suitable for a young noble or prince, and the colours he wears match those of the green earth and the golden sun. He does not look to be foolish at all, unless you take into account his precarious position atop the cliff. He is in obvious danger: he steps forward lightly, and one more step will take him off the edge of the cliff and plunge him to his death. The white dog at his heels does not help his safety as it bounds about excitedly; it would not take much for this animal companion to trip him up. Yet, despite the danger, the young man's face shows peace, not fear, as he looks out over the wide world beyond the card. This is because the danger of the cliff is symbolic (as all things are in tarot) and does not represent death or risk. Instead it represents the leap from the familiar, exoteric world that we take for granted into the immersive, wondrous, esoteric world of mystery and wisdom that is the Tarot Illuminati. From the highest point in the universe, our young Fool leaps into the other cards of the tarot, just as we do when we begin our tarot journey or start to interpret any reading.

As such, the Fool represents the chaos and possibility that comes before the beginning of anything. This is why he is a fool: he turns everything upside-down because he is the prime force of chaotic, unformed spirit on its way to becoming matter. But before he is something, he can be anything. In the card image, the young man almost seems to have stepped right out of the large, golden sun. In the Tarot Illuminati, the sun, especially one so big and stylized, is symbolic of divine light and the point of our spiritual origin. In the same way that the actual sun gives life to everything on Earth, the sun as a symbol in the tarot speaks of the divine force that gives us spiritual life, allowing us to evolve and grow in wisdom and illumination. It is this which the Fool seeks, and he has stepped out of the sun, his origin, so that he might undertake this most amazing of quests.

Over his right shoulder the young man carries a staff, upon which is hung a bag. We do not know what this bag contains; it is coloured the gold of the sun and the green of earth, like the man himself, indicating that it comes from the same source as him. Since we cannot see its contents, this bag—like the Fool card itself—contains infinite possibility. It also shows the young man in the card purposefully setting out on a journey as a wayfarer and traveller. In his left hand, he lightly carries a white rose. This rose is an alchemical symbol of purity in will and desire, and its colour reflects the dog, which therefore also represents something pure—in this case, since it is an animal, it represents our lower natures and natural instincts being as pure and full of potential as our spiritual desires (the rose).

We also see that the four elements are present: earth, in the forests and mountains; air, in the height of the cliff and the air that blows the Fool's cloak about; fire in the sun; and water in the lake behind him. But although the elements are all around him, he is not fully manipulating or using them yet, and they are found in their unrefined forms. When we reach the Alchemist, the next card of the major arcana, we find them present in manifest form as the symbols of the four suits. This reminds us that the Fool is simply in the moment, the recipient of new experience and change rather than the creator of such. The Fool does not plan ahead, does not have a goal or purpose beyond obtaining new experiences, does not yet know much of the world. We can see that he is a very young man, probably not yet beyond his teenage years. We often speak of people of this age as having their entire lives before them, or having the world at their feet because we believe that they have almost limitless opportunities to choose what or who they become and to make their own way in the world. This is what we hope for the young man who steps out onto the edge of the cliff in the card image, and although he takes a great risk and puts himself in danger, we know that this is his journey, his choice, and his free spirit will not take any other path. By necessity, for the tarot pack to exist, the Fool must take the leap of faith and step off the edge of the cliff.

Revelation

When the Fool appears in a reading, he brings with him a breath of fresh air and a rush of potential, possibility, and new beginnings. His carefree step into the querent's life indicates that the querent is on the verge of something new and big, a completely fresh stage of life and the beginning of a journey, either figurative or literal. As such, it can mean newness in any part of life: new job, new relationship, new home, new country, new school, new wardrobe, new perspective, new spiritual path, new way of being. The Fool offers the querent an opportunity to start afresh in some area, to leave behind any negativity or past difficulties, and to walk away to clear horizons.

Sometimes this card appears simply to say that the outcomes in the particular situation are uncertain, and that there are a great number of possibilities available to the querent. It may also point to a path that is as-yet-untrodden by the querent, something they may not have considered, or an entirely new perspective on the situation. It can suggest that the querent needs to lighten up and approach the situation with more joy and laughter—they shouldn't take life too seriously. It is time for them to let themselves be free from baggage they may have been carrying, or the weights of the world that they have placed themselves under, and step out into something new with a light heart.

The Fool can indicate spontaneity in life instead of planning. In relation to projects and specific questions, if this card appears, the querent is advised not to plan too much, but instead to "go with the flow," to start moving forward and to follow the path where it leads. In relation to a romance or friendship, the Fool might indicate a need for more spontaneity and fun, or a fresh way of acting and being around each other.

This card can suggest that others might view the querent as foolish, foolhardy, or careless, based on their actions. This is because the querent may be prone to rushing into things without thinking, living only in the moment and not planning for the future, and not taking things seriously. But the Fool reminds the querent that despite the judgments of others, their perspective is one that will serve them well and allow them to feel most fully themselves and fully immersed in their life's experiences. In this situation, the querent is not advised to follow the rules or stick to the guidelines, but to make their own. Sometimes it also advises the querent to regain a sense of wonder at the world, to become innocent once more and to see the possibilities and potential not only in themselves but in others.

Reversed, the Fool brings with him foolishness and folly, risk and danger. The querent is warned that they should look before they leap and consider their actions more carefully, or they may end up in trouble. It indicates that the querent is acting too rashly and being immature or naïve in the situation, and others do not respect them because they don't see them as worthy of that respect. Sometimes the Fool appears reversed to bring the querent a stark message: grow up, stop acting like a child, and take responsibility for yourself.

Keywords

Innocence, carefree, foolishness, folly, youth, adventure, new beginnings, carelessness, child, fresh perspective, freedom, potential, possibility, chaos, spontaneity, free spirit.

CHAPTER 2

The Alchemist, the Instigation of Transformation

"This is a spiritual truth: that what is established above is also established below. The material and spiritual planes have a direct correlation, and they are reflections of each other, as though we are standing between two great mirrors. You and I stand like great trees between these two planes, like pillars through which the correlations and reflections might run: we are channels of the divine energy transforming and changing state. It is within us that the transmutation of lead into gold occurs. Therefore we are also the will and direction of change; we are both the instigators and the effects of it. But you must learn the art and science of creating change: it does not necessarily come naturally. You must apply your mind and know with full self-awareness the resources that you have at your disposal and the direction you wish to move them in; you must also understand what it is to have intention. Without these, your transformation would be stunted and misdirected, your energy wasted. Come and apprentice to me, seeker of gold, and I shall teach you the movements of the stars in the heavens and the order of the natural world; I shall show you how everything has a system and all systems are One; and I shall give to you the secrets of alchemy. The universe and every particle of you are not static, but rather a never-ending series of processes and transmutations. You and I shall merely take our places amongst those ever-changing stars as heirs to the great mystery."

Astrology: Mercury

Illumination

A catalyst is required to bring the chaotic possibilities of the Fool into manifestation and actuality, in the same way that some impetus was required to cause our planet to form out of the chaos that preceded it, and in the same way that most religious traditions and mythologies have a story of the divine

9

creating the Earth from the formless void. In the Tarot Illuminati, the card following the Fool is the Alchemist (traditionally called the Magician). As the first card to be given a number, this is also the first spark or instance of creation, the moment when potential becomes actuality, chaos becomes form, and magic becomes reality.

We see in the card image a man robed in red and white, standing before an altar upon which are the four elemental symbols of the tarot. Around him, various alchemical vessels such as alembics and beakers can be seen, beneath the altar are books and tools of sorcery, and behind him are various etchings and diagrams of magical and spiritual significance. The entire scene takes place in a room that is open to the stars, and we can see the brilliant night sky outside. It is obvious from all the paraphernalia at his disposal that this man is a magician, alchemist, and enquirer into the mysteries and workings of the universe. Magicians and alchemists work from the principle "as above, so below," which means that there is a direct reflection and correlation between the spiritual and earthly realms, that human life is a reflection or earthly image of divinity, and that by studying one we can learn of the other. As such, our Alchemist, who is engrossed in a weighty tome, is in the practice of working with earthly tools that represent spiritual concepts, and performing rites and actions that are symbolic of internal, spiritual processes of change and transformation. It is for this reason that he is called an Alchemist in the Tarot Illuminati: the traditional alchemist performs a complex series of chemical operations upon various raw materials, which are then transformed into purer matter (called gold or "the Philosopher's Stone"), as a direct reflection of the spiritual, inward processes of transformation that he is creating within himself simultaneously. It is within this conception of the universe that humans have studied the stars and the planets for millennia, believing that their movement has a correlation to our lives, the horoscopes that are the charts of our birth somehow relating to our characters and life path.

A diagram of the Vitruvian Man by Leonardo da Vinci features in the background of this card. This is an example from the Renaissance polymath of what he called a "cosmography of the microcosm," in other words, the workings of the human body as a direct reflection of the workings of the universe. This reminds us that, for the Alchemist, the everyday world is a reflection of the spiritual world and vice versa, and that there is a significant order and meaning in the universe.

The phrase "as above, so below," which drives our Alchemist, is first found in the Emerald Tablet of Hermes, a text that comes directly from the alchemical tradition in Greece and the Arabic world, which claims to be a letter from Aristotle to Alexander the Great (although some of the earliest instances of it appear around the seventh to ninth centuries CE). This text tells of the means by which primal matter can be transmuted into higher matter through various stages. It claims to be the work of Hermes Trismegistus ("Thrice-Great Hermes"), called "thrice-great" because he was said to know the three parts of the wisdom of the universe: astrology, alchemy, and theurgy. The card image demonstrates these three parts of wisdom: astrology is referenced by the setting being open to the stars in an observatory-like room; alchemy is shown not only in the title but the alchemical items scattered around; and theurgy is shown by the items beneath the altar and the magical energy that permeates the scene. Given that the Alchemist is dressed in the principle colours of the alchemical process—red and white—he could be Hermes Trismegistus himself.

We see the four elemental suits of the tarot—sword, cup, wand, and pentacle—not only upon the altar in the image, but suspended in mid-air by magical energy above the altar (although the Alchemist holds the wand himself, as this is his most natural tool: the magician's wand that directs and focuses his will to create manifestation). The Alchemist therefore not only has the four constituent parts of the universe at his disposal, but also the four suits of the minor arcana as his tools. This tells us that the Alchemist has everything necessary for transformation; all the resources he needs are at his fingertips. It also reminds us that sometimes the things we need to kick-start a process of change and development are the most mundane objects, or are already inherent in our selves: the sword, cup, pentacle, and wand all relate to different parts of our psyche (see the descriptions of the four aces for more detail). These four symbols also show us the link between the Alchemist as the first card of the major arcana and the four aces.

The light blue, dynamic energy that we can see enveloping the four elemental objects forms a direct line from the lemniscate (infinity symbol) above the Alchemist's head ("as above…") and the circle of power created between the four objects ("…so below"). This tells us that the Alchemist is directing and controlling energy between chaotic potential and actual change; he is the channel for that transformation. The fact that he is holding the wand himself, not the other three objects, reminds us that as a magician he extends and exerts his will out into the world to create change. It has been said that magic can be defined as causing change to occur through the exertion of, and in accordance with, one's will; if so, then we create magic every single day of our lives. The Alchemist is the representation of that moment-to-moment transformation in our lives that is symbolized by the transmutation of base metal into gold.

Revelation

In a reading, this powerful and dynamic card signifies a time when the querent has everything they need to create positive and definite change in their life, and to channel the desired change to the place they want it to go. As the first numbered card of the major arcana, the Alchemist suggests that this is a time for new beginnings, initial action, and immense inspiration. If the querent is considering a new beginning or project, the Alchemist is one of the most supportive cards that could appear. Most importantly, it brings with it the message that the querent can do anything if they set their mind to it: they are the alchemist in their own life, changing the raw materials and resources they have into "gold": results, achievement, and change.

When the Alchemist shows up in a reading, it indicates that the querent needs to take immediate action in a situation rather than waiting around, and also that they need to be the change they want to see and create in the world. It asks the querent to assess the resources that they have available to them—both material resources and personal, inner resources—and how these can be used to effect change in their lives. Often, this card also indicates the need for a creative solution to a problem, instead of perhaps the most direct solution; intelligence, wit, and cleverness should be applied.

The Alchemist can sometimes be a communicator, but mostly it appears to signify the direction of the querent's will and energy toward a goal. If the querent has a goal in mind, then they must be aware that success begins with commitment of energy and knowledge of direction. Sometimes it can indicate that something the querent is doing or working on seems to be inspired by or linked directly to a higher cause or power, as if they are channelling a project or goal and they are simply the messenger for it or the means by which it reaches manifestation. It tells the querent to remember that the everyday world is a direct reflection of the spiritual world, and therefore they can process transformation and change on a spiritual level by acting as such on the material level. It can also relate to the querent's intentions and where they want to go with a path or project; it asks them to consider both their intention and their direction.

Occasionally the Alchemist indicates a person in the querent's life, somebody who takes on the role of instigator and inspirer. They may give the querent ideas, or give them the initial push needed to begin something, but not take any action themselves.

Reversed, the Alchemist signifies a character who may be untrustworthy or who may act the role of trickster in the querent's life. It can suggest that the querent is being misled as to the source of something, or that somebody they know has something up their sleeve. It may also indicate a misuse or lack of resources, or a misdirection of energy and will. Further, it can say that the querent has a certain skill, talent, or resource that they are neglecting or not using, when in fact it would be a useful tool on their path.

Keywords

Resources, channel, energy, will, direction, magic, intention, trickery, instigation, inspiration, tools, "as above, so below," drive.

Chapter 3

The High Priestess, Silence Gestating Mystery

"In times of old, many have walked this pathway, seeking initiation into the mysteries. Some came with wondrous words and great works, others with force and fire, still others with desire and yearning. Their footsteps were not permitted to pass, neither in nor out of the Temple of the Moon. Inscribed forever above the gateway and in the annals of history is the formula for passing: Know Thyself. Silence is the only vehicle by which you may pass, and thereby drink from the river of memory. And when the waters touch your lips, so parched from long days and nights wandering the desert, you will discover an oasis within yourself and the fallen temple shall be rebuilt therein.

I am the gatekeeper of the mysteries, the oracle within you that gestates inner wisdom in the darkest, most silent part of your self. I am the waiting womb, virgin and untouched and therein containing all potential. From the womb of silence, sealed and protected, everything comes. The first word must proceed only from the absence of words, and the first thought must be conceived without speech. Only when you silence your self can you know the subtle web of the world and its underground rivers; only when you stop speaking will your mind be truly open to knowledge. And when you have found it, you will see that it is only a process of remembering.

Here, drink this: it is the waters of the river called memory. Do you hear it? Hush now."

Astrology: The Moon

Illumination

The High Priestess in any tarot deck is one of its most mysterious cards, full of layers of meaning and depth. In the case of the Tarot Illuminati, this card represents most beautifully the purpose and goal of tarot: reflection upon symbolic images (mysteries) to reveal or articulate answers that are already present within us. Here we have the passive feminine (as opposed to the active feminine principle of the Empress), receptive and silent. The High Priestess forms a complement with the Hierophant; she represents inner wisdom while he represents received wisdom. Together they present to us two equally useful, complementary modes of learning and understanding.

In this card, we have an evocative image of a gatekeeper seated in the entrance to the Temple of Solomon, the first temple of the Old Testament, which housed the Ark of the Covenant (the container for the tablets upon which the Ten Commandments were engraved) in the Kodash Hakodashim—"Holy of Holies."[1] The Temple of Solomon was built with two freestanding pillars on either side of the entrance; these pillars were called Boaz ("strength") and Jachin ("established"). It is these pillars that we see indicated on the card by the initials "B" and "J." They tell us that the High Priestess is seated in front of the Temple of Solomon, acting as the portal through which we must pass in order to enter the mysteries within. Here we are reminded that this card represents the wisdom contained within, and that the Temple of Solomon is a structure to be built within ourselves. It is telling that the High Priestess in the Tarot Illuminati does not keep her scroll of wisdom closed and hidden in her skirts or useless in her lap, but rather she holds it out, open, toward us so that we might read it. Upon this scroll we can read instructions for rebuilding the Temple.

The pillars of Boaz and Jachin in this image are black and white respectively, representing polar opposites. The High Priestess sits between them, representing the wisdom that is attained at the point where polarities and dualities meet. This is reminiscent of various practices from around the world in which paradoxes or opposing statements are entertained simultaneously by a person until the mind reaches a point where the paradox or conflict causes it to stop thinking entirely, achieving silence and stillness. Examples include the Buddhist meditation upon "the sound of one hand clapping," or the Greek identity riddles found throughout the ancient Mediterranean world, of which the Gnostic text, *Thunder, Perfect Mind* is one, a text written in the first person as the Goddess of Wisdom.[2]

1.　1 Kings 6-8.

2.　*Thunder, Perfect Mind,* from James M. Robinson, ed., *The Nag Hammadi Library,* rev. ed. (San Francisco: HarperCollins, 1990). Also available online at http://www.gnosis. org/naghamm/thunder.html

Since the High Priestess guards the entrance to the Temple, we must ask ourselves what lies within. Any initiation into a Mystery involves a death and a rebirth, usually into an underworld of some sort. Since the High Priestess is the silence that gestates wisdom within, we can imagine that when we pass beyond her gate, we descend into a womblike, tomblike underworld cave, treading the same paths that initiates of the ancient mystery religions did. The Greek rites of Eleusis, the Roman cult of Mithras, the mysteries of Hekate, modern Wiccan initiations that enact the descent of the Mesopotamian Inanna to the underworld, and a great number of other traditions that are still practised today feature either an actual descent into a cave, underworld, or deathlike darkness, or a metaphorical one. In the Eleusinian rites, the initiates were taught that after death they were to drink not from the river Lethe (forgetfulness) as all the other dead did, but to drink from the river Mnemosyne (memory). The riverlike robes of the High Priestess remind us of this river of memory, and teach us that when we descend into the dark silence within ourselves to discover the answers, we are simply remembering what we already know: our inner wisdom.

Another well-known temple from the ancient world shares this idea of inner wisdom: the Oracle of Delphi. The entrance to this temple, in which seekers found answers delivered by a priestess of Apollo, had carved above it the words "Know Thyself," implying that to enter the temple was to enter one's inner world, and that the words of the god heard within were only one's own wisdom reflected outwardly.

The presence of the full moon above the High Priestess, and the triple moon that forms her crown, link her to the lunar forces of mystery and intuition, removing us from the glaring light of the sun and putting us in a nighttime state of peace and quiet. With the triple moon crown, our High Priestess becomes a lunar goddess, closely tied to the feminine mysteries of flux and the phases of the moon. In astrology, Kabbalah, and the ancient world, the moon is associated with the forces of birth and the soul coming down into manifestation, reminding us again that it is silence that gestates wisdom and births it.

The concept of revealed mystery is expressed by the fact that not only is the High Priestess opening her scroll for us to read, but her veil is also being blown back, as if by a strong gust of wind. This is a card that speaks of inner wisdom being received or remembered, not for its own sake so that it may be stored and hoarded, but instead so that further understanding and revelation might occur. Wisdom begets wisdom.

Revelation

The High Priestess card can be difficult to interpret in a reading, since it contains such huge, abstract concepts. It often appears to indicate silence and stillness of some kind, stating that in this situation the answers are best found in the quietest, most peaceful way. Perhaps this takes the form of simply listening: listening to another person, listening to one's inner voice, listening to one's intuition or instinct, listening to silence…Sometimes it takes the form of meditation and reflection, or any practice and process by which the mind is stilled and reaches a zone of silence. The High Priestess indicates that only when the mind is quiet and free from the busy humdrum of the situation will answers and a solution come. However, it also suggests that the querent may already know the answer to their question: they have only to listen and it will be revealed.

Sometimes the High Priestess appears to indicate a seeker's quest for wisdom, psychic ability, spiritual understanding, or a desire to find their own truth. It often represents an initiate or an initiation into a religion, mystery tradition, or spiritual path, but one that focuses on allowing its initiates to find their own answers by being given the keys to doorways rather than simply being handed the answers straight away. If this card appears in a spread concerning spiritual or mystical matters, the querent should be prepared for a period of descent into dark silence—not an underworld of pain and inner demons, but simply an underworld of pregnant silence. For those of us living in the modern Western world, sometimes silence is the hardest thing for us to practice. Not everything needs to be spoken, the High Priestess advises, and often secrets are secrets for a reason: not because they should be hoarded and kept in a process of one-upmanship, but because telling others the answers steals from them the right to undergo the same initiatory journey of discovering them for themselves.

The High Priestess might point to divinatory practices such as tarot, oracles, dream interpretation, or contemplative meditation. It also says that the querent might be in a state where they feel as though they are ready to receive something—whether it is wisdom, inspiration, the influence of another, or teaching. At times it can indicate a person in the querent's life who is well-versed in mystical or spiritual matters.

Reversed, the High Priestess hoards secrets for their own sake, and can indicate a hidden agenda. This card might represent a person (sometimes the querent, sometimes another person) who is too quiet and does not express themselves, a "shrinking violet," or somebody who retreats so far inside themselves that they lose all personality. Reversed, this card might also tell the querent that they are not making enough time to be on their own, listening to their inner voice. Perhaps they are denying their intuition, perhaps they are too busy to value quiet time and time for reflection. Because of this, they find blockages and obstacles appearing in their life. Repression can be indicated by the High Priestess reversed, and a distortion of wisdom hidden behind secrets and symbols, cloaked with an air of mystery that is not real mystery at all.

Keywords

Silence, receptivity, passivity, gestating, virgin, mystery, inner wisdom, intuition, secrecy, initiation, remembering, reflection, listening, quietness.

CHAPTER 4

The Empress, Venus Incarnate in Sensual Earth

"From impregnated silence and mystery form must come, thus I am the gateway of creation. Like a river, I carry tiny pieces of manifestation downstream until they are deposited, there to create the shapes of the earth. I have brought many things to birth, some small things negligible to most, and some things of greatness, and sometimes the entire universe. I am the creator of every moment, engendering all possibilities with active force toward manifestation. The earth we walk upon is my body as well as my child; its beauty and wonder are my works of art, my offering to all my other children that they may also walk in beauty and wonder. For what is life without beauty? What is it without love? I am the Queen of Love, and love is my war cry and my heart's shield. When you love unconditionally, you open your heart to the pains of the world, but even these pains and sorrows are of my Love Creation. No moment, no part of the world can be discounted, for it is all perfect. I gifted every being with vitality and sensuality so that it could engage with life, falling deep into its sumptuous folds and experiencing all.

How can your heart ever be truly at risk when you know that the source of pain is also the source of love? Nothing created was done so without difficulty and suffering. The river of creation is a river of blood, and the blood flows with pain yet fertilizes where it runs. The song of creativity and engendering is the cry of a woman in labour, the cries of lovers in their moment of unity, the cry of triumph at the end. Do not mistake me for a passive force, and do not mistake me for anything other than yourself. You are me, and you are creator and co-creator of every moment and every step you take upon the earth."

Astrology: Venus

Illumination

After the silence of the High Priestess, in which all things were possible, the

Empress is the first card of the major arcana to represent manifestation and creation. Where the Alchemist was the first spark of inspiration from the chaos and potential of the Fool, and the High Priestess as the passive feminine received that spark and in silence and mystery gestated every possibility, the Empress takes this energy and gives it form. In the tarot she is the quintessential representation of creation and creativity, but she is also the epitome of vitality, sensuality, luxury and love. She is a mother, and she became so through acts of sensuality and sexuality, love in action. As such, she represents unconditional love as well as the unstoppable force of creativity. The twelve stars around her head link her to the mother of the Christian tradition, Mary, who is described in the Book of Revelations as "a woman clothed with the sun, with the moon beneath her feet, and a crown of twelve stars on her head."[3] Numerologically, 3 is the number of manifestation. Whereas 1 is the initial dynamic force pushing outward and 2 is the balance and duality of union, 3 is the product of duality. It is therefore also the first number of action: the Empress isn't a passive force waiting for creation to happen; she represents the act of *being* that creativity, not just in projects such as artwork and writing, but in every moment. It is telling that she holds firmly in her right hand a golden sceptre, traditionally symbolizing power. She is consciously taking ownership and power over every moment, being its creator and co-creator, and becoming part of the vitality and essentialness of life. In her other hand she holds, more gently and less firmly, a symbol of the harvest: sheaves of wheat. These are golden in colour, representing the richness and luxury of the natural world, but they also represent the fruit of one's labour and the work and energy that must be expended for manifestation and therefore harvest to occur. It is interesting that whereas the sceptre, symbol of ownership of the moment, is grasped firmly, the results of labour are not: the Empress does not necessarily create so that she may own something at the end of it, but for the sake of the creative process.

In the card image, she wears blood-red skirts that flow over her and the earth beneath her. She is the active feminine, sister of the High Priestess. Where the High Priestess wears the quiet colours of water, totally receptive, the Empress wears the passionate colours of life and vitality. If the High Priestess is the waiting womb or gestating womb, the Empress is the birth-giving womb. The red of her skirts reminds us also that the process of creativity demands a lot from us, sometimes all. If we look closely, we can also see that her underskirt is embellished with a Tree of Life bearing pomegranates, the fruit of fertility

---

3. Revelation 12:1

and growth. The name of this fruit comes from the Latin meaning "seeded apple," and in the Graeco-Roman world it was known as the fruit of the dead; in fact, the goddess Persephone was given it to eat when she descended into the underworld. It also has links to Hera, the wife of Zeus, high lady of the gods of Olympus, who was often depicted holding a pomegranate.[4] The pomegranate was also offered to the great mother goddess of the Greeks, Demeter. In Jewish tradition, the pomegranate links the Empress and High Priestess, as the pillars of the Temple of Solomon (Boaz and Jachin) found on that card were engraved with pomegranates.[5] It is even possible that the fruit on the Tree of Knowledge of Good and Evil in the Old Testament is not an apple, as commonly believed in the West, but rather the pomegranate, which was native to the region. As such, the Empress represents fertility not only of body but also of mind and soul.

Resting gently upon her skirts we see a golden key, upon which a red and white rose (also called the "Tudor Rose") is emblazoned. The Tudor Rose is the flower emblem of England, itself called the "green and pleasant land."[6] Its presence reminds us that the land around us and beneath our feet is beautiful, our environment sacred.

There is something very luxurious about this card. The Empress' costume is sumptuous, the throne upon which she is seated is comfortable and welcoming, her headdress is regal and beautiful and she herself is a very beautiful woman. This reminds us that the Empress isn't just "Mother Earth" but also, astrologically speaking, the planet Venus, the planet of love and sensuality. Venus was the Roman form of Aphrodite, the Greek goddess of love and beauty, and the mother of Eros, the god of primal fire, eroticism, and sex. The Empress loves life! She revels in all things beautiful and luxurious that life has to offer, and engages in the pleasures of the material world, because these things not only help create life but also make it worthwhile. Thus, the heart-shaped shield that rests at her side is carved with the symbol of Venus, also the symbol of woman.

Revelation

In a reading, the Empress can represent many things depending on the question, spread, and surrounding cards. Most often she indicates that a creative process

---

4.   Pausanius, *Description of Greece*, 2.17.4

5.   Kings 7:13-22.

6.   William Blake, "And Did Those Feet in Ancient Times," a poem that later became the hymn/anthem, "Jerusalem." "Milton a Poem", c. 1808.

will be started or finished, or that the querent is undergoing the process currently. Surrounding cards will indicate the nature of this process, its success, and/or the querent's relationship with it. Usually this card suggests a significant creative project, born from the querent's passion or love. This card isn't about duty or responsibility, although it might involve them. It also says that anything the querent is currently undertaking will undergo a great period of growth.

The Empress can sometimes represent a person who acts as a mother to the querent, or the querent's own motherhood. This can be actual motherhood, or more metaphorically: what does the querent feel is their "child"? How do they nurture their life, their surroundings, their projects, other people? The Empress also asks the querent how much effort they are willing to put into something and reminds them that, most of the time, the act of creation can be painful and can require dedication.

As the Queen of Love, the Empress brings luxury and beauty to a reading, and invites the querent to assess how they engage with life and enjoy it, or how they relate to luxury and sumptuousness. In readings about love and relationships, the Empress is a very positive card, indicating great enjoyment and growth in the relationship, along with passion and sensuality.

Reversed, the Empress can show us the dark mother, the smothering mother. Sometimes when we love something, we hold onto it too tightly, destroying it in the process. This can be a person, a moment, a perspective, or a project. We stifle growth by trying to cling to stasis. The Empress reversed can indicate that growth or creativity is stifled for some reason; surrounding cards might suggest why). Writer's block and artist's existential angst are part of the Empress reversed, as is any difficulty with a mother figure or the act of nurturing. The querent may find that they are denying themselves any luxury or pampering, and that this is shutting them off from the creative parts of themselves.

Keywords

Creativity, engendering, creation, manifestation, harvest, creative process, love, sensuality, sexuality, luxury, sumptuousness, vitality, active feminine, motherhood, nurture, growth, beauty, birth.

CHAPTER 5

The Emperor, Aries Seated in his Power

"The first time a would-be warrior picks up a sword, he frequently believes power to be inherently resident in the weapon itself. In the same way, many of those who use tools to create something in their lives think that the power and ability lies in the tool itself. But when the would-be warrior learns to wield the sword, he also learns that the power lies only in him, and therefore all the responsibility for that power also lies in him and his actions. The throne upon which a ruler sits is considered the seat of his power, yet truthfully no order, no laws, no structure, and no power comes from that throne; it comes from the ruler seated upon it.

Many would-be warriors pass my way, seeking training in the skills of the sword and axe; I first teach them the art of self-control and self-discipline. Without these things, they are not warriors at all, but dangers. Many of them rage against my leadership because they do not see how my strict rules and the order I place upon them can be of use, yet how can you act with responsibility and the whole weight of your power if you do not understand what it is to create structure and order? I am the man of war that can teach you to own your power, to direct it, and to act in this world with precision, courage, force, and ambition. I am the armoured Sun King who does not need to fight, nor do I seek conflict. Conflict demonstrates the imbalance of power and the desire for power as an end rather than as a means. Power is never to be a goal, but a resource within you that you can access once you understand order and responsibility. Only when my would-be warriors learn this are they allowed to begin training with a sword."

Astrology: Aries

Illumination

The Emperor is partner to the Empress. The fact that these two cards sit side by side in the major arcana tells us immediately that they share a special relationship, and their titles give them regal authority in the world. The empress and emperor historically are sovereign rulers of an empire or imperial realm; they are generally considered to be of higher rank than a king and queen. In fact, many emperors throughout history have had some degree of divinity attached to them, such as some of the later emperors of Rome, around whom an imperial cult formed, and who were often deified after death. There is clearly a theme of power, authority, and order in this card, as an emperor's role was not only to rule his people, but also to balance the needs of his subjects, foreign affairs, the military, political leaders, economic affairs, religious institutions, and all other aspects of his empire.

In the card image, we see a regally dressed and armoured emperor seated in a relaxed yet commanding manner on a magnificently carved stone throne. He bears a wand topped by an ankh in his right hand and a bejewelled orb topped with an equal-armed cross in his left. Great red mountains rise behind him, and even the sky is red—the colour of the fiery, active nature of this card. It is also the colour of war, aggression, dominance, ambition, passion, and drive. The Emperor's innate power is further symbolized by the golden armour that he wears: gold is the colour of the sun, confidence, and outward manifestation. The Emperor is therefore our Sun King, a virile god in human form. In many ancient cultures, the king, emperor, or pharaoh was seen not only as the son of God but a form of God himself, or appointed by God to rule. This makes the Emperor in the tarot a powerful symbol of order, divine right, and authority.

The authority of the Emperor is repeated symbolically throughout the card image. The crown that he wears shows his right to rule and he wears it with ease, just as he sits on his throne with ease, showing that he is comfortable with the role of responsibility. The orb topped with an equal-armed cross demonstrates his rulership over the four corners of his domain, as well as his balanced and even hand in rulership and power. The wand in his right hand is phallic in nature, as he is the active masculine force in the tarot, the father and the leader. This ankh wand is also known as a *crux ansata* (literally meaning "cross with handle"), and represents life and the key of life. It is also said to represent the male and female united in a nonsexual form. In ancient times in Cyprus and Asia Minor, this ankh was used to represent the planet Venus and therefore the goddess of love. This is thus a poignant symbol for the Emperor to be holding: it links him directly with his partner and co-creator, the Empress.

That he wears armour is a symbol of his association with Mars, the planet that rules the zodiacal sign of Aries, which we also see in the image in the form of the ram's heads carved in the stone throne. Aries is the first sign of the zodiac (the astrological year begins at the spring equinox, when Aries also begins) and also a fire sign; it represents the first fiery force of life bursting through the virgin earth to bring spring to the world. It is intensely phallic and sexual in nature. Mars is associated with war and control, and its symbol is used today to indicate the male gender. Mars is the partner of Venus in astrology and her lover in Roman mythology, and of course our Empress is Venus herself, bearing the sign for Venus upon her heart-shaped shield. These two come as a pair. Where the Empress is creative and receptive, earth and water, the Emperor is active and controlling, fire and air. Where she is woman, he is man; she is mother, he is father; she is the raw material to which he gives form; where she is potentiality, he is actuality. This is further reflected in their respective thrones: where the Empress is seated upon soft, luxurious cushions, the Emperor is seated on a carved stone throne. This contrast shows the difference in their essential natures and the stages of creation that they each rule over.

This stone throne is an important symbol for our Emperor. A throne is not only the seat of power for any ruler, but it represents the energies of the number 4. The fours of the tarot are the cards of manifestation and concrete actuality. They are stable and unmoving, like the four walls of a house or the four corners of the world. Four is also the number of the elements of earth, air, fire and water that together make up the world we inhabit (in a spiritual sense, not a chemical sense). Therefore the Emperor is the foundation upon which we might build, our stability, the control we have over our lives, as well as our power to act. Being seated on this stable throne of power, the Emperor represents the ways in which we, too, are seated in our own power, taking responsibility for our lives, acting with full awareness and choice, ruling ourselves with an even and balanced hand.

Revelation

In a reading, the Emperor is a powerful and potent force in the querent's life. He often appears to indicate a time of action and manifestation, a time when the querent is required to assume a role of responsibility or power, a time to ground their ideas and dreams into concrete reality. It may also suggest a need in the querent's life for more stability, order, and control in response to uncertainty and difficulty. If the querent is finding it difficult to bring some project to completion or to make their life circumstances easier, the Emperor advises that they need to take control of the situation and take full responsibility themselves for it.

The Emperor often represents a stable time of certainty and the achievement of ambitions. He can appear in work- and career-related readings to indicate a boss or somebody in power who can either help or hinder the querent (surrounding cards will indicate which). It can also indicate the querent's father, especially if accompanied by one or more kings in the reading, or somebody who acts like a father to the querent. Sometimes the Emperor represents the querent as a father or in a fatherly role to another person, and indicates the ways in which they rule, give guidance, and demonstrate leadership.

When the Emperor appears, he can also advise the querent that they need to take a leading role in a project, rather than being a follower. In other situations, he may suggest that the best approach to the situation is to practice careful self-control, rather than seeking to control others. True power, the Emperor says, does not lie in having power over others but in recognizing the power within oneself. This card points to ambition, plans for achievements, and great heights of triumph, showing a querent who is ready to fight for their goal and take every action possible to make it happen. There is no room for waiting with the Emperor, no room for simply considering something or letting another person take action: there is only room for the querent to take action, and to do so soon.

Yet there is a structure and order to the Emperor that may not sit well with some querents, since he brings with him the rules and laws that create order. As such, this card may advise that the querent follow existing rules and guidelines rather than trying to find a way around them (this is especially true if the Hierophant is present in the reading too). It also suggests that the querent should create more structure and routine in their life, and give more time to projects with clear and achievable goals. And every now and then, due to the aggressive Aries nature of the Emperor, it may appear to advise the querent that it is time to stand up for themselves and their beliefs, and even to fight for them.

Reversed, the Emperor can represent a boss, father figure, or person in authority with whom the querent has problems. This person may be overbearing or misusing their power, since the Emperor also represents the misuse of power in all ways. This card reversed can sometimes point to a lack of foundation or structure in the querent's life that must be addressed, or a situation in which the querent is not being forthright and active enough.

Keywords

Rulership, dominion, power, control, structure, laws, order, fatherhood, authority, responsibility, leadership, boss, action, war, aggression, ambition, achievement.

CHAPTER 6

The Hierophant, the Institution of the Sacred

"Millennia have passed and the lives of many men and women have come and gone. In their place they left history, and in that history they left a treasure-house of wisdom, experience, knowledge, and teachings. Yes, our predecessors may have been more primitive than us or lacked the current scientific knowledge that we have the privilege of having, yet they still have much from which we can learn. It is from this collective storehouse of past wisdom and knowledge that tradition arises, and the most effective means by which these traditions might be taught and accessed: organizations and institutions. Such things were never originally intended as a means of control or oppression, but as a safe and stable environment for the passing on of tradition and the wisdom contained therein.

When you step into my church, wisdom-seeker, you step into the rich tradition upon which it is built; when you seek knowledge from me, you also take your rightful place in the long line of all those other knowledge-hungry acolytes and neophytes. And by being in my position, I am also placing myself in the lineage of every other leader of this tradition, an unbroken line back to the beginning when my tradition was founded. I am the word of God, the lamb of God, the Word made flesh, but not by birth or happy accident: I am the messenger of that great and noble wisdom that millions seek, and which is offered to them every moment by those who have taken on the mantle of Hierophant, revealer of the sacred. I can show you the mysteries and hand you the keys to the doors of knowledge, as the receiving of traditional wisdom from a teacher is a necessary step to any true path of knowing."

Astrology: Taurus

Illumination

In the major arcana, two cards of authority and leadership appear side by side: the Emperor and the Hierophant; they are also the two cards that most clearly use the masculine figure as a symbol. They follow on from the two most feminine figures of the major arcana, the High Priestess and the Empress, and thus we can see that these four cards share some kind of special relationship. There are essentially two partnerships here, with the Empress and Emperor being worldly mother and father, and the High Priestess and the Hierophant (called "High Priest" in some tarot decks) being spiritual mother and father. The Hierophant is a pope of the church, and as such he is addressed as "Papa" in Italian-speaking countries (which is where the title "pope" comes from) and "Father" in English-speaking countries. To those who follow the faith he represents, the Hierophant is a spiritual advisor and fatherly figure who cares for their souls and tries to guide them toward good, in the same way a worldly father would for his children. In these four cards, then, we have four different kinds of manifestation and process: the High Priestess is the receptive feminine, the Empress the active feminine; the Emperor is the active masculine and the Hierophant the receptive masculine.

Furthermore, the Hierophant and High Priestess are a pair because they each embody half of the necessary approach to learning and gaining wisdom: the High Priestess represents the path of inner wisdom and seeking answers through individual experience, and the Hierophant represents the path of learning from the wisdom of others and finding knowledge through an accepted tradition.

In the card image, we see a figure of religious authority wearing all the holy vestments of his position. He wears the papal tiara (a three-tiered crown that is given to popes on their coronation, but which in recent papacies has somewhat lost favour) and sumptuous red and white clothing. These colours also link him to the Alchemist and therefore to the process of channelling divine energy. The Alchemist draws energy from the divine so that he might bring it into manifestation through his magic, but the Hierophant directs the spiritual message of the divine to those who listen. Since the Hierophant also embodies the word of God on earth, he is the personification of the divine energy that the Alchemist was working to manifest. Indeed, the word "hierophant" comes from the Greek meaning "revealer of the sacred."

The crossed keys we see in the foreground of the card are the keys of St. Peter, who stands at the gates of heaven in Christian belief, representing admission to a world of religious belief and divine wisdom. As a symbol in the Catholic Church, they remind us that Peter was the first pope, and therefore the man who transformed Christianity into an institution.

The triple-cross wand in the Hierophant's left hand is a symbol of authority, but in the context of the Hermetic Order of the Golden Dawn, the occult organization that significantly influenced the development of tarot. The Hierophant in the Golden Dawn is a specific role taken by a member during certain rituals; he carries the triple-cross wand. The Hierophant in this role rules over the hall of the Neophytes (early initiates) and expounds the mysteries to them. In this way, we can interpret the two acolytes in the card image, kneeling before the Hierophant, as representing neophytes— those who are eager and willing to embark on a journey of discovery and learning from the Hierophant within the structure and order of a religious organization or institution. These two acolytes are clothed in red and yellow, their cloaks embellished with roses and lilies. These represent the two requirements for true learning: desire (roses) and purity of intention (lilies). Acolytes are part of a strict hierarchy, telling us that this card is about learning from a tradition of received wisdom and listening to a teacher, but also about the hierarchy that allows such learning to be instituted. The wisdom that can be gained is rich and deep, as indicated by the richness of the surroundings in the card: gold filigree and luxurious robes.

Another symbol of the Hierophant's position and authority can be found in the lamb that is seated gently upon his lap. This lamb is symbolic of the flock that the Hierophant leads, since priests and papal authorities are often seen as shepherds, guiding and protecting their lambs and sheep from predators or accidents, watching over them and leading them to greener pastures. This lamb is also representative of the "lamb of God," an epithet given to Jesus, who himself took on the role of Hierophant by giving people the message of God and embodying the word of God himself (he was also called "the Word made flesh"). In the card image, the Hierophant makes a sign of benediction with his right hand. (This can also be seen in the Ten of Swords, where the traditions and received wisdom are destroyed, and we see the dead man making the same sign).

Many tarot readers take issue with the Hierophant because he represents the religious institutions that have spoken out against tarot and other esoteric practices for so many centuries. However, that there is great beauty to be found within organizations, institutions, and religion, most importantly because, were it not for tradition and received wisdom from these sources, much learning would have been lost over the ages. Much of what we consider received wisdom is useful, true, and meaningful. When we learn from experts in their field, leaders, and spiritual authorities, we are learning from the Hierophant. Even when we study tarot, whether from books or directly from experts, we are learning from him.

Revelation

The Hierophant represents such an abstract concept that it can sometimes be difficult to see how it relates to a reading. However, it is also rich in meaning and has many possibilities to offer. Often, it points to a person in the querent's life who plays a teaching role, somebody to whom they have recourse, one who advises them and guides them. It can be an actual "hierophant" or priest, leader of the querent's church or other religious or spiritual community, or a person with experience in their field to whom the querent goes for guidance. More metaphorically, the Hierophant can represent the querent's inner moral compass, as the manner in which they approach authority.

Sometimes this card signifies some form of hierarchy that the querent is involved in, perhaps at work or in a spiritual or religious community. It may also represent any communities or organizations that the querent is involved in, particularly those that offer teaching in a certain tradition. Because of this, the Hierophant can suggest that the querent seek aid and comfort or a solution to the situation within their religious or spiritual community, or turn to received wisdom and tradition for the answers to a problem.

The Hierophant can indicate a time of learning for the querent, especially learning within an institution. It therefore relates to any education within a school system or higher education at college or university. It can also point to research and the need to turn to the writers and wisdom-bearers of the past for answers or inspiration. If in doubt, the Hierophant advises, the best approach to the situation is a tried and tested method that is supported by experience. Sometimes this card places the querent in the role of teacher or spiritual leader; if so, it relates to issues concerning those they teach and guide, or ways in which they manifest and channel the message of the wisdom that they wish to express.

The Hierophant can also ask the querent to consider what values and traditional wisdom they hold dear, and why. Do their beliefs aid them or hinder them? What ethics and morals do they have and how do these affect their lives? It further asks them to consider from whence they receive their wisdom and knowledge.

If the querent is on a path or undertaking a project to manifest something that is based in spiritual wisdom, then the Hierophant is a wonderful card to receive in a reading. It represents the grounding and manifestation of such goals, making definite reality from abstract concepts. The querent may need to seek advice and aid from another person to help make this happen, but the potential is there.

Reversed, the Hierophant denotes issues with spiritual authority, iconoclastic tendencies, and poor advice being received or given. It may also indicate somebody who the querent believes represents spiritual wisdom, but is in fact misleading the querent in some way, or someone who cannot substantiate their claims to knowledge. This card reversed can also signify institutions and organizations that are oppressive to the querent or holding them back from progress, dogma that the querent is stuck in, or a problem within a community.

Keywords

Hierarchy, organizations, dogma, institutions, messenger, faith, outward wisdom, received wisdom, tradition, mediation, advice, religion, authority, knowledge, experience, learning.

CHAPTER 7

The Lovers, Yearning for ReUnion

"Every man and every woman is a star: we all come from the same source, made from the same stuff, and it is that stuff that also makes the rest of the universe. When we are created, we contain within ourselves a spark of the divine, a star within our bodies of flesh that is eternal and a direct reflection of every other star contained within every other person and being upon the earth and in the heavens. Together we are constellations, and we come together in groups to create patterns in the sky. We move about in the heavens and in our orbits, and some of us collide while some of us find a mutually beneficial orbit; still others unite in the most beautiful constellations that their union will be seen and remembered throughout the ages. But we are all star-children, siblings under the canopy of heaven, and we all seek reunion with that from which we came bursting into life. The stars within us speak to their source and origin, and we yearn to return to it. The journey is long, but we find every now and then in another person a star that is closest to that which we yearn for, and we see in them the source of light, and they see it in us. We join with them, in yearning and desire and passion, and through them we are completed. This is love: the joining of two stars contained in the bodies of two human beings, expressed in their bridging of the gap between them and the gap between them and the divine. Yet do not curse the gap, Lover; do not bemoan the space that you must traverse to achieve reunion and love, for it is only by virtue of this gap that you might feel yearning and desire and love at all."

Astrology: Gemini

Illumination

Up until the appearance of the Hierophant, the major arcana cards featured only a single human figure in their images. The Fool, the Alchemist, the High Priestess, the Empress, and the Emperor were alone in their environments, representations of archetypical concepts. In the Hierophant, we met our first card containing multiple figures, in the image of a priest and two acolytes. Now here, in the Lovers, we have another image featuring three figures, but instead of a priest we find an angel, and instead of two acolytes we have a naked man and woman. The Lovers marks the point in the tarot where we move from soaring universal concepts to more personal ones of interaction, inner processes, and relationship.

The figures pictured in this card are probably familiar to most readers. On the left, accompanied by the serpent and the apple and leaning against the Tree of Knowledge of Good and Evil, is Eve, the biblical first woman. On the right, with his arms covering his face and head and his back turned to us, standing before the Tree of Life, is Adam, the biblical first man. This is clearly a scene from the Garden of Eden, before "the Fall of Man," indicated by the fact that Eve has not yet taken the apple from the serpent. Above them, with his arms outstretched in blessing or proclamation, is an angel with great wings and a countenance of light. We will meet this angel again in the Temperance card, which shows the result of the union found in the Lovers card, and also in the Devil card, with the Lovers in a fallen state. Finally, we will see him in the penultimate card, Judgement, calling forth the Lovers from their graves, accompanied by the manifestation of their love, the child. The identity of the angel is unknown, as the original account of the Garden of Eden does not designate a name, but instead states that God set a number of cherubim to guard the entrances and exits to the garden. The term "cherubim" is the original Hebrew indicating a plurality of angelic beings called cherubs, yet these are not to be confused with the winged children or babies found in later art. However, as languages have changed with time we find the term applied to such beings in art, and in particular to the being called Cupid, Eros, or Amor, the Graeco-Roman winged god of love, who carried a bow and arrow and inspired love in mortals. Therefore, the angel in this card image is not only a reminder of the biblical setting, but also a nod toward other representations of the source of love between people. As the first man and woman, Adam and Eve also represent the first instance of love.

There is more than just the idea of love in this card, however. In the story of Adam and Eve, God first created Adam and then created a mate for him out of one of Adam's own ribs. Whilst to many modern readers this may suggest that Eve was therefore subservient to Adam, being created second and from a part of him, in tarot language it says that they are both created from the same source and, more importantly, they are each part of the other. The Lovers card, therefore, is a representation of the shared source of all humankind, the fact that we are all created from the same "stuff." In spiritual thought, we are all beings that contain the same spark or seed of our divine origin within us. In terms of the Garden of Eden, Adam and Eve were said to have walked with God and spoken with him directly, indicating a state of perfection and union with the divine. Yet we all know the rest of this story. The unity and perfection is lost when Eve is tempted to eat the fruit from the Tree of Knowledge of Good and Evil, and gives it to Adam to eat also. When they taste the fruit, they are granted the knowledge to distinguish between good and evil; they are taken from a state of blissful ignorance to one of conscience, moral awareness, and choice. They are then expelled from the Garden in what is known "as the Fall of Man"—separated from God, and their state of divine union and origin removed from them.

It is through Eve's act of eating the apple and offering it to Adam that humankind was separated from God, as well as the knowledge of good and evil being imparted to them. Whilst we might initially see this act as a wrong done to humankind by Eve because of the separation it causes, it is in fact a great service done to us. Separation of the soul from the divine causes the soul to yearn for reunion; separation of one lover from another allows them to yearn for each other. It is this act of yearning for reunion in the midst of separation that gives rise to mysticism, religion, and all human relationships. In love, we recognize the divine part of the other person as the divine part of ourselves seeks its own; this could not occur if there were no separation. There cannot be re-union if unity is already achieved. There cannot be a space to fill together if there is only oneness.

The Lovers is therefore a complex card of duality, representing both the state of separation and the union that occurs when the gap is bridged between one person and another. From Eve and her choice to create separation and duality, all of humankind arose. It is for this reason that she is called Eve, which translated means "life" or "source of life." It is interesting to note that the etymology of Adam's name associates him with the colour red, linking him perhaps to the fiery Emperor, as well as mankind in general. Looking at their names, we see another instance of the separation and duality between Adam and Eve, in which they become representations of our selves (Adam) and our divine source (Eve). The gap between Adam and Eve in the card image is symbolic of the gap between ourselves and the object of love that we wish to reunite with, whether it is a spiritual concept or a human lover.

Revelation

If there is a "true love" card in the tarot, this is it. Most often in a reading the Lovers will indicate a human love of some kind, and the surrounding cards will indicate what nature the love takes. It is rare to see this card indicating the kind of spiritual reunion that it represents at its core, since most readings are concerned with everyday life rather than spiritual realities or paths.

Commonly, this card signifies a relationship. It may point to a current relationship or a prospective one (again, surrounding cards will indicate which is the case); if it does, then it also suggests that this relationship will be extremely important and long-lasting. It is especially so if it is accompanied by the Two of Cups, Ace of Cups, or Four of Wands. It says that the querent and the other person in question are made for each other, a perfect fit. The love indicated by this card is not just sexual gratification or mutual attraction: it is also a deep and intimate bond between two people, which often plays out on a spiritual level as well as on the emotional and physical levels. This type of relationship is often described as feeling as though you have found the missing piece of yourself in another person, or as having found a twin soul.

Occasionally the Lovers points to a love of some kind in the querent's life that is not another person, such as a career, a pastime, or a place. It indicates a deep passion for it, a yearning to be involved with it, to work on it, or to pursue it. Just as with a human partnership, the Lovers suggests that this passion is a perfect fit for the querent. It could be that they are working in a career that brings out their passion, the kind of work they love doing with all their being. It might also indicate a particular field of expertise or area of study that the querent loves so much they would want to dedicate their entire life to it.

As a card of separation as well as love, however, the Lovers can sometimes point to the gaps between two people, yet it also focuses on the yearning to bridge the gap. Thus it can signify a yearning for a relationship to work out, as well as the desire to work in a field of study that the querent loves, or a burning desire for a particular outcome. It can also represent the act of uniting two parts of the self, or two parts of a project, or even bringing two people together in a nonromantic context, such as working together or learning from each other.

There is a harmony in the Lovers card that often comes out in a reading, especially when asking about a current situation. It indicates balance and harmony between people and states, as well as the desire within the querent to maintain or achieve that harmony. In many cases, this card will point to the ways in which the querent feels and experiences unity and love in their lives.

Reversed, the Lovers can point to a relationship that is based not on a spiritual or emotional connection but instead exists on a purely physical level. Surrounding cards will indicate whether this will be a positive or negative thing for the querent, but usually this card reversed suggests that the querent thinks the bond is greater than it is. It points to strong feelings of love that are not returned, or that are misinterpreted, as well as imbalance in a current relationship. Sometimes this card reversed suggests that the querent needs to reunite one part of themselves with another part, or perhaps seek reunion with another person, such as an absent friend or an estranged partner.

Keywords

Love, reunion, separation, desire, yearning, passion, relationship, romance, partnership, sex, harmony, completion, true love.

CHAPTER 8

The Chariot, the Soul Extended in Action

"Lovers of wisdom have called the soul a chariot, drawn by horses and driven by a charioteer. Those that know the nature of the soul will understand that it is not a still, silent creature but rather a whirling force of fire, always extending outward in action, carried forth into the world by intention, the body, speech, and reason. The soul is like the questing hero, the Grail Knight, seeking and searching the wide world for challenge, questions, and answers. Am I your soul, brave quester? Or am I the force of your soul? Am I your faculty of reason? Or am I your faculty of control? I come forth to tell you now that I am all of these things, for force, reason, and control must be yoked to the urges of the soul so that victory can be attained. There is a long path stretching before us, seeker; be thankful that you have these allies to pull you onward, for you would fail alone. And you will not give up, because you cannot, because the quest will always be there, your road will always lie before you. Though you may close your eyes and turn away, the chariot of your soul will still be drawn forward, but the reins will be held too loosely in your hands and the momentum of your unruly steeds will drag you, in ignorance, to catastrophe. Dare to take the reins of your soul, to have the courage and strength to exert your control and will upon your self, and ride forth into the world, assured of victory."

Astrology: Cancer

Illumination

The Chariot presents us with an image that seems simple, yet contains within it a hidden philosophical depth. We see in this card a charioteer, driving his horses forward with control and a calm demeanour, his ornate chariot being drawn through the river that runs through his homeland. He is a prince or a noble, certainly a warrior, riding out from the city of his birth and into the wider world, ready for a challenge and an adventure, eager to test and prove himself, and seeking something greater than that into which he was born. This is similar to us: we are born into our situations, unable to choose to whom we are born, where, and when. Whilst some stay in that situation (perhaps because it is so good, or because they don't know how to do otherwise) for the rest of their lives, becoming only as much as they were expected to be at birth, the Chariot is the card of those who wish to surpass themselves and their circumstances, to better themselves and seek greatness. This is the card of the soul's desire to extend out into a wider universe, to expand its horizons, and to quest for a higher good.

A number of chariot images and allegories are found in history and philosophy, all of which see the soul as a chariot. The Greek philosopher Plato wrote in his *Phaedrus* that the soul could be described symbolically as a charioteer with a pair of winged horses—one horse white and noble, always moving toward the highest glory, full of honesty and modesty, and the other horse black and ignoble, always causing difficulty for the charioteer, being the lower emotions. The charioteer himself Plato called the faculty of reason and the ability of the soul to control the pair of horses.[7] If the charioteer was able to hold the reins of the horses firmly, driving the black horse in the same direction as the white horse, then the soul would achieve greatness and fly higher to the heavens; if not, it would lose its wings and return to its next life as a lower human, perceiving less truth. This allegory highlights the necessity of control, force, and will in our lives. Without them, we would not progress and would often give into actions and thoughts that are negative and self-defeating, which drag us backward rather than pulling us forward. The card image shows us the black and white horses, both decorated equally, both pulling in the same direction, suggesting that our charioteer has succeeded in obtaining control over the various parts of himself, and is now directing them toward his goal. This is important: he is not destroying or putting away his black horse (the lower self), but rather acknowledging its useful aspects and using them in his quest.

Another chariot image for the soul is found in the Katha Upanishad, a Hindu text from around 500 BCE, saying:

> *"Know the Self to be the master of the chariot, and the body to be the chariot. Know the intellect to be the charioteer, and the mind to be the reins. The senses they speak of as the horses; the objects*

---

7. Plato, *Phaedrus* 245c – 254e.

*within their view, the way. When the Self is yoked with the mind
and the senses, the wise call It the enjoyer."*[8]

It further states that the man who has discriminating intellect as the driving force (charioteer) of his soul, and a controlled mind as the reins over his senses (horses), will achieve the supreme state of being and the goal of his path.[9]

However, the chariot isn't always used to describe the soul; in the Jewish tradition, a particular kind of mysticism, called Merkabah mysticism, uses the image of the chariot to describe methods of mystical ascent toward a vision of God. So we can see the Chariot as not only the soul embarking upon its journey and quest but also the quest itself and the road that the chariot travels upon. We are reminded of the Arthurian legends in which the Knights of the Round Table embark upon the Grail Quest (synonymous with a quest for spiritual attainment). The vision of the Grail is not just the final prize at the end of their quest, but is the reason for their quest (they are given a vision of it originally, and then it disappears) and also the means by which they might attain it (the Grail represents spiritual purity and enlightenment, and the Grail stories conclude with only a single Knight truly achieving the Grail—Sir Galahad, the most pure and holy of all the Knights).

In the ancient world and the Italian world at the time of the tarot's birth, chariots would have been involved in great triumphal processions, which gives us the original name for the major arcana, *I trionfi*—"Triumphs," as if each card of the majors is a chariot bearing scenes of victory through the streets. Such chariots would have been akin to the floats we see today in carnivals and street parades, bedecked and beautified, often bearing scenes and characters upon them. Our chariot's reins double up in the card image as bunting, the decoration of celebration and triumph, reminding us that the Chariot is a card of the victory that comes at the end of a great quest, as much as the quest itself.

In the card image, our charioteer has left the safety of his home city behind him. The soul must always move out of its comfort zone in order to progress, just as in the everyday world we must push ourselves to unfamiliar places or states of being, follow a learning curve, and step into the unknown in order for any progress to be made. We cannot achieve if we just stay still. Adventure does not come to us, we go to it. Above the charioteer's head we see a directional

---

8. The Katha Upanishad, trans. Panoli, 1994. 1.3.3-4.

9. The Katha Upanishad, 1.3.9.

compass, indicating that he is in the centre; in other words, he is in control of his own direction, and all direction proceeds from him. He is seated beneath a triumphal canopy of celestial images, showing that this is a soul journey, blessed by the heavens. He wears armour because he is a hero and a warrior, ready to fight and exert his will and strength during his quest. He will not shirk responsibility or duty, nor run from obstacles, and will never admit defeat.

The entire card has an atmosphere of direction and momentum, as if we are being carried along on the quest by the speed and force of the charioteer and his horses. The power in the image is palpable, and challenges us to take the reins of our lives and take control of our own power and direction, always moving onward to greater heights, and embracing every adventure as an opportunity.

Revelation

When the Chariot appears in a reading, it can be a great blessing or a stern lecture. As an outcome card it is extremely positive, showing great success, triumph, and victory. The querent will find that any endeavour they are currently in or any journey they have embarked upon will reach a conclusion that is more than satisfactory. This might indicate promotions at work (particularly if accompanied by cards such as the Eight of Pentacles or Six of Wands), success in exams, the completion of a project the querent has worked on for a long time (e.g., a book, artwork, or screenplay), or investments that pay off (look out for cards such as the Four of Wands for investments in property, for instance, or pentacles cards to indicate sums of money). Whatever the querent has embarked upon was a good choice. They will also find that they will make great and swift progress on any current projects or situations.

On the other hand, this card can also indicate the querent being called to a task, purpose, or challenge that seems difficult or insurmountable, certainly taking them out of their comfort zone. They should be advised that this is an important opportunity for them, as it will offer potential for growth and progress as well as great results and achievements. They may feel that events around them are pulling them in that direction anyway, like momentum is gathering in their life and pointing toward a certain road. The Chariot says that they should take the hint and follow this road—it will lead to amazing things! This is the call to adventure, the invitation to rise up to a challenge.

The presence of the Chariot can often "speed up" the reading it appears in, saying that the events will happen quicker than expected and with more force. As an advisory card, it tells the querent that they must have clear focus and direction; having control over themselves and the situation is absolutely necessary for progress and victory. If they lose control, direction, or focus, they will find that they are no longer in charge of their situation but rather a victim of circumstance. This card therefore asks the querent what their goals are, what direction they are heading in, and how they plan to exert their will to achieve their goal.

In a reading about relationships or other partnerships, the Chariot can raise issues of control and power. The querent is advised that the relationship will be successful if they have control over themselves and the situation, but not power over the other person. Shared goals and achievements will aid the partnership.

If this card appears reversed in the reading, we can surmise that the querent's direction and focus is haphazard, and that they are being led by circumstance and others rather than doing the leading. They may also be cowering from a challenge, refusing to accept the call to adventure, preferring to stick to their comfort zone. In more positive circumstances, the Chariot reversed may simply suggest that the querent is refusing to receive due honour for their achievements, shying away from the limelight and hiding their light under a bushel. Generally, the momentum and journey of the Chariot is never truly blocked or slowed, as its force and speed is too great, but reversal might indicate that instead of being a charioteer driving the horses with control and the reins held tightly, the querent is a passive rider screaming on the floor of a speeding chariot, having lost control of his horses, which are now pulling the vehicle in unknown directions, leading it away from victory.

Keywords

Victory, control, force, direction, momentum, quest, journey, achievement, ambition, goal, speed, challenge, adventure, progress, focus, triumph.

CHAPTER 9

Strength, the Maiden and the Beast

"Centuries ago, as the tales say, there lived an adventurous knight who sought to prove his strength, courage, and valour. He sought far and wide for a chance to be great, and eventually he found himself in the service of a king who had one beautiful daughter. The knight fell in love, naturally, with the maiden, and sought her hand in marriage. Yet disaster fell: this maiden was taken by a terrifying beast, a dragon, to its lair, and the kingdom was in fear and fright. But the knight rode out to meet the dragon and fought it bravely, slaying it and freeing his love from its clutches. He triumphed over the animal, the beast, and therefore he also overcame the libido and passion, the animalistic self contained within his love and himself.

However, this knight did both himself and his love a great disservice; the tale is falsely glorified. To slay the beast within, to tame it and to cage it, is to destroy a part of your self. Strength is not always in the sword and the arm, but in patience and kindness: it comes from within. Neither the sharpest sword nor the strongest arm can give you courage if you do not already possess it in your heart. Know this: I do not fear the beast that lies against my body, nor do I fear its power or size. I have tamed him, but not destroyed his strength, for to do so would be to destroy my own. He is me and I am him. Such a great beast was never meant to be slain, but understood and embraced, for you must remember that it was not so long ago that we also were animals ... "

Astrology: Leo

Illumination

Strength and the card that comes before it, the Chariot, show a connection between human figures and animals in the card images. In the context of these two cards, the beasts represent various parts of our psyche or self. In the case of the Chariot, the black and white horses represented our lower and higher natures respectively, and in the case of Strength the beast represents our animal natures, our libido, our lower selves. The interactions between the beasts and humans in the cards show us different ways of approaching this part of our selves.

The title of this card tells us immediately what it is primarily concerned with: strength in all its forms. Yet we do not see what you might expect in the image: there is no strong, powerful man with muscles, nor a battle or struggle leading to victory. Instead we have what might be seen as the opposite of strength: a white-clad, delicate young woman wearing flowers in her hair and letting a large lion lick her open palm. Clearly this is not an illustration of brute physical strength, but a deeper kind of strength found within. The maiden has tamed the lion and has formed a bond with it, demonstrating the power and strength required to embrace the lower self and form a relationship with it.

The white that the maiden wears identifies her as the higher parts of ourselves, as well as the archetypal virgin, the pure self untouched by the lower self or libido, which is represented by the lion. As a beast, the lion is a powerful, forceful predator that is representative of the untamed wilds of nature, and therefore not only the lower parts of our self, but also our wilder tendencies. This white maiden, however, is also an alchemical symbol of the process known as calcination, in which the material being worked upon is put through an operation of fire, which separates the gross, lower parts of the material from the subtle, higher parts by purifying it and reducing it into a fine, white ash. This is symbolic on a spiritual level of separating the lower, grosser, unrefined parts of ourselves so that we may purify them, raise them higher, and thereby integrate them healthily into our lives. In the card image we can see that this is exactly what has happened already: the white maiden is separate from the lion, and she has acted in such a way that it now licks her hand and lies peacefully next to her.

Two symbols in this card link it to the alchemical process via the Alchemist card: the red and white roses in the maiden's wreath, and the lemniscate (infinity symbol) that she has drawn in golden, sparkling energy in the air above her. Red and white are worn by the Alchemist himself, and are symbolic of the union between masculine and feminine. This tells us that the Strength card is not simply one of taming the beast within, but of integrating it and uniting with it once it has been refined, just as the Red King and White Queen marry in alchemy (note that the lion is almost red in colour, and the maiden is dressed in white).

Although the maiden has tamed the lion, she has done so with gentleness and kindness, not brute force. This tells us that the maiden in the Strength card has learned that if you simply try and cage the beast, locking it away, it will become angrier and more fierce and eventually break free and wreak havoc; but if you tame it by raising it up, offering it kindness and learning to understand its ways, it will become an ally that will add to your strength. There is a stark contrast here between the Chariot and Strength. Whereas the Chariot, with its reins, exerts careful control over the beasts in the card, which are tied to the carriage, Strength does not seek control over the beast but simply seeks integration and understanding. This is further shown by the fact that the lion gently dips its paw in the waters of the pool by which it lies, the beast thus coming into contact with the symbol of emotion, spirituality, and depth.

The lemniscate above the pair appears to remind us that nothing in the universe is ever truly destroyed; instead, energy changes state. There is nothing to be lost in accepting and integrating the lower parts of the self. There are obvious connections between this card and the folktale that has become widely known as "Beauty and the Beast," in which not only does the beautiful maiden refine the uncouth and dangerous beast, but she also unites with him in marriage, and when she does so, he returns to his human self again. Just like the maiden in the Strength card, we must recognize the lower parts of our self, our animalistic side, our libido, and—instead of destroying it or trying to control it—learn to refine it, use it for a higher purpose, and in doing so achieve unity.

Revelation

The Strength card can be very abstract, since it speaks of inner processes, perspectives, and approaches rather than events or occurrences in the everyday world. However, when we extrapolate its more abstract meaning, we find that it is a card that offers immense depth of wisdom when applied to the everyday world. Often, Strength appears in a reading to show a particular dynamic between the querent and another person, or between the querent and a situation. This requires them to answer the question: are they the lion, or the maiden? As the maiden, the querent is in a position to recognize the more physical, gross, lower, wilder, or distasteful aspects of a person or situation, and faces the challenge and opportunity of learning to embrace those aspects and refine them toward a purpose. As the lion, the querent is living more closely with their libido, their wilder and more animal nature, and living impulsively, yet they may have another person in their life that is trying to learn to accept them as they are, and to see the beauty even in their lower nature.

Sometimes this card appears to tell the querent that their actions or some aspect of their life requires refinement, or perhaps that a project or piece of work needs refinement. It may be viewed as too coarse, too crass, too base or too "dark" for others, or perhaps even for the querent themselves. When they achieve this, they will be in a stronger position to move forward. It can also advise the querent that their situation is best approached from the standpoint of quiet strength and power, rather than obvious displays. It reminds them that "honey attracts more wasps than vinegar"—in other words, their obstacles and opponents can best be dealt with through gentle acts of kindness, calm, and inner strength.

Occasionally the Strength card will appear to indicate a specific process of healing and embracing the libido; it may point to a querent who is undertaking shamanic work with animal spirits or any other work that reunites them with an aspect of themselves that is usually pushed away in the modern world. It can also suggest a special relationship with the animal kingdom, such as somebody who works with animals or has an animal companion. It is particularly apt for veterinarians and others who heal sick and injured animals.

Most typically, however, this card speaks of strength in many different ways. It often points to the querent's own inner strength, or the fact that they are in a strong position in the situation. It also indicates the need for courage in the situation, and the need to show compassion and understanding, perhaps even kindness, at this time. There is a certain amount of self-control implied by this card that leads to the ability to face the situation with compassion. Sometimes Strength can also indicate the strength needed to overcome the hold the querent's lower self has over them, in cases such as overcoming addictions.

Reversed, Strength becomes weakness, courage becomes cowardice, and compassion becomes anger. The querent is in a weakened position in the situation and is fighting to regain control. The problem with this fight is that regaining control will not solve the problem. The querent needs to learn acceptance and understanding so they can see that there is no opposition present at all, only that which they have created in their minds. Strength reversed can also appear for querents who are timid and afraid of the direction they are going, or who believe they don't have the strength to undertake a certain task or path. They should be reminded that although the gentle maiden in the card does not look like much, even a gentle touch of her hand contains strength enough to tame the lion.

Keywords

Strength, inner strength, courage, compassion, gentleness, kindness, power, embracing the lower self, the animal self, the libido, animals, healing, strong position.

CHAPTER 10

The Hermit, the Seed of Light in the Darkness

"You have travelled a long way to find me here, seeker, just as I have travelled a long way to be here. We are in darkness, in the womb of the world, the great cosmic display of life, death, and rebirth. You can see it written in the stars and in the heavens, and deep within the earth. Above us, stars die and are born, planets move, and the face of the universe changes forever. Beneath us, the earth shifts, lava flows, the worms consume decaying matter, and seeds spring forth. This is the primal dance, yet to mortals it is a mystery to be sought after, delved into, like a man shining light into a dark cavern. I am the way-shower of this "mystery," the guide along the roads you must walk if you wish for revelation. I have walked these paths of initiation myself, many aeons ago, and the light I shine so that you may see is merely my own wisdom. It is a small light, flickering and weak, yet in the depths of darkness into which we are going it might as well be the beacon of a lighthouse or the light of the sun. You ask why I am so alone—this is the way it must be. The light shines most clearly when it is alone, and my task is one that not many would take up. It is my lot to show the ways that lead to the underworld and the temples beneath the earth; it is mine to take the hands of those who are lost, and mine to pick them up when they are at their lowest. I must brave the darkness of eternity so that others might see the light. I am the one upon whom all eyes rest when all else fails, and I am the one who will lead you out of the wilderness and the desert, to the Promised Land. This light I carry is my burden and my blessing; I offer it with open hands to all, for it is the seed that will redeem the world."

Astrology: Virgo

Illumination

The Hermit is the second of our lunar cards, in which the moon features prominently, the first being the High Priestess. These two cards share a special bond: if the High Priestess is the guardian of the gateway to the temple, then the Hermit is the guide that shows initiates the way within the temple. He is also the last card in the procession of the major arcana to feature a distinctive, human character: after this we find ourselves travelling a strange road populated by angelic, hermaphrodite beings, depictions of death and the darkest aspects of our psyche, and cosmic forces such as the stars above, the moon, and the sun. In a way, the Hermit is the last card that we can relate to on a personal level, but at the same time this can confuse the meaning of the card. Whilst a hermit is an individual who has made a choice to live alone, the Hermit in the tarot is much more than that, and his aloneness is only one aspect of his greater meaning. The moon's presence in the card gives us a clue: this is a card about the metaphorical underworld, our inner world, the hidden mysteries of ourselves.

The first thing we might notice about the card image is the age of the figure himself. His wrinkled, care-worn face and long white beard and hair tell us how old he is. Age in the tarot is an important symbol: compare this card to the Ten of Pentacles, in which we see a venerable grandfather whose wisdom and experience has benefited his family. Age indicates great wisdom, great experience, and the ability to present it to others. The Hermit has seen many things over a long period of time, and has a greater understanding of how the world works, how people work, and how the two interact. The Hermit holds a staff firmly in his left hand, yet he is not leaning on it for support as a lame man might; rather, it is in front of him, its top glowing with an ethereal golden light. Perhaps he has used the staff to help him reach the top of the summit upon which he stands, or perhaps it has some kind of magical property, like the wand of a magician. The staff is shaped much like a shepherd's crook, indicating that the Hermit is not in his position to serve only himself, but that his role serves others also.

He stands upon the summit of a mountain covered in snow. The height of this mountain tells us that he has come far and is at the height of his own experience and wisdom. Like a lighthouse, now he can use his experience and wisdom, from this great height, to better guide others when they are lost. His environment is an icy wasteland, in which many travellers might get lost or stranded. Imagine their joy were they to see the Hermit's light shining like a beacon in the darkness, leading them to the summit from which they could better see the lay of the land and plan their route! This can be seen as an analogy for the soul's evolution when caught up in darkness, lost, or simply trying to find a path. When we feel ourselves to be in a metaphorical desert, we look for guidance from those who have had this experience and come through it. With their wisdom, we reach the same position as them, where we can see our goals and paths more clearly. From there we can move on to other mountains, other paths, or stay where we are and take on the role of guide ourselves.

The Hermit, therefore, is a *psychopomp*, a guide of souls. In Greek myth, the role of psychopomp was originally given to the winged messenger god Hermes, who, with his magical staff (the caduceus, perhaps represented in the card image by the Hermit's staff) guided the souls of the dead to the underworld. Without his guidance, they could be lost and never reach the Elysian Fields, but wander instead as hungry ghosts on the shores of the river leading into Hades. This role of *psychopomp* is important for us in the modern world also. When we are at our lowest, darkest point, descending into our own metaphorical underworld (or inner world), we need a guide to aid us. This guide might be another person, or it might be another aspect of ourselves. Throughout history, hermits would take themselves away from society and live on their own, usually in a wild place or a difficult place to survive in. They would meditate, pray, contemplate, and generally engage in a spiritual way of life. Also throughout history, people would seek out these hermits for the wisdom and healing they could provide through their heightened connection to the divine. In some versions of the Arthurian legends, King Arthur is said to have sought out Merlin when Merlin was living as a wild hermit in the forest.

The word "hermit" comes from the Greek *eremites*, which means "of the desert" and comes from *teremos*, meaning not only desert but also "uninhabited." The hermits of the ancient world were typically desert-dwellers, a prime example being the Desert Fathers of early Christianity, founded by Anthony the Great, who sought complete solitude in the desert, away from human habitation. This tells us that the Hermit of the tarot is a person who has chosen to go out into the wilderness or the desert in order to find wisdom and connection with the divine. In tarot, the wilderness or the desert is synonymous with a spiritual state of darkness, such as a descent into the underworld, the "dark night of the soul." But this darkness is also synonymous with a rich fertility: within the darkness of the earth, seeds grow and minerals and precious ores are to be found. This reminds us that when we find ourselves, like the Hermit, in the wilderness or a state of darkness, if we seek wisdom therein, we will find light and truth. In the modern world, if we remove ourselves from the bright lights of a town or city and go out into the wild, we will see the stars at night like we've never seen them before. Few of us who live in cities have seen the Milky Way with our naked eye, yet it is visible from Earth if we just leave urban areas of light pollution. When we go into the quietest, darkest, inner parts of our self, we often find a richness of wisdom and an opportunity for deeper connection with the divine.

In the New Testament, we are given an example of going into the desert in such a manner. Jesus, after his baptism in the river Jordan, is described as going into the desert "filled with the Holy Spirit," to be tested for forty days and forty nights. He fasted for those days, and Satan tempted him three times; each time he refused. When the testing had been overcome, Jesus was attended by angels.[10] In the Old Testament, Moses led the Israelites out of slavery and into the desert, where they wandered, seeking the Promised Land, for forty years. This would suggest that the desert or wilderness as a metaphor is a necessary part of our spiritual growth and attainment of wisdom.

The card image's beautiful starscape, with three shooting stars and the moon shining brightly, reminds us of the vistas of the heavens that open to our eyes in the darkness. It also points to the origins of the Hermit in the earliest tarot packs: he did not carry a lantern then, but an hourglass, and he was the Father of Time. Here, our Hermit is an astrologer and watcher of the clockworks of the cosmos, but his role as Keeper of Time remains the same. He knows the workings of the universe, which points again to his wisdom and experience.

The symbol that is most prominent in the Hermit card is the lantern that he carries. This is what distinguishes him as a guide, rather than as merely an old man lost in the desert. He holds it aloft and out to the world, showing us that he is sharing the light with others. This light is symbolic of his inner light that he is externalizing, his wisdom and experience being used to guide others along the way. Within the lantern we can see a six-pointed star, created from two interlocking triangles, one pointing down and one pointing up. This symbolizes the union of heaven and earth, masculine and feminine, and links the Hermit to the Lovers, as in some tarot traditions it is he that presides over their marriage. This star also reminds us that the wisdom that the Hermit carries and offers to us is the wisdom pertaining to the union of heaven and earth—"as above, so below."

---

10. Matthew 4:1-11.

The role of guide in the darkness, a beacon or lighthouse for those lost and in need of aid, is fulfilled by many figures from history and myth, such as the *bodhisattvas* of Buddhism: people who attain Nirvana but instead of allowing themselves to be freed from the cycle of reincarnation, they choose to keep reincarnating until, with their help, all other creatures have been liberated. The Hermit uses his spiritual awareness and wisdom not to benefit himself but to benefit others, making him the hand of compassion offered to us in the darkness of the wilderness.

Revelation

In a reading, the Hermit can often indicate a great spiritual awakening, or a long process of enlightenment or illumination taking place in the querent's life. It indicates a querent who is turning inward and looking toward a deeper part of their life and themselves, or embarking on a spiritual journey of some kind. It can suggest either that the querent already has a lot of experience or wisdom on a spiritual level, which they are now able to use to help others, or that they are the one in need of help from a more experienced person (surrounding cards and the context of the question will tell you which is the case). The Hermit can therefore indicate acts of compassion toward others, as well as an inner light that the querent has that has driven them this far, and which they now wish to share with the world. Perhaps they had a burning desire to found a yoga studio and teach yoga in the inner city, and now it is about to become a reality. Perhaps they have spent most of their adult life learning art therapy, and now they wish to use their skills and knowledge to help others learn it, or put it into practice by setting up their own therapy centre. Perhaps they have written a self-help book they want to see published. The Hermit is every desire to bring inner wisdom and experience into outer reality and shine one's light for others to see.

This card often advises the querent to remove him- or herself from a situation in order to see things more clearly. Alternately, they may need to take the "high road" in a situation and rise above it. The Hermit may recommend that the querent take some time to be alone rather than surrounding themselves with others. This might indicate a retreat of some kind, a meditation practice, a vacation, or a short trip alone. It can even be something as mundane as a walk in the park. It is time for the querent to undergo some soul searching in order for their life to progress. They may be currently in a time of barrenness, and this soul searching and turning inward will give them the answers they seek, which will help fuel their creativity and projects.

The Hermit suggests that the endeavour the querent is currently undertaking or hoping to begin is best done alone, without too much help (and interference!) from others. In a work or business context, it can point to working from home, or the querent running their own business based on their experience and wisdom. If it appears in a relationship reading, this card indicates that the querent will not find a relationship for quite a while, most likely because they have other things to do alone first. Maybe they are simply not ready for a relationship or need the time alone to know themselves better.

If this card appears reversed in a reading, it suggests that the querent is going through a particularly dark time at the moment, maybe spiritually but also emotionally. They may be seeking spiritual guidance and help, or desperately seeking a life path that suits them better. The Hermit reversed can also indicate issues that the querent is having with their age, viewing it negatively as a weakness rather than positively, and it can also point to intense feelings of loneliness.

Keywords

Alone, loneliness, isolation, spiritual wilderness, guidance, wisdom, experience, seeking, introspection, turning inward, age, inner light, compassion.

CHAPTER 11

The Wheel of Fortune, the Riddle of Constant Change

"I have a riddle for you. If you answer correctly you may pass, for you will truly understand the nature of the universe and the precious wisdom of the tarot. There are four creatures of mighty power: one bears water, one soars the heights, one has the strength of the earth, and the other the presence of majesty. What can be found between them?"

Astrology: Jupiter

Illumination

Wheels are cyclical, and they symbolize the cycles of life, which are many and varied, while fortune is an abstract concept associated with luck, fate, destiny, and the ups and downs of one's life. The concept of the Wheel of Fortune pre-dates the tarot by over a thousand years, as it is found in ancient Greek and Roman philosophy, and nevertheless has remained almost unchanged throughout the centuries. Due to its prevalence in medieval philosophy, it found its way into the major arcana of the tarot.

In Roman mythology, the fate of all individuals is given to the goddess Fortuna, often depicted in control of a great wheel upon which men and women can be seen. As she turns the wheel, some rise upwards to the top, symbolizing their fortunes becoming favourable, whilst others descend to the bottom, symbolizing their fortunes failing. In some medieval versions, a king rises and falls on this wheel, with his words inscribed in Latin: "I reign" as he sits at the top, "I have reigned" as he falls to the bottom, "My reign is finished" as he lies at the bottom, and "I shall reign" as he rises to the top. Sometimes Fortuna is depicted blindfolded, because fortune seems to be utterly random and does not necessarily give to individuals what they deserve: a good man can suddenly find his life descending into darkness, whilst a man who has undertaken many bad deeds can find himself prosperous. Whilst this may seem fickle, it is in fact one of the only things in life that can be relied upon: the Wheel of Fortune tells us that the only thing certain in the universe is change.

In the card image we see two wheels, one inside the other, and in the centre of both is the globe of planet Earth (compare this to the World card). Around these wheels are the four creatures we might recognize also from the World: the human, the eagle, the lion, and the bull. Each of them has a book, and seems to be made of stars. Around the outer wheel we see three other creatures: at the top of the wheel reigns the sphinx, with a sword in one hand; descending down the left side is a snake, representative of the Greek monster Typhon, and ascending on the right side is Hermanubis, the syncretic god of Hermes and Anubis combined.

Around the outer wheel at the four compass points are the letters TARO. This obviously could relate directly to the tarot itself, telling us that the tarot is a tool to help us understand the strange workings of the Wheel of Fortune, particularly in relation to our own lives. Yet since this is a wheel, we do not know which way round to read the letters. Thus, they can also become ORAT, from the Latin "to speak," possibly indicating the oracular nature of tarot as a means of accessing individual fate, ROTA, from the Latin for "wheel," and ATOR, an unknown word that some have said relates to the Egyptian goddess Hathor. There are four other letters on this outer wheel. In Hebrew they are Yod, Heh, Vau, Heh—YHVH. This is the holy name of God, which in the Old Testament is not read aloud, but instead replaced with the name "Adonai"— "Lord." English speakers know the name as Jehovah. This is the holy fourfold name of God, which creates and sustains the universe, and which contains within it also the four elements of earth, air, fire, and water, as well as the four court cards, princess, prince, queen and king. This is yet another symbol of change and cycles, since it spirals around itself and recreates itself. In the centre wheel, we can see the symbols of the four elements, with earth in the north, air in the east, fire in the south, and water in the west, as well as the directional compass pointing to the cardinal points. In the very centre is the tiniest wheel, just over the planet Earth. This is like a sign saying to us, "You are HERE!"—in the very centre of all this rotating, cycling motion. Thus we might only notice the cyclical changes on a human, everyday level and not notice the bigger cycles represented on the outer wheels.

The number four is associated with this card, which might seems strange at first because whilst four is a number of stability (see the Emperor and the fours of the minor arcana), the Wheel of Fortune is a card of constant change. Four appears in the fourfold name of God, the four corners of the Earth, the four letters, the four elemental symbols, and the four creatures that can be seen in the corners of the card. These creatures represent the fixed signs of the zodiac: Aquarius, Scorpio, Leo, and Taurus. They are also representations of the four living creatures from Ezekiel's vision in the Old Testament, in which they appeared to Ezekiel winged and atop whirling wheels, escorting the chariot of God. These wheels were within other wheels, and represented the constant change of the universe that God rules. We can identify these creatures further as representatives of the four evangelists, St. Mark, St. Luke, St. Matthew and St. John the Evangelist (who is often considered the same person as St. John the Apostle).

Why so many fourfold symbols of stability? The answer is found in the gaps between each of the four parts of the symbol. What is found in between the four elements? What is found in between the four seasons? A state of change. One season becomes another through a state of transition, and the cycle continues on.

The three creatures on the outer wheel are the final mystery in this card. They are directly reminiscent of the king that can be found in medieval depictions of the Wheel of Fortune, who ascends and descends around the Wheel. Here, Typhon the snake is the spirit of bad fortune descending down the wheel; Hermanubis is the spirit of good fortune rising up the wheel. The sphinx is the balance between the two extremes, and even though it is sitting atop the rotating wheel, it is not moving: it has found stability in change. The sphinx also reminds us of the ancient Greek tragedy *Oedipus Rex*, in which the eponymous character meets the creature on the road to the city in which he will meet his fate (unknown to him). The sphinx asks him a riddle: "What goes on four legs in the morning, two legs in the afternoon, and three legs in the evening?" The answer, of course, is man: as a baby he crawls on all fours in the morning of his life, as an adult he walks strong on two legs in the prime of his life, and as an old man he uses a crutch in the evening of his life. This riddle not only gave Oedipus passage on the road, but it also reminds us once again of the changes that we must all endure throughout life.

Together, these three creatures represent the three Hindu qualities from Samkhya philosophy: *sattva* (balance, the Sphinx), *tamas* (darkness, Typhon), and *rajas* (air, Hermanubis). Each of the tendencies is necessary for creating, preserving, and destroying. Where *rajas* is dynamic and ever-moving, *tamas* can provide stability and slow movement, and *sattva* holds the balance between these states and their transitions.

The Wheel of Fortune is undeniably one of the least human and most cosmic cards in the tarot. When we experience changes in our everyday life, they are merely simpler reflections of the grand cycles and changes that are the fundamental nature of the universe around us. This is why the four creatures are made of stars: they are reminding us of the universal and cosmic nature of the Wheel of Fortune.

Revelation

When the Wheel of Fortune appears in a reading, it can be difficult to interpret since its meaning is so abstract and universal. Fundamentally, it indicates change of some kind in the querent's life—big changes at that. It can manifest as a complete change of career or job, change of relationship, change of lifestyle, change of life focus, change of concept of the self, or change of religion, amongst other things. This is not the kind of change found in the Death card, however, where the change requires an ending, but rather it is a change that allows transition from one state to another, one state flowing into the next.

The Wheel of Fortune can also indicate a time in the querent's life when change seems to be all they have. They may feel as though they cannot hold on to anything for long; as soon as they become accustomed to one situation, they need to adapt to a new situation. The querent should be advised that they must remain adaptable and flexible in the current situation, and learn not to cling too hard to the current state of things; it will just make change more difficult. Change is the only constant in the universe, and it is also the only constant in life on Earth; however, the querent is currently having this fact demonstrated more vividly than usual.

Sometimes the Wheel of Fortune can indicate luck and chance favouring the querent, their fortunes picking up and their life in general improving. They may become more aware of the cycles of their life, and be able to use this understanding to their benefit. As such, this card can also point to tarot readings and oracles, any attempts to divine the future or predict, including playing the stock market. Gambling is associated with the Wheel of Fortune, so its appearance can indicate gambling wins, although the querent should be made aware that fortune is a capricious mistress and their luck will not last forever.

Reversed, the Wheel of Fortune can represent great confusion in the querent's life, with endless changes making them dizzy. They may feel like they are on a cosmic hamster wheel, struggling to run fast enough to keep up, and that everything is moving too quickly for them. In this situation, we can imagine the querent on the outer wheels shown on the card, where the spinning makes you even dizzier; if they can find their centre—the most stable point in their life—they will find the changes easier to cope with. This card reversed can also bring ill fortune, a streak of bad luck, gambling losses, and setbacks.

Keywords

Change, cycles, luck, fortune, gambling, risks, ups and downs, rollercoaster ride, adaptability, flexibility.

CHAPTER 12

Justice, the Scales of Cosmic Balance

"For every action there is a reaction. For every cause there is an effect. The consequences of all acts ripple out into the universe with you at the epicentre, yet they also come back to you, though in a different form. And I? I stand at the very centre of them all, the still yet dynamic process by which the balance of the universe is maintained. I am the fulcrum at the centre. Some say I am blind, but I am not: I see all, but I do not judge, nor do I give value to one thing over another. I simply calculate, and the universe, in truth, is one great calculation. Know the formula, and you will see how one thing gives way to another, the creation of one thing will always require displacement and the removal of another. The subtle balance of your world depends upon nature, red in tooth and claw, playing its role as swift creator, preserver and destroyer.

You, mortal, know much about your human ideas of justice and reward, yet to these I give little thought. In my cosmic scales you may find a reflection of your own justice, and in that you must also know that all of your deeds have a consequence and a price—you tip the scales one way or another with every moment of your life. But do not let the talk of morality and law confound you. To pass through the veil that I guard, you must first understand that you, too, stand at the fulcrum of the cosmic balancing act, and that you are a part of the web of cause and effect, action and reaction, tied to every living being upon the earth and under the earth, in the seas and in the heavens. This web cannot be broken, and, knowing this, you might yet find your heart weighs in the balance of a feather in my scales, and pass through the veil."

Astrology: Libra

Illumination

Deities from the ancient world and medieval philosophy appear in barely disguised form throughout the tarot. We've met Venus, the goddess of love, in the Empress, and her consort Mars in the Emperor; in the Wheel of Fortune we met Fortuna turning her wheel upon which men rise and fall; now in Justice we meet possibly the most scrupulous, cold, and unyielding goddess of them all. The lady of cosmic balance, the fulcrum of the universe upon which the scales of everything are adjusted, stands before us with her weighing scales and her sword, and bars the entrance to a temple.

Lady Justice is clothed mainly in white, the colour of purity of will and intention, yet her over-robe is in the colours found most frequently in the suit of wands, the suit of will and drive. This tells us that not only is the justice and balance of the universe completely judgment-free and pure, but it is also the driving force of the universe, allowing life to continue and survival to be maintained. The balance and equilibrium found in this card can be seen as the will of the universe, the cosmic order. Lady Justice holds in her left hand (her receptive hand) a set of scales that are perfectly balanced, containing nothing, and in her right hand (her active hand) a sword, also perfectly poised and balanced. She reactively adjusts the scales of the universe to maintain balance, and actively exacts swift justice within the world to the same end.

It is important to note that when speaking of justice in the context of this card, we are not talking about human justice (that can be found in the Six of Pentacles, which shares some symbolism with the Justice card) but cosmic, universal balance and natural law. The active justice that the card exacts in the world does not necessarily mean that the just will receive rewards and the wicked will be punished; nature does not work that way. Nature is not just, but it is exact. It is purely a matter of calculation. Here we find the law of cause and effect—the effects we create with our actions. There cannot be an action that does not cause a reaction. Even the tiniest act has rippling effects out into the universe, and we cannot live without creating these effects and therefore the need for adjustment within the universe. Every breath we take consumes oxygen and replaces it with carbon dioxide, thus we have changed the makeup of the universe, and a balance must be exacted to maintain such a cycle (in this case, our planet has a built-in carbon dioxide removal system: trees and plants use the carbon dioxide and replace it with oxygen). This is more than just justice: this is symbiosis and the rich cycle of adjustment and balance that maintains the universe. Note also that we are using the term "equilibrium" rather than "equality," because the world does not necessarily create beings on equal terms or footing. Some creatures are born weak, others are born strong.

Some are preyed upon by others, some act as predator, some are at the top of the food chain and some are at the bottom. This is what is meant by the phrase "nature, red in tooth and claw…" created by Alfred Lord Tennyson in his poem "In Memoriam." As humans, we are mostly shielded from this side of nature, and we have instilled equality as a protected principle in many of our societies. Yet in nature the fine balance is maintained through constant adjustment and cause creating effect.

In the card image, we find other symbolism that further expresses the idea of balance and equilibrium. Justice is numbered 11 in the Tarot Illuminati, and thus it equates with the High Priestess (1 + 1 = 2) and the twos of the minor arcana. Further, it is found at the centre point of the major arcana. It therefore shares the properties of balance, equilibrium, duality, and polarity. Whereas the High Priestess is still in silence, the point between inception and birth, Justice is still in balance, being the infinitesimally small fulcrum upon which all extremes balance.

Lady Justice stands between two stone pillars that are identical in their height, width, carving, and decoration. Pillars are also found in the High Priestess and the Hierophant, and these two cards are each teachers of their own mysteries and guardians within or without a temple or religious building. Just like the High Priestess, Lady Justice stands at the entrance of a building, the door itself covered by a veil between the two pillars. Beyond the veil we can make out the light of burning flames, signifying some sort of illumination. What is beyond this doorway? What mysteries does the goddess of justice guard? And how might we pass between these pillars to find out? We can imagine that this is the guarded entrance to the second half of the major arcana, and we must first demonstrate our understanding of the lessons we have learned thus far before we can proceed.

There is a brief suggestion of human action and morality in this card, despite its more cosmic associations. Throughout the world, the act of judging an individual's actions and the correct response to those actions is often depicted in iconography as a set of scales. In Egyptian mythology, it was believed that after death the deceased would face Maat, the goddess of law, justice, truth, and order, who would weigh their heart, symbolic of their soul, against her feather. If their heart was the same weight or lighter than the feather, they could pass to the afterlife, but if it was heavier, they would be torn to pieces by attending deities. Maat not only watched over the justice and balancing of human action and thought, but also the order of the universe: she regulated the turning of seasons, the movement of stars, and the procession of time. This reminds us that not only is Justice a card of universal balance and equilibrium, but it also asks us to consider the effects that our actions, thoughts, and words have on the world and others around us, as well as upon ourselves. Every action has a reaction. No act is an isolated incident, and no man is an island.

Revelation

There are two distinct ways in which Justice can appear in a reading. Firstly, it can point to some sort of balance and equilibrium in a more universal sense; secondly, it can indicate the effects of the querent's actions in a more human sense. It is a matter of intuition, the context of the question, and surrounding cards to decide which aspect the card is taking for the reading.

Most often, Justice indicates the law of return playing out in the querent's life. It suggests that the querent will see the results and consequences of their actions, and the effects of past acts. These may not, however, be results that are based on the virtue or goodness of their actions, but simply reactions of some kind. This card points to events that may not be what the querent wants, but rather what they need. There is a definite sense with this card of karma coming into play in the querent's life, and a sign for the querent that their acts have effects; they do not go unnoticed by the universe.

Sometimes Justice brings with it the need for maintenance of equilibrium in the querent's life through the act of adjusting things. Depending on the context of the reading, this may manifest as a lifestyle adjustment to fit around a new job, career, child, location, or relationship. In a relationship reading, it may point to the need to adjust the balance of power in the relationship, or the way in which the partners relate to each other or divide the responsibilities within their household. This can also apply to family or friends of the querent. In the workplace, it might point to the need to balance many different roles, requirements, tasks, or interests to get a job done.

The Justice card can indicate that the querent must remain unbiased and objective in the situation at hand in order to get the best results. This might indicate that they are caught between two people or two conflicting interests, and they are being asked to choose. Justice suggests remaining as neutral as possible and finding a balance between the two, so that the best decision may be reached. There is also the need for absolute and unbiased truth in the matter, fairness from all involved, and consideration of all sides.

On a mundane level, the Justice card can point to legal matters, contracts, promises, oaths, and arrangements between people. Upright, all of these things are positive and useful for the querent. If accompanied by the King of Swords or the Six of Pentacles, Justice can represent a judge or person with the power of judgment in the querent's life.

Reversed, Justice indicates legal matters and court cases that are not favourable to the querent. It represents events transpiring from their actions that will be negative and difficult for them, or difficulty in adjusting their life to maintain balance in response to a new situation, person, or event. Sometimes it suggests that people in the situation are being untruthful, unfair, unjust, or biased—usually against the querent.

Keywords

Justice, judgment, objectivity, balance, equilibrium, maintenance, order, law, truth, legal matters, contracts, promises, cause and effect, consequences.

Chapter 13

The Hanged Man, the Dark Night of the Soul

"They called me traitor but in turn betrayed me, and now I am the scapegoat, the sacrifice. Hanged like Peter, it is not my reward to find my soul at liberty among the stars and the angels of heaven; I must let every part of me fall away, leaving only that which remains to peer, naked, into the darkness of the abyss beneath me. Into the dark night of my soul I descend, into the absence of love and the absence of God and light. But what is it that remains? Only that which can be suspended between the past and the future, between what was and what shall be, between the heavens and the earth. This is the path of the winding stair descending, the footsteps down, down, down. This is the path of sacrifice, and few walk it willingly. This is the necessity of surrender, of letting go and giving up—not because all is lost or hope is gone, but for the very reason of hope. When you can surrender yourself entirely, you will know what it is to be a tiny piece in the greater good, and to be connected to your higher self. Do not struggle, do not protest, but find serenity and peace in your surrender. There is always a higher purpose to all things, even your pain and the darkness in which your soul walks. All it takes is for you to turn the world on its head and see it from a different angle."

Astrology: Neptune

Illumination

The Hanged Man marks the point in the tarot when things begin to turn dark. Justice, the preceding card, was the balanced pivot itself marking the halfway point of the major arcana; here is the turning point itself. From here on, we are faced with cards that are more abstract, dealing with some of the biggest issues we can face, and putting us through an intense series of dark and internal processes. As such, the Hanged Man indicates the descent into the Dark Night of the Soul, the sacrifice of the self, and surrender.

Despite the name, the Hanged Man is not being hanged by his neck until dead as we might expect. Instead, he is hanged by one foot from a Tau-cross gallows, which is in full leaf. His other foot is bent at the knee and crossed behind his leg, and his arms are crossed (probably tied) behind his back. Given his predicament, you would expect to see a face showing strain, pain, or suffering, but instead the Hanged Man's face is peaceful and serene, though very serious. Around his head there is a white-gold halo that shines like the sun, lightening his countenance. He hangs in a smoky grey nothingness, suspended between the worlds. The image is a simple one that contains great depth.

There is only one other card in the tarot that portrays figures upside down: the Tower, which we will meet later. In that card we find great destruction and a forced, catastrophic loss of ego or a sense of self, and two figures fall headfirst from the tower that is struck by lightning. They wear red and blue, just like our Hanged Man, which links them to him. However, whilst in the Tower the figures seem to be in pain or suffering, one of them still clinging to his crown and attempting to retrieve what is being destroyed, in the Hanged Man there is a clear acceptance of the process. This link tells us immediately that the Hanged Man is a card of losing something, letting go of something, or finding something destroyed. Yet the peace upon the Hanged Man's face reassures us that whilst it is a difficult process, it is one that will result in a higher awareness. This is further shown by the solar halo that emanates from the Hanged Man's head, marking him as a martyr or holy man.

Martyrs can be found in many religious traditions, and in each one they share the fact that they allowed their physical, mundane, earthly body or concept of self to be destroyed or surrendered in order to attain a higher spiritual understanding and state of being. For many this meant actual physical death, often accompanied by horrific torture, although the earliest Christian meaning of the term could be given to any man, woman, or child in the church that underwent torture or interrogation and social humiliation for their faith, even if they lived. From that point on, they were awarded greater respect in the early Christian community, and were seen as having a greater understanding of God. This concept of surrendering one's ego, sense of self, or physical body in such a way is found in the main feature of the card image as it has remained unchanged through the centuries since tarot's birth in Renaissance Italy: the fact that the man is hanged upside down. This peculiar position was common at that time in the *pittura infamante,* a defaming or shaming portrait, Which was used as a social punishment for thieves, bankrupts, traitors, and frauds (although the depicted hanging itself was never carried out). These shaming pictures would be displayed in prominent places in public for all to see, and they often included a list of the depicted man's crimes. It was a form of social ridicule as well as retribution, particularly in cases where the person might have evaded punishment by law for some reason. The portraits were requested and commissioned by legal and civil authorities to support a court ruling or other punishment. There are no records of any women being depicted in this manner; most men depicted were from the higher classes, and thus they had the most to lose from being publically shamed. A person seen in a shaming portrait would lose friends, influence, reputation, power, work, business, and clients. This further points to the Hanged Man in the tarot being an image of sacrificing or giving up the mundane world or the self, yet once again the peaceful and serene face of the man indicates that instead of struggling against his defamation and shame, he is in acceptance and learning to flow with it. If he struggles, his defamation will most likely be uglier, messier, and attract more attention. But if he surrenders himself to the process, he might be able to recoup something from the situation.

Nevertheless, this is still a dark card. The grey mist of nothingness behind the Hanged Man is symbolic of a spiritual limbo, an unknown place, and the Hanged Man is suspended in the very middle of it. We can see no heavens and no earth, only the place in between. He is between the worlds, at the centre of the *axis mundi*, the world axis. His suspension, and the gallows upon which he hangs, represent a connection between the world above and the world below, a pathway that allows us to descend from the world of light to the world of dark, the underworld. Since the solar halo is reaching the world below first, the Hanged Man shows itself to be a glyph of the descent of light into darkness in order to redeem it. This is part of the mythical formula of the dying-resurrecting god, found throughout time and in all cultures. We see it personified by Jesus, Odin, Attis, Osiris, and in goddesses too, such as Inanna and Persephone. All of these figures sacrificed themselves in some way or descended into the underworld, resulting in their rebirth or resurrection, and the attainment of a greater understanding and spiritual wisdom. Many also underwent the physical mortifications associated with martyrs: Jesus was crucified, Osiris was murdered and had his body mutilated, Odin was hanged from the World Tree, and Inanna was killed and hung upon a meat hook by the goddess of death. This tells us that the Hanged Man is a card that puts us through the process of sacrifice to attain higher spiritual wisdom for ourselves or for others. In mysticism, this is a well-documented part of the spiritual journey, called the Dark Night of the Soul, after the poem of the same name by St. John of the Cross, the Spanish Christian mystic. In the poem, he described the dark of night as his guide, with the night being more loving than even the sun at dawn, offering great spiritual potential. In this darkness, though many trials and sufferings await, the mystic finds deeper unity with God or the divine, giving him- or herself up to it and surrendering to it like a virgin girl to her lover. The Dark Night of the Soul, in which the mystic feels intense sadness, loneliness, and depression, and during which he may feel as though the divine has abandoned him (reminiscent of Jesus' last words upon the cross in the Gospel of Mark, "My God, my God, why have you forsaken me?") is the womb in which the mystic gestates into resurrection.

The resurrection found in darkness and the life springing forth from the Dark Night of the Soul is symbolically represented by the Hanged Man's number, 12, adding up to 3 (1 + 2), the number of the Empress and therefore birth and life, and also by the fact that the gallows upon which he hangs is in full leaf and bursting with life. This is letting go and surrendering to the process of sacrifice within the Dark Night, but not death—that comes in the next card. This is life in suspension, not life in death. This is the point of sacrifice at which the mystic hangs in the balance between the worlds, and forms a bridge between heaven and earth with his surrendering of the self.

Revelation

The Hanged Man is not an easy card to receive in a reading, nor is it a pleasant one. However, it is an intensely spiritual and mystical card, which means that it can be quite difficult to interpret in a reading that relates to more mundane and everyday matters. Often it appears in a reading to indicate a time of standstill and suspension of activity, in which the querent may find that it is seemingly impossible to move forward, make progress, or achieve the breakthrough they need. However, unlike another card of immobility, the Eight of Swords, the Hanged Man is not bound or tied down, but rather in a state of stillness for a good reason. It may be that the querent would not benefit as much as they think they would from action or movement forward at this time; they must take the time to be still and surrender themselves to the current process or moment, rather than look to the one that may be coming.

Sometimes the Hanged Man points to a time of spiritual darkness for the querent, feelings of abandonment and isolation on their path or journey. Periods of intense depression may accompany the Hanged Man, along with a belief that the querent is suffering for no reason and experiencing the world at its cruellest. It may feel like a time of limbo, as if nothing is happening. However, if the querent learns to not struggle against this experience, but instead surrender themselves to the process, they will find spiritual wisdom and a deeper understanding of themselves.

If the querent is going through changes, difficulties, or worries, the Hanged Man simply tells them to let go and give in. It will do them more harm to fight, and they should instead become passive, receptive participants rather than trying to direct the changes or take any action. In relation to projects, the Hanged Man sometimes advises a brief pause in work so that the querent may reflect on their current progress and achievements to date, and take the time to make better plans. The main positive aspect of the Hanged Man's suspension and limbo is that it gives the querent plenty of time to think.

This card can sometimes indicate a change of perspective, seeing the issue from a different point of view, and turning everything on its head. In a relationship, it may suggest a break or a temporary separation so that both partners can assess what they want from each other and the relationship. With regard to family matters or an issue the querent cares deeply about, the Hanged Man talks about sacrifice for the higher good, particularly self-sacrifice in some way for the benefit of others. In this sacrifice the querent will find peace, serenity, and inner harmony.

Reversed, the Hanged Man indicates a martyr complex, feeling always like the victim, or a standstill that will be very difficult to break out of. It can also indicate that the querent has great difficulty taking or initiating action in their life, or acting upon their thoughts. At its worst, the Hanged Man reversed suggests a loss of faith, struggles against the process of the Dark Night of the Soul, and an intense spiritual pain that pervades the querent's life.

Keywords

Spiritual limbo, letting go, surrender, suspension, pause, thinking, reflecting, sacrifice, descent, Dark Night of the Soul, martyrdom, inner harmony, serenity, giving up, inaction, standstill.

CHAPTER 14

Death, the Sunset Roads of Metamorphosis

"When the hero's clothes are stained with blood and the river runs red as the sunset, when the body's decay becomes food for worms and the keening of the grieving mother wails across the land, I shall ride triumphant. Then I will open my mysteries to you like the wings of the raven or the butterfly from the chrysalis. Know this, and do not fear: everything dies, yet nothing is destroyed. You stepped into this world under pain of death and you are already dying. The hour of your death is unknown, but it is certain, and nobody is promised tomorrow. Death is a constant companion for those blessed with mortality; sometimes I come as an enemy, sometimes as an opposing warrior, sometimes as a friend, and most often as a stranger. But do not fear: you've died a thousand times already. Your constituent parts rotted away long ago to allow new parts to grow; your concept of self has died and been reborn as a phoenix from the ashes countless times; you have bid farewell to who you were before and what you knew, and have taken to walking the sunset roads that lead across the world to dawn. With every step you are like the corn of the fields, ready for my scythe; with every breath you are teaching your lungs the death rattle. Whilst in life, you are in death. Only the fool denies the metamorphoses and transitions on the sunset roads: he will find it hard walking. I say it a third and final time: do not fear. Remember, you must die. The small deaths of your life are preparation for that final nightfall when the shades of this world fall from your eyes and you take my hand as it reaches for you, joining me in the danse macabre."

Astrology: Scorpio

Illumination

No card in the tarot is so recognizable (and so misused by the media!) as Death. Tarot readers almost universally respond to its appearance with, "It's okay, the Death card doesn't mean death, but transition…" However, since the tarot as a whole presents us with a coherent view of the universe of human experience, death must feature somewhere in the deck. The original designs of this card were likely to refer to actual physical death, since the tarot was created at a time when death was a frequent visitor to a person's home. Modern times have blessed us with longer life expectancies, lower infant mortality rates, and better medicine, making death a stranger to us and therefore turning the Death card into a symbol for something else: transition, metamorphosis, change. This does not take away the fear of it, however, as change can be a terrifying thing. We cling so readily to the status quo that when it comes time to let go, we cannot, or we go through suffering as we learn how to do so. Death rides into our lives and tramples on our stability, reminding us that every beginning leads to an ending, and in order to change and grow we must leave something behind. Sometimes this comes as a gentle transition, like the butterfly leaving its chrysalis, and at other times it is a more painful journey, like the raven picking clean the flesh from our bones until we are left with only the bare necessities. It is easy to confuse Death and the Tower because both represent endings of some kind; but whereas the Tower is sudden destruction, Death is a natural decaying process. It is not merely change, either, like we find in the Wheel of Fortune, but rather a particular kind of change: death, leading to decay, leading to a new beginning.

When any living thing dies, it rots. This process of putrefaction, decay, and decomposition sees all its constituent parts break down and change state. In a body, the soft tissue, such as skin and eyes, decays first, and then internal organs begin to liquefy; after this, the external features do the same, so that the body is no longer identifiable. Eventually, after a remarkably short period of time, all that will be left is bones. After a much longer time, even the bones will be gone. Most importantly, although the body changes state dramatically, no longer being the person or creature it once was in life, it is not destroyed: it transforms and becomes part of something else, like the earth, or the insects and plants that fed from it. Decaying plant and animal matter creates fossil fuels that give us power, as well as fertilizing other plants, which are then consumed by other animals, some of which we in turn consume. Chalk hills were formed from the deaths of billions of protozoa around ninety million years ago, and beneath our feet within the earth are the bones of untold numbers of our ancestors. Life is built on death.

In the Death card, we see one of the four riders from the Book of Revelation, riding a pale horse, fully decked out in chainmail armour and helmet. His appearance is terrifying, since he brings in his wake that thing which most of us fear. His horse tramples beneath it an armoured king, whose golden crown—a symbol of his ego or concept of self—falls to the earth. This reminds us that no matter how great we believe ourselves to be, or how impressive our titles or reputations are, we are never immune to the force of death. This force may manifest itself in our lives as the death of the old self to allow for growth, or the closing of one door so that another may open. It can often be difficult to face, as we only focus on what we are losing. However, death as an armoured warrior tells us that we cannot conquer him, though fight him we might.

Death carries a large flag that is also a scythe, the blade created from the skull of a crow or raven. These carrion birds are known for frequenting battlefields and places of execution or burial, where they feast upon the remains of the dead and help along the process of decay with their appetites. As black birds, they are harbingers of death, as well as emblems of a certain stage of alchemy known as *nigredo* or the "black work," in which material is left to decompose in its container so that its constituent parts separate into strata. In internal (spiritual) alchemy, this allows the alchemist to remove that which isn't truly them and recognize the parts that are, so that they can be perfected into the Philosopher's Stone. In the earliest alchemical engravings, this stage depicted the Red King and the White Queen (polarized parts of the self, akin to the Empress and Emperor of the tarot) united in lovemaking in a coffin or a black alembic (alchemical beaker). In other words, the alchemical king and queen are interred together in their symbolic tomb and are left to decay. This process of *nigredo* is symbolically represented in the Death card on the flag: the red rose is a symbol of the Red King, the masculine principle, while the white rose is a symbol of the White Queen, the feminine. They are united together in the blackness of death's flag. Once again we are reminded that death, and the decay that follows it, fertilizes new life.

Incidentally, this rose has many other connotations. You can find it on the golden key that hangs from the Empress's skirts, for instance, connecting death and life. It represents the silence of the grave and the secrets to be found within the process of transformation, as it was the rose that was carved upon Catholic confessionals to indicate that anything spoken there was confidential. The rose was also hung from council chamber ceilings to swear all those present to secrecy; this is where we get the term *sub rosa*, "beneath the rose."

Featuring prominently in this card, as if carried along by the momentum of the ride of Death, is a boat sailing down a river that looks red with blood. Boats and rivers are symbols throughout the Tarot Illuminati for a journey of transition from one state to another. We see them in the Six of Swords, for instance, in which a woman and child are ferried across the water by a boatman (reminiscent, perhaps, of the ferryman in the Graeco-Roman underworld). The river of blood reflects the colourful sunset (or is it a sunrise?) that we can see in the card, where the golden sun sets behind a castle with two towers. Here is another gateway for us to pass through, like those found in the High Priestess and the Moon, reminding us that death happens all the time in our lives whenever we make changes or undergo them.

Revelation

The Death card appearing in a reading means big things. It symbolizes every ending and transition in life so that the querent can move on and find something or be somebody new. It can indicate the end of a job or career, the end of a stage of life, the end of a relationship, the end of an era or a friendship, even moving from one location to another. Surrounding cards, or the context of the question itself, will indicate the nature of this ending. If the Death card is accompanied by cards such as the Wheel of Fortune and Six of Swords, the querent can expect sweeping changes that alter their life forever. If accompanied by more destructive cards, such as the Tower or the Ten of Swords, the querent may find that they are being forced into this change by circumstances outside their control.

Every now and then, this card can actually indicate physical death, as this is one possible manifestation of ending in our lives. Such an interpretation should only be given if Death is surrounded by cards that support this, or if the question specifically concerns something that might lead to death, such as a long-term illness; however, it is always wise to be careful with such a reading, as a bereavement counsellor or medical professional is likely to be better suited to dealing with the real concerns of the querent than a tarot reader.

Sometimes this card appears to remind the querent that changes need to be made, or that if they surrender to the process of transition, they will suffer less. This card is not always easy to deal with, but the querent is reminded that the decay of one thing fertilizes something else. The process of metaphorical death allows the querent to cut away from their life what they no longer need, to take the proverbial scythe to their circumstances or personality. It may be a call to the querent to take a matter or problem down to its "bare bones."

If reversed, Death can suggest that the querent is stagnating because they are refusing to change, or having difficulty doing so. They may also be having a hard time dealing with loss and bereavement, or letting go of an old state of being, person, place, or time.

Keywords

Death, change, ending, transition, metamorphosis, letting go, decay, stagnation, stasis, bare-bones, sunset.

CHAPTER 15

Temperance, the Angel on the Middle Way

"There is fire, and there is water. There is man and woman. There is earth and sky, life and death, being and not being… and I stand between them all. Many see them as black and white, opposites between which there stands a clear divide, a barrier that neither side may cross. There is no such barrier; there is only me. I am the mediator that stands on the Middle Way, the path to unity through tempering and moderation. Everything is in flux, and when you realize this, you can adapt everything—manipulate it, mix it and mingle it, throw it all together into a boiling cauldron and create something that is greater than the sum of its parts. I am beyond unity: I am that which comes from it. Yet I am found also before the birth of that creation. I am the process by which it is created.

Walk my path, with your feet wet from the river that will never be the same when you return to it, with the many-coloured herald of perfection crowning you, and you shall know the mysteries of alchemy. You shall be given the knowing of being two things—all things—at once. Let your life be a work of art, let it be a creative process of fluidity and adaptation, never the strict rules of excess one way or the other. Understand this: take too much, and you will be greedy and overburdened; give too much and you will be starving and weak; learn to do both, be both, stand in both worlds, and you will become greater than yourself. Know also that you are truly neither man nor woman, but something bigger and less confined to such forms. Let your self be the cauldron in which the mixture brews, and let your self be the Philosopher's Stone created therein."

Astrology: Sagittarius

Illumination

From the blackness and decay of Death, we are now faced with a radiant vision of an angel, robed in white with the sun rising behind him. Temperance is

83

traditionally one of the four Virtues, and refers to the moderation of the self without going to extremes of behaviour or character. Situated just before the Devil, which represents imbalance and extremes, the Temperance card shows us the path of balance. The most prominent symbol in the card is the angel, mixing fluid between two golden cups, standing with his feet both in water and on land, with a shining rainbow above him. Behind him, a path continues through verdant fields, and the sun rises.

The angel is also found in the Lovers and Judgement, between which falls this card. It is therefore the midpoint between a beginning in the Lovers card and completion in the Judgement card. In the Lovers we saw the angel blessing Adam and Eve in the Garden of Eden, where they were separate from each other and in a state of innocence. In Judgement, the man and woman, positioned like Adam and Eve in the Lovers, are looking to the angel announcing their resurrection, being freed from their earthly bonds and achieving a spiritual state of perfection. Between them is the child that has been created from their union, the Philosopher's Stone achieved through their process of alchemy. Here in Temperance, however, the man and woman are gone and have been replaced by two golden cups, both being held by the angel, who pours watery energy from one cup to another. This is the alchemical process in action, and specifically the part of that process that occurs after the *nigredo* stage (seen in the Death card, and discussed previously). This stage is called the "Peacock's Tail" due to the rainbow-coloured emanations that arise. Once the putrefaction of *nigredo* has been completed, the substance is put through a process of distillation: this process involves first heating the substance so that it vaporizes into steam, and then cooling it rapidly so it liquidizes again, thus making it stronger and purer. During this, the "Peacock's Tail" would appear, being all the colours that are contained within white light, the next stage that follows, called *albedo*.

This means that not only have our alchemical king and queen now rotted away into each other, truly unified, but now—united—they are being put through another process involving opposites: repeated heating and cooling. In Temperance we see the unity of opposites and the flux between them to create something from that union that is greater than the sum of its parts, just as pure white light is often seen as symbolically greater than the rainbow colours that it contains within itself. Temperance is about moving between extremes; bringing together opposites and synthesizing them; taking a wide variety of influences and sources and mixing them all together in a great milieu of potential and creativity. There is no separation in Temperance as there was in the Lovers, but instead a recognition of the things shared in common, the uniting threads.

The unity of opposites and the state of being in between them during the process of uniting is also symbolized by the angel who, like the maiden in the Star, has one foot in the pool of water and one on the land. This highlights the idea of living with a foot in both worlds, living with a healthy relationship between our conscious mind (land) and subconscious mind (water), or our mundane and spiritual lives. It also brings to mind the famous quote from the Greek philosopher Heraclitus: "You could not step twice into the same river, for other waters are ever flowing on to you." This means that at every moment, not only does the moment change, but so do you. When you step back into the river, its waters have moved on and are no longer the same river, just as you are no longer the same person you were a moment ago. There is continual flux and change occurring in the Temperance card, and the angel moderates and tempers that flux. The purple irises in the card link it to the Moon, the quintessential card of flux and shifting, but also point to the Greek messenger goddess Iris, who acted as a mediator between heaven and earth, just as the angel acts as a mediator between the two cups.

The angel is less a "him" and more a "him/her," as we can see that whilst it has a man's torso, it has a woman's head and hair. This is another reminder of the unity of opposites, and a direct reference to our alchemical king and queen who are no longer separate but united as one, ready to create the Philosopher's Stone together from their marriage. Further, the angel isn't just any angel, but the archangel Michael, signified by the fire triangle upon his chest. This draws us to another interesting link between the Lovers, Temperance, and Judgement. It is the archangel Raphael that we see in the Lovers card, the angel of air; Michael in Temperance, the angel of fire; and finally Gabriel in Judgement, signified by his trumpet. These are the only three cards in which angels can be found.

Like the angel, we have also seen the two cups before. They are held by the lovers in the Two of Cups (the Lovers as they appear in the minor arcana). In that card, the cups are held upright and no flow can be seen between them, yet in Temperance the watery energy flows between them and is shared. This is the process of coming together, an internal process, indicated by the watery nature of the energy, and one that may not move along smooth lines, shown by the fact that the energy is tumultuous and choppy. To onlookers, this process looks downright messy, an eclectic hodgepodge that surely cannot work. But to the mixer, the alchemist, nothing could be more natural. We can see this in the grace and poise with which the angel mixes the fluid between the cups.

Revelation

When Temperance arrives in a reading, it is often to bring the lesson of moderation and balance into the querent's life. It indicates that there are a number of different, sometimes conflicting, extremes in their life, which are useless to them on their own. These various elements, must instead be brought together into one place, melted down in a great cauldron, and shaped into something new and better.

Often, Temperance indicates the need to take the middle road, avoiding extremes and finding a balance between them—finding the common ground. In a work or career reading, for instance, it might be that the querent needs to find the common ground between themselves and a colleague with whom they are in conflict, or the middle way between a tried and trusted method and a new, innovative one. Temperance advises them to take the best bits of both, discard the bad bits, and thus create something more effective. It can also represent testing a method or idea through rigorous application of extremes, thus strengthening it.

Temperance is the card of eclecticism in all areas of life. Spiritually, it represents drawing on a number of different belief systems to find the best of all of them which suits the querent. With regard to creativity, it brings with it an inundation of different influences for the querent to create from; most importantly, it suggests an eclecticism of skills, talents, and passions, which—on their own—might not seem like much to the querent, but when united together create something far greater and more useful. The querent should look to how they can combine their various skills and talents, rather than viewing them in isolation.

This card can indicate a need for adaptation; the querent will be required to "go with the flow" in relation to life changes—coordinating various parts of their life toward a more unified goal, whilst moderating them so that a single part does not become more important. There is a suggestion of balance and even-handedness required in the querent's life, with the querent juggling many different things and giving equal weight to all of them. In a social situation, Temperance suggests that a given group of people is a melting pot of various ideas, beliefs, skills, styles, and personalities that might seem to clash at first, but which actually work great as a team, each person bringing something unique to the table.

In a relationship reading, Temperance really comes as a blessing. It is a higher form of the Lovers, and thus brings not only unity between a couple, but also fruit being born from that union. Whilst this may indicate a child, it can also indicate a couple that work together to create things, each one using their own particular set of skills toward the goal. It represents a tremendously creative partnership, so that there is much more to the relationship than romance and love.

Reversed, Temperance indicates an inability to find common ground; the process of bringing together different sources, people, or influences being blocked; or a refusal to adapt to an ever-changing situation. The flux and balance of Temperance is unwelcome to the querent; they would prefer to move toward excess rather than moderation.

Keywords

Moderation, tempering, balance, flux, common ground, unity, synthesis, alchemy, milieu, creativity, eclecticism, melting pot, equal weight, adaptation, flow, the middle way.

CHAPTER 16

The Devil, the Chains that Bind

"When you desire nothing, nothing is what you will get, but when you desire the world, you will bring yourself great renown and riches. You must thrust yourself into life without fear and without holding back. Reservation is for the weak, and they shall only be given tastes of the weakest fruits. Bury yourself deep in the bosom of decadence and your rewards shall be glorious, I promise you. Climb to the top and glorify your self, and your achievements will be seen throughout the land. I am the desire for greatness and for worldly success, the decadence of material luxury and the excess and extremes of the physical world. What is sin to one is virtue to another. When you consume, I am there fuelling the fires within you; when you rut, I am there too, urging you on. Let lust govern your loins and ambition govern your heart! But fear not the chains that you find around your neck—you are a slave, but only to your own desires and ambitions."

Astrology: Capricorn

Illumination

The Devil is a card that invokes fear and shock in many people, since it uses as its title the name of the most evil being in traditional Christian mythology. The Devil, also called Satan, is often identified as the ruler of all sin and vice, as well as the tempter of humans. According to this worldview, the Devil is responsible for all of humankind's evil deeds and wrongdoings. In medieval times, it was believed that he could possess people and cause them to perform evil acts, and could send his minions (demons) to do the same. The Catholic Church, in response to this, had a rite of exorcism to drive evil and demons out of a person's body and cleanse them of wrongdoing. It is also the Devil who is said to have tempted Christ when he went out into the desert for forty days and nights to fast and pray, offering him worldly riches in the form of a kingdom, and tempting him to transmute the rocks of the desert into bread so he would not starve during his fast. Satan finally tried to tempt Jesus into bowing before him and worshipping him, at which point Jesus drove him away and completed his fast.[11]

In some strands of Christian thought, Satan is said to be a fallen angel, Lucifer, who was once one of God's most loyal servants in heaven. But Lucifer rebelled against God, leading other angels to fight at his side, because he did not want to serve God any longer. He is said to have had the attribute of great pride, which caused his downfall. As punishment, God expelled him from heaven and cast him into hell, where he ruled from thereon as Satan, governing the souls of the wicked and punishing them for their wrongdoing. The name "Satan" is from the Hebrew meaning "adversary"—the opponent of God. The term "devil" comes from the Greek *diabolos*, meaning "slanderer" or "accuser." Both these titles show him to be an enemy not only of the divine but also of our own true selves.

In later folklore, the Devil is depicted as a trickster, hell-bent on obtaining the souls of humans through underhanded and manipulative means. In modern parlance, we talk of "making a deal with the devil," which involves bargaining with the devil or one of his demonic servants, and trading one's soul for worldly riches, beauty, youth, or some superhuman feat, and typically plays on a human's greed, ambition, or passion. We see an example of this in the Elizabethan drama, *Dr. Faustus*; a more modern example is the folktale that grew up around the blues musician Robert Johnson, who was said to have had a burning desire to be a great musician. He took his guitar to a crossroads, where he met a "large black man" (the devil) who tuned his guitar, played a few songs on it, and then returned it to him. Johnson soon became one of the greatest blues musicians that ever lived, but he died suddenly at the age of twenty-seven. It was believed that he had sold his soul to the devil for skill as a musician, and the devil had collected his payment sooner than expected.

To give one's soul to the devil in traditional thought doesn't necessarily require a bargain or pact. It is often believed that one can give one's soul to the devil simply by indulging in sinful behaviour or vice. In tarot, the definition of sin is void, since it is up to the individual to decide for him- or herself what is right; however, the Devil card tells us that we can metaphorically chain ourselves to that which is bad for us, the worst of human nature, through acts

---

11. Matthew 4:1-11.

which are bad for us. Whereas the angel of the Temperance card advises us to moderate and temper our actions, the fallen angel in the Devil card urges us to go to extremes. The Devil in the card image is elaborately decorated with gold jewellery, indicating the love of money for its own sake, the desire to own and hoard material possessions. This is complete immersion in the earthly, material realm, as indicated by the environment of the card: here we see the scene taking place in a cavern beneath the earth, reminiscent of the Greek underworld Hades, in which the souls of the dead rest but within which all the earthly riches of gems, minerals, and ores can also be found. While worldly goods and possessions can be useful tools and things of beauty, here they become obsession, seen as ends in themselves rather than as means to an end. This is why the figures in the card have chains made from gold, a precious metal: when we obsess over possessions and money, they become our master.

The Devil himself represents all the vices of the world being offered to us. Since the man and woman in the card are kneeling at his feet, chained to him, we know that they are his slaves, subservient to him. They are no longer in control of their desires, choices, or actions. This is the most dangerous position for a person to be in. When we are in this state, we are vulnerable, often addicted to something that we believe makes us strong, or which gives us a buzz for just a little while longer. Alcoholism and drug addition, sex addiction and addiction to power are all found in the realms of this card, with their victims kneeling at the Devil's feet. Upon his exquisitely carved throne, we see the figures of people engaging in extreme behaviours, and one covers her face in despair. In the centre of the throne is a great stone goat, symbolic of the astrological sign Capricorn, which rules over this card. Capricorn's horns are also found on the Devil's outfit, and his are also those of the Devil. This cardinal earth sign reminds us of the worldliness of this card. Capricorn in turn is ruled by the planet Saturn, the glyph of which we can see tattooed onto the right shoulder of the Devil, reminding us that the devil was often depicted as a goat. As a mountain goat, Capricorn leaps from peak to peak, always seeking greater heights, which tells us that this card brings great ambition with it and a desire for the best. Goats are also in modern culture associated with sexual drive, reminding us of the lust that the Devil rules over. Lust for life can be positive, but the Devil usually takes it to extremes, where lust becomes rapacious desire and covetousness.

The sexual nature of this card is highlighted further by the fact that the chains that bind the man and woman to the Devil are connected to a giant ring that rests over his crotch. The couple is chained to their lower, worldly desires instead of being guided by a higher calling or awakened realization. If we look closely, we can see that not only does the man look away from the outside world, instead turning in toward the devil's throne, but also that the woman's eyes are glazed over, her irises white and her eyes unfocused. Their perception is blinded; they are in ignorance. Anybody who knows an addict or a person who is on a self-destructive path understands what this ignorance looks like: denial. Denial to admit anything is wrong, refusal to accept help. Whilst in this state of ignorance and denial, nobody can help and no intervention will succeed. The chains the man and woman are bound with must be broken through their own realization and effort.

The chains are also symbolic of everything that binds us and chains us down in our lives. Sometimes this is our own fear, ignorance, and hatred holding us back. Sometimes it is material forces or circumstances. Of course, not all the chains that bind us are negative: we routinely take on bondage out of choice and for good reason—the bonds of marriage or civil union with our loved one, the bonds that tie us to a child, the bonds of a contract that gives us employment or a loan, oaths and promises to friends and relatives. But when these things become a prison of our own making, we know we are in a Devil situation.

The Devil and the Lovers cards are linked in the tarot; the numbers of the Devil card, 1 and 5, equal 6, the number of the Lovers card. In the Lovers, we see an angel with a woman (Eve) on the left and a man (Adam) on the right, in the Garden of Eden before the Fall. In this card, we find the woman and man still on the same sides, but now they are chained to a fallen angel. They too have fallen. If the man and woman in the cards represent two different aspects of our psyche, anima and animus, feminine and masculine, here we find both aspects caught up in a web of addiction and imprisonment.

Revelation

The Devil is rarely a positive card, but it does have a few redeeming qualities. Sometimes it can represent the querent's ambition and desire for greatness, as well as their desire to move on from one achievement to the next, never stopping or pausing for breath. One thing's for certain with such a querent: they won't rest on their laurels! If positively aspected in a reading, this card can indicate a time of great desire and action in the querent's life, a lust for life, and a willingness to take risks and enjoy life to the fullest, which will serve to further their goals and improve their circumstances. This querent wants to make the most of life while they can and while they have the means and desire to.

In a relationship reading, the Devil, if surrounded by positive cards, can sometimes indicate that the physical side of the relationship is wonderful—the sex is great and the mundane circumstances are working very well for the couple. If accompanied by the Lovers or the Four of Wands, it might also indicate the bonds of matrimony, or other contracts between the couple that tie them together somehow. On a spiritual level, the Devil can represent the descent of spirit into matter, a focus on Earth-based religions, a reverence for the life force, or perhaps engaging in sex magic.

However, most of the Devil's reasons for appearing in a reading are negative. It indicates that the querent is, or will be, in a situation in which they are trapped or imprisoned, one they are finding it difficult to get out of. Sometimes it even suggests that they do not know they are trapped at all, as they have been duped or deceived into thinking they are free. This card can indicate the querent's ignorance in a matter, or their willingness to stand by whilst acts that would harm themselves and/or others are perpetrated. They may also be the perpetrator themselves. This card sometimes points to an addiction of some kind, such as alcoholism or drug abuse, as well as the most decadent (or luxurious) things taken to an extreme. If appearing in a reading about health or accompanied by cards that indicate health concerns, the Devil speaks of overdoing it: too much food, too much wine, too much exercise, for instance. It can indicate obesity, unhealthy habits, and an unwillingness to break out of such cycles.

Usually the Devil points toward the querent's inner demons—their fears, bad habits, or any secrets and shame they are hiding from themselves and others. This may also relate to the querent having feelings of entitlement or dominance over others, or, alternatively, feelings of powerlessness. Often it says that the querent has handed over their power to another person or agency so that they don't have to take responsibility for their actions, thoughts, or failures.

This card can indicate mind games, either on the part of the querent or which the querent is a victim of. It can also point to the querent feeling like a slave to a certain aspect of their life, such as a job, or to another person. It sometimes indicates a codependent relationship, an unhealthy one, or one built solely on one person being in control of the other.

Reversed, the Devil carries the same associations as upright, but instead of being in ignorance about the unhealthy lifestyle or the vice and entrapment, the querent is growing aware of it and feels the need to escape. They are shaking their chains and starting to pull on them. Sometimes, when reversed, the Devil can point to a breaking of promises, oaths, or contracts (for good or ill), and detachment from a situation rather than attachment.

Keywords

Vice, temptation, ignorance, decadence, bondage, lust, urges, inner demons, chains, entrapment, imprisonment, oaths, contracts, promises, attachment, dominance, slavery, habits, addiction, obsession, materialism, hedonism, desire, sexuality, ambition.

CHAPTER 17

The Tower, the Destruction of the Self at the Edge of the Abyss

"You worked so hard to build so high, to construct great walls and create beautiful things. You attached yourself to them, considering them to be extensions of your self, your personality, your ego … That was your mistake. Fool, don't you know that in the end everything must be destroyed? Don't you see that if you build false towers and unstable foundations, your creations will crumble to dust? Everything you ever strived for, everything you ever loved, everything you showed to the world as you must be destroyed. Only when all sense of self, all ego, all attachment has been cut away can you be worthy to receive illumination. For years you have looked out at a tiny world from stained-glass windows, protected behind the mask of bricks and mortar; for too long you have known your "self" and your destiny. However all your knowledge up until now is false. And the more you cling to it, the harder it will be to let go and move on, like the child that clings to its mother's breast when it should wean. Now it is time for illumination and, since you have made it so hard a task for revelation to come to you, you must now face the lightning strike. It will destroy everything you have surrounded yourself with to get to you, and when it does, you shall fall … because nothing can be left over from this, nothing spared, no mercy given. You will be liberated from your tower, and as you fall, you shall be able once again to see the stars that you have missed for so long."

Astrology: Mars

Illumination

The preceding cards in the major arcana may have seemed like things couldn't get any darker or more challenging. Well, the Tower says otherwise. However, given the ugly state of things associated with the Devil, it may be that this experience with the Tower is necessary to free us from the shackles and bonds of the previous card. This does not, unfortunately, make the experience of the Tower any easier.

In the entire tarot pack, there isn't an image as disturbing as this. The card image is one of destruction and upheaval. It shows two figures, a man and a woman, falling headfirst from a burning tower. The tower has been struck by lightning and seems to be exploding from the inside out, spewing flames and black smoke into the sky. Even the rocky foundations of the tower have caught fire, and there seems to be no soft landing for our falling couple. The destruction and ending pictured here can sometimes be confused with the decay and ending found in the Death card; however, there are important differences. In Death, the upheaval, change, and destruction is natural and gentle, a decay that serves to fertilize life with its process; in the Tower, on the other hand, the upheaval and destruction is sudden and swift, tearing down everything we have built. It feels needless, pointless, and very painful. It is not a gentle process that we can learn to face or cope with, but one that we just have to try and survive.

The main symbol in the card is the tower itself, being struck by lightning. In ancient Greece, lightning was considered a sign from the heavens of the gods, particularly Zeus, intervening in the mortal world. Even today, we talk about a "bolt from the blue" to describe a sudden occurrence that shocks us and turns our world upside-down. Symbolically, the strike of lightning can also represent divine inspiration hitting suddenly, or shocking illumination coming from an unexpected source. Here, the lightning is striking the very top of the tower, thus the topmost part of it endures the most damage. This tower can represent many things, however generally it is everything that we have built, everything stable in our lives, all our plans and achievements, our authority, and our reputation. Given that it is also phallic in nature and therefore linked to the suit of wands, this tower can represent our concept of self, our ego, or the persona we portray in the world. It is all these things that are destroyed by the lightning, yet this lightning seems like it should be a force for good, coming as it does from the heavens and the divine. As such, we are reminded that although the destruction and devastation in the Tower card is painful and destroys much that we hold dear, it may be for the best, and sometimes what we have built is wrong or leading us down the wrong path (as in the Devil, the preceding card). Sometimes we cling so much to our concept of self, driven by ego, that we don't take the gentle hints life throws at us to implement any change, so instead massive and sudden destruction is the only thing that will cause us to change. Given that this card follows the Devil, the card in which we built up material wealth and ego, and became addicted to the pleasures of the material world in excess, the Tower can often be seen as a card of necessary destruction that leads to liberation.

This idea is made even clearer by the appearance in this card of twenty-two little flames in the shape of the Hebrew letter Yod, which we also meet in the four aces. This letter in the Hebrew alphabet represents both a hand and a seed, as it is included within every other letter in the Hebrew alphabet. It therefore represents seeds of wisdom or life, and numbering twenty-two means we have one Yod for each of the major arcana of the tarot. These flames are being released because of the destruction, as if they were trapped within the tarot and now they are free to be expressed in their true spiritual nature (fire is often synonymous with spirit in tarot). The card after the Tower is the Star, a card of illumination and spirituality, as well as renewal and rejuvenation, continuing this theme.

Throughout the Tarot Illuminati, we have seen male and female figures appearing as pairs in the cards. Together they represent the entirety of our psyche, and in the context of this image they are both falling headlong from the tower, both being thrown down and destroyed. There are two ways we can view this: we can seem them as undergoing destruction, and even as he falls the man is still reaching for his crown, the ego and sense of self, showing denial and a need to clutch onto the things that are being destroyed. However, we can also see them as being liberated and released from the constricting confines of what the Tower represents. As the different parts of our psyche, our anima and animus, they are being released from all the negative thought processes we have accrued throughout the earlier cards, released from the wrongly built ego and false persona we used as a mask to hide ourselves, freed from false ambition and allowed to start again with a blank slate. When the Tower has been completely destroyed, the rocky foundations beneath will be revealed and there will be room to start building again. The Tower is the reset button of the tarot.

Revelation

To receive the Tower in a reading can be both an unwelcome message and one of great possibility. Wherever it falls, the Tower indicates sudden and difficult destruction in the querent's life; surrounding cards and the context of the question can indicate the nature of the destruction. It points to upheavals that are unwanted or unpleasant for the querent; changes that the querent does not want and will fight against if possible; and the removal from the querent's life of something they hold dear or place great value in.

If the Tower appears in a reading about work or career, the querent may suddenly find themselves unemployed or demoted, forced to take a pay cut or forced into a different job role that is unwelcome. If it shows up in a reading about love or romance, the querent should be warned that the relationship could end in a most unsavoury fashion, with a great number of secrets coming to light that will be painful to know. However, the Tower might also have a less devastating meaning, such as simply a situation in which one or more people "blow their tops" in an explosion of anger. Health-wise, the Tower advises that the querent may be on the verge of some sort of breakdown, though they may not realize it because they may be in denial, or an unpleasant event may tip them over into illness.

For a querent who is busy with a project or enquiring as to the direction they should take, the Tower indicates that they will find themselves needing to scrap all progress made so far because the nature of the goal, the premise of the project, or the situation it pertains to, has been lost, destroyed, or changed so much that it is no longer recognizable. The Tower may also point to the destruction of the ego or the persona the querent is portraying to the world, and any false concepts they have built up around themselves.

However, the Tower can sometimes bring its own strange form of blessing in its wake. Often, despite the fact that the process of destruction is painful and difficult for the querent to undergo, once they have picked up the pieces (or others have picked up the pieces for them!) they are liberated and freed from a situation or relationship that was negative or holding them back. Sometimes the Tower appears for a querent who has felt trapped or unable to move forward because of outside obstacles, and the Tower's destruction clears the way for them. Unfortunately, it clears everything else out also; it is like throwing the baby out with the bathwater, but at least the dirty bathwater is gone. It is important to remind the querent, when the Tower appears, that these processes do hurt and it is natural to find them difficult, but there is support available for them. The reading should indicate via other cards or the context who or what might be able to help them pick up the pieces. However, the querent will still need to ride out this storm.

Reversed, the Tower represents the process of sudden upheaval continuing in the querent's life for longer than it should, holding the querent in a constant state of disruption and pain. It may be perpetuated by a vicious cycle of behaviour in the querent's own life, or by another person, or simply by the nature of what is being destroyed, but the querent will definitely be growing exhausted by it. It can also signify destruction and upheaval from the past that is still having a negative effect on the querent's life. For them to move on, they must accept that some things have been or will be lost, and that inevitably certain elements of their life must be let go before they can move on. If they refuse to accept this, they will be stuck reliving the destruction over and over, but once they let go of what was lost, they are free.

Keywords

Destruction, devastation, upheaval, disruption, ruin, loss, change, endings, letting go, liberation, freedom, explosion, release.

CHAPTER 18

The Star, the Guiding Light of Renewal

"There will always be times of darkness. There will always be moments of spiritual pain and suffering. But there will never be a time when light is truly absent. The sun does not die at night, and even at the sunset of our lives, our glimmer of starlight is never extinguished—it merely changes form. Knowing this, weary traveller, I offer you the chance to quench your thirst and soothe your fire-burned body in the deepest pools of the world; upon the surface they reflect the starlight above, and beneath they house the well of healing and rejuvenation. But do not think that the healing comes only from the waters that I pour: outward healing only reflects the inner process, as the pool reflects the stars in the heavens. I know this because I was there in the beginning when the Creator fixed the stars within every being and sent them down to earth in trails of fire. You are meteor-born, shooting stars streaking brilliant golden fire across the heavens and leaving your marks upon the world, and some of you are lucky enough to have your soul's immortality reflected by the constellations at night and the tales of men. Yet it is so easy to forget, so easy to let your light grow dimmer, so easy to cause the lights of others to do the same. When we see the light fading in the world, it is I who descends, following the paths you blazed all those aeons ago, to usher in a new dawn of awakening and renewal to soothe the wounded world. Will you be the one who welcomes me, star-born one? Will you be the one who proclaims the age of peace and harmony?"

Astrology: Aquarius

Illumination

The major arcana has given us quite a rough ride in the previous few cards. Beginning with the Hanged Man, we saw a descent into the underworld, painful self-sacrifice for a higher purpose, the death and decay of the old self, our darkest inner demons and most base desires holding us prisoner, and the complete and sudden destruction of everything we thought we knew. After the turmoil of the Tower, it might seem like nothing can ever be good or right again. Yet here we have a light shining in that darkness, guiding us out, helping us find a way to navigate beyond the destruction and upheaval. The Star shines beautifully in the Tarot Illuminati, her beneficent light pouring down upon us like the waters of renewal and life, and we may quench our thirst and soothe our burned, fire-cracked throats after our ordeals.

The image in this card is one of rich blues and turquoises, golds and whites. Water is a predominant element of the card, and we see a naked young woman with one foot in a pool, pouring water from the jugs she holds in each of her hands. One jug pours water back into the pool, whilst another pours it onto the green earth that she kneels upon. The woman is nymphlike, her body petite and lithe, and she is barely covered by swathes of light blue material that seem to originate from the water itself. Light blue swirling tattoos climb up her legs and thighs and over her torso and shoulder, and she bears an otherworldly quality that suggests she may be a water nymph or even a goddess descended from the stars and taking human form. Behind her, the valley is green and lush, an Egyptian bird of paradise, also called a Bennu bird, perches atop a tree, and above her the first reddening light of dawn begins to spread across the sky.

Her posture and actions are immediately representative of the zodiacal sign of Aquarius, the water-bearer. Aquarius represents rebirth, renewal, awareness, awakening, and humanity, and is also said to rule over the New Age movement. However, it is not a water sign but rather an air sign in the zodiac, making the Star a dual glyph of the elemental qualities of air and water. The water that is being poured from both pitchers is falling both into the pool of water and onto the earth; here, since it is a woman in the pose of Aquarius that is undertaking the action, the water represents a force or process of healing, refreshment, rejuvenation, and awakening. It is being given simultaneously to the emotional and spiritual self as well as the body and the everyday world. The duality of water and earth in this case may also represent the subconscious and the conscious minds. The water itself sparkles with silver, diamondlike energy, indicating that it is not just any water, but the waters of new life and renewal. After so many difficult, earthy and fiery cards, it is refreshing to find a card of water and air.

The main symbol of the card is, of course, the stars themselves. They are eight in number, with seven of them surrounding a much larger eighth one. Each has eight points. The main star is roughly the same height as the woman and therefore is given equal importance to her in the image. These particular stars are reminiscent of those found in Islamic decoration, in which they represent spiritual perfection and the light of God reaching out in all directions of the world. The star as a symbol has a rich history. It often appears in mythology as a sign or omen designating the birth of a special leader such as a legendary king or spiritual teacher (as is the case for Jesus, King Arthur, and Siddartha Gautama, who would become Buddha). It is therefore a sign of fame, fortune, and greatness, as well as the ability to lead others or bring about the dawn of a new era or awareness. Stars have also been used as means of navigation by travellers upon the sea and on land, particularly in wilderness where the lack of artificial light enabled them to see the stars more clearly. Coming out only at night, stars thus represent a guiding light in the darkness, and a means by which we can find answers. This supports the concept of the star being a symbol of the light of God, or the light of the divine, as often it is this force that we turn to in the metaphorical darkness. As a source of light in the darkness, the Star and the Hermit share a bond, yet it is the Hermit that guides the way into the darkness and the Star that guides the way out. The number of stars and their points reminds us that numerologically the Star and Strength are also linked: 1 + 7 = 8. In both cards we find maidens, and both cards share the theme of healing. Another aspect of the star as a symbol is that in our modern world we make wishes on stars, and give the name of this symbol to the famous idols that we look up to, or who represent luck and fortune. The Star is the height of luck in that it shines light favourably on us all.

The Bennu bird, also called the Egyptian Phoenix, perched on the tree in the background has meaning in both Christian iconography and ancient Egyptian myth. It is sometimes used as a symbol of Christ's resurrection and the immortality of the soul, indicating renewal and rejuvenation on a spiritual level. In the Egyptian Book of the Dead, this bird is closely associated with the sun rising out of the underworld each night, just as we rise up out of the darkness of the preceding major arcana cards into the light of the Star. The sun god Ra was called "Lord of Jubilees" to mark his joyous rising at dawn. It is in this celebratory thread that we can identify the female figure on the pitcher held in the maiden's right hand: it is Euterpe, the Greek muse of lyric poetry, whose name means "rejoicing well" or "delight." She holds to her lips her signature *aulos* or double-flute. The dawn that the sun brings after being reborn from the darkness of the underworld can be seen in its nascent form in the card image; it represents the dawning of a new spiritual life, the dawning of self-awarenesss and a renewed perspective, and the dawn of a day that brings with it long-awaited healing and refreshment on all levels.

Revelation

Perhaps the Star could be called the luckiest card in the pack, but it is also a deeply spiritual card. It often appears in a reading to indicate a querent who is going through a time of intense renewal in their life, usually after a difficult time or experience. They feel like they are being led out of the darkness and into the light, being given renewed hope and opportunity, guidance and direction, and their mind is set on rising higher into spiritual awareness and understanding. When the Star appears, it reassures the querent that no matter how bad things may become, or how dark they feel inside, there is a glimmer of hope that, if it is nurtured, will grow and spread its light to all parts of the querent's life. They are being given a chance at new life, a rebirth of sorts, through increased awareness and rejuvenation of energy, hope, and direction. This is a breath of fresh air, a spiritual pampering of the soul, a restoration of faith.

Often the Star signifies the end of a difficult time or a period of conflict. In a social situation, it indicates peacemaking, with rivalries and enmities being healed and all participants moving on. Any pettiness between people is let go so that they might all move on, heal, and seek higher things. In a reading about love, the Star indicates the kind of relationship that heals both parties, provides them with inspiration and hope, renews their passion and ability to love, and ushers in a new era of peace and harmony.

For work, projects, careers, and goals, the Star is a truly wonderful card to receive. It signifies hopes, dreams, and wishes coming true—not necessarily through the efforts of the querent, but instead through synchronicity or chance or a bit of luck. Everything just seems to fall into place and the querent has a clear path toward their goal. This card might also indicate the querent achieving some sort of recognition, fame, or fortune, and their light will shine brightly to all who see them. Sometimes the Star can also represent the querent "following their star"—carrying within themselves a glimmer of a dream that they nurture and listen to, letting it guide them toward achieving the dream and making it bigger and more manifest. The querent is encouraged to chase their dreams and wishes, and to take every opportunity that comes their way, as it will all lead toward achieving that dream.

The Star can also point to a movement toward a more spiritual way of thinking and being. The querent may have an interest in the New Age movement, spirituality, religion, mysticism, ecology, and any associated practices, such as meditation, crystal or sound healing, or Reiki. Anything concerning healing is of particular interest to the querent, as they may wish to help others through the difficult, wounded feelings they themselves have undergone and overcome. Occasionally the Star can also signify a querent who has a spiritual gift of some kind, such as the ability to see auras or talk to spirits.

Reversed, the Star does not take on any negative qualities as such, as its energy is so pure and spiritual that even reversed and surrounded by poorly aspected cards it sheds a glimmer of light upon the situation. However, at its worst the Star reversed can suggest that the querent is ignoring the guiding light in their life, whether it is in the form of an inner dream or hope, a person, a spiritual teaching, or an experience that holds rich wisdom for them. This may be due to a feeling of inadequacy or feelings that they don't deserve such guidance, so the Star reversed also reminds the querent that they are made of the same stuff as the stars, and they have an inherent beauty and power of self-renewal and guidance contained within them.

Keywords

Hope, healing, renewal, rejuvenation, refreshment, rebirth, peace, harmony, beauty, guidance, direction, luck, fame, fortune, opportunity, success, spirituality, dreams, wishes.

CHAPTER 19

The Moon, the Silver Road of Shadow and Tides

"It is time…Now you must return the way you have already been, through the valley of the Moon, treading the winding, shadowy path of illusion upon which everything—even your self—will shift and flow. There are tides throughout the universe, and you are not only part of them but you also have them deep within, and it is by my light, therefore, that you love and hate, fear and feel joy, fall in love and out again. Yet my light has no power of its own, borrowing light from the sun, and it is my honour to transmit this truth to your weak eyes so that you might not be blinded…But the light never reaches you complete; there is bound to be distortion: this is inevitable when it passes through the lunar gateway. So do not fear—yet do not tarry, either—for even in the shadows there is a resemblance of truth. The shadows owe their existence to the light. Move quickly now: the wolves are baying for blood and soon the hounds will follow…but the thing to truly fear is neither wild beast nor allies turned enemy: fear only fear itself, rising up from your own subconscious, a strange, primal creature made only of survival instinct, left over from when the world was nothing but thrashing teeth, ripping claws, and interminable darkness. Walk through the valley of the Moon and fear not the shadows; know that this silver road is a promise and preparation for what is to come."

Astrology: Pisces

Illumination

Our journey in the darkness is not quite over, even after the beautiful light of the Star shone through the devastation of the Tower and reminded us that there is always hope and guidance, no matter how dark things get. Here we travel onward on the path of the Moon. It is a strange path, filled with mystery and the unknown, strange creatures and the subconscious, lunacy and tidal flow. The card image is just as strange: a giant moon with a face sits close to Earth between two stone pillars. In the foreground are a dog and a howling wolf, and between them, out of the depths of a pool, crawls a lobster. From here a path winds over a rugged landscape, leading through shadow and flanked here and there by purple irises. Behind the moon, on the path beyond, the landscape looks illuminated, hinting at what is to come when we have successfully traversed this lunar landscape.

Yet that's no moon: we can clearly see that there are solar rays shining brightly behind it. It's either an eclipse, or the moon itself is a gateway to the sun, or an obstacle in the way of illumination. It's almost as if the back of the sun's head is the moon. This does not necessarily make this a negative card, as a brief foray into ancient philosophy will show. For the Greek Platonists and Neoplatonists, the sun represented the light of truth whilst the moon represented the reflected light of truth, the light that humankind was able to see. In Plato's philosophy, he described a "world of true forms" in which the "true form" of everything could be found; our world, being the manifest world, was a copy of the world of true form, and therefore a reflection—often a poor one—of the light of truth. Yet a seed of truth was still present for these forms to exist in our world at all, no matter how poorly they reflected the light. Later, around the second century CE, philosophers such as Porphyry wrote that the sun was the source of light, but that it was only through the moon that light could come into manifestation, since the moon was a gateway through which souls passed on their way to birth.

The moon, being closely tied to a woman's fertility cycle, is an obvious symbol for birth. Yet in tarot we have little application of this particular association. Instead, tarot looks at the moon from the other side: if the moon is the force through which our souls come into being and through which divine light and truth passes, it is also the gateway through which we must pass a second time in order to reach that light and achieve illumination. The moon, then, is at once a gateway for manifestation and an obstacle in the way of apotheosis. This is why we see in the card image the solar rays shining out from behind the moon: the moon and the sun are directly connected, but the moon in this card not only reflects but to some extent hides the solar light of truth. In the tarot, the Moon and Sun cards are directly next to each other in the order of the major arcana, reminding us that there are two celestial gateways and rulers of light that we all face in our search for illumination.

The manner in which the moon reflects the light of the sun is both positive and negative. On the positive side, it provides a gentler, less harsh way of seeing the truth. Whilst we are unable to stare directly at the sun, we are able to stare directly at the moon, even when it is full. The moon filters the light of truth into a form that is more readily accepted and easier to access. On the negative side, however, this often means that the truth is distorted slightly, just as light refracts when it passes through water. It doesn't mean the reflection is not true, just that it is not being shown in its original and truest form. As such, the moon can have a misleading effect, but it can also have a gentling effect.

The relationship between the moon and the sun, and their associations with various kinds of truth or perceptions of truth, can be found in Plato's "Allegory of the Cave," in which he describes a cave that is populated by people who are chained with their backs to a rock, and their faces to the wall of the cave. Behind them, on a bridge, their captors walk every day, and behind that bridge are giant fires. The prisoners have never known anything else, and every day they see the shadows of their captors cast by the fire onto the wall in front of them. They watch this shadow-show and believe it to be truth. This part of the allegory is the moon: the reflection of light and the distortion of truth. However, one of the prisoners escapes one day and manages to find his way out of the cave, into the light. At first he is blinded by the bright sunlight that he has never known before, and he crawls upon the ground, blind and in pain. Eventually he acclimatizes to the light, and returns to the cave to bring the truth to the other prisoners. This second stage of the allegory is the sun: the bright daylight of truth, which brings illumination yet can also be harsh and blinding. Through this pairing in the major arcana, we too go through the same process of perceiving only partial truth to fully perceiving the actual truth, but often the reflected light of the moon is necessary to "work up to" the full truth of the sun.

The dog and wolf in the card image are a reference to the fact that much lunar folklore concerns the full moon creating madness of some kind, in both humans and animals. In past centuries, the moon was said to bring about a particular kind of madness, lunacy, which later gave its name to those classed as "lunatics"—the mentally unstable or disabled, and often those who expressed political or social views that were disliked by those in power. In the image we see the wolf is howling at the moon, a common motif in art, and we are reminded of the wild side of nature, and therefore the wild side of our own nature. The dog, sitting calmly on the left, is simply a domesticated descendent of the wild and dangerous wolf, and like that dog we too have wildness within that can be brought out in certain circumstances. In the past, women specifically were seen to be more prone to such wildness, by virtue of having a womb—itself intimately connected to the lunar tides. Women who spoke out or refused traditional societal roles were sometimes called "hysterics" (the name, like that of lunatics, being taken from that which was viewed as the instigator of the "madness": the womb, in Greek, *stera*); some of them were even forced to undergo hysterectomies as a curative measure. The link between the moon and the womb brings us back to the idea of the moon as a force of genesis and birth, bringing souls into existence, and the two pillars forming a gateway either side of the moon in the card are supportive of this. They are the point of no return, the legs raised in birth posture, and the path between them is the birth canal through which the child passes.

We can see purple irises scattered about the landscape. The iris symbolizes a warning to be heeded: apt for the wildness that threatens in this card, and for the distortion to be found in the reflected light of the moon. Iris was the name given to the Greek messenger goddess, whose role was to guide young girls to the afterlife. The lobster that crawls out of the pool is a symbol of the primal aspect of our nature emerging from our subconscious, which the moon also rules over. There is a strong connection in this card to the wilder, primal, and intuitive side of the self; it is this aspect of us that is tidal, subject to ebb and flow, rise and fall. The moon, being the creator of tides in the ocean, is also the creator of tides in our lives.

Revelation

The Moon card has many faces that can appear in a reading, and as such it can be difficult to interpret. Often it indicates a reflection of the truth in the querent's life that is not complete, or distorted in some way. It may point to something being hidden from the querent or the truth being misrepresented. However, there is a seed of truth present, which the querent should be able to access if they are astute and perceptive, although sometimes it can be difficult to find that truth hidden beneath many layers of distortion. Since the moon appears as the back of the sun's head in the card image, it may also represent another perspective, a situation that the querent may not have considered, or which is not seen as a traditional approach. There are two sides to every coin, and the Moon is the side that lands face down.

Sometimes this card can point to secrets. In the context of a relationship reading, it may signify a clandestine romance, as well as secrets being kept from one another. It can also represent secrecy in emotions, with one person in the relationship hiding their true feelings from their partner, for one reason or another. This could be because the partner feels as though their emotions are too confusing, deep, or personal to be able to share with another, or it could be because they fear the reaction of the other person should they share them.

The Moon can often relate to fears that the querent has, particularly fears related to, or manifesting in, their emotional relationships. Thus, this card might indicate something from the querent's subconscious influencing them in their choices perhaps more than it should, and probably without the querent fully realizing the extent to which this aspect of themselves in is control. It suggests that fear is the driving force for the querent at this time; the querent must seek out the hidden side of themselves in which their fears lie so that they might shed light on them and learn the truth. The only way out of fear is through it in this case, and the pathway of the Moon is, unfortunately, the pathway through fear also. This card can also raise issues concerning the querent's shadow self and their primal nature, as well as all the deep-seated and intense emotions that they have. Further, it hints at the ebbs and flows of the querent's life, pointing to recurring waves of a theme or challenge, opportunity or feeling, which rises on a regular basis and then recedes, just like the tide.

On a spiritual level, the Moon points to psychic ability and being able to listen to intuition. It also indicates an interest in witchcraft or Wicca, the divine feminine, women's mysteries, psychic healing, scrying, visions, dream work, and blood magic. Occasionally, especially if accompanied by the Ace of Pentacles, the Nine of Pentacles, or the Queen of Cups, the Moon can relate to women's health issues.

Reversed, the Moon suggests deliberate hiding or distortion of the truth, misguidance, trickery, and madness. It indicates emotions that are so extreme that they have the possibility of becoming potentially harmful neuroses, psychoses, or mental health issues. It may also point to the repression of emotions and a refusal to face deep-seated fears, which can lead to a worsening of the situation. Sometimes this card reversed suggests imbalances in the querent's life of a tidal nature, an ebb and flow that the querent finds difficult to handle.

Keywords

Illusion, deception, reflection, intuition, ebb and flow, recurrence, secrets, hiding, clandestine romance, primal nature, fear, the subconscious, magic, witchcraft, madness, strong emotions.

CHAPTER 20

The Sun, the Light of Truth

"Let the darkness flee and the shadows melt away, let damp and cold not threaten old bones, and let life spring forth where my rays of light touch. I am the centre of all life and the source of it, and I am also the destination. As once you came forth from me, little spark, so you desired awareness of me and unity with me, and now you are no longer a spark but a bright, blazing flame, wondrous to behold, riding triumphant and bearing the banner of my light. You are the child of my golden dawn, the little sun upon the earth, but you have always been thus: you merely lacked the awareness of it. You have walked through many shadows, seen many kinds of truth, been offered many sorts of illumination, but it is only I that can grant you true enlightenment. Never let your gaze turn from me, follow truth and illumination with every step henceforth, and take my hand, sun child, as we herald the light of truth to the world. Watch us rise!"

Astrology: The Sun

Illumination

It has been a long time coming, but now the darkness and shadows are passing. We have walked the long paths of night and have come again to the gates of dawn, and now the sun is rising in its fullest, blazing glory and vitality, heralding the day. Where the moon was the light reflected and perhaps distorted, the sun is the light directly revealed, the light illuminating everything, the light without and within. As with the moon, it is useful to examine these as a pair, since they represent two parts of the same process and two faces of the same cosmic force. If the moon is the back of the head, then the sun is the face looking directly at us.

The card image of the Sun, like that of the Moon card, features the titular cosmic body as one of the main symbols. Here, an orange-golden sun with a woman's face within it blazes hot over a walled garden surrounded by sunflowers. Within the garden, a naked child with white-blond hair rides a white horse, covered only in pearlescent swathes of material and carrying a standard of gold. The child looks at us, yet points directly to the sun.

Throughout the Tarot Illuminati, children symbolize new beginnings, youth, innocence, and joy. Yet this particular child is not just an infant, since he is arrayed in such a fine manner and riding a horse. This would seem more apt for a king or a ruler, perhaps even a champion. The clues to the infant's identity can be found in an ancient text called the *Chaldean Oracles*, a series of fragmented texts dating to around the second century CE, which were held in high regard by Neoplatonists. Recall that the Moon and the Sun as a pair in the tarot are influenced by Neoplatonism and its ideas of truth and reflected truth, and whilst the sun was seen as the origin of the soul's light, it was the moon that acted as the birth canal and gateway into manifestation. Since the sun in Neoplatonism symbolically represented the source of divine light, it also represented the goal with which seekers wished to obtain unity. One fragment in the *Chaldean Oracles*, which speaks of a union with, and epiphany of, Godhead, bears a striking resemblance to the image in our Sun card:

> *"Having spoken these things, you will behold*
> *either a fire leaping skittishly like a child over the aery waves;*
> *or an unformed fire from which a voice emerges;*
> *or a rich light that whirs around the field in a spiral.*
> *But [it is also possible] that you will see a horse flashing more*
> *brightly than light,*
> *either also a fiery child mounted on the swift back of the horse,*
> *covered with gold or naked;*
> *or even a child shooting arrows, upright upon the horse's back."[12]*

Here is the "fiery child," mounted on a horse that is "flashing more brightly than light." We can see that he is naked as well as being covered with gold. This is a bright and bold statement within the tarot, again, of our divine origin and a reminder that to become illuminated and enlightened, we must find a path back to union with that source. Physically, we owe our continued existence as well as our collective origin to the actual light of the sun, and symbolically we speak of

---

12. *Chaldean Oracles*, Fragment 146.

gaining knowledge and wisdom in terms of light to acknowledge the importance of the sun in our lives. Many religions also use solar language to speak of their god or prophet, such as Christianity, which sees Christ as the "Light of the World," and the emperor and Mithras in ancient Rome as the "Unconquerable Sun." "Good" deities are given epithets and realms of light and sky, whereas "bad" deities are given the darkness and low places away from sunlight. In every culture throughout the world, the sun is given a prominent (if not paramount) place in the pantheon, and often worshipped with special devotion.

Thus, this fiery child upon its flashing steed is not just innocence and rebirth, but the awakened consciousness in the spirit, recognizing its unity with the divine source of light, and receiving the light of truth directly rather than through a mediator or distortion. The child is restored consciousness after its long and arduous journey of discovery in the major arcana. We have here the reawakening of our selves in the midst of the light that we thought we were so separate from, a reunion with the source of life. The Roman emperor Julian wrote of the sun as the source of all the world's forms of life, describing it as bringing forth life from darkness into manifestation:

> *"The Sun's resplendent deity I sing,*
> *The beauteous offspring of almighty Jove,*
> *Who, thro' the vivifying solar fount*
> *Within his fabricative mind conceal'd,*
> *A triad form'd of splendid solar gods;*
> *From whence the world's all-various forms emerg'd*
> *From mystic darkness into beauteous light,*
> *Perfect, and full of intellectual goods."*[13]

This parallels the relationship in the tarot between the Moon and Sun, with the Sun illuminating everything that the shadows of the Moon's light had concealed or distorted, allowing us to return to the origin of our selves, in perfection, light, and beauty.

There is more that can be said about the sun in symbolism than there is room for. It is one of the greatest symbols of light, life, and truth; it is the source of all growth and life on Earth, a source also of intellectual and spiritual growth and illumination. It provides warmth and light, chases away the darkness,

---

13. *Two Orations of the Emperor Julian: To the Sovereign Sun.*

shows everything clearly, and brings happiness and joy in its wake. There is a quintessential enthusiasm and vitality that blazes from the heart of the sun. The sunflowers in the card represent this enthusiasm as well as optimism, since the sunflower head will follow the path of the sun throughout the day, and is designed to absorb as much light as possible. The sunflowers also represent always looking toward the light and toward truth, never turning away from it. However, since the sun is so bright and blazing, it has a negative effect in our world: sometimes it parches the earth, drying things up too much. Truth can be brutal, and sometimes it causes more pain than lies.

Revelation

The Sun card brings a blaze of energy and warmth to a reading that is always welcome. It radiates joy and enthusiasm, happiness and optimism, making everything else in the reading a little brighter, no matter how dark everything may seem. When the rays of the Sun touch the querent's life, they can expect light to be shed on the truth, opportunities to pour forth, and vitality to be renewed.

When the Sun appears in an outcome position or to indicate the future, there are few better cards to see. It indicates that the future that awaits the querent is bright and filled with happiness. They will be walking a path of truth and awareness, being given the opportunity to make conscious and fully aware decisions, and to act with clarity in their life. Whilst the Sun does not indicate specific outcomes (other cards in the reading might do that), it does suggest a general atmosphere of joy, happiness, and brilliance that is coming in the querent's future.

Sometimes the Sun points to the querent standing out from the crowd, their light shining so brightly that it is impossible for others to miss them or ignore them. They are a force to be reckoned with, a sight to behold, and somebody who is likely to have or gain great reputation and fame. Since the Sun's rays reach so far across the world at any given time, this card also indicates that the effects of the querent's actions, particularly in relation to work or career, will have wide-reaching influence across a large spread of society or the world. Work that the querent does might also involve bringing truth to situations or the lives of others, helping in the uncovering of things, or dealing with the revealing of information.

If the querent is having a difficult time at the moment, the Sun advises them that optimism will get them further than they think and will bring them to the point at which they can begin to move forward again. It says that the querent should look on the bright side, turn their face toward the truth, and keep moving. It often appears in a reading for people who lack confidence, and combined with other cards it can indicate specific methods and techniques for gaining confidence. However, most of the time the Sun points to immense self-confidence and confidence that the querent has in their work, skills, knowledge, or talents. It also indicates that the querent feels intense happiness in their life and in their work. If it appears in a relationship reading, this card suggests joy and a bright future for the couple, built on truth and happiness shared with each other, as well as confidence in each other.

There is a definite feeling that life is good when the Sun shows up in a reading. Anything the querent was planning is bound to turn out for the best and bring great success. Whatever they were hoping for will come to pass. It brings good health, wellness and well-being, positive outlooks, and healthy friendships. There will also be some excitement and good luck thrown into the mix. In situations where the querent feels stuck, the Sun provides an opportunity of seeing the way forward, and anything unclear will become clear in the near future. It also bodes well for any querent who is studying, since it indicates all forms of clarity, truth, and wisdom. On a spiritual level, the Sun can sometimes suggest a mystical experience of unity, or an affinity with light and forces of goodness, with the querent desiring to bring light to others with their optimism and joy.

Reversed, however, the Sun can shine too harshly. It indicates truths being revealed that can be painful for the querent, or the querent blazing so brightly that they burn out or draw the unwanted attention of those who would be jealous of them.

Keywords

Confidence, optimism, happiness, joy, enlightenment, illumination, origin and source, renewal, consciousness, awareness, well-being, luck, positivity, success, vitality, radiance, brightness, enthusiasm.

CHAPTER 21

Judgement, the Call to Awakening

"From your birth to your death you are caged in worldly trappings, weighted down by the world. You are encased in rock, in a cold tomb, and you see little beyond the cave in which you were born. You are lead—ugly metal for everyday use, unworked and touched only briefly by the light. But you may, having glimpsed the light in the shadows of your tomb, crawl toward it, put your self through the alchemical process that transmutes lead into gold, create of yourself the cosmic egg of possibility and potential. You are rock-born, coming from the dust of the earth, but you need not return to dust at the end of your days if you but strive toward the light. One day you will hear my call of awakening and resurrection, and you will break free from the earth and rise up, rejoicing. You will cast off your chains and let go of fear, moving from darkness into light. You will stretch your arms to the heavens and cry out that you are free, and the tears that fall down your cheeks will take fear with them.

In times gone past, those who sought after the mysteries would bury themselves alive, as they knew that until that point they were just the walking dead: moving upon the face of the earth yet not truly living, not awake. They were sleepwalkers and lived in ignorance, but saw enough of the promise of light to know they could be free. So they went deep into the earth, entombed themselves in womb-like caverns and coffins, there to stay while they gestated and grew in knowledge, wisdom, and desire for rebirth. And when the time was right, the angel would break open their grave and blind them with the true Light. Because in the beginning, the Earth was without form and void, and darkness was over the face of the deep, and the angel hovered over the face of the waters and said, 'Let there be light!'

And there was Light. This is only the beginning, not the end."

Astrology: Pluto

Illumination

The Judgement card depicts the traditional Christian Day of Judgment, which is said to come at the end of the world, when the dead will rise from their graves and be reunited with their souls, and thereafter judged based on their acts in life and sent to heaven or hell. In the tarot, this image bears deeper significance, however, beyond that of judgment and punishment or reward (that is better found in the Justice card). The resurrection of the bodies in the Day of Judgment is symbolic of the liberation of the spirit from that which entraps it, and the awakening of the self to a higher calling.

In the foreground of the card, we see three figures rising from their graves: a woman on the left, a man on the right, and a child between them. This is an important image. Two other major arcana cards of the Tarot Illuminati also depict a man and woman together as a pair, the Lovers and the Devil; in each, the woman is on the left and the man on the right. This puts the Judgement card at the end of a process that occurs in these other two cards. In the Lovers, we saw the distinction between One and the Other, and the reunion of them; it was also a paradisiacal scene of the Garden of Eden before the Fall. In the Devil, these figures were no longer presided over by an angel, but by a fallen angel; they had chains around them and were in a state of fallen grace. Now, in Judgement, the man and woman are both free from their chains, looking upward toward the heavens, and between them they now have a child who stands in a similar, uplifted pose. They have been united, they have undergone the woes of the world together, and now they can show the result of their efforts. We get a clue about this result in the Death card, in which the red and white alchemical rose upon Death's flag tells us about the marriage between the Red King and the White Queen within the earth of the grave, an alchemical symbol of the fertility that comes from the decaying process. In the darkness of the womb babies gestate, and in the darkness of the earth seeds germinate. When the king and queen are released from their deathly marriage bed, they come forth having borne a child—the Philosopher's Stone, the Alchemical Egg. This is what we see in Judgement: the man and the woman have risen from the grave of Death and *nigredo*, and not only are they now free and liberated, but they also have created something greater than the sum of its parts. On a symbolic level, we can see the child in the card image as representing a new awakening and a new beginning, highlighting the rebirth that is taking place in the card.

Rebirth is an important process in any spiritual path or religious endeavour. It is therefore found in the earliest written records as well as in modern spiritual practice. Any initiation ceremony or series of ceremonies will include an element of rebirth. Even the idea behind "born again" Christianity is that the individual undergoes a baptism that not only cleanses them of their sins but plunges them into the waters that, symbolically, they came from originally (water, wombs, and tombs are synonymous in symbolism). The Greek story of the phoenix that is born from its own ashes reminds us that we not only must free ourselves from our old self in order to be reborn, but that the old self provides the fertile material that can form the seed of the new self.

Many deities are said to have gone down into the earth to undergo trials that led to rebirth, such as the Sumerian goddess Inanna, who descended to the underworld and faced death there, being born anew afterwards, and the Christian Jesus who, after crucifixion, was placed in a rock tomb from which his body disappeared at his resurrection. In ancient Egypt, the sun god Ra was seen as dying every night and descending into the underworld on his Boat of Millions of Years, fighting the demons therein that tried to stop him being born again, and then being born at the morning from the body of the sky goddess Nut. Later this myth became syncretized with the idea of the pharaoh's afterlife, allowing for his rebirth in a similar manner, and even later this rebirth became available to all the dead, regardless of status. The rebirth of deities throughout mythology helps humans see the possibility for rebirth in themselves, but it also highlights the fact that we must first undergo a process of death, which we see in the graves and tombs of this card image.

The graves in the card image are representative of any state in which we are trapped or not awakened. There are so many situations that can be indicated by this, and to some extent the everyday world itself can become a tomb. If we get caught up in the mundane, ignoring any spiritual ideals or higher calling, allowing ourselves to sleepwalk through life, then we are truly dead. Another form of the resurrection of the dead can be found in horror movies: the zombie. Zombies are the walking dead that have risen from the grave but lack their soul and mind or will. We can also use the term to indicate people who go through life without any semblance of free thought or understanding of a higher spiritual reality. The Judgement card calls us to rise in awakening to a fully conscious awareness.

The angel that dominates the card, carrying a trumpet, is Gabriel, who in the Christian tradition calls the dead to rise from the grave. He does not judge the dead but merely calls them up, hinting at the fact that the Judgement card isn't really about the act of judgment at all, but the act of rising. The angel can be seen as symbolic of our higher self or higher calling, pulling us toward a higher state of being. Sometimes we do not need an external force giving us cause to look to an awakening, but an internal one. Angels can also be seen as humans but with immortality and wings, so they are a symbol of a realization of a better way of life and a more evolved perspective or way of being.

Revelation

The Judgement card can be difficult to interpret in an everyday situation without downplaying its meaning or power. Nevertheless, it is likely to appear in a reading for mundane questions at some point. In these cases, the idea of rebirth and awakening must be interpreted metaphorically and applied to the situation and context.

In a reading, this card could indicate a time of rebirth and reawakening. The cause of this is not indicated by Judgement but by the surrounding cards and/or the context of the question. Examples might include the ending of a long-term relationship, the ending of a job or career, or the ending of a stage of the querent's life. This is a time of reassessment of the self, of rebirth from the ashes like the phoenix. The querent may have been undergoing a painful process of letting go or loss, and the Judgement card appears to let them know that these events will fertilize a time of growth and awakening for them, and that they will leave behind the cause of pain and rise above it. This card usually points to a movement toward a new sense of self, one that is better for the querent and more fitting for their life's goals and aspirations. Thus Judgement can also indicate the act of breaking old habits and habitual thought processes in order to move on unfettered in life. Sometimes the Judgement card appears to indicate the querent's aspirations and long-term goals, or it suggests that they have reached the end of a goal or cycle and now need to move on. It might also indicate that one opportunity is closing off to them, but that this will lead to a new, better opportunity instead.

Everything to do with the querent's higher self and higher calling is discussed with this card. They may be on a spiritual quest for rebirth, or seeking a radical change in their life that will allow them to feel more in control and free from limitations. It can also point to an epiphany or "eureka!" moment in the querent's life, one that has happened or is about to happen, and a dawning realization. It suggests that any answers the querent is searching for currently can be found if they let themselves undergo the process of rebirth and awakening. They need to pay attention to a deep calling within themselves and allow it to lead them to a higher understanding. It may also be that something has been lying dormant within them or in their lives, and it is now time for it to be released. The querent will also find that learning from the past will be beneficial to them and allow them to move on and rise higher.

In situations the querent is finding difficult, the Judgement card suggests that the best response is to rise above it and move on. They must not let themselves be drawn back down into the mire of ignorance.

Reversed, this card can suggest that the querent is refusing to answer the call of their higher self, or a call to become greater. They may be so caught up in the past, or in old habits and old thought processes, that they are unable to move on, grow up, and evolve. They may be trapped in past wounds or circular arguments, or too comfortable in their habits. They have become zombies in their life, shuffling from one moment to the next without any true awareness. They must break out of this state of being, for their own sake.

Keywords
Rebirth, awakening, reawakening, liberation, freedom, letting go, higher self, higher calling, aspirations.

Chapter 22

The World, the Cycles of Completion and Beginning

"The great road is long, and you have walked its dirt forever and a day. Did you think, in the darkness of the night, when the path disappeared and you thought yourself lost, that there would be a destination still awaiting you? No. But that was a necessary experience. All of life's trials and tribulations are lessons and opportunities that allow you to grow and become a fully aware participant in the dance of life. You know now, looking back, how much can be learned from them. And you can see also how much you have changed. Change is inevitable, and you can never go back the way you came, can never return to the point of origin, though you may still be inspired by it and you may yet find your feet being set on a new path, toward a new destination. There is always more out there, waiting for you, traveller, and you will never be too weary for the treading. Now you are a dancer to the rhythm and joy of life, knowing what it is to move with the beat of your self and the universe, knowing the reflection between the two, and embodying all that is to be found between them. Now you and I both stand at the infinitesimally small point between ending and beginning, and here you are the centre of the world, the product of all your experiences and the synthesis of all your learning. Dance with me now, in this moment, with no past or future, just the now, just your birthright being danced out in the beat of your world: it is awareness, and it is illumination."

Astrology: Saturn

Illumination

Here at the end of the major arcana, after all our trials and tribulations and a journey to end all journeys, we are given the World. This is our prize for reaching completion—as if completion itself wasn't prize enough! It's been a long, strange journey of upheavals and challenges, learning and illumination, sorrow and joy, and we've found ourselves pulled between extremes. Now, thanks to all these experiences, we reach a point not only of completion and conclusion but also synthesis, where everything we have experienced and learned comes together to create something greater than the sum of its parts.

In the card image, we see a naked woman dancing with orange material flowing and spiralling around her. Behind her is a laurel wreath, the traditional symbol of victory, decorated with stars and red ribbon, and she holds two double-ended wands in her hands. In the setting, we see a water-bearer in the top left of the card, an eagle in the top right, a lion in the bottom right, and a bull in the bottom left. Within the circle of the wreath is the world itself, our planet and our home.

Dancing is one of humankind's quintessential expressions of joy, happiness, and celebration. It can be seen in other cards of the Tarot Illuminati that represent joy and success of some kind, such as the Ten of Cups or the Three of Cups. It is made clear by the fact that our woman is dancing that there is reason to celebrate, but this dance in the context of the World is far more than that: this is the dance of life, the dance that we are all participants in, yet many of us are not aware of it. When we reach the World, we have become aware that we are dancers, and we are also aware of the steps, the moves, and the rhythms of our life and the universe. We've grown to understand these rhythms through previous major arcana cards, and now they come as second nature to us. Once we know the rhythm and the steps, we are able to move more gracefully and with ease through life. The nudity of our dancer illustrates that this is a natural state of being, and since we come into this world naked, it also reminds us that this state of being is our birthright, which we came into this world with an inherent claim to. Awareness, understanding, illumination, and wisdom are ours to take, and a goal to strive toward that every human being should have the opportunity to pursue.

The laurel wreath is a symbol of victory, given as the prize to the victors of the Olympic Games in ancient Greece, representing also a height of achievement and greatness. Here it does not indicate victory over others, but instead a victory over ourselves—we have pursued our path to completion. It is wrapped with red ribbon, the colour of passion and desire, showing what instigated the journey, and decorated with the stars that have guided us in the darkness, which represent all our highest goals and aims. This laurel wreath almost creates the shape of a circle or 0, a cosmic egg, which links the World back to the Fool: although an ending has been reached, there will always be another beginning. We never quite return back to 0, the beginning; instead we spiral onward to a new path or journey with new lessons to learn and integrate. The double-ended wands that the dancer holds in her hands tell us that she has learned the dual powers of receptivity and activity, masculine and feminine, and in them she has found her balance. There is no place in the World for extremes: all the extremes have been thoroughly explored in the previous cards. Instead, we have synthesis, complete and perfect, between all states and elements.

The four beasts in the four corners of the card are the symbols of the four fixed signs of the zodiac and the four elements: the bull for Taurus and earth, the lion for Leo and fire, the eagle for Scorpio and water, and the water-bearer for Aquarius and air. We've met these elements before when they appeared in a natural form in the Fool, as the Alchemist's elemental tools, and in their animal form in the Wheel of Fortune. Here, they are once again in their animal form, and as such they represent the four elements as living, active components of our lives, allies in our journey toward completion. With the dancer and the globe of Earth in the centre of them all, we are reminded that we must integrate these four elements fully into our lives so that we can be whole and complete, just as the earth is a complex synthesis of many different elements. This represents the drawing together and synthesis of all we have learned throughout the major arcana, and the result thereof: us, participating wholly and with full awareness in our lives, dancing with life's rhythms, and claiming our birthright as illuminated and aware individuals.

Revelation

This wonderful card most often signifies the completion and conclusion of a very important path, journey, or project, which will leave the querent in a position of having reached a landmark or milestone, yet also being given the opportunity to move on to something new. The querent should be reminded that even though they have completed something and reached the final stages, a new journey will always await them, with new lessons to learn, and new opportunities.

There are many other cards in the tarot that indicate completion and conclusion. The Four of Wands, Ten of Pentacles, Ten of Cups, and Three of Cups, for instance, all indicate some sort of successful ending to a project, goal, or path. However, the World is different: this isn't just the ending of a short-term project or the reaching of an everyday goal—this is a life-changing conclusion. It is so important that the World can often signify the completion of the querent's life's work (or one of them!), the conclusion of all the lessons that they have been learning and processing over many years.

On a more mundane level, the World brings with it opportunities to gain great wisdom and understanding, as well as an indication of the mundane world that the querent surrounds themselves with. It suggests that they possess all the elements required to create something big and important or life-changing. The querent needs to draw together elements from a wide variety of sources to create this, such as pulling together very different people in a work situation or on a project to create something that is greater because of their differences and varied approaches. It might also be found in drawing on very different historical or textual sources during research or while seeking inspiration, and finding the common thread that ties them together. The querent will be going through a process of integration, outwardly as well as inwardly.

Often, the World reminds the querent that as they complete this journey, a new one will be offered to them. They cannot cling to their success and rest on their laurels; they must move forward once more. We can never know everything, and there is always much more out there for us to learn and to be. Although achievement and completion is indicated here, it is not the end.

If the World appears alongside cards of victory, such as the Six of Wands or the Chariot, it suggests that this is going to be a time of overcoming obstacles to achieve victory, winning out in something, and being recognized as a paragon of excellence in one's field.

Reversed, the World—like the Star—rarely takes on a truly negative aspect. Instead, it points to a delay in victory, a goal that was once in reach but, for some reason, has been put off and delayed or taken just out of the querent's reach. It usually suggests that the querent thought they had reached the completion of something, only to find that there was more work yet to do before reaching the end.

Keywords

Completion, conclusion, ending, final, circular, integration, synthesis, victory, triumph, celebration.

PART 2

The Minor Arcana:
Illuminating the Mundane

Traditionally the minor arcana cards relate to the everyday world and our daily lives. If the major arcana cards are the grand concepts, then the minor arcana can be seen as the details; these two parts of the tarot are always interacting with each other, like one big family. Where astrology contributes its symbolism to the major arcana, numerology and the four elements contribute to the symbolism of the minor arcana.

The Four Elements in the Suits

Each of the four suits is associated with one of the four elements: pentacles with earth, swords with air, wands with fire, and cups with water. You can see these elemental associations clearly in the card images, as each suit features the colours of its element, or the scenes will be set in an environment corresponding with that element.

Pentacles/Earth: Earth is the bedrock and foundations of our everyday life, the mundane world, and our physical bodies. It asks us to think about our daily survival, money, fortune, family, home, environment, health, and work or career.

Swords/Air: Air is the element of our breath, and therefore the element of communication and particularly the spoken word. It is further associated with the world of ideas—thoughts, attitudes, and beliefs.

Wands/Fire: Fire is the element of desire, drive, passion, ambition, creativity, and sexuality. It corresponds to ego and individuality, and the power of manifestation.

Cups/Water: Water is the element of our emotions and intuition, as well as everything that connects us to others. It is concerned with our romantic relationships as well as our and social ones.

In the Tarot Illuminati, we see that each suit is also set in its own *cultural* environment, which further evokes the elemental ideas of that suit. All of these cultures are based on real-world examples, but in many cases are enhanced with a little bit of fantasy to spark our imaginations.

Pentacles: an Oriental-inspired culture with an emphasis on fortune, prosperity, family, and duty.

Swords: a culture based on the Elizabethan era of England, with cold, sweeping mountainsides, craggy beaches, and cloudy skies.

Wands: a Persian-inspired culture, set in hot deserts, with views across vast oceans of discovery and the sun blazing down from above.

Cups: a fantasy culture filled with beautiful beings that seem otherworldly, set in an environment of waterfalls, glittering oceans, fountains, lakes, and rivers.

Numerology and the Minor Arcana

The cards within each suit of the minor arcana are numbered from 1 to 10, and thus they share clear associations with numerology. Any time you have more than one of a given number appearing in a reading—for instance, more than one five—the energies of that number are stronger and contribute to the overall interpretation.

One: Beginnings, instigation, focus, pure potential.
Two: Duality, balance, opposition, relationship.
Three: Manifestation, creativity, community.
Four: Foundation, establishment, strength, structure, order.
Five: Conflict, imbalance, struggle, aggression.
Six: Harmony, balance, synthesis, fairness.
Seven: Flux, uncertainty, flow, illusion.
Eight: Strength, boundaries, trapping, stagnation.
Nine: Completion, achievement, awareness.
Ten: Endings, return, renewal, fullness, overkill.

In the tarot, the energies of each suit begin at their most pure and focused form in the aces, and then flow outward to the tens, at which point they have gathered more momentum and layers of meaning. Two of the suits, pentacles and cups, are considered feminine and passive, thus they can "catch" all of this energy as it flows through the suit; see the symbolism of the Ten of Pentacles and the Ten of Cups. On the other hand, swords and wands are considered masculine and active, thus they do not receive energy well—they impale or bludgeon it, which can be seen in the Ten of Swords and the Ten of Wands. In the cups and pentacles the endings are joyous, while in the swords and wands they are filled with struggle and pain.

Of course, numerology also pertains to the major arcana. Starting with the Wheel of Fortune (10), you can add the two digits of a major card together (e.g.

1 + 0 = 1) to find its numerological association; this again shows that the major and minor arcana work together as one big family.

Making Light Work 3

By uniting numerology with the elemental associations of the four suits, you can you create simple short sentences to remind you of the card meanings. For instance, the Five of Swords unites the energies of the number five with those of the element of air. Using the correspondences above, we might create the phrases "aggression in the mind," "conflict of words," or "struggling ideas."

You can go through each of the minor arcana cards to create key phrases that speak to you. Here are some easy ones to start with:

Two of Cups
Six of Pentacles
Eight of Swords
Five of Wands

Making Light Work 4

Consider how the major arcana cards are related to the minor arcana cards that share a numerological association. How do the minors of a given number elaborate upon the message of the associated majors? What features of the card images reflect this numerological correspondence?

One: Aces, the Alchemist, the Wheel of Fortune, the Sun
Two: Twos, the High Priestess, Justice, Judgement
Three: Threes, the Empress, the Hanged Man, the World
Four: Fours, the Emperor, Death
Five: Fives, the Hierophant, Temperance
Six: Sixes, the Lovers, the Devil
Seven: Sevens, the Chariot, the Tower
Eight: Eights, Strength, the Star
Nine: Nines, the Hermit, the Moon
Ten: Tens, the Wheel of Fortune, the Sun (also compare these to the aces: 1 + 0 = 1).

Kabbalah in the Minor Arcana

In the Hebrew mystical system known as the Kabbalah, there are twenty-two letters of the Hebrew alphabet that have their own meanings and themes; these are ascribed to the twenty-two major arcana cards of the tarot. These letters are seen as pathways between ten spheres on a diagram of the universe, called the Tree of Life, and each of these spheres—called a *Sephira*, or plural *Sephiroth*—represents the building blocks of the universe. Since they are ten in number, they fit nicely into the numbered cards of the minor arcana. Thus, taken together, the major arcana and the minor arcana create the whole universe.

Each Sephira has its own "personality" and planetary association:

1. Kether, "The Crown": Unity, oneness, source
2. Chockmah, "Wisdom": Abstract wisdom, duality, the Father
3. Binah, "Understanding": The Divine Mother, creativity (Saturn)
4. Chesed, "Mercy": Expansion, mercy, stillness, creation (Jupiter)
5. Geburah, "Severity": Aggression, severity, action, destruction (Mars)
6. Tiphereth, "Beauty": Connection, harmony, the centre (the Sun)
7. Netzach, "Victory": Kindness, leadership, flux, emotion (Venus)
8. Hod, "Splendour": Intellect, the mind, thought (Mercury)
9. Yesod, "The Foundation": Reflection, transmission (the Moon)
10. Malkuth, "The Kingdom": Experience, manifestation, the everyday (Earth)

Starting at the top and working down, we ignore Chockmah and Kether, since they are so far above the process of manifestation that they do not rightly have a planet that can be associated with them.

Malkuth also is not assigned a planet, for it is too close to Earth. Instead, all the other planets influence it in varying combinations, just as the element of earth itself is a combination of the other three elements.

Binah as Saturn—This may seem the strangest home for Saturn, as Saturn is usually considered destructive in nature. However, Binah is called the Great Sea, and is as much a great destroying Dark Mother as she is a nurturing creative mother. She is at once the great womb that births and the great maw that consumes; she is the womb and the tomb; that which we are born from, we will return to in the end. The Beginning is the End.

Chesed as Jupiter—Chesed is often considered to be the All-Father of the Tree of Life, the god that takes the *logos* or wisdom directly from Chockmah and rules and governs creation with it. So Jupiter, the benevolent all-father of astrology rules this Sephira. He is generous, loving, merciful, and jovial. However, Jupiter/ Chesed can also fall into the trap of becoming a *demiurge*, believing himself to be the absolute and highest creator, since he cannot see the supernal Sephira above him, seeing only what is below him, and therefore forgetting that he is not the highest.

Geburah as Mars—Mars, the aggressive and passionate, is at once dynamic and fiery, as well as destructive. Mars never stops, moves quickly, brings disarray and chaos to life, but it also provides impetus and drive. It shakes up what is stagnant and urges people on in strength. Mars can be either an unbalancing force or a dynamic, passionate force, depending on where it is found.

Tiphereth as the Sun—As the sun is the centre of our universe, so Tiphereth is the centre of the Tree of Life. Tiphereth connects all other Sephiroth and shines the light of Kether down upon Earth. The sun connects the planets together, providing a single source of light and life for each of them, and it shines the light of God upon us. The sun is a life-giving, positive, and energetic force, but balanced—unlike the dynamism of Geburah and Mars. Under the energies of the sun, everything flourishes and grows. But the sun can also burn and dehydrate that which is overexposed to it.

Netzach as Venus—Emotional and fluid Netzach is a perfect description of the planet Venus, ruled by the goddess of love herself. Venus represents not only the emotional content of our lives, the relationships and social aspects we share with others, but also every feeling we have and every intuitive response. It is watery, fluid, and constantly in flux. Venus also rules luxury and sensuality. Whilst this is a very positive planet, bringing a gentle glow to everything, it is also unstable and changeable, and therefore reacts unpredictably in certain situations.

Hod as Mercury—The Sephira of the mind and organizing intellect finds a natural partner in the planet named after the Roman god of communication, speed, messages, and trickery. Mercury is well-placed for academics and thinkers, but not good for lovers and poets! The forces of Mercury and Hod serve to limit and overanalyse, and when this process is applied to the realm of ever-expansive feelings, emotions, and intuitions, things tend to go badly.

Yesod as the Moon—Just as the moon only gives off reflected light from the sun, so too does Yesod only give to Malkuth the light it has in turn received from Tiphereth. Here, the moon is a reflection, an image, a mirror. But it is also the foundation: the ancients believed that it was through the moon's gateway that souls came into their human bodies, therefore whilst the moon is a planet of flux and shadow, it also provides a more solid foundation for earth and Malkuth. Although its waxing and waning is always in flux, so it is also predictable.

Astrology and the Minor Arcana

Like the majors, the minor arcana cards have astrological associations, but since they are representative of more mundane themes, they do not have a single planet or zodiacal sign attributed to them; rather, each card is assigned a combination of one planet and one zodiacal sign. Just as our astrological birth charts are made up of myriad combinations created by the planets moving in and out of the zodiac signs, with each planet's influence being colored by the sign in which it is placed, so it is with each minor arcana card. The resulting partnership between planet and sign can be a happy one, a so-so one, and sometimes a detrimental one, just as some friendships or working relationships can be in the human world.

Rulership, Exaltation, Detriment, and Fall

Each planet has a natural home (its rulership), where the concerns of the planet and the zodiacal sign in which it is placed are mutual or shared; an exaltation, where the zodiacal sign bestows extra energy upon the planet, almost like a party hostess greeting a very special and honoured guest. A detriment is when the planet is in the zodiacal sign directly opposite its rulership; this planet will have great difficulty operating and expressing its energy in that sign. And finally, a planet in its fall is debilitated and handicapped, its energy stunted, stymied, or weak; the sign of a planet's fall is directly opposite that of its exaltation.

Planet	Rulership	Exaltation	Detriment	Fall
Sun	Leo	Aries	Aquarius	Libra
Moon	Cancer	Taurus	Capricorn	Scorpio
Mercury	Gemini & Virgo	Aquarius	Sagittarius & Pisces	Leo
Venus	Taurus & Libra	Pisces	Aries & Scorpio	Virgo
Mars	Aries	Scorpio	Libra	Taurus
Jupiter	Sagittarius	Cancer	Gemini	Capricorn
Saturn	Capricorn	Libra	Cancer	Aries

The sun rules Leo, the sign of the ego and the self, the sign of the king, or man at his highest. It is in its detriment in Aquarius, the sign of selflessness, community, the group mind, and the global village. The sun is exalted in Aries, because it too is a sign concerned with the self; Aries shares the sun's fiery nature, takes command easily, and grabs all the attention. The sun is in its fall in Libra, because such a self-serving and confident planet does not go well with a sign that is traditionally associated with peace, harmony, and cooperation.

The moon rules Cancer, and is associated with the generative process, birth, motherhood, nurturing, and family. It is in its detriment in Capricorn, which represents the strict control of the emotions, a trait that doesn't sit well with the moon's fluctuating energies. The moon is exalted in Taurus, because in this sign its emotions are grounded and steady, finding a firm foundation. The ancient writer Porphyry further wrote that the bull is representative of the moon's power of genesis. The moon is in its fall in Scorpio, where the passion and broodiness of that sign amplifies the moon's negative emotions and causes them to become even more fluid and unstable.

Mercury rules Gemini, as they both represent thought, communication, and the element of air. Mercury is in its detriment in Sagittarius because their modes of thought are so very different: where Sagittarius sees the bigger picture, its mind wandering far and wide, Mercury sees the details and flits about, making very short journeys. Mercury also rules Virgo, where thinking becomes very analytical. Thus Mercury's other sign of detriment is Pisces, since its logical, organized way of thinking does not sit well with the psychic, intuitive mind of Pisces. Mercury is exalted in Aquarius, the sign of the inventor and innovator, allowing for creative thinking and intellectual advances. It is in its fall in Leo, where details are often overlooked if they do not serve the ego.

Venus rules Taurus, the sign of beauty, luxury and sensuality, providing it with a steady foundation. It is in its detriment in Scorpio, which transforms the gentle, sensuous love of Venus into an intense, often jealous and possessive love that can quickly become obsession. Venus also rules Libra, the sign of cooperation and interpersonal relationships. Thus it is also in its detriment in Aries, because Venus's love of peace, beauty and harmony is in direct contradiction to the self-interest of the warrior Aries. Venus is exalted in Pisces, because the ruler of Pisces is Neptune, the planet that is considered the higher expression of the energies of Venus. Whereas in most signs the love represented by Venus is expressed on an individual level, with Pisces the love is universalized and extended to humanity. Venus is in its fall in Virgo, where its gentle, loving nature is rendered picky and critical, and where free expression of the emotions is often blocked by considerations of practicality.

Mars rules Aries, and they share an intense love of action and control, as well as a fiery masculinity and ambition. Both are capable of pushing forward regardless of any obstacles, and are well known for having a virility and lust for life that pervades all matters. It finds itself exalted in Scorpio, where its penchant for destruction can be used to transform base matter into something with greater depth and wisdom. Mars finds its detriment in the airy, balanced sign of Libra, where the scales must always be balanced and peace maintained, and it reaches its fall in Taurus, the slow-moving, materialistic sign of possessions and value, where the fast action of Mars becomes total destruction for the sake of destruction.

Jupiter rules Sagittarius, both planet and sign embodying the outward expansion of power and ideas, searching for truth and justice. Since Jupiter is the "great wanderer" of the zodiac, it finds itself in its detriment in Gemini, the planet with a short orbit that rules brief journeys. Jupiter is exalted in Cancer, the sign of nurturing and mothering, as these benevolent traits are expanded under Jupiter's influence. It is in its fall in Capricorn, as this sign rules self-discipline and controlled emotions, again limiting Jupiter too much.

Saturn rules Capricorn because they both relate to worldliness, achievement, discipline, and control. It is in its detriment in Cancer, the emotional sign of motherhood and nurturing, as Saturn's stoic, constricting nature does not sit well with caring Cancer. Saturn is exalted in Libra, where it seeks to create balanced structures and balanced judgment. Aries, where it is in its fall, stifles the earthy nature of the sign.

Triplicities

A planet is also said to be strong, or to have "essential dignity," when it falls in its own *triplicity*, which is another way of saying its ruling element:

Earth—Taurus, Virgo, Capricorn
Air—Gemini, Libra, Aquarius
Fire—Aries, Leo, Sagittarius
Water—Cancer, Scorpio, Pisces

The planets are likewise given an elemental nature:

	Day Ruler	Night Ruler	Participating Ruler
Earth	Mercury	Saturn	Venus
Air	Saturn	Venus	Mercury
Fire	Sun	Mars	Jupiter
Water	Jupiter	Moon	Mars

(Note that this is one version of the planetary triplicities; it seems that astrologers just can't make their minds up about it!)

So when the Sun falls in Leo or Aries, it has "essential dignity"—in other words, it is particularly strong, has more influence, and is more benevolent. This does not mean that if a planet falls in another sign that it is weakened; it's like when we work in a team with other people—our own skills are not usually lessened by those around us, but with the right combination of skills, and with each team member working toward the same ends or sharing the same interests, together we will strengthen each other and the work produced will be better and more useful.

Putting Together the Jigsaw Puzzle of the Minors

So, let's start to piece this jigsaw puzzle together! Not only does each minor arcana card have associations with a Sephira and an element, but it also has associations from the astrological sign and planet it is ruled by. Within the latter, we need to look for essential dignity (whether the planet falls in its own triplicity) and whether the planet is in its rulership, exaltation, detriment, or fall because of the astrological sign it is paired with on the card.

Here are some questions to consider in our astrological assessment:

1. Is the planet happy in this element?

- Does it have essential dignity?
- Is it in an element that directly contradicts its interests?
2. Is the planet happy with the zodiacal sign it is paired with, and vice versa?
   - Do they share common interests?
   - How do they both move energy?
   - Is the planet exalted in this sign?
   - Is the planet the ruler of this sign?
   - Is the planet in its detriment in this sign?
   - Is the planet in its fall in this sign?
3. Is the planet happy with the Kabbalistic Sephira it is placed in?

In the following chapters, as each minor arcana card is introduced, you will find that the astrological, planetary, and Kabbalistic associations are cited but not explained. This is so that you can consider these associations yourself and make the connections you find most relevant. You may also find that the astrological associations are contained within the first-person speech of many of the minor arcana cards, so be on the lookout for those too.

The Suit of Wands

Ace of Wands, the Thrust and Lust of Life

"From the depths of the primal light I came, whirling in tongues of fire and terrible visions. With the fullest force of life I explode into your dreams and inspire all the urges that course in your blood: the urge to thrust yourself into the world, bold and bright and golden; the urge to set your mark upon history with great deeds and mighty reputation; the urge to roll up all your energy into a ball with another soul and shout the culmination of your pleasure to the stars. I am the lust and desire in life that drives you ever onward to greatness, challenges, pleasure, and pain. I am the force of will at its purest and most focused, the strength of your will and energy and desire all directed to one purpose… I am magic, and I am unstoppable. In my hands I grasp the fires of passion that can inflame or injure you, and from that passion, from that spark of inspiration or danger, everything else proceeds. If I cannot have release, if I do not achieve my goal, I will not weaken, but instead I will consume you from within and you will be the fuel for my ever-burning fire."

No astrological associations for Aces / Kether in fire

Illumination

All the aces, as the first card of their suit, share a special relationship as not only the source of the cards that follow but also as the purest representation of their elemental powers. In the case of the Ace of Wands, we find fire at its purest and most primal, the origin of the concerns of the suit of wands: energy, the self, ego, ambition, drive, passion, desire. All the aces feature Yods, the Hebrew letter that means "hand," which is also the seed of the other Hebrew letters. Thus the Ace of Wands can be seen as a seed that is planted and then bursts into life, releasing its fiery force into the world. As primal fire, this Ace relates to the world of inspiration and desire, as well as our urges, whether they are sexual, creative, destructive, or ego-driven. Just as the wand is thrust out in the card image, so we have the urge to thrust ourselves out into the world and into new experiences, immersing ourselves in everything life has to offer. There is an undeniable lust for life radiating from the Ace of Wands that fills us with desire to do, to be, to will, and to act.

As elemental fire, it is interesting that an item traditionally made of wood is used to represent this suit. We see that the Ace of Wands is fuel for fire—a great stave of wood that burns bright and long, which can be used to aid survival at its most basic, as well as a torch to guide and inspire. The image of a fiery wand or torch is found throughout the ancient world symbolizing the fires of lust and desire, and in medieval Christian mysticism we see the fiery arrows of divine ecstasy being driven through the heart of St. Teresa of Avila, causing her intense spiritual pleasure as well as pain. As an arrow, the Ace of Wands also reminds us of focus and direction as well as aim, and this card is nothing if not a card of aims, ambitions, and goals set with purest intent, will, and desire. The Ace of Wands is also a magician's wand (or, the wand of the Alchemist card). A magician's wand is not merely a stage prop that is wiggled around for show; it is the extension of the magician's will out into the universe. Through the wand, the magician directs the full force of his will, intention, and energy to enact change within and upon the universe: this is the act of creation at its most dynamic. Of the wand, Aleister Crowley writes, "To strike with the wand is to utter the fiat of creation…"[14] *Fiat* here comes from the Latin, "let there be," used in particular reference to the creation of the world in the Old Testament, *fiat lux*, "let there be light." Echoing this in the card image, we find that our Ace of Wands is not a dead stick, but rather a living branch from which beautiful flowers blossom and leaves grow, with tendrils of golden light sprouting forth and seeping out into the world. From this card, inspiration is fuelled and seeded in a primal form in one's life, whether in dreams or ideas, urges or creative processes. This is a fiery muse that not only engenders inspiration but also the desire to act upon it, often manifesting in the unstoppable urge to express that inspiration outwardly. The hand that holds the wand in the card is strong, well-defined, and certain, the muscles delineated and tensed: this is not a receptive inspiration, but rather a firm, active, passionate thrust of inspiration into life and being.

---

14. Aleister Crowley, *Magick: Book 4, Part 3* (York Beach, ME: Red Wheel/Weiser, 1994), page 198.

We can also see blooming—almost ejaculating—from the tip of the wand, a golden tree. Here is obvious phallic symbolism, as the wand represents the phallus in its erect state, pulsing with lust and life and the need to expand outward into the universe. It is driven to a heightened state of direction by fire, and just like any build-up of energy, it must eventually burst out, too big to be contained any longer. Thus the Ace of Wands represents great and intense passion that burns within and requires expression without. Any endeavour undertaken without this passion, going forth without the powerful, ejaculating drive of the Ace of Wands, lacks the necessary momentum to reach completion in a whole and perfect state. Anything that lacks the pure, primal fire of the Ace of Wands cannot maintain the primal desire for action.

Being the extension of will into the universe, the Ace of Wands can also be seen as the ego, the self, the concept of "I." It is the first delineation of personality, the ego that pushes us onward to greater heights. Often the ego is viewed as a negative aspect of the self, but when applied correctly it can be a positive force for change and dynamic action. It is the ego that is responsible for giving us drive toward our goals and ambitions, for instance. Since the Ace of Wands is a card of enacting change in the world according to one's directed will and energy, this is a potent reminder that we are the beginning of that change. Action is required for anything to happen. The great, gleaming building in the background of the card began as a dream, inspired and fuelled by desire, will, and intent, and all these things were then focused into action and driven ever onward by passion. When we think about magic, often we see it as the creation of something out of "thin air," but we have a better example of that principle right here: from the most abstract of inspirations and sparks of dreams, a beautiful building stands testament to the unique ability of mankind to express passion and conceive beyond necessity.

Revelation

The Ace of Wands in a reading is always a welcome sight! It brings with it great fire and passion, indicating a driving force or inspiration that fuels the querent, either currently or in the near future. It indicates that great projects will be started with an intensity of action that allows them to go far and succeed; if it appears in a reading concerning a current project or endeavour, it suggests that it is dynamic, fast moving, and active. If the querent is concerned about a possible endeavour or path, perhaps a business decision, job change, house move, or starting a family, then the Ace of Wands in their reading tells them that moving ahead will be based on passion, pure will, and intent—the best start! Whilst this card usually suggests that an endeavour or project will continue in a dynamic manner, the presence of other cards in the reading might indicate otherwise, so check the spread for factors that might suggest the energy and drive at the beginning of the path could peter out, get stuck, be overdone, or create burnout.

Sometimes the Ace of Wands appears in a reading to indicate matters of the self, or concerns with personality, sexuality, and the ego. It also points toward issues surrounding the querent's ambition or passion in life, and asks them to consider what it is that they are passionate about. What can drive them to greater achievement? What inspires them and fuels their passion? This card also shows up to tell the querent to "go for it" and make action paramount in their decisions. If they have a new idea or are feeling inspired, they should not feel they need to hold back: there is an energy behind this idea that will propel them forward. The querent should act while the fires are burning within, using their passion to feed them along the way.

If this card appears in a relationship reading, it clearly indicates great desire and passion between the partners, and they are likely to base their love on a shared project, goal, desire, or pastime. However, due to its phallic nature and creative impulse, if it appears alongside a number of other "fertile" cards, such as the Empress and/or Ace of Cups, the querent might find that pregnancy isn't far off! If the Ace of Wands appears in a reading about an artistic or creative endeavour, then the querent is well-placed for such a task. However, this card advises the querent that they must focus their energy, passion, will, and intent in the right direction, as otherwise everything will be for nought.

Reversed, the Ace of Wands can sometimes indicate energy directed to the wrong goal, or in too many directions at once. A lack of focus in the querent's life or a lack of ambition is indicated by this card; surrounding cards may speak to the cause of this. Sometimes this card appears reversed for querents who are finding that they are so shy that their creative or business undertakings are suffering, or it may indicate a lack of confidence in a particular area, most often concerning sex or personality traits.

Keywords

Inspiration, spark, drive, passion, will, intent, focus, ambition, achievement, energy, direction, sexuality, personality, ego, self, impulse, desire, action, dynamism, fuel.

Two of Wands, the Conqueror at the Edge of the World

"Bring me a horizon of splendid colour, a shore of unknown sand, strange treasures of far-away kingdoms, and the mysteries of the mind of man … I command a vast and brilliant empire, and can see my dominion from the grandest tower in the land; I won it through the power of my desire. The strong will, by necessity, must be expansive in nature, not happy to be cloistered and shut away. The strongest wills in the world always seek more: not through greed or lack, not through a need for ownership or ego, but because the will is a fire that must be fed and fuelled, lest it be extinguished. Its fuel is discovery, success, stimulation, and strength. When fed, desire creates further desire, and when fuelled, will creates a stronger will. It began with a spark, an idea, a passion that burst into life with the force of the universe, seeking release into the world. I am that release, that natural extension, the point drawn into a line. And when the line reaches its end, it must conquer new ground, extend further, push its will and desire deeper into the waiting universe. I know the limits of my dominion, and therefore I know what is not my dominion, and what is waiting for me. But knowing it is not enough, because I know also that I have not yet expanded my will and desire far enough. I am the explorer, the entrepreneur, the leader, and the conqueror. I do not seek to take from others, but my influence will be felt to the farthest regions of the world."

Mars in Aries / Chockmah in fire

Illumination

In the Ace of Wands, we saw the initial fiery spark of inspiration and divine light bursting forth with will, intent, passion, and energy directing it toward its goal. The Two of Wands, therefore, is the direction itself, the force of will and desire exerted upon the world, the nature of expansion and extension. If the Ace of Wands is the first point, the Two of Wands is the line you can draw between that point and the next. It is thus also the ability of the self to "put two and two together," to move from the singular moment of inspiration to a plan of action. All the ideas in the world, and all the passion, will not bring success unless there is also the ability to act and create the necessary changes in the real world. In this card, we see action being taken and the dominion of the will expanding to include new ground.

In the card image, we see a man standing in a beautifully designed room with large, open windows that allow him to look out over the ocean, upon which several ships sail off to new lands. It is possible that he is a wealthy spice merchant, sending out ships loaded with his precious wares to merchants in other lands. In due course, the ships will return laden with money and other items precious to him that he cannot find in his native land. These exotic items he will perhaps trade on again, or sell in his country for high prices, using some of his profit to obtain yet more spice and fund the next voyage. Trade such as this was extremely important in the ancient and medieval world, not just for merchants who made a living from it, but also for the possibility of cultural expansion. It was via trading that languages and skills were learned and passed on, religions shared and converts made, common practices and values discovered between strangers, the borders of kingdoms expanded and contracted. Such trade may have begun as long as 150,000 years ago, and we can see that the earliest culture from which we have written records, the Sumerians, made long-distance trades with the Harappan civilization in the Indus Valley. For several centuries, a trade route brought various spices from India and China to Europe. However, when the so-called Dark Ages began in Europe, such trade almost died out (one of the reasons the era was called the Dark Ages in the first place!) and Europe fell into decline while the kingdoms of Africa, the Middle East, Asia, and the Orient continued to trade and interact. When the European spice trade was brought back to life and pioneered by Vasco de Gama in 1498, it helped kick-start the Age of Discovery (also called the Age of Exploration), during which Europeans engaged in extensive exploration of the world beyond their borders, establishing contact once more with other kingdoms and creating detailed maps of the world.

The spice merchant in the card image is dressed elaborately in the bright colours of wealth and life, gold and green. He holds two staffs firmly in his hands and his chin is raised in an attitude of control, command, and perhaps arrogance. This is a man who knows his strength of will, knows his success, and is certain of the further expansion of his empire. How is he certain? Because he knows his success. How does he know his success? Because he knows his strength of will. The famous and oft-quoted poem, usually called "The Victor," attributed to C.W. Longenecker (but probably written by D. Wintle, and also found in more than one version) reminds us beautifully of this:

> *"If you think you are beaten, you are;*
> *If you think you dare not, you don't.*
> *If you'd like to win, but think you can't*
> *It's almost a cinch you won't*
> *If you think you'll lose, you're lost,*

For out in the world we find
Success begins with a fellow's will;
It's all in the state of mind.
If you think you're outclassed, you are.
You've got to think high to rise.
You've got to be sure of yourself before
You can ever win a prize.
Life's battles don't always go
To the stronger or faster man;
But sooner or later the man who wins
Is the one who thinks he can."

This is true dominion. Not dominion over the self, as if there were something in you that must be tamed or overcome, but rather power to know your capability and to truly understand yourself to be powerful. "Success begins with a fellow's will," which is not a tangible thing but can be affected purely by one's own thought processes. Our conqueror standing at the edge of the world is standing on the edge of his own world, eager to expand his dominion, not because he wants to take things from others, but because he wants to extend himself. In the card image, the ships sailing out across the ocean and away from their homeland remind us that we must always be on the lookout for opportunities to extend ourselves and stretch our wills further, to achieve more and to broaden our horizons. We should not desire to stay cloistered away with no need for progress or growth. All the wonders and riches of the wider world are out there waiting for us, a vast treasury of beauty and ideas and challenges. The force of our passion and desire in the Ace of Wands pushes us outward so that we become like the spice merchant holding firmly his two wands, sending out his ships to explore, discover, and return richer than before.

Revelation

Like the ace, the Two of Wands is also a favourable card to see in a reading. Although it does not have the celebratory, loving, or joyful images found in cards such as the Four of Wands or Three of Cups, it brings with it good reason to celebrate and be happy. It will often appear in a reading concerning a project, goal, plan, or endeavour, where it indicates expansion, the extension of an idea into action, and the opportunities that arise from it. The querent is in a time of great growth and progress as their plans are driven forward and outward by their inspiration, passion, and will. They have an excellent and solid business plan or plan of action that will succeed and bring them many further opportunities. Sometimes the card indicates simply that the querent will have an opportunity come into their life soon, and surrounding cards will indicate the nature of that opportunity.

Often the Two of Wands suggests that the querent has a desire to explore and broaden their horizons, whether in a metaphorical or actual sense. This may manifest as a desire to move to another country or go travelling to discover new cultures, learn a new language, or gather more knowledge. If accompanied by cards such as the Six of Swords, it can point to a move overseas. This card often represents entrepreneurship and the search for aid in establishing a new business, such as applying for loans or grants. It can also indicate a business partner or creative partnership; where the Ace of Wands is one person's desire and will, two wands coming together are two wills working toward the same goal. It might also be time for the querent to start bouncing ideas off another person or brainstorming, externalizing their inspiration in an accessible format.

In general matters, the Two of Wands suggests that the querent feels as if the world is at their fingertips and they have lots of opportunities for growth, plenty of ideas, and are in control of their destiny. They can see their domain clearly and have a realistic understanding of their life's inventory. The Two of Wands also reminds the querent that they need to "think high to rise,"—in other words, thinking in a manner befitting a successful businessman will help them to become a successful businessman.

If this card appears in a question regarding business or work, the outcome couldn't be better. The querent will be given the small business loan for which they applied, for instance, or will receive an investment from a big company to support their nascent business, or will secure the funding for their Ph.D. If accompanied by the Six of Wands, the Sun, or the Ten of Pentacles, this meaning is heightened and things will really start to take off for the querent. They are in an excellent position at this time, and they must take advantage of that.

If reversed, the Two of Wands becomes a card of domination—a desire to dominate others through the power of will. The querent may be the instigator of this, or the victim; the surrounding cards and the context of the question will indicate which one. It may also suggest that the querent is in a state of mind where they wish to exert their influence upon something for the wrong reasons, using their power or will just because they can or because they want to demonstrate it to others. There is also great arrogance suggested by the Two of Wands reversed, with the querent's ego growing, rather than their experience or opportunities. They are advised not to rest on their laurels, and to avoid the pitfalls of believing that simply having a great idea will make them great. Ideas don't change the world: action based on ideas does. If this card is reversed in a reading, but otherwise surrounded by positive and supportive cards, it might simply indicate that the upright meaning stands, but results will be delayed or there is some sort of obstacle in the way that must be overcome before any progress can be made. If this is the case, then the querent is reminded that if they think they're beaten, they are.

Keywords

Dominion, expansion, extension, business, business partnership, creative partnership, will, dominance, exploration, discovery, opportunity, entrepreneurship, endeavour.

Three of Wands, the Ships Coming In

"I had a dream and a vision of a great empire of wealth and power at my disposal, of my inspiration seeing new horizons and foreign shores. I took every opportunity, changed my perspective and took the long view. Many people will tell you to live in the moment and not get ahead of yourself, but when you have the passion behind you and your plans are taking off, how can you think only of today? How can you not envision yourself in the future, several steps ahead? If you think only of what will serve you today, you cannot succeed. You will squander your energy on frivolity and small profits, tiny investments, and little return for your efforts. But if you think on a grander scale, truly consider the possibilities and potential of your vision, energy, passion, and talents, you will find that you could begin to change the world and make a true name for yourself. Fortune, fame, renown, influence— aren't these the things everybody with talent wants? Not just to be known in your place of origin or your place of work, but to have a reputation that spreads far and wide, even to places you have never seen. I am not the kind of man that works for another. I am not a slave or an employee. I am the driving force behind a business plan, and I am the leader of others. And so, my ships are coming in. Not yet, but soon. I took every opportunity and took the long view, looking far to the distant horizon, and now I see there, riding that horizon, my ships coming in. I ensure that you too may move beyond plans and into direct action."

The Sun in Aries / Binah in fire

Illumination

Continuing the creative process of the suit of wands, we have the three of this suit. Threes, numerologically speaking, are associated with results, birth from duality, the group, and talents and skills. They share the creative qualities of the major arcana card numbered three, the Empress, who also brings things to birth. In the suit of wands, the three represents birth from the expansion and plans of the two, as well as group desire and group passion toward a common goal. In the Three of Wands we start to see the results of efforts, though they are not yet fully realized.

In the card image, we see a man standing on the edge of a cliff, looking out to sea. Five ships are approaching the harbour as he watches, and his stance is one of power, control, and expectation. Two staffs are planted into the ground either side of him, whilst another rests over his shoulders and he holds it across the length of his arms. Golden material from his outfit drapes over this staff, showing us that he has not just picked it up, and it is not in motion but at rest. He is definitely waiting, watching the ships approach.

The two staffs in the ground have a different cap than the staffs in most of the rest of this suit and the third staff across his shoulders. These caps do not feature the golden tree of life motif bursting from the tip of the staff, but instead look like closed points or buds. Since they are planted firmly in the ground, they indicate the parts of the man's plans that have already been acted upon, which have taken root and form a foundation for his future plans. The closed tips show that their creative energy has already been fired off, so to speak, and they are now efforts that have been and gone. The staff that rests on the man's shoulders, then, is the staff that is still "active," indicating plans made for the future, or action that is ongoing.

It is clear that this is our spice merchant from the Two of Wands. In that card, he sent out his ships to start trading, filled with spices from his native land. He had a plan then to create a wealthy spice trading empire, and in the Three of Wands we see his ships returning (note there are five ships sent out in the Two of Wands, and the same number returning here). It is likely to have taken a long time for this trade route to be completed, as sea travel and trading was a long, arduous process in the ancient world. But our spice merchant had his plan and executed it; he knew how to think big and to think beyond the borders of his native land. If he had only thought within the area he knew, he would not now be seeing five ships laden with unknown goods, treasure, and payment arriving in harbour for him. He would have been a local, small-time trader, content with doing little deals here and there and remaining comfortable.

It takes foresight and vision, in addition to a plan and a desire to act upon it, to create something great. True creative thought isn't just about getting from A to B, start to finish, but in thinking outside the box, and in assessing how best you can use your talents, skills, and resources. In the Two of Wands, we saw that the spice merchant was standing within a cloistered room looking out to sea, yet in the Three of Wands he is out in the open, upon a verdant cliff-top. He is thinking and acting outside the box now, and has a view farther out to sea than before.

It is important to note that, because the ships haven't yet arrived back in port, this indicates the plans are still in action. Results are not here yet, manifestation has not quite occurred fully (we'll see that in the Four of Wands). In between the initial plan, action, and expansion of the Two of Wands and the results and completion of the Four of Wands, our spice merchant must wait and have the confidence to keep stoking the fires of his dream. Opportunities are likely to present themselves to him, and plans might change slightly, but the need for creativity, passion, inspiration, and foresight will always be there.

Revelation

In a reading, the Three of Wands indicates that the querent's plans have been put into action and are progressing smoothly. They are in a time of growth and expansion, as well as abundant creativity in thought and action. This card suggests that the querent has inspiration feeding and fuelling their endeavours, and that they are thinking outside the box in order to create something original and authentic. However, the Three of Wands reminds the querent that at this stage results may be a fair way off; they should not expect overnight success, and there may not be much action they can take at this time to speed things along. They have done everything they need to get matters moving, and now they can simply support that action.

In any situation, the Three of Wands suggests that the querent needs to be taking the long view. If they have a choice between an action that would benefit them in the short term with immediate and definite results they could count on, versus an option that has the possibility of offering results in the long run but which isn't certain, they should choose the long run possibility. The querent needs to think beyond the here and now, beyond surviving today, and make plans for the future, as well as plans beyond the mediocre. The Three of Wands indicates that the querent has something great going for them, whether it's a talent, skill, experience, desire, or dream, and that it is bigger than the limited way in which they are currently viewing it.

This card says it's time to re-evaluate business plans (and plans of any kind), and to start brainstorming ways in which the querent can expand further than they have as yet considered. This may involve taking on new employees or volunteers in a business situation, becoming a leader or boss instead of an employee, or pulling in others for a think tank. Since the threes are often about the group mind, the Three of Wands recommends or indicates teamwork of some kind, with a few people pulling together to create something based on a shared dream or goal.

The Three of Wands usually brings with it major opportunities in the querent's future, so they need to be on the lookout for them. They may not seem like much when originally offered, but they will grow exponentially as time goes on, resulting in great things for the querent.

Reversed, the Three of Wands indicates delays in plans and outcomes. The expected results will not occur, the situation has changed dramatically, or results will take far longer than originally anticipated. This card reversed may also suggest that the querent is closing off their dreams and passion by thinking too small, focusing too much on the present, not considering the future, and not taking what they consider to be risks (anything not certain is a risk for the reversed Three of Wands querent). When reversed, the Three of Wands can also point to a lack of inspiration and creativity, or teamwork going awry and individuals fighting with each other during the creative process.

Keywords

Progress, plans, vision, foresight, opportunity, ships coming in, awaiting results, inspiration, creativity, teamwork, growth, long-term plans.

Four of Wands, the Thanksgiving of Hearth and Home

"When you have planted your seeds in spring and worked the land in summer, tending and weeding, letting the warmth of the sun nurture your labours, in the autumn you may harvest and enjoy the fruits of your work. It is a joy to set a

strong foundation beneath your desire and see it grow in strength and beauty, so set your will to the four corners of the known world and see it returned a thousandfold. Yet when you have built a grand empire from the results of your labours, you must pause to give thanks and make merry, and fill the walls of that empire with passion and love. And you must give thanks also when desire finds a solid grounding in the lives of others: when two people are joined in union, when the harvest of the community is brought in, when great honours are achieved. Thanksgiving marks the recognition and acknowledgement of completion and results. Without it, nothing is truly complete. When you build a dwelling and fill it with all you need to live within its walls, the final thing you must fill it with is love, so that around the first lighting of the hearth fire you may share your joy and achievement with another. When you are joined with your chosen love, the first thing you shall do is offer a banquet to all those in attendance, because your joy and achievement is increased a thousandfold when you offer it to others to share in."

Venus in Aries / Chesed in fire

Illumination

After following the creative process through the Ace of Wands, the Two of Wands, and the Three of Wands, we see the glorious results and manifestation in the Four of Wands. The fours of the tarot all carry connotations of stability, strength, and structure, so this number in the suit of wands—the suit of will, passion, and desire—sees the foundation being built upon which a life can grow in passion and desire, as well as the previous fiery energy and effort of the suit finding a home and grounding. Solid material and the element of fire also share a positive relationship in this card, as the fire of the suit is fuelled by the solid foundation provided, and it also contains the fire so that it becomes domesticated. Here we find the hearth fire, the cooking fire, and the fire upon which ancient cultures made sacrifice in thanksgiving.

This makes the Four of Wands not only the result of the energies of the first three cards of the suit, but also the focal point from which all further successes can emerge. Like the heart of the home, it is the hearth where the food is cooked and around which the family gathers, and which warms them on the coldest nights.

In the card image, we see in the background a grandiose palace, its spires almost touching the sun, bordered by a golden gate that is shut. The palace is evidence of the empire that has been built in the previous cards of this suit, and the strong foundations that have been laid, as well as the strength of will required to lay them. The golden gate that is closed reminds us that in the Four of Wands, the fires of our passion and will are contained and locked away, but not out of greed as in the Four of Pentacles but because when we contain fire, we can put it to far greater use than when it is let to run wild. Tamed fire forms the basis for modern civilization and ancient survival.

This contained fire was so important in most ancient civilizations that there was a deity specifically given to the overseeing of the home hearth or the public hearth fire. In Lithuanian mythology, Gabija is the hearth and fire goddess who is the protector of the home and family that dwells therein, as well as the provider of fertility. She was seen as the fire itself, thus the fire would be "fed" with bread and salt, and "put to bed" every night (covering the charcoal with ashes, thus containing the fire) to prevent it from causing a house fire. In Chinese folk religion we find the kitchen god called Tsao Chun (or Zao Jun, as well as other variants), meaning "Stove God," standing at the head of a group of other domestic gods that protect the hearth and home. Ancient Greece and Rome had Hestia and Vesta respectively; Vesta not only looked after the family that gathered around each hearth, but she also looked after the city that was gathered around her sacred temple fire, tended by her temple priestesses (the Vestal Virgins). If she was not served correctly, or if one of her priestesses broke her vow, it was believed that a great plight would befall the city.

In Hinduism, the god of fire is Agni, one of the most important deities in the Hindu pantheon and one of the oldest. As fire personified, he accepts the sacrifices made to the gods, which are usually burned, transforming them from physical food into spiritual food in the form of smoke. Hindus today still perform the Agnihotra ritual, during which they make offerings to the fire that go to the gods, and which also serves a blessing and purification purpose for those in attendance. It is usually performed by a family unit or a community, and often as a means of offering thanksgiving to the gods.

This reminds us that the Four of Wands isn't just a card indicating a house or a place to live, but a home in which people can thrive and flourish, share and love, and an environment in which dreams can be achieved. The home and hearth is a microcosm, an everyday representation of the universe and the divine, in which the four walls of the house represent the four corners of the Earth, the floor is the earth that is our home, and the ceiling is heaven. The home and those that dwell within are sacred.

In the card image, we see a wedding between an elaborately costumed man and woman. They wear complementary colours, he in mostly white with touches of gold, and she in mostly gold with touches of white. It is interesting to note that metal, when heated, has different colours; the two hottest colours are yellow and white. This is symbolic of the fact that the fuelled nature of the fire in the Four of Wands is so hot that it must be contained and put to use, or it will become destructive. The wedding that is taking place is an obvious symbol of joy and celebration, in which passion and desire are united in material reality. A wedding also is usually a community event, bringing people together to mark the occasion. In most religious marriage services, the couple will not only give thanks to their guests for attending, but to their god(s) for bringing them together.

It is tempting to imagine that the man in this card is the same man from the Two of Wands and the Three of Wands, our wealthy spice merchant and entrepreneur. We could imagine that he and the lady had a long courtship, and that her father banned the marriage until the young man had built a wealthy empire through his trade, had proved his worth and could provide a stable home for his bride. In this card we see their joy at being able to celebrate their love and the beginning of their lives together, as well as the beginning of the home they will build together. The staffs that create their wedding canopy are bedecked with flowers and greenery, another symbol of completion and manifestation of results. These four staffs have the same tips as two from the Three of Wands: the closed bud that indicates efforts and energy expended in the past, which now forms a firm foundation for the future. Behind their palace, the sun sets, marking the ending of the day during which we work, and the beginning of the evening, during which we celebrate our day's work.

Revelation

The Four of Wands is the culmination and completion of all the energies of the suit of wands up to this point, and therefore indicates a time in the querent's life when everything will come to fruition, when some plan or project is nearing completion, conclusion, or a satisfactory end. If the querent was working on a project, or working toward a goal, the Four of Wands suggests that it will bear fruit and they will see the results of their labours in the near future. All their efforts will pay off, the creative input will bring manifest results, and the future they have dreamed of will become tangible.

In business or work-related readings, the Four of Wands points to a happy work environment or business team; it can also suggest the coming together of two investors or businesses to work toward a common goal. The work or partnership will greatly benefit all involved and yield excellent results.

This card suggests that this is a time of harvest for the querent. This is an opportunity for them to enjoy what they have created, to celebrate it with others, and to give thanks where thanks are due. It is time for them to acknowledge any help they have received along the way, but also to acknowledge where they put in hard work and effort. Sometimes the Four of Wands can indicate the celebrations themselves, such as a thanksgiving dinner, a New Year's Eve party, or a birthday.

If the Four of Wands appears in a reading about love and romance, it usually refers to an existing relationship, one that has strong foundations and has been around for a while. This card not only suggests that the relationship will be happy and filled with joy, but also that it will be long-term. It sometimes indicates a marriage or an engagement, or buying or renting a house together. If accompanied by the Two of Cups and/or the Lovers, the querent should be advised that this relationship is a match made in heaven.

Often this card shows up in a reading to indicate a house, property, or real estate. If near cards that indicate movement, it can point to a house move or a desire to change location; if near cards concerning money or investment, it might suggest getting on the property ladder; if near cards that indicate people or a social aspect, the Four of Wands is more likely talking about the home life of the querent, and any details can be further ascertained from surrounding cards.

Reversed, the stable foundation of the Four of Wands becomes the earth that smothers the fire. Instead of fuelling the querent's passion and containing it so that it might be put to good use, the querent's passion and desire is smothered by the humdrum activities of their daily life, in particular their home life, which may be difficult at this time. Reversed, this card can also indicate uncertainty in a marriage or otherwise stable relationship, or point to a marriage of convenience. Sometimes this card reversed simply tells the querent that they are not showing gratitude where it is due, and ungratefulness will create a bad impression at this time.

Keywords

Gratitude, thanksgiving, celebration, harvest, yield, outcome, results, manifestation, completion, marriage, wedding, home, hearth, household, community, happiness, joy, contentment, strong foundations, prosperity, culmination.

Five of Wands, the Test of Contest

"Contentment is an enemy that dulls the mind and blunts the sword. Peace is the enemy of progress. Without something to fight against, we become complacent, taking everything for granted. The reality is that we live in a harsh world that exacts a harsh price and demands only the best from us—or at least it should. Those of us hidden away in comfort, enjoying the luxury of stability, are not called to the battle and the fray; we are not called to the testing grounds or the initiation chamber. These people see life as a river upon which they float blissfully, being carried toward the ocean where they will become one with the infinite. This is a lie. This is their excuse so they do not have to exert themselves in any way. They are weak, and will remain weak. Conflict and contest tests us and forces us to excel above ourselves and others. When we do not exercise our bodies and push them to their limits, we do not know our strength and our bodies become weak and pathetic. When we put our bodies through the rigours of martial practice, exercise, and discipline, we not only know our strength but also develop it. When we stretch our wills and energy beyond our expectations, they strengthen just like the muscles of the arm. It is said that to live in interesting times is a curse and a burden, as if the wide variety of challenges that life's manifold experiences bring are a danger to us. It is no curse, only a blessing. May you be given the opportunity to test yourself. May you have the chance to prove yourself. May you see your strength and will grow and expand as you overcome each challenger and opponent. May you live in interesting times."

Saturn in Leo / Geburah in fire

Illumination

After the wondrous manifestation of results and joyous celebration of the Four of Wands, the five comes as a shock. Weren't we happy in our stable harvest state? Wasn't everything perfect once we had grounded our desire in action and results? Yes, we were. But after the harvest of contentment comes the winter of stillness, and then by necessity there must be a bursting forth of new life through the ice and snow to bring spring to our lives. However, the fiery burst of renewal cannot come from stability or contentment, but must come instead from contest, conflict, imbalance, and the aggressive fight for strength.

The Five of Wands at first seems to be simply a card of conflict, of pointless fighting and war, but it is a necessary stage in the creative process of the suit of wands. It's conflict is actually contest—will set against will to determine the strongest. It is this strength that comes out of the Five of Wands, furthering the energies of the suit so they don't get stuck and stagnate in the four.

It is sometimes said that contentment is the enemy of progress (or, variously, that it is the enemy of invention). Contentment can lead to complacency. When we have always had peace and stability, we do not fully appreciate what it is to strive, to have to fight for something that we believe in, to have to struggle for survival. Without this knowledge, if ever we were to find ourselves in such a situation, we would not be prepared and would find ourselves failing and lost. It is interesting to note that all the fives of the tarot depict some sort of imbalance, conflict, testing, or sudden upheaval, but they are followed by the sixes that bring some sort of rebalancing, harmony, and peace.

In the card image, we see five warriors fighting against each other with double-ended staffs, their hands firmly grasping the centre of the staffs, their postures in direct battle stance. They battle atop a hill with the sun shining through the clouds above them, and their clothing spreads swathes of bold colour around the card. We can see no reason for their conflict in the image, no hint at a prize to be won or an offence being taken. In fact, their facial expressions are not angry but determined, their eyes set on their opponents in fierce concentration. This is clearly not a battle born of anger, bitterness, resentment, or deception (unlike the Five of Swords, perhaps), but a battle between equals in order to test their strength against each other and improve their skills.

Sparring occurs in all martial arts traditions. It is almost impossible to study a martial art to a high skill level without engaging in friendly combat with one of your peers (or sometimes, against somebody slightly better than you). Any competitive skill is best learned through friendly matches, including sports, online gaming, chess, and card games. Nobody ever found themselves vying for big money as a professional poker player without first testing themselves vigorously against others for little or no prize. In times of peace, it was common for the Roman army to continue with daily training, military drills, contests between units and individuals, swimming practice, horse-riding practice, and weapons practice. It was expected that they would maintain not only their bodily fitness level but also their skill and courage during peacetime as much as during war.

The staves in the image tell us a lot about this card. Firstly, they are blunt, telling us that nobody in this fight is going to get seriously hurt—unlike the Five of Swords, in which the swords' sharp edges have potential to do great damage. Secondly, these staffs are double-ended, and they must be held in the centre for maximum efficiency as weapons. This reminds us that in contest and competition or friendly conflict for training purposes, we must maintain a sense of personal balance: this is not a battle for the purpose of building ego or weakening others, but for the purpose of testing and improving the self. The shape of the five staffs as they are wielded in action form the shape of a lightning flash, like a bolt out of the blue or the raw power of atmospheric electricity.

The combatants all wear different colours of clothing; these bold swathes of colour bring vibrant energy to the card and remind us that the forces competing here are all very different and unique. Although they are equal in rank, experience, or value, they are different in nature or state of being. It also serves to highlight the fact that action and competition brings colour, metaphorically, into one's life. The height of the hill upon which they compete also tells us that their contest serves a higher purpose and that it will strengthen their wills, keeping them at their peak.

Revelation

Depending on the context of the question and the other cards around it, the Five of Wands has the potential to be a beautiful, positive card, or one of great negativity. Whenever it appears in a reading, it points to action, competition, or disruption of some kind. Sometimes it suggests that the disruption will serve a higher purpose, with better things coming out of it. The querent may find that they are currently stuck in a stagnant state, unable or unwilling to move, progress, or break out. The Five of Wands tells them that any conflict in this situation will serve to give them the boost and drive they need to move forward; to break out of captivity, it's usually necessary to fight.

The Five of Wands shows up to indicate any kind of competition the querent may be undergoing, whether they are aware of it or not. This could include competing in an area of expertise, in sports, or by entering into a contest that showcases their skill and talents. It might also relate to unseen rivalry such as from others who may be applying for the same job or funding. On a more abstract level, this competition may be from people or forces that are trying to actively oppose the querent, sometimes to see how they rise to the challenge and sometimes just to cause them problems.

If accompanied by cards that indicate family, the Five of Wands can point to conflict within the family unit, often the kind of conflicts that occur between siblings. Such conflicts can bruise egos and hurt feelings, but will rarely cause any real damage; when the time comes that one of the siblings is threatened by an external force or person, the other will defend them with devotion and strength. At times, therefore, this card appears to tell the reader that any conflict the querent is currently having within the family or with a close friend will soon be resolved, it is merely there to test them; once some actual conflict occurs outside of them, they will join forces to fight against the threat, stronger and more united despite their petty battles.

The Five of Wands urges the querent to test themselves in this situation, and to not let their guard down. It also advises them that their current struggles should be viewed as a test of will or strength, as well as an initiation into a new part of their life or a new understanding of their self. But they must not become stagnant or rest on their laurels; any peace or contentment they are currently experiencing is not guaranteed in the future. Sometimes the Five of Wands signifies inner conflict rather than outer conflict, showing an ego or self divided, or the querent's desires and urges being drawn in different directions, or competing factions fighting for their attention and time.

Reversed, the Five of Wands is a negative card, bringing with it conflict for conflict's sake, competition not born from the need to improve but from the need to belittle or embarrass another, or to establish power over them. It might also point to a person who is so accustomed to being in a state of conflict or battle, either with others or themselves, that they are unable to relate to others peacefully. The querent may also be feeling as though everything in their life is a struggle or as though every day is a battle.

Keywords
Struggle, strife, battle, conflict, competition, testing, contest, battle of wills, training, war, aggression, action, fighting.

Six of Wands, the Heroic Return of the Sun King
"From the fierce contest of wills and the competition of strength, fresh from the battlefield and arrayed in the light of a thousand suns, I ride forth into my kingdom

in triumphal procession. I have overcome the finest warriors and the most cunning magicians for this position, and it is now mine by birth and divine right. I came from my mother's womb already a hero, bursting with light and blessing, and I tested my strength and desire through many hardships and years. This is what I truly mean when I speak of divine right, not grace from God handed to me on a golden platter, but the foresight of God to give me strength and will, and the desire to direct them. Only the best may rule, only the wisest and most powerful, power given by virtue of proof. When the king is no longer fit for his office—and we all come to this in the end—he must step down from the throne and choose his heir. I am that heir, the king reborn in glory and majesty. Before me, the crowds throng and shout my name, pledging their allegiance and swearing fealty and love. They do not love me because I am king, but for the virtues that make me king: my will is the strongest, my achievements the greatest, my ambition the highest. I will accept their love, and in return I swear to protect my people, to rise up against the enemy when the horn of battle sounds, to give them a voice, and to allow the light of a thousands suns to shine as brightly upon them as it does upon me."

Jupiter in Leo / Tiphereth in fire

Illumination

After the conflict of the Five of Wands, here we find a glorious triumph given to the victor, and to the victor go the spoils. Where the five golden staffs were levelled against others in the Five of Wands, in this card we see one staff crowned with the wreath of victory and splendour, setting it apart from the rest. The Six of Wands brings us a celebration of victory, sandwiched between two cards of conflict and battle. Here we see the radiant Sun King returning from battle, bedecked with his solar conquest and returning to his people, where he renews his pledge to protect them and rule them beneficently.

We can see that there are five figures all clothed similarly, wearing blues, reds, and yellows, who greet the arrival of the leader. On the right, one waits on bended knee—perhaps he is pledging his service to the lord or simply showing the correct respect to him—and his left hand opens out into a gesture indicating the path before the leader, inviting him to pass. On the left, another is also on bended knee, his head bowed, clutching his staff upright and with his other hand behind him in a clear posture of deference. These two figures in the card image give the man on the horse power and authority, showing us that he is in charge and deserving of their respect. Around him, three other men greet the leader, staffs upraised, looking directly at him. They seem to be welcoming him and hailing him. The city is bedecked with red banners to celebrate the leader's return, red being the colour of achievement, passion, and will. This shows us that the leader is not leader by virtue of being born into the position, but by virtue of his own strength and character.

The horse upon which the leader sits is white and well trained, with excellent step for a parade horse. A man in control of a horse in this way must have a strong will and focus, as well as the ability to remain calm and poised even in the most difficult situations. We can see from the leader's demeanour that he is in control, his entire posture and expression one of command and confidence. If there were any doubt over his ability to rule, the other men need only look at his countenance to see the shining faith he has in himself, the confidence he has in his own abilities, and the certainty he carries with him. This reminds us that when we believe in ourselves and have confidence in our own abilities and character, we have already won the hardest part of the battle.

The leader carries a staff that is identical to those of the men, but it is distinguished with the decoration of a wreath. The wreath is a symbol of victory in contest, being the traditional prize awarded in the original ancient Greek Olympic Games, held every four years in the city of Olympia. These games ran from around the eighth century BCE to the fourth century CE and are recorded by Homer, who also recorded similar games being held at the funerals of heroes to celebrate their great deeds and honour.[15] It was not only athletic games that were held at the Olympics, but also contests between artists and poets who would showcase their work to would-be patrons. It was also a festival in honour of the great god Zeus. Although the prize for winning the games was a simple wreath of laurel leaves, victory represented an opportunity for the winner to show his ability, skill, and strength and to achieve fame and political weight for the city-state or country that he represented. Due to the political nature of such triumphs and losses, the contests and games became a nonviolent way of gaining power over other states and countries, forging alliances or destroying them, and showcasing one's own strength via a proxy hero.

The triumphal return of a leader as seen in the card image is found throughout history and even today. In the UK, a monarch will be driven through the streets of London (today in a car, but in older times a carriage) on their coronation day, and will do so also on other special occasions, such as a wedding

---

15. Homer, *The Iliad*, 23.

or jubilee. In ancient Rome, a *triumphus* was held to celebrate and offer to the gods the military achievement of an army commander who had proven his worth by winning several battles or completing a foreign campaign. For the procession, he would be dressed in a manner more befitting a king or a god, and would be accompanied in the parade by his army and any spoils of his campaign; this included not only the worldly goods that had been gained, but also any prisoners of renown (such as Vercingetorix the Gaul, who was paraded in Julius Caesar's *triumphus* in 46 BCE before being executed). The commander would then be taken to the temple of Jupiter, the god of triumph and rulership, on Capitoline Hill, where he made a sacrifice to Jupiter. This procession awarded him great honour, not just for the day of the parade but for the rest of his life, as he would thereafter be called "man of triumph," and after his death he would be represented at his own funeral and the funerals of his descendants by an actor wearing his death mask, clad in the lordly colours of purple and gold. The *triumphus* not only celebrated the successes of this great military commander, but also served to further establish Rome's wealth, power, and grandeur, and to provide the public masses with a reason to celebrate and love Rome.

These triumphal parades tell us that the Six of Wands is firstly about the victory and promotion of the leader, providing him with an opportunity to show his greatness to the public, and secondly about the needs of the public. Triumphs are rarely awarded to those whose achievements only serve their own interest; in fact, most of the world's awards and medals today go to those whose achievements improve the lives of others in some way: the Nobel Peace Prize, the Purple Heart, an OBE or MBE, the Medal of Honour, or the Navy Cross, to name a few. We see this occurring in the everyday world also, where it is most often those who would best serve the greater interests of the company or business that are promoted in the workplace, as opposed to those who would simply serve their own personal ends. It is wise to remember that although the Six of Wands highlights a single individual as worthy of praise of victory, that individual is given power by those they would in turn serve, and thus we see that the balance of power is reciprocal.

Revelation

In a reading, the Six of Wands brings the rebalancing energies of the sixes into the querent's life, making them an unstoppable yet stable force for good. The number six is a solar number, associated with the sun, and therefore shines great light on all areas of the querent's life. Generally speaking, when the Six of Wands appears in a reading, the querent will find that obstacles will be overcome with ease and advancement in their life will occur quickly. They seem blessed at this time, with people praising them and offering them golden opportunities.

The truth is that the querent is not blessed *per se*, but rather they have such an air of confidence, power, and ambition that those around them know they can and will do great things. This is vital for the querent: anybody who has applied for many jobs will know that even if you list all your qualifications for the position, you may not be hired, as the employer will give preference to the applicant who has an air of confidence and command. It is self-confidence and display of it that the querent needs at this time in order to get their foot in the door and make progress. Everything else will follow from that.

Often the Six of Wands shows up to indicate some kind of promotion, usually at work, which is especially supported by the presence of cards such as the Eight of Pentacles or Ten of Pentacles, but also sometimes in voluntary positions. The querent will find that their work is praised by their superiors and peers, and they receive acclaim for what they have done. If they have applied for a job or position, they will be successful. If they are concerned about a social situation, the Six of Wands assures them that they will come out on top, and prove to themselves and others that they are in control. Situations that could result in either a win or a loss will result in a win, and all problems will be overcome. Sometimes this card can point to a person in the querent's life who has the power to grant them success or promotion, such as a boss or a judge. The Six of Wands gives the querent the advice of being confident in themselves, in whatever situation. Confidence will take them far, and others will place trust and faith in them based on it. In romance, they will find that confidence will win them their desired partner.

This is also the card of the protector and warrior, indicating that the querent may be called upon to use their power and influence to aid another. They are reminded that although they may be superior in some situations, such as at a higher management level at work or having more experience in a certain field of expertise, they are not required to have an ego that accompanies it. They will not always be given position and authority, or power and acclaim, by virtue of the fact that they are themselves, but only by virtue of their continuing achievements and efforts, as well as based on how well their achievements serve others.

Reversed, the Six of Wands points to arrogance and an expectation of success and promotion regardless of effort or skill. The querent may be in a situation where they are using their power or position to bully others or use them, rather than to serve and help them. They may have also obtained power or a position of authority through underhanded means, or their position may be begrudged by others. This card being reversed can also suggest that their power is by no means stable, and that there may be a conflict over it. The balance of power is in flux, and whilst the querent may be the named leader currently, they may not be for long.

Keywords

Victory, triumph, conquest, celebration, jubilation, crowning, coronation, success, achievement, confidence, hero, leadership, praise, promotion, acclaim.

Seven of Wands, the Heart of the Warrior

"I may not have much, but what I do have I will defend. In the face of betrayal I have honour; in the face of weakness I have courage; in the face of offence I am the defence; in the face of my enemies I am an unholy creature of war. When I fight, it is only in response to those that seek to harm those I am sworn to protect; and when in battle, I am bloodthirsty and incessant, my war cry shattering the ears of those that hear it, calling the ravens to feast upon their banquet. What do I fight for? Everything. What do I fight with? Everything. I am the protector of the weak and those unable to fight for themselves; I will make a stand and speak for them when they would otherwise be unheard. I will beat the raiders from our borders and stop invaders from entering our lands. I am the freedom fighter and the bodyguard, the rebel and the soldier, the hero and the adversary. Where liberty would be imprisoned, I will break the chains. Where voices will be silenced, I will shout the truth from the mountaintops. Where life is taken, I shall exact it as a price in return.

We stand now, fellow fighters, on the eve of a glorious battle, the outcome of which will decide the fate of human history. We must fight with all our power and all our strength, all our will and all our courage, on the side of liberty, for if we stand by and let it be slowly taken away person by person, place by place, before long there will be nothing left to fight for. I call upon you now to take up the weapon of your will and stand at my side to fight in the cause of freedom, to face the multitude of enemies that would tear us down. It is said that if you have nothing you would die for, you have nothing to live for. But sometimes it takes greater courage to defend your values with your life than with your death. So know this, fellow warrior: I ask you to stand beside me and fight in the greatest battle of history—the battle to live courageously and never cower from protecting that which you hold dear. And as your life becomes a testament to overcoming in battle, a war cry will rise greater and louder in your throat, until finally it can be heard across the span of the years. What will your war cry be, warrior?"

Mars in Leo / Netzach in fire

Illumination

We can see a clear progression in the suit of wands, from the initial spark of inspiration and the creative process of the first three cards, to the manifestation and comfort of the Four of Wands, followed closely by the contest and competition of the five that kick-starts will and strength once again. In the Six of Wands, we saw the reigning champion of that contest riding through the streets triumphant, but here we see him called upon to put everything he has to the test and defend those he is sworn to protect. The Seven of Wands is the card of every individual who has ever stood up for a cause or a person, faced up to a challenge that might overcome them, or stood in the way of danger to help others. This is the card of every political activist, freedom fighter, soldier, petition writer, protester, wartime peacekeeper, martyr, and cultural hero, and the card of every cause that campaigns to protect those that are unable to speak for themselves. It is also representative of anybody who fights to keep their liberty.

The battle in the Seven of Wands is not the same as found in the Five of Wands or the Five of Swords. Firstly, it is not a testing ground or practice run, and secondly, it is not a manipulative fight for egotistical or petty reasons. We know this because the suit of wands is concerned with the will, desire, passion, and the things that drive us onward in life. This is a battle to protect that which we hold closest to us.

In the card image, we can see a single man standing precariously upon a stone structure that arches above his head and behind him. Aimed at him from below are six staffs, and he raises his own staff with both arms as he prepares to strike down his attackers. The edifice upon which he stands could be a gateway, indicating that he is a bodyguard protecting his country or kingdom at the front line by keeping invaders out. It might also be a religious building or cultural landmark that he defends, this being symbolic of fighting to defend his beliefs or values.

It is clear that the warrior is outnumbered and overwhelmed. Although he has the advantage of higher ground, he is also in a precarious position and might easily be toppled from his stance by the attackers. This reminds us that often the battles we find ourselves in are against an army that vastly outnumbers us, but because we are fighting for something precious to us, we will enter the battle anyway. Examples of this from history include the nineteenth-century abolition of the slave trade in the United States (which that took many years and many abolitionists to bring about), the women's suffrage movement of the early twentieth century in the United Kingdom, the anti-Apartheid resistance in South Africa, and the African-American civil rights movement of the 1960s and 1970s. In all of these examples, the few stood against the many and fought against the reigning ideological mores of their country and culture, which treated them as lesser citizens (if citizens at all) and did not afford them the same rights as others. In all of these situations, people gave up their lives or their freedom for their cause, and what today we take for granted, like women's right to vote and the equality of all races, had to be fought long and hard for.

Today we see such fights manifesting in different forms and centering on different issues, but still firmly rooted in the same concepts of liberty and equality; among them are the animal rights movement, the fight for marriage equality regardless of sexual orientation, the Occupy Movement, and more. There are also fights taking place on an individual level, as one family battles to find funding that will enable their daughter to undergo a lifesaving operation they otherwise cannot afford, and another fights to allow their Muslim son the right to absent himself from Christian prayer at school, and still another couple fights strict adoption laws that make it difficult for them to adopt a child simply because they are gay. The Seven of Wands asks us to consider what we would fight for, what we value most in the world, and how far we will go to protect what we treasure the most. Who among us would not fight with everything we've got to protect our children? Who among us would stand down at the first hurdle when faced with a challenge to our most basic values?

Although the warrior in our card is overwhelmed and in a precarious position, all he need do is muster one valorous blow and he will dash all his opponents' staffs to the ground. All it takes is for us to be courageous and brave, and we can stand against any threat or obstacle. But it is necessary to remember that the wands suit is about the vital energy of life, not death, and thus although the iconic moments of courage are those in which one brave hero stands against the many and dies to defend liberty (think *Braveheart*), it takes just as much courage to defend your cause with your life, and to live every day as a steadfast battle for what you believe in.

Revelation

In a reading, the Seven of Wands says that great trials and battles are coming the querent's way, and they will be called upon to go into those battles with courage and bravery, rather than running from them or avoiding them. The exact nature of these struggles will be indicated by the context of the question and the surrounding cards, but it could be a battle to get their child into their school of choice, a battle to be heard at a parent-teacher meeting, a battle to overcome a bully at school, work, or home, or a battle against illness. The Seven of Wands is often a card of the underdog, suggesting that the querent is overwhelmed and outnumbered, but if they can muster every last bit of strength and will they have, they may yet succeed if they give it their all.

This card can indicate that the querent will be in a situation where they need to fight for something they believe in or hold dear, or defend themselves or a loved one from some sort of attack. This card may suggest that what they value most is being threatened by external forces. In a business reading, or concerning an endeavour the querent is undertaking, this card suggests they will meet with great opposition and conflict along the way, which they must defend against. They will also be called upon to speak out against some wrongdoing they see, to give a voice to another who is unable or less able to speak for themselves, and to brook no argument. The only way the querent can face the onslaught that is coming is to stand fast and strong, to take decisive action, and to not let such things pass unchallenged. In a way, the querent is being called to act as a guardian of their situation, place, or family; they are the sole defence and first port of call in times of distress, need, and danger.

The Seven of Wands can point to the querent taking part in political activism and campaigns, fighting for their rights or beliefs. It might also suggest the act of going to war, metaphorically or literally. If surrounded by negative cards and cards of oppression, the Seven of Wands might indicate bullying being experienced by the querent; in a relationship, this may take the form of domestic abuse or emotional abuse. They must face this with strength and take action, not letting it happen again. Once they stand up for themselves, their strength will be clear to the other person.

If this card appears in a reading about a social situation, it suggests that the querent is in a position where they feel the constant need to be on the defensive or to apologise for who they are or what they do. They may also be seeing some struggle or strife in their friendship group or community; as always, the Seven of Wands advises them to not let the perpetrators continue with such actions. In short, in all situations the Seven of Wands advises the querent to be courageous in how they act.

If this card appears reversed in a reading, the querent is a victim that feels powerless to prevent further harm being done to them, and powerless to speak for themselves or stand up for themselves. They may be on the losing end of a fierce battle for something they value, or they may be unable to stop something they care deeply about from going to ruin. If reversed, the Seven of Wands is a very negative card, and often points to a self-defeatist attitude that will prevent the querent from being able to take any action to make things better.

Keywords
Valour, bravery, courage, fight, defence, protection, threat, battle, standing up for one's self, the underdog.

Eight of Wands, the Heights of Ambition

"There is nothing better in this world than to let your dreams and ambitions fly free. There is nothing more perfect than being released from doubt and conflict, strife and difficulties, to rush forward with the gathered momentum of your will and bring your success ever closer. Oh, to be a free spirit, to breathe the free air, to blaze trails in uncharted territory! Yet be warned, ardent traveller: once you start this bold path, you must not falter and you must not pause. It is all or nothing: no half-measures. This demands every ounce of will and desire and energy from you so that you can send your dreams off into the universe with suitable momentum behind them. They've got a long way to go, so they need a lot of energy. And when the wild ride of your passion toward progress takes you to unknown places, be sure to hold on tight, or else you will be left behind. But do not fear: even if you fail and fall, there will be more dreams and more chances. It is free to try, and free to be free! Set your sights on the highest goals... aim for the stars, and who knows where you might find yourself?"

Mercury in Sagittarius / Hod in fire

Illumination

It seems that we just can't stop moving in the fiery suit of wands. After our battles in the seven, now we find in the eight that we are being carried forward so fast by our dreams and ambitions that we fear we may not be able to keep up! The eights of the tarot are "double fours," and therefore represent the most expressive force of their suit. In the case of the wands we see fiery, active, passionate drive thrusting itself forth with immense power and swiftness.

The image of this card is simple and beautiful. Set against an expanse of clear blue lake, dark green pine forest, and grey and white mountains, eight staffs fly through the air with exceptional speed. We can almost smell the pine and the fresh, clear air, bringing us relief from the battles and scuffles of previous cards. It's as though our hopes, dreams, and energy have been set free from strife and conflict, allowed freedom to move forward and to progress once more. Once again we have a clear shot at our goals and dreams, and we can direct our energy ever onward to reach them. The staffs flying through the air represent our will, our actions, and our passion all being thrown headlong together toward the same goal. There is a decisive focus here, with everything that we have being driven toward one single unified point.

The mountains that stand proud in the card image are symbolic of our own pride and ambition. They represent the heights we are willing to climb, the obstacles we are willing to overcome, and the lofty paths we are willing to tread in order to reach our goals. They also indicate how great the goals themselves are: we are creating in the Eight of Wands something truly amazing, something that could change the world and revolutionize our lives. This is one of few images in the Tarot Illuminati where the suit's main symbol is set or partially set outside the confines of the card. In the Seven of Wands, the staffs are being aimed at the warrior in battle, and their source, from outside of the card, shows that they come from unknown assailants; here in the Eight of Wands, it is most notable that the head of one of the staffs is outside the card, telling us that the Eight of Wands has a destination that is vast and beyond our current way of thinking or plans. This is the ability to think and act outside the box, and to be unafraid to venture onto untrodden paths and blaze trails so that others may follow.

Yet there is a danger hidden in the card image. We do not see from where the staffs have come, and we do not see where they are going. How far will they fly? Will they go too far? Do they have the energy behind them to reach their destination? What if they fall? The swiftness and power of the Eight of Wands requires us either not to start the process at all, or to make sure we go the full distance. If we enter into this venture half-heartedly, we will not have the energy and power to keep up with the direction our dreams are flying. It takes an immense amount of energy and effort to keep flying this high, and it can take its toll. We are reminded of the flight of Icarus's sons, who were so taken with pride at the invention of their wings that allowed them to escape prison, that they flew too close to the sun. The wings, held together with wax, melted in the sun's heat and they fell to their deaths. It's possible to set our ambitions so high that we get burned along the way, exhausted from the energy our efforts consume.

Revelation

When the Eight of Wands appears in a reading, it brings a swiftness to the entire situation, much like the Chariot does. Fast movement and swift progress in all things is signified by this card, and it often suggests that the querent is the kind of person that is always rushing around, always on the go, always doing something. This card indicates that the querent may find that they are being given the energy or drive in a sudden burst to push forward in a project or on a path that has been dragging on for a while. They may also find that circumstances conspire to push them onward, perhaps faster than they anticipated, and put them in a position where they will be able to achieve great things. This can make the querent feel like their life is running away from them, or that they are having to run to keep up with everything that is happening, but simultaneously they will feel like it is positive and a step in the right direction.

If the querent is at the start of some venture in their lives, the appearance of the Eight of Wands suggests that it will "take off" and progress quickly to further stages of development. If it appears in a relationship reading, it points to fast movement and a passionate, quick-burning romance that sweeps the querent off their feet. They may make moves in the early stages of the relationship that are traditionally taken slowly, such as moving in together or getting married.

Often this card indicates that the querent will be involved in a number of events that could be described as synchronicity, carrying them forward in a series of coincidences that they could never have expected. It may also suggest that the querent will best approach their situation by thinking outside the box and allowing themselves to dream big and start working toward their bigger goals and dreams. The querent may need to be the trailblazer in the situation, not the follower, and the tried and tested methods may no longer be applicable.

However, the Eight of Wands often brings with it exhaustion and burnout. The querent must be careful, when chasing their dreams so rapidly, that they do not climb so high that they cannot get back down, or lose all their energy before the end and not have the momentum behind them to continue.

Reversed, the Eight of Wands points to the risk of burnout and warns against pride and arrogance as their ambitions fly higher and higher. Just because they have achieved great things does not give them the right to look down upon others.

Keywords

Trailblazer, swiftness, movement, momentum, progress, achievement, lofty ambitions, dreams, synchronicity, pride, burnout.

Nine of Wands, the Strength of the Will

"A true warrior is never done. A true warrior fights on, even with the gravest of injuries, yet he knows how to choose his battles carefully. You can feel the burn and the ache of a wound, know your weakness, and acknowledge the strength of your enemies, but this is not your own weakness or vulnerability. This is your deepest and most dependable strength. What kind of warrior would I be if I surrendered using my injury as an excuse? To do so would be to misunderstand the nature of battle. The real battle does not take place in the gaps between blades or the gaps that are closed between body and blow, but in the will and mind of the warrior. When your will is strong and you wait, watching the tide of battle, awaiting the opportune moment for all your conserved energy to be released toward your goal, then you are a true warrior fighting a true battle. Yet be warned: do not trick yourself into believing that to stand firm is half the battle. It is not. To stand firm is to deny yourself the essential knowledge of your wounds, and you must never overestimate your abilities. But if you remain always with your weight more to one leg than the other, your muscles not relaxed nor tense but in between, then you are in the strongest position. From here you may act as the tide of battle flows, and no movement or blow shall be wasted. Yet be prepared for the pain of the burn as you wait, as you maintain your defence, as your muscles protest for

want of either stillness or action, and know that this pain you feel now serves to remind you of the most vital of all things: you are still alive."

Moon in Sagittarius / Yesod in fire

Illumination

After the battle of the Seven of Wands and the swift movement of the eight, by necessity we must find some rest in order to push onward. The nines of the tarot are all about approaching completion: they have the fullness of the energies of their suit, but are just one step away from full manifestation of that energy. In the suit of wands, the suit of will, energy, passion, and drive, this is the point of no return and the final push toward the goal (yet, as we can see from the Ten of Wands, it isn't the hardest part of the journey by any means!).

The card image in the Nine of Wands is one of stillness, so you would be forgiven for thinking that it indicates rest and peace. However, we can see that the man in the image bears the belt, armour, and well-toned muscles of a warrior who has already fought many battles. There are few figures in the Tarot Illuminati as physically imposing as the warrior in this card, immediately telling us that there is an immense strength intended in the image. Further, his feet are planted firmly and he clutches his staff tightly. We can see that although his feet are both firmly on the ground, indicating steadfastness, he leans more of his weight to his right foot than his left, suggesting that he is ready to leap into action at a moment's notice should he need to.

The Nine of Wands has a lunar quality about it—represented in the image by the large moon behind the archway—that reminds us that we can often achieve true strength in progress through awareness of the changeability of a situation, other people, and the world around us. Responding effectively to the changes in a situation puts us in a stronger position. Where the moon appears prominently in the Tarot Illuminati, it represents flux and change, and requires adaptability and flexibility to find strength in the ebb and flow of the tides within our lives. Battles are not won through simply rushing in and hacking through masses of enemies, but through being able to change tactics in response to their actions, to use their weaknesses to our advantage, and to respond to their tactics.

The sand at the warrior's feet is not smooth but shows signs that there has been much movement in this area recently. The warrior has trodden this path many times before and fought many battles on this spot. He is a veteran, and his survival is testament not only to his strength of arm but also his strength of will. After so many battles, he must be exhausted, injured, weary of fighting. Perhaps he is, as we can see that his facial expression is one of being on guard, and his arms and hands are completely tensed, though not in anger—in readiness. He stands defensively, holding the staff across his body in a shielding fashion, and is ready to fight to defend his position. The other eight staffs that are embedded in the ground, standing upright, not only point to the strength of the warrior's position and all the efforts he has thus far made, but also show us that he has his back guarded. He guards his own front with his vision and the staff he holds, and his back with his previous efforts. He is clearly in defensive mode, yet ready for action and attack if required. Perhaps he is conserving his energy, knowing that he is at the tail end of many battles, so that when he does have to fight once again he will do so more effectively.

The suit of wands is full of battles of varying kinds, yet this is the only card that shows the tension and intense concentration required for victory. This demonstrates that it has been a hard struggle to this point for the warrior, and he may not have won every battle he entered into, yet he is not giving up, he is not surrendering, and he is more than ready to continue the fight. He is not rushing in and making a lot of noise as in the Five of Wands, nor is he in a precarious position fighting against several assailants as in the Seven of Wands; instead he is prepared and ready, stronger not just in body but also in will.

It is easy to imagine this warrior leaping into action when it is time to fight. The animal furs he wears at his thighs and loins hint at his potential ferocity. Here, toward the end of the suit, he has everything to fight for, and he also has all the experience and strength of will gathered from previous successes and losses. This warrior is strongest under pressure and most effective when responding to an attack rather than initiating one. In the same way, the archway behind him is built so that the top bricks maintain the shape of the arch due to pressure and force placed upon them, which they could not do if they were not arched. The arching shape reminds us of the moon's flux and its gentle shifting qualities, reiterating that strength will be found in response to changes and conserved energy will be put to better use in this manner.

Revelation

In a reading, the Nine of Wands brings an immense strength to the situation. It does not necessarily indicate that the querent is in a strong position, but rather that they are facing their situation with a strength of will and experience that will put them in good stead. However, the Nine of Wands comes with mixed messages. On the one hand, it speaks of strength, and on the other hand it speaks of a wound that weakens the querent in some way. This could indicate past experiences that have left the querent in pain and with battle scars, or it could point to an aspect of their physical body that makes doing a certain thing more difficult. Yet if the querent perseveres, presses on, and learns to choose their battles, instead of fighting every battle on principle, they will find themselves more effective.

In a relationship reading, the Nine of Wands points to either the querent or the partner being wounded from past relationships and suffering from emotional pain, which may put them into a defensive mode in this relationship. Their actions may thus be dictated by the desire to defend themselves or prevent further injury, and they may be reluctant to open up, viewing it as showing weakness and vulnerability.

In other areas of life, this card indicates the querent going through a lot of events or situations that require a lot of them, putting immense amounts of energy into things only to encounter obstacles and hindrances, hard slogs and battles to fight. When the querent eventually reaches their goal, it will be hard-won and hard fought for (though probably worth it!). This card also suggests ongoing projects or situations that are demanding upon the querent and their energy, perhaps something that began as a passion, driven by inspiration, and is now proving difficult to push toward completion. The querent may feel as though the end is far away and it will be too difficult to get there, but the Nine of Wands reassures them that they do have the strength and wisdom to do so. They just need to dig deeper within their resources to find their reserves of strength and will. Perseverence is the key.

The Nine of Wands can sometimes suggest that the best way to respond to a situation is to wait and see, to conserve energy before acting in response, rather than initiating action. The querent may find it best not to throw the first punch, but you can bet they'll throw the last one! They must be dedicated to flexibility and adaptability in this situation, as they will be able to respond with more strength and a firmer foundation because of it. Otherwise, they may find that they end up initiating the wrong battles, fighting for things that are not worth their time or energy, and wasting their inner resources. Often this card appears when the querent is under great stress, to indicate that they should see the stress and pressure as an ally, goading them to action, pushing them faster and harder toward their goal.

Reversed, we find that the querent has expended all their energy on pointless battles, and now they are in a weakened position. Their foundations are not firm, their intentions unsure, and all of their passion and drive are gone. They are responding to threats by lashing out, and often taking out anger and frustration on others instead of channelling their high emotions toward something positive. It can also point to past wounds or injuries (emotional, spiritual, or physical) that are holding them back.

Keywords

Strength, will, perseverance, energy conservation, defence, adaptability, flexibility, battles, wounds, injury, strong position, inner reserves.

Ten of Wands, the Burden of Choice

"Nothing worth doing in life was ever easy, and we are simply glorified working beasts. Unlike the oxen at the plough and the horse beneath the saddle, though, we choose the burdens we carry and the paths we walk. Every responsibility, every choice, every project, every goal, every dream, every ambition is another weight on our shoulders, and we carry them with us until the day we die. There is never an end to the work, for when one goal is completed, another one arises, calling us back to action, pulling us back into the fray. And we answer the call, because we don't know how to do anything else. We are conditioned to be this way.

But many of our burdens in life are the ones we judge worthy of our effort, and we will gladly strain our aching muscles and take those extra steps to carry them. Thus I offer you a chance to be great, not through virtue of birth or happy accident, but through the honest sweat of your brow and back, the determination of your path. I am the testing and the stretching. I am going to see just how far you can be pushed before you break. I am going to see how much weight you can carry. I will follow your every pained, aching step uphill, and when you most desire to drop your burden, I am going to allow you no respite. I am there when you think you cannot take another step or your shoulders will break from the strain, because I know you can always take another step. You are stronger than you ever believed, and I will force you to see this through gritted teeth and bursting lungs. And in the end, when you can finally place down your chosen burden, you will turn to me and through parched, cracked lips ask, "More weight…"

Saturn in Sagittarius / Malkuth in fire

Illumination

We reach the end of the suit of wands, but we don't find the joy of the Ten of Cups or the material success and wealth of the Ten of Coins. On the other hand, we also don't find the complete ruin of the Ten of Swords. Instead, we find a depiction of the way most of us live in the modern world: trudging from one responsibility and choice to another, usually exhausted, carrying our burdens with us. Sometimes we carry our burdens with pride and we become martyrs to our cause, and sometimes we need to ask for help because those burdens are too much. Here in the Ten of Wands, we see not only the act of carrying our burdens but also the encouragement needed to continue to do so, and the process of realizing our strength.

In the tarot, burdens are often frowned upon. We applaud our Fool because he carries little baggage with him, and the happiest cards are not weighted down by concerns like work, chores, obligations, large bundles of heavy wands or piles of sharp swords. But we cannot go through life completely unburdened, and the Ten of Wands is here to remind us that most of our burdens are those we have chosen to take on, and there are very few instances in life where we are forced. Having a bad day running the kids here, there, and everywhere? You chose to create a family. Hating your current job and the long hours? You applied for that job and accepted it, and you continue to show up for it. Feeling exhausted from expending all your energy into a project that still seems so far from completion? You got the project going; you can drop it at any time if you choose to. Of course, this does not mean that you cannot feel tired, pained, annoyed, upset, and complain loudly about your burdens, but the Ten of Wands asks us to remember that we have picked up the bundle of disarrayed wands and are walking up the steep hill through choice. Further, great things have been created from the weight of such burdens: liberty is founded upon the sacrifice and responsibilities of the past. Michelangelo's work on the Sistine Chapel required him to paint it while lying in back-breaking position on scaffolding suspended from the walls, and every woman at the end of pregnancy carries the weight of her child and the weight of her own pain as she brings life into the world.

In the card image, we see a man hunched over from the weight of the ten wands he carries. He wears the blue of aspiration and a small amount of the red of passion and desire, but the blue mostly covers the red, telling us that at this late stage in his journey toward completion, his passion and desire has been dimmed, oppressed, weighted down so that all he has left is a half-forgotten memory of why he began the journey in the first place, and the hope of what will happen once he reaches the finishing line. His burden is a heavy one, as his body posture shows, yet the wands he carries are the same ones found in most of the other wands cards, reminding us that this is still a card of great energy and drive. The exuberant bursting forth of passion in the Ace of Wands has dissipated down to the Ten of Wands where it has become determination and grit.

Our man walks uphill, treading his way up thigh-breaking stone steps. Anybody that has attempted such a walk will know the pain as the muscles protest at every strain with each new step. This is also near the top of a great hill, telling us that not only is the end in sight (though the last part is always the hardest!) but also that the man has aimed so high and come so far that perhaps he bit off more than he could chew: up here oxygen is thin and even breathing is more difficult. But if you set your sights on the stars, what do you expect? Nothing great ever came from mediocre goals.

It is sunset in the card, and ahead a sturdy stone tower awaits the man. Culmination and completion is close, but there is still some way to go before arrival. The going gets even tougher from here on in, as he is already exhausted and lacking in energy, the weight of his burden getting heavier and heavier, his mind beginning to allow doubt in. He could very well give up, drop his wands, and trudge down the hill again, but then he would have come this far for nothing. This is a valid choice, but the other option is to grit his teeth, gird his loins, and make one last final push with everything he's got.

Revelation

In a reading, the Ten of Wands can indicate the completion of a long and arduous task, a project that has been some time in coming, a great work that has taken up the querent's energy and time for so long. It often indicates that the querent's path is a difficult and demanding one, but one that is worthwhile despite how hard they are finding it. Being at the end of its suit, this card says that completion is assured, but that the querent needs to make yet more effort and expend a little more energy and time before they can finally lay down their burden, hand it to somebody else, or see it transformed into their goal.

Often the Ten of Wands says that the querent has bitten off more than they can chew, taking on a massive task that at the time seemed easy, but now is looking like the most difficult thing they've ever done. Perhaps they took it on as a challenge to themselves, to prove themselves to others, to feed their ego, to boost their résumé, or because they simply needed something to do. The fact is that now the querent is faced with a choice: drop it and admit defeat, or "man up," stop complaining, and just do the work.

In a reading about a possible goal, project, or endeavour, the Ten of Wands advises the querent that it will be a long journey and require everything they have. If they are not prepared for a challenge or battle, they should not begin. But if they think they've got what it takes to walk the road before them, then this is their call to arms. It also advises the querent that they must be aware of their level of energy or tiredness, as often health problems can result from this card's weight and exhaustion. It indicates that the querent is going through, or will go through, a time when they will not be allowed respite or dropping their burdens: greater things depend on them, or perhaps others depend on them.

Often the Ten of Wands asks the querent to consider the nature of the burdens and responsibilities they have in their life, and which ones they are willing to keep. What is worth it? What is not? It also reminds the querent that whatever it is they are doing, they must be prepared to work for it.

Reversed, the Ten of Wands can be a negative card, pointing to oppression and martyrdom. The querent may be in a situation where they are being forced to do something they do not want, either by circumstances or another person, or that they are being expected to give too much of themselves. They are exhausted, but there is no end in sight, and they do not consider what they are doing worth the energy and time, yet they feel they cannot let go. Sometimes the Ten of Wands reversed suggests that the querent is carrying baggage from the past with them, and that their present and future is being shaped in a certain way by negative influences from their past actions or mental state.

Keywords

Duty, responsibility, burden, weight, strength, determination, oppression, baggage, exhaustion, tiredness, struggle, task, work.

CHAPTER 24

The Suit of Swords

Ace of Swords, the Breath of Life

"In the beginning was the word, and the thought, and the idea. At the start of all things there was the first sharp intake of breath and the following cry of the newborn child. From the clouds of unknowing I pierce through to the light, and thrust truth into life, for I am not a sword wielded in war but a sword wielded in peace. Yet even in peace I may cut to the quick, and many are the casualties: for no idea, proposition, or statement may go unchecked and untested; all weakness and imperfection is revealed, and careful critique embarked upon. Upon my blade all oaths are made, with my knife's edge I distribute justice, with my motion and my stillness I am the maker of kings. Speak the truth and I am with you; conceive the first whisper of an idea and I am there. Set me at the highest places, upon windy mountains and peaks, and there I shall carry your prayers swiftly to the gods. For a pure idea and the words of wisdom to express it create the world anew. I am the triumph of wisdom for wisdom's sake, the true lover of wisdom, the philosopher, and I penetrate to the core of all things so that I may dare to know."

No astrological associations for the aces / Kether in air

Illumination

As all the aces are the beginnings, roots, and seeds of their suit, the Ace of Swords is the most pure and unified form of the elemental forces of air. Air in the tarot represents the mind and everything that comes from it: thought, intellect, knowledge, wisdom, communication. But the Ace of Swords is more than just the seed of an idea or the beginnings of communication: it is the sacred breath of life and the holy trinity of truth, liberty, and justice. Here we find thought and word at their purest, with intention and will directing them in a single focus toward the light of truth. Surely this, then, is the quest for knowledge and wisdom at its highest.

It is interesting to note in this card that the Ace of Swords is the only ace to feature two hands holding the elemental object. To hold a sword with one hand might allow for the sword's position to be weakened, easily pushed aside, deflected, or disarmed. But a two-handed hold upon the sword shows a firm intention and direction, as well as strength to maintain balance and position. This is further expressed by the general appearance of the card: it is fresh, clear, open, and balanced, the hands raising the sword high above the misty clouds so that it catches the glinting rays of the sun, symbolic of divine light. Unlike the Ace of Wands, this elemental weapon is not held by a strong, muscled male arm but rather the gentle hands of a woman, in a posture that is reminiscent of the Lady of the Lake from Arthurian tales. It was the Lady of the Lake who bestowed the sword Excalibur upon King Arthur, thereby offering him sacred kingship and power. In the same way, the qualities that the Ace of Swords represents—truth, justice, pure thought and intention—grant power of the purest kind to their wielder.

On the position and holding of the sword, Aleister Crowley writes:

> *"The Sword may, however, be clasped in both hands, and kept
> steady and erect, symbolizing that thought has become one with the
> single aspiration, and burnt up like a flame."*[16]

This is, in other words, the unity of thought with intent. One wonders if the employment of all four Aces together would lead us to achieve miracles: the Ace of Wands being will and energy, the Ace of Cups being love and the divine, the Ace of Pentacles being action and manifestation, and the Ace of Swords being thought and intent. No wonder the Alchemist has these elemental tools upon his table!

As in the other aces, we see Yods falling like golden droplets from the blade of the sword. Yod means "hand" in Hebrew, and is the seed letter of all the other letters of the Hebrew alphabet, reminding us of the nascent and seedlike nature of the aces. They can also be seen as little pieces of divine light that filter down from the aces to the rest of the suit, showing us that each suit starts with its

---

16. Aleister Crowley, *Magick: Book 4, Part 2* (York Beach, ME: Red Wheel/Weiser, 1994),
    page 87.

purest form. In the suit of swords we find the purest form of thought, intention, and word, but as it becomes more manifest and caught up in the world, heavy with mundanity and its concerns, it loses its purity and develops into the petty aspects of the mind—jealousy, cruelty, manipulation, politics…

However, the olive branch and palm fronds that rest within the crown in the Ace of Swords should always remind us that in the beginning of the suit of swords there is peace and truth. These two plants are traditional symbols of peace, the olive branch being the plant brought back by the dove that returned to Noah in the ark to signify that it had found land, and the palm frond being a symbol of victory and triumph in pre-Christian times. It is also found in the Bible to celebrate Jesus' triumphant entry into Jerusalem, commemorated today on Palm Sunday. The Christian writer Origen calls it "the symbol of victory in that war waged by the spirit against the flesh."[17] This is not necessarily to say that the mundane world is bad, but rather that sometimes it is easy to get so caught up in it that we find ourselves falling down below the misty clouds of the Ace of Swords again, unable to see the light of truth, our thoughts and intentions divided and scattered to the winds. Entwined with the palm fronds and olive branch is a golden crown, symbolic of the highest attainment and power of the senses (since the crown rests on the head, the highest point of the body).

We see on the sword's hilt the jewelled wings of a dragonfly. This beautiful insect is symbolic of agility, and the ability to rise above and see beyond the surface of an issue, as it hovers above water. It exhibits iridescence on its wings and on its body, meaning that it shows itself in different colours depending on the angle and polarization of light falling on it. This reminds us that the mind is capable of conceiving of a vast number of different perspectives almost simultaneously, and also mirrors the act of the creation of colour through refraction of light. All colour comes from pure light, just as all words and thoughts come from pure mind.

As unrefracted, pure light and thought, the Ace of Swords can be seen as the initial urge toward knowledge and the love of wisdom. We get the term "philosophy" from the Greek *philo sophia*, "love of wisdom." It is the pursuit of philosophy that teaches the mind to conceive abstract ideas, to pursue logic to its highest end, to apply critical thinking to all statements and propositions. The ability to do this allows us to apply our mind to the purpose of maintaining peace, promoting equality and liberty, freeing ourselves from ignorance, and

---

17. Origen, *Joan* XXXI.

offering justice. This is why the sword in the Ace of Swords is not being wielded in battle, but instead held aloft in peace: to destroy others for the sake of an ideology is done with neither pure intention nor a love of wisdom.

Revelation

In a reading, the Ace of Swords can be difficult to interpret as it is quite an abstract card, relying therefore on surrounding cards and the context of the question to add the specifics to its broader ideas. When it appears, it refers to all issues or concerns surrounding communication, thought, ideas, and studies. It also indicates that the querent's mind is paramount in this situation, perhaps because they are embarking on a course of study or a journey of knowledge, such as university or a vocational training course. The Ace of Swords often suggests the very beginnings of a knowledge-based project, such as the writing of a thesis, a new scientific study, or an outline for a book. Any way in which the querent applies pure intention and their mind together is signified by this card. Sometimes it can represent that one great idea that will change the querent's life forever, or an entirely new perspective and outlook that brings the querent to a greater understanding of truth and wisdom.

Generally the Ace of Swords brings clarity to the reading. As such, the Ace of Swords asks the querent to consider what their intentions are. If it is surrounded by cards that signify confusion or imbalance, it might indicate that the querent's intentions are not as pure as they could be, or their words and actions are not guided by a higher truth or wisdom. With this card in the spread the querent also needs to consider how they express their thoughts—through writing? Through the spoken word? More importantly, how might their ideas be more eloquently and clearly expressed? Clarity of thought and word is necessary in this situation. At times the Ace of Swords also suggests that the "pen is mightier than the sword"; the querent may find that they will have the greatest effect in their situation by writing and communicating via the written word.

In a reading about a relationship or any situation involving other people, the querent is advised that communication must be as clear as possible for any growth or stability to occur. Depending on surrounding cards, it can also indicate whether justice is being served to or by the querent, and whether in a fair or an unfair manner. In matters concerning contracts, promises, or oaths, the Ace of Swords is a positive card, as it suggests that both sides will keep their part of the bargain.

If the Ace of Swords is reversed in a reading, this places the golden crown of highest ideals at the bottom, with the cloudy mist of confusion at the top, and the sword of truth is also reversed. This makes for an unhealthy application of the mind, a mind geared toward overturning truth and replacing it with confusion, the sowing of the seeds of doubt. It might also suggest that the querent is having problems engaging with their intellectual side due to the concerns of the everyday world; perhaps they are being distracted from their studies or writing that book by their job, family, health worries, or even an annoying neighbour that plays loud music at night. It might also indicate that they are having difficulty communicating or being heard, either because they have an inherent problem with expressing themselves or because someone or circumstances are silencing them. Sometimes the Ace of Swords reversed can simply indicate the same quest for knowledge as it would upright, but here knowledge is not sought for the love of it, but rather as a means to an end.

Keywords
Intention, thought, mind, knowledge, ideas, wisdom, peace, communication, intellect, philosophy, critique, justice, equality, liberty, freedom, clarity, words, writing, messages, speaking.

Two of Swords, the Fulcrum of the Mind

"Come to find me on the shores of the world and all the in-between places of life. Meet me at the crossroads of every possibility, and at the turning point of every tide. Find me at the birth of paradox and between paradoxes, for I am that which occurs in the state between changed states. When your mind conceives of the idea, I am the intake of breath and the pause before you speak it; when you entertain a choice, I am the moment of stillness before the decision. Change begins in the fulcrum of the mind: with a decision. Decision tips the scales so that change is already manifest. Come to meet me at the moments between the waves and the times between lunar changes, and we shall draw down the moon together. Then we shall leave footprints in the sand for mere moments in time as we choose which path to walk and which to leave behind, and within moments the stillness of our past impressions shall be washed away by the incoming tide…"

The Moon in Libra / Chockmah in air

Illumination

The twos of the minor arcana are divided in nature; the Two of Cups and the Two of Wands show us the union and harmony between the pairing in their cards (e.g., two hearts, or the extension of creative impulse) but the Two of Swords and the Two of Pentacles present us with images of change and how it occurs. The latter suits show us transition and balance through adaptation between things or states, and the Two of Swords in particular teaches us about the moment between states of being or the point before decisions are made. From the Ace of Swords' focused, pure thought and initial idea, the Two of Swords represents "two minds" or two states of mind, two possibilities of perception.

There is an overall sense of liminality and quiet in this card, as if time has stood still for a moment and everything fallen silent, as the woman stills her mind in order to make her decision. She is seated on the shoreline, a place that is in between places, not a place by its own virtue but through the virtue of its setting: she is between land and sea, but also in both and at the same time in neither. She is sitting at one of the world's many natural crossroads, and she holds two identical swords in perfect balance across her chest, amplifying the liminal nature of the card.

The presence of the moon brings to the Two of Swords the concept of flux and the ebb and flow of tides; in the suit that is concerned primarily with the mind, thoughts, and ideas, this flux places us in the shadowy realms of the moment decisions are made or choices are considered. When we are first presented with choices, all of them are possible and the future is completely open to us, which leads many people to stay in this peaceful state of possibility for longer than necessary. When we stand still on the wet sand of the shore, our footprints cannot be washed away, but as soon as we choose to walk in a certain direction, we leave behind footprints that will be washed away by the waters of flux. As soon as we make a decision, the other options are no longer possible. This is what we see in the Two of Swords: that infinitesimally small moment in time that is, for our viewing convenience, frozen, when the mind is between states, between possibilities. It is the scales of decision-making completely balanced, and the silence and stillness before the mind commits to a path.

The two swords being held so perfectly by the woman in this card can represent many things. Most obviously, they are balance, and the stillness required to hold them in this manner. They are more specifically the balance of the mind—the inner peace found therein, and the concentration required for balance. They also symbolize being "in two minds" about something, torn between options, which gives us another perspective on the position of the woman at the shoreline: she is caught "between the devil and the deep blue sea." Here we find a dilemma, this word coming from the Greek meaning "double proposition." Perhaps the woman in the card is carefully weighing all the options, meditating upon both sides of the story, bouncing ideas back and forth in her mind. Certainly the moon in the card is waxing (growing toward full), suggesting that after this moment has passed and a decision has been reached, forward motion can proceed. However, if we see this image as a freeze-frame of a very specific moment, remaining indecisive will not bring any growth.

Blindfolded, our woman is in a peculiar position. What are the reasons for covering her eyes in this the situation? Perhaps it is so that she can focus better on her other senses, suggesting that initial impressions might be misleading. Perhaps it is so that she can turn inward to her thoughts, rather than being distracted by the colours of the world. Have you found that meditation is easier and more successful with your eyes closed? It puts you into a state that mimics sleep, drawing darkness over our vision and relaxing our eyes, yet our mind remains awake and attentive. By blindfolding herself, the woman in the Two of Swords voluntarily puts her mind into a liminal state in which answers can be reached more clearly, removing confusion or distractions. This state of being is a temporary peace that seldom occurs in the modern world, and most often when we are between states, decisions, or possibilities.

In the image, her red hair is the only splash of colour to stand out against the grey-blue, stormlike colours of the sky, sea, and her dress. It is mostly contained in a hairnet, but we can see that wisps of it are flying free, blown backward by the wind. This is the wind of change, at the moment only a gentle breeze. Since this is only the Two of Swords, early in its suit, the winds are barely a whisper, but storm clouds are gathering above. A storm will break if the decision required in this card is ignored.

Revelation

In a reading, the Two of Swords is a clear message that a decision or choice needs to be made. It can also refer to the process of decision-making. It usually suggests that the querent is currently in an in-between state, such as between locations, jobs, studies, or relationships. They may also be of two minds about something, caught trying to decide between two distinct options that are nevertheless equally weighted in virtue and application. The querent may find that they are bouncing back and forth between options without being able to make a decision. If this is the case, the Two of Swords advises them to still their mind and remove distractions from the equation. They must be focused and aware of what is relevant to the decision-making process and what isn't.

Often the Two of Swords indicates that the querent has made the choice *not* to make a choice, thereby preserving the peace of their situation. This may be due to fear of what they will leave behind once they make their choice, as they may be conscious that other doors will close if they step in a certain direction. This card might also say that they are having difficulty adapting to changes in their life, finding themselves instead in an unproductive state of limbo.

If the querent has specifically asked about a situation where there is more than one possibility, this card advises them that all the possibilities are equally good, useful, or achievable. They will not get any further guidance beyond that which they give themselves. They must pause to assess the situation and then make their decision firmly and fearlessly, accepting that change is a necessary part of growth.

Sometimes, especially if accompanied by cards that suggest other people or a social situation, the Two of Swords puts the querent in the role of peacekeeper during times of conflict or quarrel, either between themselves and another person, or between others. Only a completely calm and considered approach, listening to all sides of the story and weighing it up with fairness, will resolve matters.

If reversed in a reading, the Two of Swords says that the querent is caught in limbo, finding it difficult to make a transition from one state to another, and has grown so accustomed to their current position that they will happily stay there until they stagnate. It also suggests that, regarding any choices or decisions that need to be made, they are caught between a rock and a hard place, between the devil and the deep blue sea, and their choice must be the lesser of two evils.

Keywords

Balance, equanimity, peace, peacekeeping, limbo, standstill, liminal, betweenness, decision, indecision, choice, flux, crossroads, dilemma, meditation, concentration.

Three of Swords, the Existential Sorrowing

"At the dawning of mankind, there was suffering. The moment life began, so did pain. Even the universe cried out in the throes of birth to bring the Earth, sun, and moon into existence. This is the nature of things: to hurt and be hurt. You forget this, my child, protected as you are from the lash of suffering by wealth and comfort. You do not waste away in hunger nor shrivel in thirst; you do not find yourself lost in an arid wilderness, nor put to death at sea. There are those that would keep the truth of the world from you, keep your eyes from seeing the reality of humankind's existence; these are your enemies. They would halt your understanding and keep you as an infant, blind and ignorant. They would let you believe you are immortal and invulnerable, making you forget that humanity itself, even more so you, are but brief shadows passing over the face of the Earth, and the Earth is but a brief shadow passing through the universe. You are as nothing. But know it, truly, and the nothingness will not matter. When you are wounded by the deep sorrow in the face of suffering, you will rage like the storm, feeling the gales and torrential rain rip at your heart and soul. Then I shall open my arms to you and pull you close, but there will be no comfort found in me, only pain more acute and a realization of a path forward. This is the sorrow that teaches harshly, the sorrow that smothers in its pain, the sorrow that reveals the truth. This is the mourning for the loss of ignorance, which some call innocence, and the keening for the inevitable fate of humanity and your own pitiful soul. I will let you cry in rage and terror, I will revel in your anguish and pain, for in the darkest, deepest moment of your existential sorrowing, you will find the way to redeem the world."

Saturn in Libra / Binah in air

Illumination

The Three of Swords is the only card (apart from the four aces) that does not feature in its image a living creature or person. It is also a terribly vicious card image to look at! It is easy to confuse the meanings of the Five of Cups and the Three of Swords, since both focus on sorrow of some kind, but the difference is explained by the lack of living creatures in the Three of Swords: whereas the Five of Cups represents grief on a human level, such as loss of a loved one or the painful ending of a situation, the Three of Swords represents sorrow on a more existential level, not connected with a personal tragedy. This card seems to be in direct opposition with the Three of Cups, which declares existence to be pure joy; the Three of Swords declares the nature of existence to be pure suffering.

Here we find the deep sorrow of existential angst. This is the profound sadness felt when seeing the state of the world and the suffering of mankind. Some of us may have felt it: a deep depression in the face of a realization of our inevitable death, or a sense of impending doom when thinking about the fact that at some point in the future, the race of humankind will be extinct, probably due to the inevitable death of our solar system's sun. On a smaller scale, we may have felt it when becoming aware of the plight of the developing world, knowing that people in other parts of our world starve every day, or die of thirst, or develop diseases that in our Western culture have died out due to the availability of vaccinations and medical technology. We may have felt it when looking at the state of our own culture, seeing human rights being ignored and the pleas of those who would try and change the world for the better cast aside. The fact cannot be ignored that even if our individual lives are happy and comfortable, and we rarely face suffering on the same level as those in the developing world, the world in general is filled with suffering, and people undergoing it.

In the card image, the main focus is the heart, which is pierced cruelly by three swords. The heart is embellished with three red and gold gems, and in the centre of it is a crucifix also embellished with red gemstones. The heart in the Tarot Illuminati is not the cartoonlike, simplified heart of many other tarot decks, but instead the heart is anatomically correct and realistic. It therefore makes us aware of the real pain of this card, the profound feelings of suffering and wounding. It makes the sorrow more personal, more applicable to us. This isn't just the suffering of others and the suffering of humankind, but the sorrow we feel in response to our realization of it.

The suit of swords is primarily concerned with the mind, thought, communication, and ideas. The three swords that pierce the heart in the card image therefore represent this realization, this deep process of thought associated with it. This isn't just an emotional pain, but one that takes place in our mind as well: an existential suffering, a philosophical angst, a balking of the mind at the sheer sadness of the state of things. In the centre of the heart, the golden crucifix reminds us that the angst is not just on a mental level, however, but also on a spiritual level.

In the background, we see a stormy ocean, above which heavy, black, pendulous storm clouds have gathered. The wind and rain lashes, and the waves break powerfully upon the rocks that form the foundations for two pillars either side of the heart. As the rain falls onto the pierced heart, it pools at the top in various indents and runs down over it, washing the swords clean of blood. The blood falls from the tips of the swords onto the rocks below, where it will be washed away in due time. This washing away of the blood by the rain symbolizes the process of sorrow and grief washing away pain. The Three of Swords serves as a powerful reminder that this kind of suffering and sorrow is the same that was felt by many mystics and great thinkers throughout history, who went on to change the world for the better based on their awareness. Mother Teresa (now Blessed Mother Teresa, one step away from being canonized as a saint in the Catholic Church) began her work helping the poorest and sickest people in the slums of Calcutta. It was her realization of the suffering of these people, and her resulting sorrow from it, that spurred her to found the Missionaries of Charity, the work of which still continues today. Siddhartha Gautama, who would later become the Buddha, began life as a wealthy prince from whom all the sorrows of the world were kept. He was not shown death, age, or sickness until one day, on a tour of the city, he beheld all three of them: first he saw an old man, a sight he had never before seen. His charioteer, Channa, explained that all men and women grew old, and Siddhartha was horrified. He then saw a man struck by disease, and Channa explained that sometimes the body suffered illness and injury, causing pain and suffering. Finally, he saw a corpse, and Channa explained that all men and women eventually die, as do all living things. This was the way of the world; suffering was a part of every person's life. Siddartha felt great anguish at this realization, until he saw an ascetic holy man. He resolved then to try and find a way to remove suffering and break out of the cycle of rebirth into continual suffering that was humankind's lot, by pursuing a holy life. His enlightenment and subsequent teachings founded the Buddhist religion, and according to the tradition allowed many others to break out of the cycle of reincarnation and suffering.

The sorrow depicted by the Three of Swords is the mystic's sorrow. Compare the pierced heart of this card image to the stigmata phenomena of the Catholic faith, in which the deeply devout bear the same physical wounds that Christ suffered at his Crucifixion (symbolized by the cross in the card image). The suffering they undergo is both a physical pain and an emotional and spiritual one, but in that suffering they find the bliss of union with God and an understanding of the sacrifice and suffering of Christ for humanity. The wounded heart can also be seen in other Christian iconography, such as the Sacred Heart, which is the burning heart crowned with thorns associated with Christ's suffering, as well as the various accounts of later mystics who described visions and feelings of their hearts being pierced by fiery arrows or swords, representing the intense love of God born from Christ's suffering and death. It is this intense spiritual sorrow and pain leading to realization and cleansing that St. Theresa of Avila was referring to when she said, "Lord, either let me suffer, or let me die."

After the Three of Swords comes the four, an image of peace and repose within a religious setting. From the suffering of the three, we are brought to a profound realization and enter into a gestation period in which we may find solace and peace. Our tears wash away our pain, but the wounds never truly disappear.

Revelation

In a reading, the Three of Swords indicates a vast amount of pain and suffering, yet has the potential to lead to peace, wholeness, and healing, not just for the querent but for others. This card indicates that the querent is undergoing a time of suffering and great sorrow. This may manifest as inexplicable sadness, fits of depression, angst, emotional pain, and feelings of being lost or powerless in the face of pain. The querent may be faced with a dawning realization of something being wrong, or might be slowly coming to see the extent of the pain of a situation. They may have recently become interested in work that tends to those most in need and seeks to alleviate suffering in others.

In a spiritual reading, the Three of Swords points to a state of deep spiritual and mystical suffering, such as a Dark Night of the Soul or contention with the darkness of the self or others, although it suggests that the pain has a purpose for the querent. This pain and the emotional wounds they are currently feeling will instigate a deeper understanding as well as a desire to improve things in the world around them. Sometimes this card can therefore indicate one who works with those who are feeling such sorrow, such as a volunteer on a suicide prevention hotline, in a women's shelter, or in groups that help people cope with depression. If the reading is specifically concerning magical or mystical matters in the querent's life, then the Three of Swords indicates the vision of the vale of tears, a descent into the abyss, and an identification with the suffering of a spiritual figure or deity.

On a more mundane level, the Three of Swords can suggest pain coming into the querent's situation, the details of which will be revealed by surrounding cards and the context of the question. However, this card focuses on the letting go of pain through engaging with it. Here are the querent's tears purifying them and cleansing them, sorrow performing a healing function in their life.

Reversed, the higher qualities of the Three of Swords are brought closer to earth. Here we see heartache and heartbreak, the ending of a relationship or a romance, as well as betrayal in relationships. The Three of Swords reversed can sometimes point to a love triangle, or it can indicate the processes of the mind overcoming the heart and causing sorrow. Reversed, this card shows us the potential for the mind to betray us and lead to suffering in our emotional life.

Keywords
Sorrow, suffering, pain, heartache, heartbreak, existential angst, darkness, mourning, healing, letting go, pain, depression.

Four of Swords, the Oracle of the Fertile Mind

"Oh, my weary, worn truth-seeker, don't you tire of your mind wandering like an ascetic, weeping and feeling the pains of realization? The mind can only entertain so much thought and activity before it begins to fray, and no truly good thought was ever born from a mind that did not pause. Quiet your mind, philosopher, and be still. In that chamber of stillness, let your mind lie down in the fertile fields of rest. There it will take root and its seeds incubate and germinate in the rich earth. Your mind is the womb of the Mother of God, filled with potential, but like the babe from the woman's belly your thoughts must be given time to become fully formed. To bring them to birth now would be to bring weak ideas and half-realized thoughts into the world. So sleep, rest, be still. In the mind of your sleep I shall bring you visions and great words to fertilize your mind. You have fought so long and hard with your thoughts and for them, struggling to reconcile perception and manifestation, it is time now to lay your swords aside. If your mind is already filled with many thoughts, how can a new one form? If you are always living in the conceptual world, dallying with theories and hypotheses, what are you creating? Let your thoughts seek peace and resolution, and you will become the temple of the Oracle of the Mind, in which stillness and the quieting of thought and speech brings to birth truth and wisdom."

Jupiter in Libra / Chesed in air

Illumination

In the tarot, the fours share the earthy qualities of manifestation, grounding, and stability, and in the suit of swords the cards are primarily concerned with the various facets, qualities, and acts of the mind or thought. In the first three cards of the swords suit, we saw the birth of thought. In the ace, the initial birth of an idea in abstract form occurred, but it was merely an idea and nothing more. In the two, we saw the moment at which an idea became decided upon, fixed in the present by extension and expansion into reality. With the Three of Swords came the fruition of the logical extension of the mind in the world: the realization of suffering and the resultant sorrow, which leads now to the Four of Swords and its manifestation of peace, resolution, and incubation. This is the grounding of thought into reality, the act of contemplation in the everyday world, but it also carries with it the fertile aspects of the four's earthiness. The setting of this card is a room surrounded by brown, wooden panelling and decorated with wooden features, making this scene one of womblike incubation, from which all things can be born.

In the card image, three swords hang on the wall, presumably belonging to the knight who lies in gentle repose. To hang up your sword is to lay it down to rest for a while, knowing that you will need it again in the future. The knight in this card accepts that resting his mind, symbolized by the swords, is a worthy task at this time, but also that he will need to put his mind into active mode again in the future. The mind cannot stay still forever. It might be tempting to think that these three swords are hanging over the knight's head as a potential threat, but if we look closely, we can see that the two lowest swords' tips are hidden by the knight's body, indicating that they are suspended to the side of him.

The pose of the knight is an interesting one. He is in the act of praying—but who prays lying down with hands clasped like that? Praying itself is a potent symbol. It is the act of communicating with the divine, as well as quieting the mind and finding a state of peace. It is known to bring hope and emotional, spiritual, and mental healing to those who undertake it, and it brings about a contemplative state of mind. Yet this pose is more reminiscent of the carved stone chest tombs found inside churches and cathedrals, built to contain the remains of important members of the parish, upon which detailed effigies of the deceased were carved. They were always depicted in the pose of our knight: lying on their backs with their heads raised by a cushion, with their hands pressed together in prayer. If the deceased was a military man, he would sometimes be depicted in his full armour.

To have your remains entombed within the sacred building of your god is not merely an indication of your influence and power. It is also symbolic of your soul being taken into the "house of God," or the presence of God. In mystical tarot language, the mind is being placed into a state of divine presence or contemplation, as symbolized by the stained-glass window of the Virgin Mary in the background overlooking the knight. Once again we have a symbolic tomb, which is synonymous—as always in tarot!—with the womb, and therefore here we see the act of incubating the mind in a state of peace and contemplation. This is why the fourth sword is lying in a similar way to the reposed knight, and pictured beneath him—this sword-mind is resting within the womb-tomb. The mind is allowed to rest in mystery.

In the ancient Mediterranean world, incubation oracles were often sought by those looking for answers and healing. A seeker would enter a temple (particularly that of Apollo) set up for this purpose and would go to sleep in a specially prepared chamber, after purification rituals and offerings. It was believed that during sleep, the god of the temple would send them dreams with answers and revelation contained therein; if the purpose of their incubation was for healing, they would be healed upon waking. The knight in the Four of Swords seems to be undertaking a form of this incubation oracle, finding peace and sleep in a place of his chosen god. In the moment when his mind is still and grounded, peaceful and at rest, God puts into it ideas and thoughts, inspiration and guidance.

Revelation

The Four of Swords can have a multitude of meanings and applications in a reading. Most obviously, it can indicate that the querent is in a time of rest and standstill that provides some much needed peace and quiet. This could be a holiday, a short break, or simply a period of time when they have less work to do. If it falls in a future position, the Four of Swords suggests that this is a time yet to come. It can also advise the querent to find some rest and relaxation, to enable them to function more readily and efficiently. If they continue to work and apply their mind so much and for such a long time, they will find that they grow so tired that their thoughts are haphazard and fragmented. This manifests as difficulty in focusing or staying on topic, finding it hard to concentrate, and lacking motivation to do anything challenging. Giving the mind a rest is essential for the querent to be able to create anything further.

This card may indicate a time when the querent specifically needs to take a break from their everyday world and activities so that they can seek answers or inspiration that they are searching for. It suggests that their answers will not come from rushing about in the everyday world; contemplation is required. On a mundane level, the Four of Swords can point to actual holidays and time away from work and duties to allow the querent to recharge their batteries and refresh themselves. It can also raise issues concerning the querent's sleep and dreams, in particular advising them to pay attention to their dreams, as they come from a fertile state of mind that might be able to provide insight and answers.

At times, this card says that the querent will bring their thoughts and ideas into reality and practical application. They will take their thoughts from an abstract and theoretical state to a practical one that has use in their everyday life.

If accompanied by cards that point to spirituality or seeking, the Four of Swords can raise the possibility of a contemplative life, the act of meditation, or dream oracles. The querent is advised that they must still their mind and silence their thoughts in order to allow creative thought to blossom. The querent needs to be in a state of incubation for their endeavours to progress, and whilst this may seem to the querent as though they are at a complete standstill, achieving nothing, it is a much-needed stillness during which they can gather momentum and new ideas.

Reversed, the earthy power of the fours oppresses the airy power of the suit of swords. The querent's mind will be so caught up in the material world and everyday life that it will have precious little time to give to seeking contentment and peace or thinking about anything beyond the mundane. It can also suggest that the querent's mind is stuck in a certain way of thinking; habitual thought patterns, dogma, refusal to entertain new ideas, and being "old-fashioned" or a "stick-in-the-mud" can be indicated by this card in reverse. Since upright the Four of Swords has the fertility of the earth on its side, reversed it is the arid and barren desert: the querent may have run out of ideas or is completely lacking in inspiration. The may also be finding it difficult to get their head around a new concept or idea.

Keywords

Stillness, respite, peace, repose, holiday, time-out, incubation, contemplation, prayer, meditation, sleep, dreams, rest, relaxation, standstill.

Five of Swords, Victory at Any Cost

"I came into this world with no special advantage save for the brains in my head. I didn't have a silver spoon in my mouth or a wealthy uncle in the shipping industry, nor any special education or an inheritance to look to. I'd be a fool not to use my mind to its highest and keenest abilities! And when you need to get ahead, well, what is there standing in the way of a clever chap like me except his own vague concept of 'honour'? I'll tell you this for free: honour will see you rot in the gutter and starve in the streets; honour will see you pass from this world in mediocrity. And mediocrity is one of the greatest sins of them all. I have no qualms about attaining victory at any cost. Some might call it dishonour, cheating, or betrayal, but I call it cleverness. If my opponent shows weakness, I am not to blame. Only a coward would let him show such weakness and not use it to his advantage. In this world we need every tiny advantage we can get—it is do or be done, kill or be killed. I am not killed, and I am not done. So, accuse me and slander me, hate me and despise me, but one day you, too, will be called to take the advantage and to use it against another. You will see the necessity in it; you will know what it is to need to defeat another and take everything you can, giving nothing back. Only you and your 'conscience' can judge how you will act. I certainly won't. But one thing you can be sure of: when you've beaten your opponent to the ground and taken everything he has, he won't make the same mistakes again. Never again will he show weakness. Never again will he trust implicitly. I know, because it was done to me. That which does not kill us, as they say, makes us stronger…"

Venus in Aquarius / Geburah in air

Illumination

There are few people that can look at this card and not dislike it. The figure in the card is decidedly unsavoury, sharing this quality with the figure from the Seven of Swords, as well as the qualities of all the fives of the tarot. The fives bring with them the energies of imbalance, conflict, upheaval, and aggression; here in the suit of the mind, thoughts, and communication, this creates an unsettling combination. In the Five of Swords, we see the imbalanced mind that seeks conflict, always looking to take advantage of another person, seeking victory no matter what the cost, and using it to fuel the ego.

In the foreground, an elaborately dressed young man is walking away from two other men. He is carrying three swords, and two swords rest at his feet, crossed. The scene is on a beach as evening begins to set in, and the waves are lapping at their feet. The man is dressed in armour, covered by clothing that would not look out of place on a prince or a wealthy merchant, and his face bears a look of arrogance.

The fact that he is wearing armour and fine clothing is in direct contrast to the men in the background. We can see that these two men have been defeated by the armoured prince, with one consoling the other. One wears simpler clothes, with no armour; the colours he wears are muted and look less costly. The man that is being consoled looks slightly better off, wearing green and a helmet that may be from a foreign land. He wears no armour either. It is tempting to think that the green-clad man was a merchant bringing back wares from a foreign land—in this case, beautifully carved, curved scimitars— and the poorer clad man was his escort, son, or helper of some kind. They were waylaid by our armoured prince as they arrived upon the shore, and he used his advantage (influence and power, as well as armour and possibly military skill) to unfairly take their wares for himself. The look on the prince's face suggests that he felt it was his right to do so, and he walks away feeling pleased with himself, showing no remorse.

It is almost certain that the prince does not care that the merchant has just lost items that are worth three months' wages. He doesn't care about the time and effort wasted now that the items are not to be sold at market. He doesn't care that the merchant may have a family to support, or customers expecting delivery that will cause trouble if they do not receive what they have already paid for. In short, the prince cares for nobody but himself.

The two swords that lie at the prince's feet are a specific type of blade: the sword cane. Sword canes are blades that are concealed as canes or walking sticks, easy to pull from their scabbard. They are deceptive, since to look at them no blade can be seen and they appear to be a normal walking cane. Anybody wielding such a weapon can have it go undetected until the crucial moment when they are in the desired position, at the desired time. It is a classic weapon for gaining an unfair advantage in a situation. The Five of Swords is all about unfair advantage, though the prince in the card probably wouldn't see it as unfair. Traditionally, this card is associated with defeat rather than victory at any cost, so the gloating prince will no doubt be partly attributing his victory to the weakness of his opponents, feeling that he simply did what any other person would do in his situation: take an opportunity. The sword canes in this image also indicate a hidden threat or a hidden wound, and somebody deliberately attempting to deceive others.

The incoming tide of the ocean reminds us of the mutability of the fives, and also indicates that soon, within minutes, the footprints of the armoured prince will be washed away, and all proof of his presence there will be gone. This card really is a card of everything unfair about the world! The imbalance of the fives lends itself to the suit of swords by manifesting as the armoured prince's attitude, which could be ascribed to ego, arrogance, or even mental illness of some kind. His thoughts are not right. His actions are not right because his thoughts are not right.

We can guess that there may have been a fight over the swords, with the merchant trying to protect his property. This is symbolic of the conflict of ideas, as well as a mind in turmoil with itself. Whether such a fight can ever be truly won or lost is a matter for debate, but the answer is suggested by this card: yes, but at what cost?

Revelation

In a reading, the Five of Swords is never really a welcome card, yet it can have some positive aspects. The positive aspects only manifest in a reading where other cards surrounding the Five of Swords are very positive and supportive. In cases like this, it suggests that the querent needs to learn how to make the most of the skills or talents that they have which others don't. It points out that the querent has a unique advantage in the situation, and they need to make the most of it. It also says that it's time for the querent to put themselves first instead of putting others first. Sometimes it can indicate a philosophical conflict within the querent, ideas being explored through debate, or a group of people testing ideas and points of view through logical argument.

However, it is more common for the Five of Swords to appear in a reading to point to a defeat in the querent's future. It suggests that the querent will be on the receiving end of a conflict that ends with them on the weaker side. This card often indicates a cheat, so in a relationship reading it might point to either the querent being unfaithful to a partner or being the victim of unfaithfulness.

If the querent is not currently in a relationship, they may find themselves becoming the third party in an affair.

In business and work, the querent should be wary: the Five of Swords indicates cheating and unfairness toward them. They may find their pay docked unfairly, accusations made that are untrue, or somebody spreading malicious gossip or rumours to ruin the querent's chances of a promotion or positive relationships in the workplace. If the querent is the perpetrator of such things, they should be advised that they are "cutting their nose off to spite their face," and they will only dig themselves into a hole from which it is difficult to get out in the future. In a similar vein, it indicates that the querent may be engaging in, or on the receiving end of, behaviour from a friend, partner, or family member acting in such a way that is designed to hurt them or another before they are hurt themselves—this is the "do, or be done" attitude of the Five of Swords. This card advises the querent that in all situations it is wisest not to show any weakness, lest it be used against them.

At times, the Five of Swords suggests that victory is possible for the querent, but that it would be a pyrrhic victory, and the querent should assess the cost and ask himself if it would be worth it. They should also be aware of their ego and arrogance, and ensure that their decisions and actions are not being made based on these things alone. This card can also point to a mind that is filled with turmoil, with the querent being uncertain what to think or believe.

Reversed, the Five of Swords usually indicates abject defeat, as well as all the upright meanings. However, sometimes this card reversed, if accompanied by more positive cards, can point to a betrayal or loss from the past that is still having an effect on the querent in the present.

Keywords
Defeat, loss, betrayal, arrogance, gloating, cheating, ego, turmoil, uncertainty, victory at any cost.

Six of Swords, the Escape of the Mind

"Your mind is your greatest gift, and it can carry you to the farthest reaches of the world and beyond. With your thoughts alone you can solve the deepest mysteries and behold the finest beauty. With your words you can bring people with you on a journey of discovery, open their minds and guide them in wisdom. Your mind

is the silver thread of Ariadne showing you where you have been, and it is also the labyrinth through which you wander, searching for the centre. Let yourself get lost in this labyrinth, truth-seeker; do not be afraid to follow your mind to the place it leads; never fear the journey nor the destination. For I am there with you; I have always been here and will always be until the end of your days. I am the ferryman, the ability of your mind to guide itself through the troubled waters of uncertainty and doubt. I am your thoughts as they take you on a passage through enquiry and reconciliation. Your mind will never stop seeking: you will be forever upon the ship at sea, forever crossing the river from one shore to another.

The mind in true harmony and balance understands that ideas are impossible to hold for a lifetime, truth is only true until it is proven wrong, facts are mere hypotheses that best serve our current paradigm. Thus, you must learn to love the labyrinth, but also know when to escape it. Know when to move on and let your mind transition, know when to leave behind old thoughts, and know what you can bring with you on your next quest. And never stop seeking."

Mercury in Aquarius / Tiphereth in air

Illumination

It can be difficult to see how the harmony and rebalancing of the sixes of the tarot applies to the Six of Swords. At first the scene in the card looks like a sad one, with a woman and child in a mournful pose being ferried across a misty river to an island on the other side. However, we must ask ourselves what the nature of a harmonized and balanced mind is. We can see throughout the annals of history that ideas are constantly changing and shifting. What was accepted as fact seven hundred years ago is not today. Once we believed the world was flat and the sun revolved around it. Once we did not know that the heart pumped blood around our bodies through arteries and veins. Once we thought that anybody believing something different from our own religious ideas should be burned at the stake as a heretic. We didn't think these things because we had a lower IQ or brains that were less able to process ideas, but simply because the evidence at the time, working on the scientific models and with the paradigms of the time, led to these "logical" conclusions. In another seven hundred years, who knows what "facts" of our time will be disproven? As such, a truly balanced and harmonized mind should know the mutable and changeable nature of ideas and thoughts, even the mutability of what we call facts and truth. We can never know everything; there is always more to learn because there is always an undiscovered mystery, like the island in the distance in the card image. The Six of Swords, therefore, is a card of transition and movement from one state to another, recognizing that the mind will always be moving on, changing its focus and ideas.

We can see a difference between the Six of Swords' harmonious acceptance of change and the imbalanced nature of the Five of Swords and the Seven of Swords. Both these cards show figures grasping at swords, trying to cling to some aspect of their mind or other's minds. In the five, the armoured prince was trying to grasp more for himself, with an arrogance and perspective that demonstrated a truly imbalanced mind in turmoil; in the seven, the thief in the card image is stealing other people's ideas and using them for his own ends. The Six of Swords shows the swords in the card simply balanced at the prow of the boat, not being grasped or carried by any of the figures, not being used as weapons nor for defence. In fact, being at the prow, the part of the boat that cuts through the water, these swords are symbolic of ideas and thoughts that we already have being used to help us move on to new ideas, new territory of the mind.

There is an element of sadness to the card image, however, as the manner and posture of the woman and child in the boat suggests. The woman is slightly bent over, her hands clasped in her lap, and the child is gripping the woman's arm, looking up at the ferryman almost expectantly. There can be a sadness when you move from one state to another, as we often find comfort in what we know best and what we have become accustomed to. Transition can bring with it fear, as well as a desire to look to another for aid, just as the child looks to the ferryman. The Six of Swords, being in the suit of the mind, on a higher level represents the journeys of the mind and the transition to new ideas and ways of thinking; on a lower level, it relates to any transition we undergo that involves leaving something behind. We can imagine that the woman and child in the boat are being ferried to a new life, away from something in the past that may have hurt or threatened them. The ferryman may be the father of the child, or he may be a stranger they have hired for help in getting across the river. We can see that, whilst they do not have all of their possessions with them on this journey to a new life, they have retained a few chests that contain some belongings. When we move to a new state of mind or being, or undergo a spiritual transition or a physical move, we never truly leave the past behind; the trick is being able to differentiate between good baggage and bad baggage.

Sometimes we can use the past, and all we have learned and gained from it, to propel us forward in momentum across the river to the other side. Sometimes we cling only to the baggage from the past that weighs us down, and in that case the weight may be too heavy for the boat and start to sink it. It is, ultimately, our choice as to what we pack in the chests that we take with us on the journey.

The river is a recurring symbol in the Tarot Illuminati. We see it as the main focus of the card in the Five of Cups, and it also runs through the Death card. Both these cards are about an ending and the need to let go and move on. However, the Five of Cups shows us a river down which the past flows, away from us, cleansing us, and the river in the Death card has a ship sailing down it—again, flowing away from the past. In the Six of Swords, the river is being crossed from bank to bank, showing that this is a transition from point A to point B. We are not shown from where the travellers have come, and are only given a glimpse of where they are going: the mysterious island in the distance. The river is slightly turbulent and covered in mist, showing that the journey may be a little difficult, but not impossible. The mist reminds us that while we are in the midst of undergoing a transition, things may not seem clear, but we should be assured that when we push through the mist, we will find clarity on the other side: the destination island is not surrounded by mist at all.

The ferryman in the card image is an archetypal figure in folklore and mythology. In ancient Greek myth, Charon ferried the souls of the recently deceased from the shores of the living to the shores of the dead, across a river sometimes called the river Styx, though the earlier sources call it Acheron. He required payment of a coin for his services, and if the dead person could not pay him, they were left to wander the shores of the river for a hundred years. These spirits would be described as very unhappy, wailing, crying, and begging to be ferried across. They were in limbo. This was why it became a custom to bury the dead with a coin in their mouths, or a coin on each eye. Later folklore tells of a ferryman that offers to take people across a river, and at some point asks for them to take up his oars for a little while so that he might rest. As soon as they do so, he immediately leaps up, free from a curse that forced him to ferry people across the river until somebody else offered to do it, and the traveller is stuck as a ferryman for hundreds of years.

Ferrymen are both helpful and fear-inspiring, since they are the guides that know the places between places. They aid people who are in greatest need of passage, and they also have the power to refuse that passage. They themselves can be seen as stuck in between, always at the transitional stage and never reaching either side fully and stepping out onto the shores of certainty. Yet everything in tarot is symbolic of something else. The image of the Six of Swords is an image of the mind that moves from one state to another in perfect harmony and balance. The mind is the traveller, with the past and chosen baggage in tow, and it is also the child, slightly fearful but ready for new experiences. It is the boat in which they travel, for the mind provides the means by which we can escape or move on, and it is the river upon which the boat sails, the milieu of ideas and thoughts. Finally, the mind is the ferryman, as it has a tendency to guide us even when we are not conscious of it doing so, by leaving us hints and clues upon our journeys and quests, allowing us to make the connections between point A and point B, between one shore and another.

Revelation

The Six of Swords has various layers of meaning when applied to a reading. In a metaphorical sense, it usually indicates the journey of the mind and a quest for knowledge or understanding, as well as the leaving behind of old ideas and the search for new ones. It may indicate that the querent has discovered that certain thought processes, habits, or ways of thinking (e.g. beliefs, ideas, facts) are no longer useful to them and it is time to find new ones that benefit them more. This may manifest as a religious or spiritual conversion, a change of focus in one's research, an acceptance of a different scientific paradigm in which to work, or the changing of courses at university or college.

Often, this card appears in a reading relating to studies and exploration of an intellectual nature, suggesting the stage of research and exploration where the querent is at: the immersion in the labyrinth. When we start to study something, it is simple, and it is easy to think that we know everything there is to know about it. But at a certain point, we suddenly discover just how much we don't know and how much more complex it is, how much more there is yet to learn, and we start to explore all those routes also. We get lost in it, immersing ourselves in all the various strands of the subject, and the deeper we go into the labyrinth, the more depth we discover. The Six of Swords tells the querent that this is a natural stage of learning and discovery, and they should persist, as eventually they will come to the centre of the labyrinth. Thus, this card can point to any kind of enquiry or research, indicating all the questions that the querent wants answered.

On a more personal level, the Six of Swords can point to a state of transition or a rite of passage. This can sometimes be an actual rite of passage, during which a change in the querent's life is marked by themselves and/or others, after which things will change forever. Examples of this include graduation from university, moving to your first home away from your parents, becoming a parent or grandparent, reaching retirement, and preparing for death. This card indicates that the prospect of such a transition may be presenting difficulty for the querent, not because of any obstacles in their way but because of fear and what they are leaving behind. They should be reassured that they can choose to take with them anything from their past that will aid them and benefit them, as the past can form a foundation upon which we can build our future.

Sometimes this card relates to actual movement, such as journeys (usually over water) and relocation. It can also point to a need or urge within the querent to make changes in their life or to move on from something. They may be aware of something in their life that they need to move away from and leave behind, especially if this card is accompanied by cards such as the Eight of Cups or Death.

Reversed, the Six of Swords indicates a change or rite of passage that the querent is finding extremely difficult. It may be causing them pain of some kind, and they are so busy clinging to the past that they are forgetting the necessity for the transition. It also suggests that the querent may be carrying with them baggage from the past that is negative in nature, which is weighing them down and causing them to find the transition even more difficult. At times this card reversed points to a delayed or blocked transition, or possibly a feeling in the querent of an urgent need to escape. If accompanied by cards that suggest current matters are very bad, then the Six of Swords reversed advises them to escape, to get out of the situation and move away. With this card reversed, sometimes running away is the best option, allowing the querent to make a clean break and move on.

Keywords

Escape, transition, rite of passage, enquiry, research, science, journeys, running away, moving on, destination, relocation.

Seven of Swords, the Cunning of the Shadows

"Don't look at me like that; you've no right to judge me. A thief I may be, but a criminal I am not. Didn't you know that humankind has a debt of life owed to the man that stole fire from the gods? And that once upon a time, a spider was tricked into pouring wisdom all over the Earth? And what of the soul that descended to the underworld and tricked her way through the gates of hell with sweet oat and honey cakes and two gold coins? Or the cunning serpent in the tree that gave us the fruit of knowledge? You would be wise to avoid such black-and-white thinking, honourable one: deception is not always how it first appears. Are there not circumstances in which you would do the same? What would be your price? What would it take before you took the silent, sneaky road, the cunning solution to a problem, the path of secrecy and manipulation? Everybody has their price. Know this, while we stand here in the shadows: away from the light and attention, we can see so much more. People are different when they think nobody's watching. Most people are more honest and true to themselves. In the shadows, without detection, we can also act more effectively. Do you really believe that the decisions that govern your life have been made openly and in all honesty in the public eye? Don't be naïve! The real decisions are made behind closed doors, open to bribes and persuasion, manipulation and the calling in of favours. Yet those who undertake these matters are not criminals. Sometimes the end justifies the means—right?"

Moon in Aquarius / Netzach in air

Illumination

The rebalancing and understanding we saw in the Six of Swords was welcome after the turmoil of the Five of Swords. But sadly, the swords suit doesn't get any brighter from here on in; in fact, the Seven of Swords marks the point at which matters really start to go downhill. We are now on the dark road that leads to the Ten of Swords and its image of utter ruin. Where the sixes hold the qualities of harmony and balance, the sevens bring with them fluidity, flux, and instability that causes great trouble in their respective suits. When fluidity and instability is applied to the suit of the mind, thoughts, ideas, and speech, we immediately get a sense that things aren't what we think they are: they are misrepresentations, half-formed, changing so rapidly that they easily mislead people. These are the flitting, fleeting words that are so quick we cannot keep up with them, and ideas that are easily taken away from us, stolen, misused. The Seven of Swords therefore is a card of thoughts and words being used to manipulate others, to control and mislead them; it is a card of trickery, deception, underhanded dealings, secrecy, and politics.

In the card image, we see a scene set in a military camp. Here, soldiers would be stationed during a campaign so that they were closer to the battle, often far from home in foreign lands. Some military camps would stay set up for years, especially in the Roman world where campaigns such as those under Julius Caesar could take a very long time. A great number of weapons, horses, and armour would be stored in these camps, within easy access of the soldiers stationed there. From these camps also the leaders and commanders would plan their course of action and battle tactics, as well as undertake negotiations with enemy commanders. These camps were not just centres of battle preparation, but also centres of political movement and influence.

In the background, standing in the light of a fire, are two soldiers, possibly guards on night watch, discussing previous battles. One raises a sword in his hand as if reliving the action, boasting about his exploits, while the other listens intently. These guards have made a tactical mistake: standing in the light, they immediately give away their position to anybody watching, waiting to strike. They also accustom their eyes to the fire's light, and therefore when looking into the shadows they will be less likely to see what is hidden there. Finally, the sound of the fire—and their talking—means that they are unlikely to hear any intruders, and if they do, they will be disoriented and unsure where the sound comes from at first.

This mistake has allowed the incident in the forefront of the card to occur: in the shadows, a thief silently sneaks, carrying five swords from the camp's weapon cache. Two more swords lie outside a tent. It is likely the thief intends to come back for them once he has placed his current loot safely out of sight. He is being quiet, and on his face is an expression of quiet happiness: he is pleased with himself. However, this thief is a young boy, and he bears no malice on his face. This suggests that he is actually doing the work of somebody else who has hired him for this purpose.

This entire scene adds up to a card that symbolizes every underhanded dealing that has ever happened. The intention behind this thievery may not be to obtain the swords for their own intrinsic value, but to disadvantage the enemy through their lack. Since swords in the tarot are symbolic of the mind, thoughts, and words, we have here the theft of ideas or the misrepresentation of words. However, the ability to undertake actions in the shadows, in secret, may not always be negative: it certainly won't be for the recipient of the stolen swords! Sometimes it is best to do things secretly, or away from the public eye; sometimes it is in our best interests and the interests of others not to tell the whole truth, or to keep secrets, or to go behind somebody's back, especially if that person would cause problems otherwise. We see this in world mythology in the vast array of trickster figures and deities who manage to benefit others through using deception, cunning, trickery, and thievery.

Greek myth gives us three prime examples. Firstly, Hermes, the messenger of the gods, is also the god of thieves owing to his airy, fluid nature. Following an incident in which he stole Apollo's cattle, he invented the lyre and the musical scale, which he then gave to Apollo in return for his actions. Secondly, we have Psyche, the mortal woman who was married to the god Eros, who had to descend to Hades as part of her quest to get Aphrodite's help in finding her missing husband. She had to trick the guardians of Hades into letting her pass, despite the fact that she was not dead, by distracting Cerberus with sweet oat cakes. Finally, we have Prometheus, the original thief, who stole fire from the gods on Olympus so that he could give it to humans, so that they might be able to see in the dark, cook, and warm themselves in the cold.

Most people will also be familiar with the antics of Br'er Rabbit, the central figure of the Uncle Remus stories from the American South, whose cunning, trickery, and deception variously gets him into trouble and gets him out of it. This is similar to the Norse trickster god Loki, who uses his cunning and manipulative words to both hinder the other gods and help them. In this tradition, we can imagine our childlike thief running with the five swords he has just stolen, turning to look back at the two left behind and tripping, or dropping a sword, or gripping too tightly and slicing his hands upon on their blades. Whilst there are positive aspects to cunning and guile, the Seven of Swords comes with the warning, "If you live by the sword, you die by the sword." Act deceptively, and you will end up moving in deceptive circles, and you may well find yourself as the victim of the very thing you have perpetrated.

Revelation

The Seven of Swords is usually an unsavoury card in a reading. It brings with it all kinds of deception, deceit, trickery, thievery, and underhandedness. Of course, it does not say whether the querent is a victim of these things or the person undertaking them!

Often, this card appears to indicate that the querent is doing something secretly or in the shadows, trying to keep something hidden. This might be something as nice as a surprise birthday party for a friend or partner, or it might be something as nasty as the secrets of a crime or an extramarital affair. These secrets don't necessarily have to be the querent's: they may also be the secrets of another person, told to the querent.

Sometimes the Seven of Swords suggests that the querent needs to take themselves out of the spotlight or stop drawing attention to themselves and their activities. Surrounding cards will indicate the reasons for this, but their endeavour is not one that should be made public just yet. It needn't be kept secret, but it also shouldn't be shouted from the rooftops. They may also need to approach a situation or person with care and stealth so as not to cause alarm or confrontation. The Seven of Swords might point to the avoidance of confrontation or conflict, the querent trying to get out of doing something they don't want to do, or getting away with something they have already done.

At times, this card can indicate the querent using their clever words to manipulate events and people in their favour. Persuasion of all kinds is indicated here, as well as an engagement with politics and the need for politics in a group setting. If this card appears in a relationship reading, the querent may find themselves in an unsavoury seduction situation, or they may find that they are being manipulated in some way. It might also indicate a betrayal of some kind in a romantic involvement, or that one close to the querent is keeping secrets from them.

In a business or work context, the Seven of Swords can suggest workplace espionage, the stealing of ideas, or somebody taking credit for the querent's work, ideas, and effort. Perhaps the boss is passing off the querent's ideas as their own, or perhaps the querent is the one doing this. There is also an element of going behind somebody's back to do something. If this card is accompanied by cards indicating money or the home, the querent should take extra care with home security and personal items they carry with them, as it indicates burglary, intrusion, and theft.

Generally speaking, the Seven of Swords points to anything in the querent's life that they are doing secretly or underhandedly. They might not realize the extent to which they are doing it, but this card can often indicate the little ways in which they manipulate others or take advantage of them, such as emotional blackmail, misrepresentation, not telling the whole truth, or somehow going missing when the real hard work needs doing, only to turn up at the end to take credit.

Reversed, the Seven of Swords warns the querent that anything they are trying to hide, all the secrets they currently hold, and anything they are doing in the dark, underhandedly, will be brought to light and out in the open. If they are engaging in activities that are manipulative, they will be called out on it. If they have been hiding their true colours, their mask will be pulled off. Truth will out, no matter how hard the querent tries to hide it.

Keywords

Deception, trickery, deceit, manipulation, politics, secrets, secrecy, shadows, theft, misrepresentation, underhandedness, blackmail, espionage, stealth.

Eight of Swords, the Prison of the Mind

"Have you come to rescue me? Did you hear me crying out for help? In the darkest recesses of your mind, there is always a glimmer of something that is begging to be set free; there is always an idea that is restricted and oppressed. How it got there you might not know, but then again you might … How did I get here? Did I walk in my sleep from a nightmare and surround myself with a barrier against the cruel world? Or was I brought here, put in chains, and left by another? Either way, the result remains the same: you must break open the prison of your mind and release all that is within. You cannot hoard ideas. The mind must always be free and at liberty. When you cage it and embed it so firmly in one way of being, you silence its true voice, like a bird of paradise kept in a cage, its song dying with its longing to be free. But I hear already the threat of the tide coming in: there is no time. Don't let yourself be mired in the situation of my fate: go, and leave me. And from this day forward you shall not be blinded like I am, nor allow yourself to take on such bonds and restrictions, nor cage your mind and ideas and limit yourself with the very tool that should be used for liberty and truth … Go on, run!"

Jupiter in Gemini / Hod in air

Illumination

Since the suit of swords is about the various ways our mind acts and works, we see a number of cards that appear to be very negative. This is simply because our own mind can often be our greatest enemy. It is not only the source of our fears that keep us prisoner, but the prison guard as well. When we think and make a decision, we automatically limit ourselves, as the Two of Swords demonstrates: thinking one way means that we are unable at that moment to think a different way. This is natural and necessary for any progress to be made. But there is a vast difference between deciding to choose one thought over another, and choosing to think in ways that limit us. The former is discipline, the latter is a prison.

The suit of swords does not sit well with the extra-strong, extra-grounded qualities of the eights, which are "double fours." The eights can be about strict discipline and strength in manifesting, but when applied to the airy suit of the mind, which began with freedom and liberty in the Ace of Swords, the energy doesn't mesh. The eight becomes a prison for the free mind, restricting and constricting it in a prison of its own making. Our minds have the power to give us great freedom from ignorance, but they can also bind us to dogma, negative thoughts, and habitual thought patterns and perceptions that not only entrap us, but also make it impossible for us even to see we are trapped, or to see a way out.

The card image is evocative and makes this point easily. A young woman, dressed in white, stands barefoot on a beach. She is bound with thick rope and blindfolded, and she is surrounded by eight swords that have been driven into the sand. She looks afraid, cowering, tilting her head toward the sounds she can hear, fearful of what might be coming. Behind and above her are looming chalk cliffs, upon which an ancient castle is situated, and the tide is coming in all around her. The bindings upon her are symbolic of being trapped in some way, tied up, powerless, and a victim, but there is another trap here in the form of the eight swords, which form a cagelike circle around her. They are driven sharpest point down into the sand, symbolizing the freedom and sharpness of our mind being dulled and stuck in the mud. This is the prison of her mind, the prison she has created from her thoughts. The blindfold covering her eyes shows us that she is blind to the solution, and possibly blind to her situation: sometimes we limit ourselves most when we are unaware of our limitations in the first place.

However, the pattern of the swords is important: there is a clear gap in front of her, through which she might be able to pass if she wished to—if she could see that option and if she could get herself free from her bonds. Looking closely at her predicament, we can see that she is not securely bound; she could slip the rope easily and thus free her hands and arms, then remove her blindfold to be able to see with clarity. However, she is dressed and acts in the manner of the typical "damsel in distress." She is clearly waiting for rescue. But we cannot be rescued from the prison of our mind by external aid alone; there must be impetus on our part for liberation. Further, if the knight in shining armour did come to rescue the damsel in distress, there is only one weapon he would use to free her from her bindings: a single sword, like our Ace of Swords, which represents the truth and the freedom of the mind. The truth, as they say, will set her free.

One thing is for sure: our damsel cannot afford to wait much longer for rescue, as the tide is coming in and threatening her. This is a symbol of all that can overwhelm us when our mind is limited in such a way. Above her, the chalk cliff is also ominous: chalk is one of the softest rocks, and erodes particularly quickly when exposed to the constant motion of breaking waves. The building situated atop the cliff is reminiscent of an old asylum, another symbol of the mind as a prison, yet it looks like it wouldn't take much more erosion before it fell into the sea. Perhaps this is saying that unless the woman gets herself free, she will be overwhelmed, yet the overwhelming may be final incentive she needs to break free and let the prison of her mind crumble. The most shocking, devastating occurrences are often the most potent wake-up calls.

Revelation

In a reading, the Eight of Swords most often indicates a feeling of being trapped or limited. The querent may find their circumstances are making it difficult for them to move freely, but this is not heavy burdens in the form of projects and responsibilities slowing them down, as in the Ten of Wands, but rather obstacles that restrict them completely. It indicates that in their situation they do not have a choice, or lack the choice that they would prefer, possibly because of the actions and impositions of others, or possibly because of their own self-imposed restrictions.

Often this card appears in a reading to indicate the ways in which the querent is holding themselves back. This can include their own beliefs or ideologies, ways of thinking that have become habitual and no longer useful, but which they keep nevertheless because that's what they're accustomed to. It might point to a situation they've put themselves in, such as a relationship or a friendship, which keeps them down or holds them back, in particular preventing them from achieving their true potential. It can also indicate things that have been said that now cannot be taken back, but which have effects that lead to the querent being committed in a way they don't wish to be, or which come back to haunt them. Generally, the Eight of Swords suggests that the current course of action or situation will lead them to being restricted in some way.

At times, the Eight of Swords says that the querent has a victim mentality, feeling powerless in their current situation to take action to help themselves. They feel as though their hands are tied and that they cannot even speak out or ask for help. They may fear reprisal if they try and escape. There is also a self-defeatist attitude present; the querent is facing a situation, challenge, or obstacle and simply saying, "I can't." Unfortunately, if they think they can't, then they will be correct. Negative and self-defeatist thinking will be their undoing and will add bars to the prison they are building for themselves. Occasionally the Eight of Swords can point to actual imprisonment.

In a reading regarding a specific project, goal, or endeavour, the Eight of Swords does not bode well. It indicates obstacles standing in the querent's way or something holding the project back from reaching completion. The querent is stuck and is finding it difficult to move forward; they have no fresh ideas, and the ones they do have are so firmly engrained so as to be no longer useful. There is also a lack of clarity and a lack of foresight suggested by this card, which might indicate that the querent is walking blindly into a situation they do not want to be in.

In a reading regarding a relationship, the Eight of Swords is a "red flag" indicating trouble. It says that the relationship will simply trap the querent, turning them into a victim, making them powerless, possibly even holding some sort of threat over them. This will be reinforced over and over again by the partner, so that in the end the querent will not even be able to see how trapped they are, so will make no moves to escape. In a reading about work, the Eight of Swords suggests that the querent finds their current job extremely limiting and they wish to move on to something else, but cannot see their way clear to do so.

Reversed, the Eight of Swords indicates that the restrictions that the querent has experienced recently will be lifted, and they will achieve the mental clarity and vision required to get themselves out of a bad situation. Reversed, this card sees the victimized person walking out of the situation or relationship that is victimizing them, one who previously believed themselves to be powerless regaining their power, or the querent leaving behind old ways of thinking that are limiting their creative thought processes. This card reversed reminds the querent that they have the power to release themselves from their bonds and the prison of their mind; they need not wait for another person to rescue them.

Keywords

Bondage, limitation, restriction, obstacles, cage, victim mentality, self-defeatist attitude, prison, lack of clarity, lack of vision, awaiting rescue, traps, being held back.

Nine of Swords, the Things That Go Bump in the Night

"I had another nightmare … It's the same one every night, the one where I'm falling, falling, falling into a pit of blackness and cold. I think I'm never going to reach the bottom, like I might just fall forever with nobody to hear my screams, but then I hit the earth and I'm dead. I'm dead and my body is already rotting and I know that my skull has split open and all my thoughts are pouring out … and the maggots come, and the animals, and the birds, and I can feel them crawling over me, clawing at me, consuming me, and getting inside me, but I can't stop them because I'm dead. And then I can hear them, screaming in my head; their voices are the voices of everything I've ever done wrong and all the people I've ever hurt. I wake up then, sweating and frightened, shaking and terrified, and I pull the covers up to my chin and sob, but there is nobody to comfort me. In the darkness of my bedroom I can still see the creatures of death on my skin; I can still hear their accusations and cries, and all my past wrongs come flooding back to haunt and torment me, no longer subconscious processes but conscious thoughts. In the morning, when I am sleep-deprived and restless, I consider telling others of the recurring phantasms that plague me … but I never do, because I think maybe I deserve the anguish, maybe I'm guilty after all … "

Mars in Gemini / Yesod in air

Illumination

You will notice that as each suit in the tarot reaches its culmination, a dichotomy develops between the two suits of the feminine elements, cups and pentacles, and the two suits of the masculine elements, swords and wands. Whereas the final cards in the suits of cups and pentacles depict life's most wonderful things, the final cards of the swords and wands depict far more unpleasant scenarios. It as if the power and manifestation of the energies of the masculine suits have run down from the ace, in which the suit is at its purest and most unified, along the way getting heavier and more divided, until at the end the sword and the wand cannot uplift this intense, extreme energy as the cup and pentacle do. Although the energy fills the cup like wine and fills the pentacle like a platter of food, it is torn to ribbons by the sword and smothered by the wand.

The Nine of Swords depicts a scene that is easy to understand and relate to: we are presented here with a young woman waking up in the middle of the night in terror from her nightmares, with all the woes of the world on her shoulders and weighing on her mind. In her waking life, her mind whirs round and round frantically, worried and anxious over some thing or another, and at nighttime sleep gives her no respite from the cruel machinations of thought as fears and anxieties creep into her subconscious and pursue her into the dream world. Thus a vicious cycle is perpetuated: anxiety feeds sleeplessness, and when sleep comes, it is fraught with anxiety that breeds nightmares; the nightmares cause more sleepless nights, and the mind returns to the pillow the following night even more anxious than before. If this card were a film, it would be *Nightmare on Elm Street*.

The setting is evocative and dark, almost oppressive, with blood-red drapes for the woman's bed chamber and gargoyles carved into the canopy of the bed. Etymologically the word "gargoyle" comes from the French *gargouille*, which has connotations of throat, gullet, and swallowing. Whilst this originally referred to the function of the decorative gargoyle in architecture to catch rainwater and guide it away from masonry to prevent erosion, it also reminds us of the main physiological responses to fear: the throat tightens, the breath quickens, we swallow or gulp. In church architecture, these grotesque-looking carvings were also used to depict creatures of evil, and their fearsome appearance led to many stories of them coming to life at the "witching hour" to roam the streets. As grotesque, demonic images, they represent our most primal and archetypal fears: unknown evil that watches over us with ill intent.

Perhaps a more troubling image is that of the nine identical swords that are suspended horizontally above and behind the woman, as if barring her from exiting the bed in which she is experiencing her torment. If we imagine this as a film scene, the woman may just have sprung awake to find herself narrowly escaping being pinned to the bed posts by nine swords in gory horror fashion. In the tarot, swords represent the mind and one's intellectual world, so here we are reminded that the woman's own thoughts are acting against her, seeking to destroy her, and preventing her from freeing herself from the vicious cycle.

In most cards of the Tarot Illuminati, the figure pictured looks at their surroundings, at another character in the card's scene, or out of the card directly at us. Here, the character simply closes her eyes, not engaging with the outside world of her card or with us, and retreats deeper into darkness. She does not seek help; perhaps she cannot see it, or perhaps she does not want to. The mind can play strange tricks on you at its darkest. Imagine what terrible, horrifying shapes it could create, in the dark and sleep-deprived, when faced with the blood-red drapes, the grotesque gargoyles, the swords looming and the shadows beneath the bed lurking… When fear grips our mind, panic sets in, distorting reality into even more terrible shapes. Fear feeds fear. However, the only thing we have to fear is fear itself, and the best way to conquer fear is to wake up.

Revelation

The Nine of Swords appearing in a reading is rarely a good thing, as it brings with it a plethora of difficulties and warnings. Any tarot reader seeing this card in a spread should be particularly concerned if it falls with the Ten of Swords, the Ten of Wands, the Tower, or the Devil. Alongside these cards, the qualities of the Nine of Swords are exacerbated. This is the kind of card that reminds us why it is often useful as a tarot reader to have some basic training in counselling, or at least an understanding of mental illness and anxiety.

Most often this card indicates anxiety and worry, usually from the everyday world and the querent's daily life, which builds up and draws their focus, making the situation seem worse than perhaps it is. This is the card of making mountains out of molehills, but don't let this cause you to ignore the source of the anxiety; the source is real and some anxiety is justified, but anxiety to this extreme will just cause more problems and create a vicious cycle. Sometimes the Nine of Swords specifically indicates problems with sleep and dreams: the querent may be having difficulty sleeping, may wake up frequently during the night, may have nightmares or night terrors, or may even experience sleep paralysis or sleep apnea. The experience of waking up from sleep feeling smothered and suffocated, occasionally accompanied by the terrifying hallucination or waking dream of a hag or other monster sitting on your chest is also represented by this card.

At times, especially if in the context of a relationship or social question, the

Nine of Swords can indicate the cruelty of another toward the querent. Cruelty can come in many forms, some of them overtly harmful (domestic abuse, for instance) and some of them more insidious, like emotional blackmail, deliberately negative language, verbal abuse, and fear mongering. Sometimes the victim doesn't realize they are a victim until it is too late, and they are so demoralized or dehumanized that they cannot protest. If issues such as these arise in a reading, the tarot reader is strongly advised to provide the querent with links to groups, organizations, and individuals that can help.

The Nine of Swords can point to mental illness and the querent's battle with it. It can also relate to problems with depression, and in extreme cases (such as those accompanied by other negative cards) might suggest self-harm of some kind. This can come in many forms, from physical harm (cutting, bulimia, anorexia, over-exercising) to harmful thoughts (guilt complex, martyr complex, self-denial). Every now and then, the Nine of Swords takes a gentler approach, simply telling the querent to get more sleep, stop worrying so much, and wake up from the nightmare they've found themselves in. It might also advise the querent that they are exaggerating a problem, and that things really aren't as bad as they seem. The querent's mind is likely to be in a darker place than it should be, however, making accurate perception (the first step to breaking a vicious cycle) difficult.

Reversed, the Nine of Swords isn't much better. Often its meaning stays the same as upright; however, it can indicate that instead of cruelty and negative thoughts being turned inward on themselves, the querent aims such things at other people. They may be verbally abusing another, causing great worry and anxiety in someone's life, or promoting somebody's negative self-image with their words and actions. Instead of showing us the querent in fear, the reversed Nine of Swords puts the querent in the fear-causing position.

Keywords

Cruelty, anxiety, worry, vicious cycle, fear, terror, night terrors, nightmares, sleeplessness, sleep deprivation, sleep paralysis, negativity, mental illness, self-harm, abuse, fear-mongering, depression, victimization, demoralization, phobia, worry.

Ten of Swords, the Death of God

"In the end, even the strongest of men will find themselves torn by the ravages of the mind. Perhaps it is because they are the strongest that they are called, over and over again, to stare deep into the abyss and discover what stares back at them from the darkness. Even you, warrior of truth, who have come to the farthest reaches of the Earth in your quest, must be taken apart, ritually slaughtered, all the pieces of your self scattered to the four corners of the Earth like a new Osiris. But look—before your eyes close upon the old world for the final time, here is your heart, beating, and here, your lungs breathing. Over there are your limbs and still farther, your torso. And what is in between, in the spaces? What can you see? Let your eyes close, fall into the truest death, allow your self to be destroyed in the abyss, and then rise anew with the dawning of the sun on the golden horizon…

What can you see now? Every detail, good or bad, beautiful or terrible, is laid bare for your analysis and critique. Sort through it carefully and be ruthless in your casting away of the old, the useless, the old-fashioned ways of thinking. Only the weak require such things to cling to. And yet, it hurts, doesn't it? More than anything else. It must. It has to. Those pieces of your self that you are destroying will forever be destroyed; you cannot regain them. This is amputation and cauterization, swift and effective, and you are the god that must be slain so that he may be reborn as the light of the world. This is inevitable; you cannot escape it. You can try and run from it, but it will catch up with you and you will die screaming and writhing and fighting a losing battle. Or you can face it and hold the weapons of destruction yourself, and thus face your death and the abyss with courage. Some have said that the things that do not kill us make us stronger. This is false, lies told to children. That which kills us, that which rips us apart and tears into us, readying us for rebirth, makes us far stronger, even through the pain. And so, warrior, truth seeker, are you ready to die?"

The Sun in Gemini / Malkuth in air

Illumination

You thought the seven, eight, and Nine of Swords looked bad? Here we are, at the conclusion of the suit of swords, and the image is the worst of them all. As the suit has progressed, we have come from a united, clear-thinking, focused mind to an ever more fragmented one, with unfocused thoughts and an over-reliance on the process of thought. The energies of this suit have become more manifest and heavy, more varied, and have culminated in the ten. Here, the swords have reached their final destination: point down, impaling the body of a cold, dead knight.

The card image is one that will be familiar from pop culture images of tarot, and indeed there are few querents that will see it and not be immediately worried. In fact, it is difficult to find anything good in the Ten of Swords, yet if we delve deep enough we can discover the seed of hope within the darkness.

We see in the foreground of the card a knight dressed in armour (even his head is covered with chainmail) and a red cloak, lying upon the rocks on a sandy beach. Ten swords of varying design are embedded deep in his body, mostly in his back, and here and there we see his lifeblood seeping out. Waves lap at his cold, pale body, and the sand in front of him bears no footprints, indicating that either he was washed ashore like this or that the tide is coming in and washing away all traces of activity from around him. On the horizon the sun is rising, its golden rays starting to touch the edges of the clouds overhead, with a canopy of stars still dark beyond.

The knight here is already dead; that much is clear. He was a warrior in life, so this card indicates a fight that has already been fought, and lost; there is no coming back from this loss. There is a finality to this card that cannot be overcome—nothing can be done to rectify the situation. We are reminded that swords are often symbolic of words, and words, once spoken, cannot be taken back. They have immense power to do good or to hurt, and when they hurt we are unable to unspeak them. Sometimes we can heal the resulting wounds, but these kinds of wounds have a tendency to always remain a little open; some even become infected and vile.

Since swords in the tarot are symbolic of the mind, thoughts, and words, the ten swords in the knight's back represent the mind being overly active and obsessive. This is too many thoughts, too many words, over-thinking and second-guessing at its most dominant. Whilst careful analysis of a subject can lead to illumination and knowledge, overanalysis of something can kill it, destroy the wonder within it, and lead us away from the path of success and completion. By thinking too hard about something, we can destroy it. Yet here we also have an opportunity: the overanalysis can take the form of a conscious breaking down of the artificial constructs in one's life, the taking apart of one's own mind or thoughts piece by piece to allow a thorough examination of them. This is mind-surgery. The Ten of Swords offers us a chance to cut apart our innermost self so that we can see it for what it truly is, critique it, and then put the best parts back together.

While this process is being undergone, it is extremely painful. This is reflected by the wounds of the knight in the card image. When we take ourselves apart, we inevitably discover things we do not like, and the taking apart itself requires a ruthless approach. Since the suit of swords is concerned with the pursuits of the mind and the application of the intellect to our lives, thus it is also associated with the act of applying critique to one's life so that we may come to useful conclusions on how to perceive the universe and our own actions. It is this pursuit of philosophy that has led to the breakdown and destruction of many viewpoints, perspectives, and worldviews. With each new philosophy, an old way of thinking was destroyed. Arriving at a personal philosophy can be a difficult and painful process, since it causes us to shed the most difficult thing of all to shed: the mind's constructs. Yet when the process is done, we are set free from the concepts that held us back, our mind is given a new lease on life, and we can view the world from a fresh perspective. Thus, when Nietzsche introduced his moral treatise that would destroy what he viewed as old-fashioned, childish, and useless Western morality, he wrote:

> *"As for us, new philosophers, we feel inspired by the news of the death of God as if greeting a new dawn …and although the horizon is not clear, it seems clear enough for our ships to set sail again and venture out toward new perils: the sea of knowledge is reopening itself to new pioneers; maybe the open sea has never offered so many new promises… To fathom this mystery I voyaged across the sea: and I saw the truth naked, verily! Barefoot up to the neck."*[18]

Indeed, we can see in the card image the open sea waiting in the background, and the horizon beginning to clear of clouds while the sun rises on a new dawn. In the Ten of Swords we have killed "God," —in other words, we have killed our ego, and now we are free to explore anew and afresh. This "death of God" is further highlighted by the fact that the knight's left hand is held in the same gesture as that of the Hierophant, two fingers held straight together and the thumb extended, in a form of blessing. Here, this gesture relates the knight's

---

18. Friedrich Nietzsche, *The Gay Science,* trans. Josephine Nauckhoff (Cambridge University Press, 2001), pp. 199.

death to the death of the mind's dogma and constructs, the static and old ways of thinking that can easily be relied upon too much. With the gesture of blessing, we are also reminded that although the image of the Ten of Swords is horrible and the related experience painful, it is an opportunity to start from scratch and reinvent ourselves.

The dawn that slowly builds from the horizon upward reminds us of the old saying, "It's always darkest before the dawn." The Ten of Swords marks the lowest point of the tarot, so from here the only way to proceed is up.

Revelation

When the Ten of Swords appears in a reading, it is not bringing good news. Generally, the Ten of Swords indicates ruination—the querent reaching their absolute lowest point. This is the card of bottoming out. The querent may feel as though they are completely ruined, at an impasse, certain that things can't possibly get any worse than this. On an emotional level, the Ten of Swords brings with it feelings of a complete lack of self-worth, as well as a martyr complex: the querent may habitually put others first all the time, never think about their own needs or desires, and feel as though they are unimportant in comparison to other people.

If the Ten of Swords appears in relation to prospective projects, investments, or plans, the querent should be warned that those things will not end well. Any investments will be poor ones, losing the querent a lot of money; a job offer will result in being overworked and underpaid; the project will see the querent's mind stretched to the point of breakdown. Breakdowns of various kinds are indicated by the Ten of Swords; however, at its worst it specifically points to mental breakdown and emotional burnout. In regards to a romance, the querent is over-thinking things and second guessing themselves; matters will go from bad to worse, eventually leading to a breakdown of the relationship.

This card points to the complete failure of a plan or venture, or the querent's defeat in a competition. It can also suggest that the querent is fighting a fight that has already been lost, and there is no way they can win or come out on top in their situation.

In a reading about a social situation or an area of the querent's life in which other people play a role, the Ten of Swords can suggest the querent metaphorically being stabbed in the back. The querent may find themselves the victim of character assassination or a particularly nasty campaign to defame their character. Gossip will be used against them, and rumours spread about them; this is the card of words and thoughts hurting the querent deeply.

If surrounded by positive cards, or as an advisory card, the Ten of Swords tells the querent that the current situation is an opportunity for them to undergo rigorous self-analysis and assessment of their own mind, self, personality, ideologies, and perspectives. They will need to cut themselves apart and examine themselves piece by piece in order to build something new and fresh for themselves. This might include the support of therapy or counselling, or undergoing the process within a particular school of thought. The things the querent will discover about themselves may not always be pleasant, and the process will involve a lot of pain, but it will be for a worthy cause; eventually the querent will find themselves free from old ways of thinking and unnecessary ideologies.

Reversed, the Ten of Swords represents old wounds and past hurts that are deeply buried within the querent's life, heart, or mind, which are still hurting in the present. These issues will have a strong effect upon the querent's future, and will keep bringing the querent back to them, time and time again, until the querent resolves them and finds reconciliation or healing.

Keywords

Ruin, failure, loss, bottoming out, ending, destruction, breakdown, overthinking, analysis, backstabbing, defamation, gossip, character assassination, past wounds, hurt, defeat.

CHAPTER 25

The Suit of Cups

Ace of Cups, The Soul Receiving Love

"From the limitless light of the heavens I open myself completely to receive the light of the divine. I am the vessel for the soul and the soul itself; I am the continual flow that allows the cup of the soul to be always full and always emptying simultaneously. I am the cup that runneth over with joy and bliss, as the divine light fills me completely; yet you cannot fill a cup that is already full and so I am in a constant state of receptivity and emptiness. What do you do when the purest form of love fills you completely, runs through your every pore and vein and limb? How can you possibly contain it? You can't. It bursts out of you in a torrent, love becoming compassion, bliss, love toward self and all others. In this state of pure love, untainted, you are connected to everything and everyone, and the great web of the world is revealed to you. From the fullness of the divine light, understanding and wisdom flows, and in that flow there is a channel for peace."

No astrological associations for the aces / Kether in water

Illumination

The Ace of Cups, like the other aces of the tarot, is the origin of its suit. Not only does it represent the beginnings of all things that the element of water symbolizes, but it also represents those things in singularity or unity, at their most pure, undifferentiated, and focused. We have in this card an evocative image of divine light descending from a singularity down to more manifest and differentiated forms, the light here being synonymous with water. Water in the tarot is symbolic of emotion, feeling, spirituality, wisdom, love, and compassion. In the Ace of Cups, all of these things burst forth and flow outward into the world, as if the cup is the womb that engenders and pushes forth these qualities into the physical. But before it can do so, the cup must first receive these things from the source, and thus the Ace of Cups represents a direct connection to the divine. The streams that flow from the cup in the card image are five in number, representing the four elements of the manifest world (earth, air, fire, and water), plus the fifth element created from all of them combined, spirit. Thus the flow of love, wisdom, and emotion from the cup permeates all aspects of existence: the physical world of the body, the world of the mind, the world of the emotions, and the world of the soul.

As a symbol, the cup is full of meaning drawn from history, religion, and myth. It can be equated to the Holy Grail from Arthurian myth, the cup of the Sacrament in the Catholic Church, and the chalice in modern Wicca. Further, as a receptacle that contains liquid, it can be seen as a cauldron, with links to the Cauldron of Rebirth in Welsh myth. Most of the meaning attributed to the cup as a symbol focuses on its ability as a vessel to contain, and its contents are viewed with increased importance. For instance, the cup of the Sacrament contains the wine that is transubstantiated into Christ's blood; as the Wiccan chalice, the cup is a sacred womb that contains all life; and as Cauldron of Rebirth it holds the process of life, death, and rebirth within itself. From the latter perspective, the cup can be seen as merely the vessel, unimportant in and of itself, given virtue only through its contents and its ability to contain and dispense. However, in the Grail tradition, the cup represents a goal that is to be quested after, representing God and union with God. Thus the Ace of Cups is both the source (container and dispenser) of light and love, as well as the ultimate goal of immersion back into the source.

Surrounding the cup and dripping from it are golden shapes known as "Yod," after the smallest of the Hebrew letters, its name translating as "hand." From this letter all the other Hebrew letters come, not because it is first in the Hebrew alphabet but because in writing the letters out, they all include Yod in their design. Yod is a seed letter, symbolizing here the nature of the Ace of Cups as the seed of its element, generating all the other cards in the suit of cups from itself. It's almost as if the rest of the suit is flowing from this cup in great streams of water, dividing into little parts of the ace's expression of love and manifesting them in a more concrete form in the world. Yod as a hand also relates directly to the hand that holds the cup aloft, coming straight from the unseen heavens, and forming the basis of giving and receiving, fullness and emptiness. A hand held out can both give and receive, but until the hand is held out, no action can be taken at all. The outstretched hand can also be symbolic of an act of compassion, or of achieving unity with another.

Above the cup, surrounded by golden Yods and sparkling silver energy, hovers a white dove, holding a branch covered in white flowers in its beak. The dove is a symbol and messenger of peace and love in the Western world. In the Old Testament, it was a dove that was released by Noah on the ark to find dry land, and it returned carrying an olive branch to indicate that it had found land.[19] In the New Testament, the Holy Spirit is compared to a dove, and this continues into the Christian tradition today, in which a dove (particularly one descending) represents the descent of the Holy Spirit into the holy Sacrament or into a person. In modern occult thought, this dove represents the descent of spirit into matter, or the illumination of divine light. By extension, the Ace of Cups can be seen as the soul or person into which light, love, and spirit descend, filling up him or her. This can relate to concepts of mystical experience, spiritual illumination, and pure spiritual love.

It is telling that the water from the cup is almost bursting out of it in streams, and rushing downwards. Anybody that has felt full to the brim with love and pure joy will know this feeling: as if you are so full of these things that you are too small to contain them, and they must burst out of you. Pure happiness comes from this, happiness not tainted or given an agenda. Love creates love.

Beneath the cup, we see an abundance of pink lotus blossoms and their lush green leaves floating upon a still pond. The lotus is a flower filled with meaning. In Buddhism, it is the symbol of purity and divine birth, the origin of divine light. It is born from muddy waters, yet when it arises and blossoms it is radiant and no mud touches it. The Egyptian Iamblichus wrote that it "expresses enigmatically an exaltation above the slime, and likewise denotes spiritual and empyrial supremacy."[20] Here is a source of divine light as well as a representation of it.

Revelation

As the first of the suit of cups, this card often brings with it the beginning of a relationship or a romance, but not just a fling: this is a deep connection between two people that begins in such a way that they can't help but wonder if

---

19. Genesis 8:6-12.

20. Iamblichus, *Theurgia or On the Mysteries of Egypt*, trans. Wilder (London: The Metaphysical Publishing Company, 1911), page 240.

it was "meant to be." When it appears in a reading about a current relationship, the Ace of Cups is a blessing, suggesting that the relationship is built on love, true and genuine, and makes the partners feel divine! However, since it relates to all forms of love, it can also indicate relationships other than romantic ones, in particular the querent's relationship with the divine and their connection to the source. Where does the querent find peace? Where do they find true happiness? What fills them with a feeling of connection to the universe and others?

It also acts as advice for the querent to be open to all experiences, and to remove any preconceived ideas from the situation. You cannot fill a cup that is already full, so the querent must be prepared to receive wisdom and love by first emptying themselves of stagnant water (emotions). To love another person, you must first love yourself; to give love you must be open to receiving love. Any projects they are working on or paths they are walking will grow only through the querent consciously choosing to receive light, love, and wisdom into themselves and their lives, so that they can then pour it outward to others. In any type of reading, the Ace of Cups brings the message of happiness, bliss, and joy, with the feeling that the querent's "cup runneth over." In some cases, it can indicate the possibility of a pregnancy, or the recent or imminent birth of a child or grandchild.

Reversed, the ace is a cup that does not allow water to flow from it; instead the water stagnates and blocks up, gets muddy, or even dries up. If the Ace of Cups is reversed in a reading, the querent may find they are having issues expressing their feelings or emotions, or they may be feeling spiritually bereft. Alternatively, sometimes the Ace of Cups reversed can indicate that the querent is giving love but not allowing themselves to take love in, so eventually they will have nothing left to give. Depending on surrounding cards, the Ace of Cups reversed may also indicate a problem in the querent's current relationship.

Keywords

Love, bliss, happiness, joy, emotion, feeling, source, divine light, compassion, receptivity, flow, purity, peace, connection.

Two of Cups, Hearts United in Balance

"Our souls were created when the divine shattered into billions of tiny pieces, little flames and droplets of divinity, that scattered throughout the universe. Some of these pieces became the sea, some became fire, some became the trees and mountains, and some became souls. When two people fall in love, their spark of the divine sees and recognizes the other's spark, and their relationship reunites two pieces of God. The moment our eyes met, I knew you. The moment our hearts met, I knew myself. *You complete me.* You are like a mirror in which I see all things reflected. *Let me share myself with you.* Let me offer myself to you. *My love, my sweetness, my true one…* My heart, my soul, my dear one… *When you are weak, I shall bring you strength.* When you are cold, I shall bring you warmth. *When you are lost, I shall find you.* When you are joyful, I shall increase your joy. *Where you are the lock, I am the key.* Where you are the rain, I am the sun. *We are two rivers flowing into one another.* We are two hearts beating as one. *Yet our love does not rush forth like impetuous youth…* No, it grows gently and flows steadily, each word, each kiss, each touch making us more a part of each other. *As the rivers flow together, they wash away all pains and sorrows, and so our love becomes the cure for all ills. Our love gives me strength and meaning, tender heart.* Our love is my purpose upon this earth."*

Venus in Cancer / Chockmah in water

Illumination

Where the Ace of Cups is the singularity and purity of love and emotion, divine love being received into the cup of the soul, the Two of Cups is two hearts joining together to express their love for each other. If the suit of cups represents souls receiving love, then a pair of cups is a union between two people who not only receive love but also express it in some form. Between the two cups the divine light can be shared, poured between the two vessels without being lost. The ace's inability to contain its bliss is remedied by the light that bursts forth being reflected back by another.

In the Two of Cups, we have an image that would not look out of place in a Shakespearian love story or an Arthurian romance. A man and a woman are caught up in each other, swooning and entwined, eyes staring deeply into each others' souls, breath taken away. You can almost hear their soft sighs and whispered words and promises. The Western world has a strange relationship with love like this. It portrays it on a regular basis in the media, in Hollywood movies, and in literature. We are raised on fairytales and fantasy stories that teach us that there is such a thing as a happy relationship, true love, and "The One." Yet as we grow older we are re-educated, taught that "love at first sight" is an old-fashioned trope, that there probably isn't "one" true love for us but many, that love does not actually conquer all. Too often what begins as a perfect meeting of hearts suffers at the hands of daily life, human weakness, and demands from others. Yet here in the tarot, being represented as a possibility in our lives, is a portrayal of true love, romantic love, courtly love, and healing love.

This card shares with the other twos in the tarot deck the qualities of balance, union, reunion, and equality. Harmony between two forces is represented in the twos, but most strongly in the Two of Cups. In the suit of emotions, love, and the social world, having equality, harmony, and union is not only the source of a loving partnership but also the goal. Although the couple in the card image look very similar, sharing the white-blonde, otherworldly hair and pale features of their people, their bodies wind around each other like the snakes around the caduceus behind them, reminding us that they are two different people with distinctive personalities, dreams, goals, and ideas. When liquid is shared between cups, it allows their contents to be mixed and united, while the form of the contents—the liquid—remains unchanged. It might be said that the perfect relationship therefore is one in which two hearts can share with each other and entwine, yet still retain individuality. Strength comes to the partnership because of the differences between two people as much as the similarities. Kahlil Gibran wrote in "On Marriage":

> *"Love one another but make not a bond of love:*
> *Let it rather be a moving sea between the shores of your souls.*
> *Fill each other's cup but drink not from one cup.*
> *Give one another of your bread but eat not from the same loaf.*
> *Sing and dance together and be joyous, but let each one of you be*
> *alone,*
> *Even as the strings of a lute are alone*
> *though they quiver with the same music.*
> *Give your hearts, but not into each other's keeping.*
> *For only the hand of Life can contain your hearts.*
> *And stand together, yet not too near together:*
> *For the pillars of the temple stand apart,*

And the oak tree and the cypress grow not in each other's shadow."[21]

Romantic love as depicted in the Two of Cups is echoed in many well-known love stories, such as Shakespeare's Romeo and Juliet, Arthurian legend's Lancelot and Guinevere, and Irish myth's Diarmiud and Grainne. In all of these tales, the love between the couple is deep and true, existing and growing despite unfavourable circumstances and different cultures, families, or social positions. This is the swooning, romantic love that we hope for and idealize, the kind of love that allows us to be caught up in something greater than ourselves. For the ability to love another person is a reflection of our yearning for reunion with the divine.

The Two of Cups can be seen as another form of the Lovers card, but on a more mundane level. It brings the concepts of reunion, harmony, and love from the abstract world into the reality of a partnership, but does not necessarily represent a romantic pairing. The qualities of this card are often found in close friendships, the kind of friendships that stay with you for your entire life, or spiritual partnerships that help each person grow. The caduceus in the card image reminds us that what each person brings to the relationship or partnership helps it to grow in its own unique fashion, creating strength and an alchemical union of beauty and healing.

Revelation

In a reading, the Two of Cups most often represents a partnership, usually a romantic one, which is between two people on equal terms, based on mutual respect and harmony. Sometimes it appears to signify the beginning of a relationship that will be extremely influential upon the querent, such as a long-term romance or one that inspires them and changes them for the better. This is the kind of relationship that makes the querent want to be the best they can be, not necessarily for the sake of the other person, but simply because love and connection inspire us to make ourselves better. If the reading is concerning a current relationship, the Two of Cups says that it is the best relationship it can be, and the partners are deeply in love with one another. In fact, there are very few cards that could top this one in a relationship reading. It would be even better if accompanied by the Lovers, the Ace of Cups, the Three of Cups, the Four of

---

21. Kahlil Gibran, *The Prophet: 26 Poetic Essays* (CreateSpace Independant Publishing Platform, 2010), page 10.

Wands, or the Two of Wands, as any combination of these might indicate the possibility of permanence, shared joy, and marriage or moving in together.

Often this card indicates the process of sharing, whether it is sharing oneself with another person, sharing ideas, sharing a home, sharing emotions or creative energies. It can indicate a platonic relationship between creative partners or those who work in a spiritual context together, or perhaps best friends who know each other better than anybody else. At times, if accompanied by other cards indicating pain or wounds, the Two of Cups can point to a relationship or a friendship that heals the querent in some way or allows them to open their heart again. This card can also indicate all forms of physical affection, from a gentle kiss or holding hands to passionate lovemaking.

If the Two of Cups appears in a reading not to do with relationships, it can indicate the love the querent has for something like a hobby, a project, or a job. It can also suggest the process of bouncing creative thoughts off another person for mutual inspiration, or the need to reunite with a complementary force, perspective, or state of being. This card might also suggest that the querent works with love or relationships in some form.

Reversed, the Two of Cups can indicate a relationship or friendship that is being overly idealised, so that the idea of the relationship becomes more important than its reality. The querent may be getting caught up in a vision of the future that is founded in a fantasy of love—such as a fairytale wedding— instead of taking actions that contribute to creating a lasting love. If found amongst cards that are negative or destructive, the Two of Cups reversed might point to the breakdown of a relationship that was once truly wonderful, or the loss of a friendship. If it seems to be a gentler form of the reversed Two of Cups, it can point to a blockage standing in the way of the sharing of love or emotions between two people (surrounding cards will indicate the nature of the blockage). More simply, the Two of Cups reversed can sometimes represent a past relationship that still has influence upon the querent and their life.

Keywords
Love, romance, courtship, romantic love, sharing, union, reunion, lovers, healing, friendship, relationship, harmony.

Three of Cups, Joy in Abundance

"There is naught but happiness in the world, and existence is pure joy! There is no reason for sadness or disappointment, pettiness or despair, because life is a testament to bliss. Where there is sorrow or failure, joy is not absent—you must simply perceive differently to find it. Make every day a holiday, every act one of celebration, every word a song of triumph, and you will join us in the dance of the Graces. As sisters we are one, united in our gratitude and thankfulness, offering the first of the harvest to the gods—for it must always be unto them. To place even the lowliest of wares upon their high altars is to make it sacred, bringing the divine down to earth and imbuing it with reason for celebration. Join us and offer the red rose of your desire to the heavens in a joyous crescendo; dance your carefree feet to the beat of grace; sing abundance into your life. But do not do it alone: your jubilation serves a higher purpose when it is shared with others. Join them to revel in the past, create a festival of the present, and welcome the future and all its potential with gaiety. Be in the moment, be the joy you wish to see in the world, and know the rich abundance of your life."

Mercury in Cancer / Binah in water

Illumination

Since cups is the suit of our social world and emotional ties, as well as our ties to the divine, we see a definite progress from the ace to the three. In the ace, the soul has a relationship with the divine, filled with the bliss of holy light, so much that it bursts out into the world. In the two, we see this bliss expressed to another vessel of light, another person, and a deep, loving relationship between partners is formed. When we reach the three, that love extends to a group, in this case a community of friendship, united in celebration. The threes of the tarot are concerned with manifestation and creativity, as well as community. Here in the Three of Cups, we not only have a group united in celebration, expressing love and happiness together, but also the manifestation of the forces of the Ace of Cups and the Two of Cups. What happens when two hearts come together in love? They share and celebrate love.

In the card image, we see three women in the process of celebrating. They raise their goblets in a toast or perhaps an offering, and they are surrounded by the colourful fruits of abundance. The stone steps behind them—maybe those of a temple, or leading to an altar—are bedecked with red roses, and three torches light the way up, burning brightly. There is a definite feeling of festival and party in this image, as well as a sense of sacredness along with the joy. This is not just any party, held because the attendees want to get drunk; these festivities celebrate something they consider sacred, and make sacred the thing they are celebrating. It could be that these three women are giving thanks for their bond, the unity found in true friendship being blissful and wonderful. But they could also be celebrating the bountiful harvest that surrounds them. Maybe they are priestesses of a temple, offering the first fruits of the harvest from their community to the gods, or maybe these are the fruits they have grown themselves that they are celebrating with joy.

The presence of three women in the card image is reminiscent of the Three Graces (also called the Charities) of ancient Greece. Most commonly depicted as three in number, and often shown dancing together around a central pillar, they were called Aglaea ("Splendour"), Euphrosyne ("Mirth"), and Thalia ("Good Cheer"). They were said to be the daughters of Aphrodite, the goddess of love, and Dionysus, the god of wine and ecstatic celebration. These beautiful goddesses were the patrons of festivities, laughter, amusements, and happiness. The Orphic hymn "To The Graces" says of them:

> *"Mothers of mirth, all lovely to the view,*
> *Pleasure abundant pure belongs to you:*
> *Various, forever flourishing and fair,*
> *Desir'd by mortals, much invok'd in pray'r."[22]*

The term "grace" is full of meaning. It can mean a favour given freely, often from the divine, as well as an act of thanksgiving, or a type of elegant, poised movement. We can imagine that the women in this card are giving thanks for something— an abundant harvest, the blessing of a new child to their community, a stroke of luck, or the safe return of a traveller who has been away for a long time.

The abundance of fruit in the card, symbolic of bountiful results, also signifies the sweetest things in life. A harvest could be shown as clearly by the depiction of wheat, or savoury foods, but fruit is not only nourishing but also sweet to taste, juicy and luxurious. Yet fruit can be such an insignificant thing to most of us, we might eat it without appreciating it. The Three of Cups asks us to remember that even "little" things, like an apple, a pomegranate, or a bunch

---

22. *The Hymns of Orpheus*, trans. Thomas Taylor, 1792.

of grapes, are blessings, joyous moments in our everyday life. Not only humans but also the gods also partake of them; we share the food of the gods.

Decorating the stone steps of the card are red roses, signifying desire, passion, and love. They are there not only for aesthetic reasons but also to remind us that joy and desire, joy and passion, joy and love go hand in hand, dancing together like the Graces.

Revelation

The Three of Cups is a joyous card, bringing a lightness and joy to the reading that suggests many good things are coming the querent's way. Most often it appears to signify a friendship group or community that the querent belongs to, such as a social club, church group, book club, family, or close group of friends that have been there for each other for years. It can also, therefore, indicate siblings that are close. Because of this community aspect, the Three of Cups can speak of celebrations that take place in a group setting, particularly those that celebrate love, such as weddings, ceremonies welcoming a new baby, or engagement or anniversary parties. If it is accompanied by the Four of Wands, it is highly likely that the Three of Cups points to a wedding.

This card says that the querent has reason to celebrate; the context of the question and the surrounding cards will indicate what. It could be something as life-changing as the news that they are expecting a baby or moving to a new home, or it could be the smaller triumphs of life: an exam being aced, a deadline being met. It can even be the really little things in life, like an opportunity for relaxation, for instance. The Three of Cups therefore advises the querent to let their hair down once in a while and not to take life too seriously. If they look, they will see that they have so many reasons to be thankful and joyful, so many sources of happiness around them. It might take the support of a social group or community to help them see it and engage with it, however.

When the Three of Cups shows up in a reading concerning an endeavour, it is always a positive sign. It suggests that the results of the endeavour will be successful and abundant, with positive outcomes that even the querent couldn't foresee. Their efforts in the present assure them of the best and sweetest things in the future, but they are reminded that they should share their harvest with others close to them to make the most of it.

In a reading about family, home life, or a relationship (including a business partnership or a friendship), the Three of Cups is particularly good. It indicates excellent communication based on trust, respect, and mutual love and affection, as well as shared commitment and goals. Home life will be peaceful and contented, with lots of fun and reasons to celebrate. The querent may also find themselves the recipient of lots of invites from their social group for parties.

Reversed, the Three of Cups sees the reasons for celebration and the act of celebration itself degraded and debased, as well as a delayed harvest. Here the querent may find themselves getting caught up in festivities and forgetting the reasons behind the celebration. They may be engaging in drunken, careless behaviour to forget about or retreat from themselves or an issue in their lives; it may also represent a distraction from problems they are currently having. The querent should be advised, if this card appears reversed in their reading, that the results they are going to see are not from their own work alone, and should be shared with others. The querent will have a tendency to hog the credit or the spoils, not allowing anybody else to share in them or the joy that they bring.

Keywords
Celebrations, parties, festivities, joy, happiness, friendship, community, group, grace, thanksgiving, results, abundance, mirth, dance, song.

Four of Cups, the Closed Doors of the Heart

"The human heart is filled with immense depth; it has the capacity to love and seek joy, to laugh and celebrate, to hate and seek anger. It thrives on the strong emotions that define our lives. When we lose the ability to feel those things, the heart begins to stagnate, and when it does so, it closes all doors to any further possibility of love, joy, laughter, and romance. After being hurt, the heart closes its doors to stop further pain from entering in—maybe it thinks it cannot survive one more blow. And from there, there is nothing. The colour drains from the world and nature loses its beauty, food tastes bland and eating or drinking is for simple survival and no more. Friends are cold comfort, and the heart seeks only its own company instead. But it is poor as a friend on its own, for it has become harsh and unfeeling. Instead it draws you in, pulling you deeper into the stagnant pit of bottled-up emotion. Here, every failure, every moment of rejection, every death of your dreams, every ending of love can be dwelt upon and recreated over and over again. Then, despite the heart's coldness, even the smallest memento can remind you of a certain smell, taste, voice, image... It is then that it is hardest, when you are reminded of what you

do not have. So there you find yourself, drawn into the depths of what you don't have, or what you do have that you hate, and you do not see the joy of life around you or the golden opportunity that is banging at the closed doors of your heart."

Moon in Cancer / Chesed in water

Illumination

What a sorry sight to see after the joyous festivities of the Three of Cups! A young man, clothed in rich fabrics, sits at the base of a tree looking dejected and sad. He stares down, and one hand gently holds a purple flower. Around him are three golden cups, and above and behind him is a fourth cup, illuminated and more richly bejewelled than the others, being offered to him by a spectral hand. But the man is so caught up in his thoughts, thinking about his cause for sadness, that he does not turn to see the wondrous sight.

The threes of each suit bring with them action leading to results, while the fours show us the grounding and manifestation of those results. However, in cups, the suit of water, emotions, love, and our inner world, the energies of the fours sit unhappily. Their earthy and grounded nature is counterintuitive to the watery nature of the cups, which prefer to flow and move. Similarly, the fours have a desire to root and bring things into being outwardly, while the watery cups prefer to explore inwardly. So instead of any joyous results or manifestations of love in this card, we find stagnation and disappointment caused by love and emotions that have become stale.

The scene is one of clear despondency. The young man in the card is idly holding a purple flower as he stares at the ground, deep in thought or self-pity. It is easy to imagine that he has just discovered that his lover has grown bored of their courtship and moved on to more exciting offers, or perhaps he is feeling dejected for want of someone to love. Maybe he himself has grown bored or tired of courtship, and has lost his passion for life. Maybe he is simply wishing his life were different. It is important to note, however, that the feelings of sadness represented in this card are not those found in the much darker Five of Cups; we can see in this card that the sun shines upon green grass and blue skies are overhead, whereas in the five all is snowy and grey. The Four of Cups instead points to feelings of despondency, boredom, stagnation, disillusionment, and discontentment.

The blue that he wears reminds us that he is in the cups suit and tells us of his emotional nature. It is also the colour of forget-me-not flowers, adding even more to the sense of dejection. The cups that are set on the hillock next to him are lacklustre in comparison to the one being offered above, indicating that his current state of emotion is just as lacklustre, and he has lost his lust for life, his spark; he feels like giving up. Next to him, a tree trunk reminds us of the earthy nature of the fours, and his position at its base tells us once again how stagnant he is. He is not moving on and will not turn to see the opportunity and joy that awaits him. He even seems unmoved by the beauty of his natural surroundings, the green fields and hills stretching out into the distance. In fact, everything seems quite beautiful in this card, apart from the look of sadness on the man's face, telling us that the cause of his sadness is to be found within, not without.

Reminiscent of the vision of the Holy Grail, the golden cup that is being offered to the man is being ignored. We can tell that this is the most important cup in the card because of its golden light and beauty, but it is made extra special by appearing on a spectral hand; note that these also appear in the aces of the four suits, so we can see this as indicating that the man is being offered a reminder of his original purpose, his bliss, the origin of his emotional world. Yet he does not see it. He does not turn to reach for it. He doesn't even realize it is being offered to him. When we get caught up in our inner turmoil, pitying ourselves and choosing to sit dejectedly in stagnation, we potentially lose chances at wonderful opportunities and avenues opening up in our lives.

Revelation

The Four of Cups can often bring disillusionment, dejection, disappointment, and stagnation to a reading. It can be particularly difficult to face if the question concerns a relationship or the querent's emotions. Often, the Four of Cups indicates that the querent is going through a period when they feel stuck and unable to move from their current situation. They are unhappy with the present state of things, unhappy with themselves and what they are doing in life, and they feel as though no matter what they do, they will just fail—so what is the point of trying any more? This may be preceded by a series of events that pushed the querent away from their goals or ideals, and forced them into situations that were necessary but far less than the querent feels they deserved. This is the card of the writer who is getting disheartened because publishers won't even read his manuscript, or the dejected actor who never gets a call back, or the person desperately seeking love who can never get beyond the third date.

Concerning love or relationships, the Four of Cups points to a romance that has become old, tired, and boring. The feelings that were once there aren't gone, but they are not supported by passion or novelty or a desire to progress and move forward together. Either the querent or their partner feels like the relationship is going nowhere, and may be considering cutting their losses and ending it rather than risk spending more time in a hopeless situation. For the querent without a relationship, the Four of Cups indicates that third-date scenario, rejection after rejection, and a lack of positive self-image that is fed by such incidents but also in turn feeds them. This card reminds the querent that if they think negatively and spend their time feeling sorry for themselves, they will not be acting in ways that encourage romance to blossom. In fact, the querent may be driving potential lovers away simply by being so depressing to be around.

In work-related matters or questions about projects, the Four of Cups again indicates stagnation and a lack of progress. It also suggests that the querent will become disillusioned with their work or project, or bored with it, or perhaps even view it as another sign that they are a failure. The work they do is boring for them, whatever they study is boring, and the thought of spending any more time in that area sends the querent into a depressive state. However, this card does remind the querent that if they wish to get themselves out of this situation, they must start thinking in new ways and making changes. By thinking and acting in this negative way, they are exacerbating the situation and making it more stagnant and boring. With the Four of Cups, the querent is strongly advised that they have a golden opportunity waiting for them, which they are at risk of losing if they do not pull themselves out of this slump.

Reversed, the Four of Cups sees the querent taking steps to move away from the stagnant point of their life and start to make improvements, both in the world around them and within themselves. By doing so, they will recognize the richness of their reality, rather than the boredom of the reality they thought they were living in, and make opportunities for themselves. This card reversed can also indicate a golden opportunity is being offered to the querent.

Keywords

Stagnation, disappointment, disillusionment, depression, boredom, stifling, self-pity, dejection, rejection, opportunities being offered.

Five of Cups, the River of Tears

"When your heart is open to another, you become vulnerable. When you open your life to another, you expose your weakest spot. Sooner or later, you will lose that person. Whether it is through a natural ending and fading of love, or a sudden betrayal, or perhaps even at death, everything we love eventually turns to dust and we are left alone to mourn for our loss. I knew this, I knew it well, and yet I still let myself love, still immersed myself in the joys of life with another. The highs, the jubilation, the excitement! They seem like cruel comparisons, allowing my pain to be all the greater now. I am distraught still with love, yet also with anguish. How can the world be so cruel as this? And how can we guard against such pain? Ah, ah! We cannot. It is in our nature to love and to feel the loss of our loved ones, for nothing lasts forever. It is only our foolishness that lets us live as though it does. But knowing now how much it hurts, would I do it again? Would I open myself in vulnerability to the joys of love? Yes. Again and again yes. Nothing lasts forever, no, not even the pain, and in time even the sorrow will pass as a shadow into my past, and I shall love again and return my heart to a state of beauty and acceptance. But now I grieve. Now I mourn my loss. To everything there is a season, and a time to every purpose under heaven."

Mars in Scorpio / Geburah in water

Illumination

As with the other fives of the tarot, the Five of Cups has the qualities of upheaval and imbalance, destruction and conflict. Since it is in the suit of cups, this upheaval and imbalance is brought into the world of the emotions, love, and friendship. This is a card of loss, and the grief felt over loss. However, it differs in its form of sorrow from that found in the Three of Swords, which represents a philosophical or existential sorrow in response to the general suffering of the world; here, it relates to human tragedy and the pain caused by personal loss.

In the card image, we see a stark image of a cloaked man who turns away from us, standing at the side of a river. Upon the banks of the river are five golden cups, three of which have spilled their contents onto the ground, two of which still stand upright behind him. The man's posture is an immediate clue as to what is happening in this card: he isn't only turned away from us, but his gaze is also cast downward and inward; he is not looking at his environment. This indicates that he has turned in on himself and is undergoing some sort of thought. If his gaze can be said to be anywhere, it is upon the three cups that lie upon the icy ground with their bloodlike contents spilled out. This indicates that he is focusing solely on the cause of his pain—loss—and not looking at that which remains, ignoring the two full cups behind him. This is natural when loss and grief occurs in our life: we focus on the pain and the cause of it, as well as that which we have lost. Often, some time must pass before we can turn around and look at our blessings instead.

The heavy grey cloak that the man wears evokes feelings of sadness, depression, grief, and mourning. It is covered in snow, suggesting that feelings of isolation and cold have also crept into his life. The only bright colour in this card, in fact, is the spilled red liquid, once again highlighting the fact that the man is looking only at what he has lost. As with any form of grief, it is easy to look at the past and the thing that has been lost and to hold it up as the pinnacle of beauty and joy, ignoring any of the negative aspects of it.

Is the liquid spilling from the cups blood, or is it wine? Its viscosity would suggest it is blood, indicating that something extremely important to the man has been lost. Being in the suit of the emotions, the thing that is important to the man must be related to another person. Has somebody he loves passed away, putting him in a state of mourning? Has he been through the breakdown of a relationship? Grief occurs in the same way, regardless of the cause of loss or what has been lost. There is also a similarity in this card to the Eight of Cups. All the cups on the left of the image can be seen as representing the past, whereas the cups on the right represent the future. The man in the Five of Cups looks only at the cups representing the past, ignoring the possibilities waiting for him in the future.

In the background is a castle or stronghold. The man is not near to it and not inside it, but situated far away, on the opposite side of the river. This tells us that he reached this point of loss and grief through stepping out of his comfort zone and away from his defences, making himself vulnerable. We all do this when we enter into a relationship of any kind with another person. In order to truly let another person into our heart, we must open it, and when we open it to them, it is also open to pain and hurt. This is the risk everyone takes when they love another. But has that ever stopped anyone from loving? At the moment of loss we often wish we hadn't left the safety of our stronghold, our well-defended emotional life, but as the two cups on the right of the card remind us, there is always a future, even for the most broken-hearted.

The river appearing in this card is a potent symbol that also appears in the Death card, the Six of Swords, Temperance, the Chariot, and the Empress. In Death and the Six of Swords, the rivers are a symbol of transition and transience; in Temperance it is a symbol of mutability; and in the Chariot and the Empress, there is a life-giving quality of movement about it. Here in the Five of Cups the river is one of the most prominent features of the card, and it travels underneath a bridge. Rivers are a body of water and thus represent a form of emotion or an emotional state, in this case one that is in a state of transition or movement. This reminds us that the emotions being felt in this card are only temporary, and eventually they will be carried downriver and away from the man's life. This also brings to mind the saying, "water under the bridge," which indicates something that belongs to the past and isn't important anymore. Soon enough, the pain and grief in this card will lessen and become a thing of the past, no longer taking up all the man's time and energy. This isn't necessarily because the emotions being felt by him now are not important, but because time heals all wounds and emotions are very fluid. We are reminded that the fives of the tarot are all about movement and states of upheaval and upset that very soon— in the sixes, in fact—return to a state of harmony.

Revelation

The Five of Cups is never a happy card in a reading. It indicates all kinds of loss, and the sorrow and grief that come from that loss. It might appear in a reading to indicate the breakdown of a relationship, either through a long, drawn-out death or a sudden upheaval. Sometimes it points to upheaval in a relationship that causes sadness, but which isn't necessarily an end, such as one partner moving far away. It can signify an ending of a platonic friendship too, sometimes caused by social upheaval or a betrayal. Mostly, though, this card talks about the resulting emotions of such loss, specifically the emotion of grief. The querent is undergoing a grieving process of some kind, though this grieving process can also be metaphorical. For instance, if accompanied by cards that talk about the querent's children, the Five of Cups might point to grief associated with children leaving home. If associated cards suggest travel, then the Five of Cups may indicate feelings of sadness at moving to another place, and about what or who is being left behind. Very occasionally, the Five of Cups can indicate the death or a loved one, and the resulting bereavement.

Often, the Five of Cups appears when the querent is focusing too much on what they have lost or are leaving behind. It suggests that by doing so, they are missing out on opportunities for important progress and growth, and may be neglecting their life in the present, including other people. The querent is likely to isolate themselves from others with the Five of Cups, preferring to lose themselves in their sadness. It is a lonely, solitary card that sees the querent desiring to be left alone in their grief. This can become a vicious cycle, as the querent is likely to turn inward and find it difficult to get out of their sadness. They need to let other people into their emotional world in order start to move out of their grief.

Sometimes the Five of Cups suggests emotional upheavals and imbalances, such as those caused by depression, anxiety disorders, or mental illness. The querent's emotions may be so fluid that they experience mood swings, making them unpredictable and driving people away. In a reading concerning an endeavour, the querent will find that they experience a loss of some kind, or that things don't go according to plan and they are left to try and pick up the pieces alone.

However, this card also offers the querent advice and a solution: they need to stop crying over spilled milk and move on. The grieving process for anything that has been lost is important to engage with and undergo fully in order to come to terms with it, but it cannot last indefinitely. The Five of Swords in a reading indicates that there is something in the querent's life that will allow them to move on and let go of their pain, but they have to look up, out of their darkness, to see it. If accompanied by cards of healing, such as the Two of Cups, the Six of Swords, or the Star, this message is amplified.

Reversed, we find the eternal widow, the querent constantly in mourning and refusing to come out of a state of sadness. This is a very dangerous position for them to be in, which will make matters worse for them; staying in this state will prevent anybody from getting close and will prevent any possibilities and opportunities for the future arising. The Five of Cups reversed suggests that this is exactly what the querent wants this way they can get the attention of others (attention-seeking behaviour is sometimes indicated by this card, reversed) without putting themselves in danger of being hurt again. If accompanied by any other cards that point to sadness, grief, and mental anxiety, such as the Three of Swords, the Nine of Swords, and the Ten of Swords, it is time to advise the querent to seek professional help, as they may be on the verge of a breakdown, or may be having depressive thoughts leading to considerations of self-harm. The power of grief in the Five of Cups, reversed, can be overwhelming.

Keywords

Grief, loss, sadness, depression, anguish, bereavement, emotional upheaval, pain, hurt, vulnerability, letting go, imbalance, unpredictable emotions.

Six of Cups, the Pleasure of the Sun-Child

"Do you recall how it felt to be young? Can you remember the endless summer days you spent in freedom and happiness, with no cares or worries more pressing than the time of your evening meal? What did it feel like to get lost in the moment, to be able to create wonders and amazing visions from nothing, and to be entertained for an entire day with just a single notion? Back then, a day seemed like a lifetime, and the future stretched before you like a wide and inviting land filled with promise. Our occupation was play, our currency was imagination, and we knew instinctively what was most important for a happy, long life: simple joy. Ah, how frail must the heart be for it to let the happenings of life wear down that awareness! If we were to let our child selves see us now, to watch us for a day, what would they say? And what could we learn from them?"

The Sun in Scorpio / Tiphereth in water

Illumination

Finally the clouds have parted and sunlight is shining through once more, illuminating our hearts, minds, and actions. As with the other Sixes, the Six of Cups offers a rebalancing and harmonizing of the forces that were previously imbalanced, in conflict, and in stagnation. All the sixes also bring with them a quality of happiness and brightness that shines through particularly brightly in the Six of Cups, since the suit is primarily concerned with emotions, relationships, and our inner world.

The card image is one of sweetness and simple beauty. In the background an older man rests his hand gently on a walking cane, his other hand upon his belt, as he looks down a set of stone steps at the scene that takes up most of the card. There, beside an ornamental pond covered with pink lotus flowers, a young boy and girl interact. The girl makes a dainty and well-executed curtsey, while the boy remains seated and holds a golden cup overflowing with flowers. Both wear the colours of their suit, blues and whites, and around them are five other cups just as filled with flowers as the one the boy holds. If we look closely, he may be smelling the flowers in his hands. Behind them a series of stone arches covers a walkway, and at the very back of the card, behind the watching man, we can see the flow of a waterfall.

It would be nice to think that the man in the background is an older version of the boy in the foreground, looking back at a vision of his past self with nostalgia and happiness. Certainly the stone steps that run between him and the children indicate a connection or continuum between them. The man is looking back at a simpler time in his life, observing his roots and past experiences that have led directly to where he is in the present. He does not appear sad, however, merely observant. There is no suggestion in this card of something being lost and grieved for (as in the Five of Cups), nor of dissatisfaction with the current state of affairs (as in the Four of Cups); instead, we sense an immense amount of joy. Often, when we understand that the past cannot be changed, and realize that it led directly to our present moment, we reach a sense of peace and harmony with our inner processes. Happy are those of us that can look back at our past experiences, actions, friendships, and words and be glad of them, remembering with fondness those times gone, remembering with happiness any friendships long since past.

The children in the card image are representative of innocence and simplicity. Adults often find pleasure and happiness in complicated things: achieving goals for which they have worked, or appreciating the emotions expressed in Stravinsky's *Rite of Spring*, for example. But children can find joy in the smallest, most simple things: they can be entranced by the movement of a bug among the grass, or engrossed in their own imagination, playing without the need of any material goods or items; even the most mundane of objects— like a box or a stick—can result in many hours of entertainment. A child's mind has not yet had the chance to become disillusioned with the world, or jaded, or to make assumptions as an adult's often does. Everything is still new and, by extension, filled with wonder. Yet, even as adults, we can often think back to the way we looked at the world in our youth, the experiences we had, the way we acted, and recover some of our innocence, joy, and wonder.

Children are found throughout the tarot to indicate something new being born, or to indicate the childlike state of initiation and a new beginning. Most notably, we see them in the Ten of Cups, the Ten of Pentacles (both cards that are simultaneously an ending and a new beginning), Judgement, and the Sun. In many mystery traditions, in both the ancient and modern worlds, candidates for initiation are referred to as a child, or put into a state of childhood, and even in exoteric religion members will be called "child." Further, it is worth noting that for almost every card in which we see a male and female pair, the female is situated on the left and the male on the right: Judgement, the Devil, the Lovers, the Ten of Pentacles, the Six of Pentacles, the Two of Cups. The left side is associated with the receptive principle and the right side with the active; feminine and masculine share those traits as well. The child pair in the Six of Cups can therefore be seen as representative of our inner world undergoing a process of regression into a childlike state: not a state of helplessness or disempowerment, but rather a state of innocence and potential from which further understanding can flow. The receptive-feminine girl child and the active-masculine boy child also represent the giving and receiving of joy.

This generosity of pleasure can be seen in the overflowing cups filled with flowers. Flowers are almost universally symbolic of happiness and beauty in the natural world. The phrase "stop and smell the flowers" indicates taking time away from a busy schedule to enjoy the journey, rather than rushing toward the finishing line. It also refers to a simpler, easier way of being. The sunflowers in the cup on the far right of the card can also be found in the Sun card and the Queen of Wands, and they are a reference not only to the solar energies of this card but also to optimism and light. A sunflower takes its name not only from its vibrant colour, but also from the fact that it will follow the sun with its head as it travels across the sky, so that the flower is always facing the sun. This is symbolic of always "looking on the bright side," turning our hearts and minds toward light, joy, and illumination, rather than negative emotions. The pink lotuses that we see in abundance in the pool are also to be found elsewhere in the tarot, such as in the Ace of Cups. They bring the purity of emotion from the ace to this card; they also represent beauty in the mundane world, and remind us of their origins, since lotus flowers root themselves in the mud before rising to the surface of the water to bloom in the light of the sun.

The actions of the children might be seen as mimicking adult behaviour, with a genteel curtsey reserved for court and an act of generosity. It would be easy to imagine that these two children are playing make-believe, and looking forward to the time when they are old enough to apply these actions in the adult world. Until then, they are simply enjoying themselves, not seeing their actions for what they represent or what they can bring them. There is an inherent joy being demonstrated in these acts, and thus in this card. This is not the pleasure found in celebration in the Three of Cups, nor the joy in achieving a goal or reaching the completion of a project as in the Four of Wands and the Six of Wands. This is true pleasure found in the moment, happiness found in life's simpler things, joy instilled inherently in our very beings.

Revelation

The Six of Cups promises a time of balance in the querent's emotional life, a time of harmony within themselves and with others. It is particularly positive if it appears in a relationship reading, as it suggests that the querent, if they are already in a relationship, will find that the partnership is one of honesty, generosity, happiness, and balance, with emotions being shared and reciprocated. If the querent is not currently in a relationship, then the Six of Cups suggests that they soon will be, and it will be a very happy one; at times it suggests that the prospective partner comes from the querent's past or is an old friend. It can also indicate anything from the querent's past coming back to help them in the present.

There is a gentility to the Six of Cups that often comes out in a reading. It advises that the querent's situation is best faced with openness, honesty, and simplicity. Complicating matters unnecessarily, one-upmanship, keeping secrets, or manipulating the situation or people in it will work against the querent in the end. It may be time for them to open themselves up to receive a gift from another person as well—not usually a material gift (that would be better indicated by the Six of Pentacles) but a gift of love, friendship, truce, or advice. It may also be time for the querent to return affection that is being offered to them, and not be afraid to love and love openly. If they have been through a difficult emotional time, perhaps having faced a relationship breakdown or the loss of a loved one, then the Six of Cups tells them it is time to open their hearts once more. They have had difficult experiences, and now they understand the pain of loss, and negative emotions such as anguish, jealousy, or anger. These emotions do not, however, define the querent: they simply add to the deep and never-ending pool of their inner world, their inner understanding of themselves as an emotional being.

Sometimes the Six of Cups points to a return to a simpler way of living. Perhaps the client is considering selling their large, busy house so that they can move to somewhere smaller, quieter, and easier to take care of. Perhaps they are undergoing a process of removing complications from their lives. This is especially true if this card is accompanied by the Six of Swords, Death, or the Wheel of Fortune. It suggests that it is time for change, but in the form of gentle change that serves to simplify things and make life easier.

At times this card appears in a reading to indicate any children in the querent's life, or a desire for children and plans to start a family. It may simply be suggesting spending more time with these children, as well as learning from them: they have a lot to offer the querent, just as the querent has a lot to offer them. This card can also refer to the querent's inner child, and any activities that the querent can undertake to re-establish a connection with their own joy. It might be time for the querent to start perceiving the world with more wonder, giving up a jaded view for a more innocent one.

If the Six of Cups appears in a reading about work, money, or business, then it raises issues of the querent's happiness. Are they happy with what they do for a living? How can they bring more joy to their job? When we are children, we often mimic the jobs and occupations of adulthood, and we take great joy in doing so. When do we lose that enthusiasm and happiness about work? This card also recommends that to get ahead in work or business, the client should not rush ahead: it's not a race. Instead, they should be taking their time to enjoy what they are doing, demonstrating their passion through immersion and happiness. They should enjoy the journey as much as the destination.

Reversed, the Six of Cups sees the querent going into a nostalgic state, looking back to the past with a mixture of fondness and bittersweet regret. Maybe they wish they could have acted or spoken differently in a particular situation, or maybe they are simply reflecting on their life now and wishing that times were simpler, just as they were when they were younger. They may feel as though they have far too many cares and worries now, and are yearning for an easier, more innocent way of looking at the world. The Six of Cups, even reversed, does not lose its positive nature, however, so the querent will still find that they are in a position of emotional strength and harmony; they should just be careful not to dwell too much in the past, or to sugar-coat it and see it through rose-tinted glasses.

Keywords

The past, nostalgia, innocence, children, childlike, naivety, play, playfulness, joy, wonder, pleasure, happiness, emotional balance, reciprocity, generosity, simplicity.

Seven of Cups, the Power of the Imagination

"Come closer, dreamer. Come closer so that I might whisper sweetly to you of the joys of the universe within you. Come closer that you might taste the fruits I offer you. Here, gaze deeply into the cup before you: what do you see? What imaginings are whirling there in the depths, waiting to be given form and life? Do you see the sunlight dancing on the surface of the water, or do you see the creatures lurking and hulking in the depths? Do you see your future here, spirit-walker? Are you granted visions of all that will be, or visions of all that can be? The distinction is important. Daydream your inspiration, seeker, and bring your visions into your waking sight. Are they hallucinations now? And can you really tell the difference between what is real and what is not? Are you sure? No. You can never be sure. Certainty is not the blessing of mortals, except insomuch as they are certain they have it. Oh, but in dreams and hopeful imaginings you can create a better world, and populate it with your wildest desires. Would you be the brave slayer of dragons or the charmer of snakes? Would you command great power or great riches? Would you be the victor of glorious battles or the servant of God? Or would you give up everything for that great unknown possibility that stands always in peripheral vision, never calling, only waiting for you to come? Know this, dream-weaver: everything begins in the imagination, and nothing can become reality without the mind first conceiving of it. Some say we cannot simply dream things into being, but they are fools. Do they think famous explorers set sail for new shores without first dreaming of doing so? Do they believe inventors and artists put pen or paint to paper and canvas without first holding in their inner vision a concept or image? What a world humankind has created with their imaginations! With it you have the ultimate seduction and temptation away from your true path, as well as the most fertile waters from which your new creations are born..."

Venus in Scorpio / Netzach in water

Illumination

It is quite possible that the Seven of Cups is one of the most mysterious cards of the tarot pack. It is difficult to ascertain what is happening in the fantastical, otherworldly card image, though the scene is clear. We have no context for the events unfolding, nor a facial expression in the character with which to judge. The sevens of the tarot bring with them the qualities of flux and shifting power, and the number seven in traditional thought is seen as a magical and spiritual number. Add these qualities to the suit of cups—concerned with the emotions and the spiritual self, and filled with its own connotations of flux and fluidity—and we find that the Seven of Cups is an ever-changing, shifting creature that doesn't quite reveal everything. It's like the judgment of distance in water: because of the way light refracts through water, what we see is not the exact truth, yet we see enough to know what is there. We are being shown half-truths, but not-quite-lies.

In the card image, we see a man being shown (or possibly creating) a vision of seven golden cups, each bearing a different scene or creature within it. Perhaps this is a vision of the future, appearing suddenly to him in a moment of great need, or perhaps it is a hallucination created after the consumption of certain substances. It might be that he has asked the gods for help and this is the answer they granted him, or it might be that he is imagining in his mind's eye all these strange images, in an effort to brainstorm his options.

In Western culture, the imagination is undervalued. It's seen as useful only to children when they play make-believe, or when people idly picture what they would do if they won the lottery or suddenly became famous. Many view daydreams as a waste of time, and those who have visions as untrustworthy or suspicious. Hallucinations are even more frowned upon, being seen as unnatural products of a mind that is either unhealthy or under the influence. But the Seven of Cups asks us to think differently. The imagination, it says, is a powerful tool for creativity and actualization. Everything begins in the imagination. When an artist paints, they have an image, even if only half-formed, in their mind's eye that they wish to bring to life. When an inventor sets to work building a new machine, they already have a concept of the invention in their head. Many of the world's famous inventors and thinkers describe moments when an idea came fully formed into their head, and they knew they had to make it a reality. Thus the imagination can be our greatest creative asset and a necessary tool for creating change in our world. It is with this in mind that many people today use practices such as creative visualization, guided meditation, lucid dreaming, and creating vision boards to improve their life and bring their dreams into reality.

Since the mind and the imagination are so easily influenced, the Seven of Cups brings with it all the means by which we might find ourselves under such influence. Mind-altering substances and hallucinogens are found here, for instance. Some cultures make use of hallucinogens to create spiritually receptive, heightened states of consciousness in which the seeker embarks on a spiritual journey. One example of this is the ayahuasca brew used in some parts of South America, a psychoactive infusion made up of various plants containing dimethyltryptamine (DMT), which is used as a religious sacrament with medicinal properties. It induces hallucinations, both visual and auditory, a blurring of the senses, and introspection. Those undergoing its effects might experience a "eureka" moment, great inspiration, a sense of oneness, elation, illumination, or sometimes fear. It is worth noting that in our Western culture, psychedelic substances that contain DMT are illegal; yet in cultures where such a substance is used for a spiritual, religious purpose, it is not. This highlights the fact that the visions granted by the Seven of Cups (which may not necessarily be through the use of such substances, but can also be gained through meditation, visualization, fasting, or dreaming) can be seen as negative if they are used merely as a form of entertainment, or positive if used as a means to self-improvement and inspiration.

So, is the man in our card image having a hallucination? Is he dreaming? Is he consciously imagining possibilities? More importantly: does it matter? We can see what kind of visions he is being granted from the symbols within the cups. The castle or tower represents worldly power and influence, a kingdom over which to rule. The cup filled with treasure represents material wealth and riches, as well as comfort and life's finest luxuries. The head of a man with his eyes closed in contemplation represents a life of peace and spirituality, whilst the cup containing a red dragon represents a life of great challenges and heroic deeds. The laurel wreath, symbol of victory, represents fame and renown, and the snake represents a life of danger and travel to exotic lands. Finally, the cloaked, faceless figure in the central, highest cup is a mystery: it could represent death, or simply the unknown, since imagination can never account for everything.

The clouds that hold up and surround the cups remind us of the pitfalls of the Seven of Cups: sometimes we cannot see a situation clearly, and sometimes things are hidden from us. Unfortunately, since the mind and emotions are in such a fluid and easily influenced state in this card, it can be almost impossible to discern reality from fantasy.

Revelation

The Seven of Cups can be difficult to interpret in a reading, since it can mean so many different things. It is a card of flux and uncertainty, change and fluidity, indicating first of all that there is some issue in the querent's life that is uncertain and in a state of flux. If found in a general future position, it suggests that too many things are still undecided in the present for any possible future to be discerned, and that the querent therefore has the choice in the here and now of what to create in their future. It might suggests that some element of their current situation is still "up in the air," or unresolved.

This card can often bring with it inspiration based in a rich and fertile imagination. It can indicate that the querent is a dreamer, often with their head in the clouds, with a brilliant imagination and great capacity for creativity. If they were to apply this gift to a project or otherwise start manifesting it in reality, they could be a talented artist, poet, writer, or inventor. However, they may have difficulty committing to any specific plan or goal, or sticking with something once they have started it, since they are easily distracted by their next interesting idea or their next imagined world. Usually the presence of the Seven of Cups in a reading says that the querent has a great idea and they should now start to make it a reality, rather than just dreaming about it—but with the Seven of Cups such a thing is easier said than done.

Sometimes this card appears in a reading to indicate a range of possibilities open to the querent, perhaps in a career or relationship situation. The querent should be advised, however, that not all their options are equal, and some would be bad choices. They must be careful to tell the good from the bad. However, with the Seven of Cups, we also find that somebody may be trying to trick the querent in some way, not by manipulating them or lying to them as in the Seven of Swords, but by not showing them the whole truth, or distorting the truth slightly. The situation the querent currently finds themselves in may be revealed as all smoke and mirrors, or they may find that where they thought there were many options, only one option was real and the rest were just distractions.

The Seven of Cups can often be a wake-up call for the querent if they are being lazy about making changes in their life. This card brings with it the message, "Don't dream it, be it!" The querent can build castles in the air if they wish, but it is time to take their head out of the clouds and start building foundations beneath their dreams. If the querent is looking for methods of improving their life or finding direction, the Seven of Cups suggests creative visualization, meditation, dream work, or vision boards would be effective means of doing so.

If this card appears in a reading about a current relationship, it may suggest that one person is trying to use subtle emotional manipulation to hide something or change the way the other views things. It can also suggest that the querent may be making more out of this relationship than there is, or seeing only an idealistic dream of what it could be in the future, rather than what it is now. This idealism can be found in other areas of the querent's life, too, and other cards in the reading will tell whether the idealism is serving a good purpose or a bad one.

If reversed, the Seven of Cups can be a very dangerous card. It is seductive and can change the state of the emotions and the mind easily and quickly, suggesting that the querent's will is weak and that they are easily influenced by peer pressure. It might point to somebody whose perception of life is so skewed that they can be a danger to themselves or others, or simply that the querent's perception of a particular situation is skewed. There is an air of deception and trickery to the reversed Seven of Cups, particularly on an emotional level. Sometimes it can indicate that the querent's plans are merely pipe-dreams, or that they will not progress beyond hopeful imaginings. At its worst, this card reversed—especially if accompanied by cards such as the Devil—can point to substance abuse, drug addiction, alcoholism, escapism, mental illness, or debauchery and decadence—and not the "good" kind of debauchery and decadence, but the kind that seeks escapism, pretends it is somebody else, and hides away from reality.

Keywords

Imagination, visions, dreams, hallucinations, smoke and mirrors, flux, fluidity, uncertainty, mystery, choices, options, possibility, idealism, substance abuse, skewed perspective, emotional weakness, debauchery, decadence, escapism.

Eight of Cups, the Vision Quest in the Wasteland

"Do you hear it? Can you smell it on the air? Can't you taste it, on the tip of your tongue, palpable and unrelenting? It is the call to walk the unknown pathways, to tread the roads that only open before you when you step into the other world, to walk through the Gateway of the Moon, to pass through the doors of the Temple

of the Priestess. I am on a love walk, a spirit walk, a walk to find my self. I seek wisdom on strange shores and in the oases of deserts. I embrace the wasteland, the no man's land, because it can offer me the wisdom I seek within myself, for I too am barren. I once had so much, so many trinkets and distractions and worldly pleasures. I could boast of the greatest friends and the highest achievements, the most influence and the necessary material worth. But it gave me no answers, no realization, no truth. I lost my self in the glamour, the smoke and mirrors, until I could no longer feel a call to something greater than myself. What use are all the treasures of the world, even all the treasures of your loved ones, when your self is missing? Some say I abandoned my life, leaving behind all the world's best things. They don't understand, and they won't until they too hear the song of the vision quest calling them, pulling at their loneliness, as if their self is out there in the wasteland and urging them to come and find it. I am not walking away. I am walking toward."

Saturn in Pisces / Hod in water

Illumination

Like the Seven of Cups, the Eight of Cups is somewhat puzzling, since it is hard to tell what is happening in the card image and what has led up to this point. We see a man cloaked in red, leaning heavily on his staff, as he walks through a gap in the foreboding rocks toward a barren wasteland, under the waxing moon. Behind him are eight golden cups, and around him all is ice and snow. We don't see his face—unusual in the tarot pack, and a feature found only in a few mournful, sorrowing cards such as the Five of Cups, or cards that invite the viewer to turn inward on themselves, such as the Seven of Cups. He is clearly moving away from us, but we cannot see his intention, nor whether he has a goal or destination. Unlike the Ten of Wands, which clearly shows the burdened journeyman's goal in the form of the tower at the top of a hill, the wanderer in the Eight of Cups could be on his journey indefinitely.

The moon itself dominates this card, bringing to mind two major arcana cards in which it features just as prominently: the High Priestess and the Moon. When the moon appears in a card image, we know that some form of flux and change is occurring, specifically a change concerning the inner world or shadow world, rather than any changes in the material world (although the link between material and spiritual means that they do often reflect each other). The moon is often a call to follow intuition, to seek a deeper understanding, to look within for answers and seek the unknown. That the figure in this card is walking toward the moon, rather than having his back to it, indicates that he is moving toward a deeper spiritual understanding, a more intuitive way of thinking, or simply moving toward change. The moon is also in the waxing gibbous phase: growing, almost full, symbolically representing the growth and fullness that the figure in the card will have in the future if he continues on his journey. In astrology, the waxing gibbous phase is a good time for overcoming obstacles, suggesting that the figure in the Eight of Cups is currently trying to overcome difficulties of some kind.

It is interesting to note that the moon is sometimes called "the wanderer" in modern astrology, since it moves around us so rapidly, changing its face over a brief period of time. The Eight of Cups can be typified as "the wanderer" or "the wayfaring stranger," who finds himself continually called to new places and new experiences so that he might obtain a deeper understanding of self. Yet the archetype of the wayfaring stranger never stays in one place for long, finding that he is always missing something, no matter where he is or who he surrounds himself with, always choosing to try and fill the gap in his heart or soul by moving on to another place. In the card image, we see the eight cups in the foreground are split with a gap between them—five on the left and three on the right. This gap reminds us that the wanderer is missing something, and he is moving from a place of lack to what he perceives to be a place of growth. Symbolically, the fact that five cups are found on the left (the place of the past) and three on the right (the place of the future) suggests that by making the choice to embark upon this quest for deeper meaning, the figure in the card is moving from a past of restlessness and conflict to a future of hope and fullness. Nevertheless, the cups are currently empty.

The icy wasteland around and before the figure further indicates this missing something, reflecting his own inner state of being. He feels barren, cold, with nothing in his life growing or progressing. He needs to go into the wasteland so that he can find out what is missing and how he might fill the gap.

We can see that the figure leans heavily on a staff as he walks. He is in need of immense support at this time, but is choosing to seek it within himself rather than from another person. He's also got a long and lonely journey ahead of him, and the staff is going to be much-needed. The staff is one of the universal signs of the wayfaring stranger or traveller, shown throughout history with deities who wander the worlds and seek the pathways, or help other cross them. In Greek myth, Hermes was given the caduceus with which he guided souls on their journey between the worlds of the living and the dead; Odin from Norse myth was given a staff with which he walked in the different worlds in varying disguises; and a Haitian Vodou spirit called Papa Legba carries a walking stick with which he travels all the pathways and roads between the worlds.

The Eight of Cups is another gateway card in the tarot, as indicated by the pillars of rock that loom on either side of the figure in the image. This represents a choice that the figure is making from which there is no turning back; once he has stepped across the threshold of his decision and into the lunar wasteland of his inner world, he is committed. The gateway here also reminds us that this is a card of transition from one state to another, a journey from outer to inner and back again, bringing back the fruits of the quest.

Revelation

In a reading, the Eight of Cups often appears to indicate the desire of the querent to leave or go away in some form or another. This might relate to the desire to change location or home, to leave a relationship, to change jobs, to leave a community they currently belong to, even to change religions or adopt a new philosophy. This desire comes from an inner need that the querent may not recognize, but which is playing out in their life in some way. Often, when we are in need of a change, our conscious mind does not immediately register it, but our subconscious mind starts breaking the news gently to us by urging us to perform certain actions that eventually make us realize what we need. This might take the form of withholding affection in a relationship, becoming emotionally distant from a person, distracting ourselves from a problem through escapism, losing the desire to attend events held by a certain group or in a certain place, doing less housework in a home that we need to move out of, and so on. The signs may be there in the querent's life and they have not yet registered them, or they may have done so and now are attempting to make the changes.

Often this card indicates a feeling the querent has that they need to turn inward rather than outward, exploring their inner world more deeply. This usually manifests as a spiritual journey of some kind, such as retreats, a pilgrimage, or meditation. Certainly it signifies an inner change, such as releasing old thought patterns, habits, and processes. Sometimes the Eight of

Cups speaks of the querent needing to let go of the past so that they can return to a state of spiritual well-being. There is a strong suggestion that they are wounded in some way, feeling a lack in their lives, and knowing that their current state of being or lifestyle is not feeding them spiritually or emotionally. It's time for them to acknowledge the lack or the wound so that they can begin to move forward. But they must learn to listen to their intuition and inner guidance in order to do this.

This card can also point to a general characteristic of the querent: they are prone to moving on quickly from situations, never staying in one place or with one person for very long. They may be serial monogamists, moving from one relationship to another in rapid succession, or they may always be looking for a new job from their current one, or looking for a new house to rent instead of the one they are currently in. The person indicated by the Eight of Cups may also have difficulties committing to anything, as they don't like being tied down; they like the freedom of being able to "up sticks" whenever they need or want to. Surrounding cards or the context of the question will indicate if this is having a positive or negative effect upon the situation.

If the Eight of Cups appears reversed in a reading, it indicates abandonment, either that the querent is abandoning somebody or something, or that they themselves are being abandoned. This can take the form of walking out on a relationship instead of facing problems, even when the relationship is worth saving and the problems are minor. Reversed, this card sees the querent throwing their hands up in despair and leaving a situation because they can't be bothered to expend effort or energy solving it. Here, they are running away in fear or out of weakness, rather than moving onward and letting go of some limitation in order to deepen their own inner landscape.

Keywords

Moving on, change, inner world, abandonment, letting go, spiritual quest, retreat, journey, wayfaring, wandering, wilderness, leaving, running away.

Nine of Cups, the Blessings of Satisfaction

"Welcome! Come in, come in! Let me pour you a cup of my finest ale—it is brewed to perfection and full of flavour, and once you've tasted it, you'll feel the joy bubbling up inside you. Here, let me sate your hunger with my most delicious

foods, prepared carefully and with a skill that is better described as art. Ah, how marvellous life is! How fortunate we are to have met, for now we can share life's finest things together. They say that the man that eats alone, dies alone, and food and drink is made all the sweeter and more satisfying by good company. Don't you agree? Oh, isn't life grand? Isn't the world just right, right now, as it is? We are often told to count our blessings, and look how many there are! What more could we want, friend? Well, perhaps just a little more, but that does not mean that our current position is not the best position we can be in. There is always more—more being offered, more being wanted, more being taken. However, the secret is not to have what you want, but to want what you have. That is true contentment."

Jupiter in Pisces / Yesod in water

Illumination

Our emotions have gone through a lot so far in this suit: we've experienced unity, love, joy, celebration, dissatisfaction, nostalgia, daydreaming, and a need to turn inward, and throughout, we've been given brief tastes of what true and perfect happiness is like. In fact, that's the aim of this suit! So, when we reach the Nine of Cups, the almost-full energies of the nines find a happy home in the suit that is concerned with our emotional, romantic, and social worlds; here they give us many cups that are full of blessings, but not so full that they no longer have room to receive more.

We are welcomed into this card by a jovial man grinning from ear to ear. His arms are folded across his chest in a stance of pride, and he puts his best foot forward in a pose that is designed to inspire warmth and welcome in his visitor. Behind him sits a throne—presumably his throne—and on the walls we see ornate wood panelling. From the back wall, two large swathes of gold fabric fall down the walls and to the floor, and above him, on a shelf that follows the walls, are nine golden cups presented for all to see.

It is the man's smile that tells us the most about this card: he is extremely pleased with himself. He is so happy that he wants to show us exactly what he is happy about: the nine cups that adorn the room. These are his cups, a representation of his accumulated emotional and spiritual wealth, understanding and wisdom, and he is quite right to be satisfied with them. But most importantly, he wants to share his happiness with us, and thus he draws other people into his world of joy. This is not a card of celebration, however, as we find in the Three of Cups, nor of perfect happiness, as we find in the Ten of

Cups. Instead, the Nine of Cups is about sensual joy and satisfaction with the way things are. We can imagine this card coming to life and we watch as the man, grinning to himself as he thinks of everything in his life that is good, seats himself on his throne, folds his arms over his chest, looks around, and says, "All's right with the world."

In this card, every wish comes true, as it has done for the man in the image. But since we see so many cups that they can barely fit on the card, we are reminded that we should be careful what we wish for; sometimes it is better to count our blessings and see that everything we currently have is wonderful, rather than wishing for what we don't have. The smile on the man's face also symbolizes the earthier, more sensual joys of life, the things that bring humour to the world and make us laugh. Laughter is one of the most emotionally fulfilling acts that we can engage in, and—just as the man in the card does—it welcomes other people into its circle of warmth and brings them emotional fulfilment too. Here we see "the good life," and the joy of the moment.

Despite this card being found in the suit of emotion, the gold material cascading down the walls and onto the floor is reminiscent of liquid gold; it's as if wealth is pouring into the man's life, covering even his drab and mundane world in fulfilment. This can be any kind of wealth, not just material: emotional, spiritual, social, intellectual. It comes not necessarily from having everything or hoarding possessions, but rather from enjoying what you do have.

Revelation

There are few better cards to receive in a reading than the Nine of Cups. When it appears, the querent can be assured of satisfaction and happiness in their life. This does not necessarily indicate success, wealth, or fortune, but rather contentment with whatever it is they do have. The Nine of Cups indicates that the querent knows how to be happy—an unusual thing in the modern world. It reminds them that happiness is a choice and a state of being, rather than a possession.

Generally the Nine of Cups reminds the querent that they should count their blessings, since they have so much in their life to be happy about. It also advises them to look on the positive side and affirm their happiness on a daily basis. If it appears in a relationship reading, it is extremely fortuitous, as it suggests that the relationship is a happy, joyful, and contented one, in which the partners do not look elsewhere or to each other's negative traits, but instead share happiness together. Socially, it suggests the querent extending their satisfaction and happiness to friends and family, playing the host or welcoming people into their circle. It might also indicate helping cheer up another person.

In a work, career, or money context, this card does not necessarily point to great riches or the perfect position in a high-flying company, but rather it points to a genuine love of the work that the querent does. They are happy in their current position and satisfied with the work they have been undertaking. Their happiness is also infectious, and will get them noticed by others who will be inspired by their example.

The Nine of Cups brings with it delight in the senses and indulgence in some of life's finest pleasures. It advises the querent to enjoy these things rather than feeling guilty about them or viewing them with contempt, but most importantly to welcome others to enjoy them as well. There is an extremely social nature to this card that points to fun and jollity, laughter and humour in the situation, and often asks the querent to simply lighten up and stop taking life so seriously. The querent's situation would be more easily solved or responded to if they laughed at it a little.

This card is sometimes called the Wish Card. As such, it often appears in a reading to suggest that whatever the querent wishes for will come to pass— particularly if it is accompanied by the Star. Of course, the querent must be careful what they wish for: this card also asks them to consider what it is that would make them truly satisfied, rather than wishing for what they think they want.

Reversed, the Nine of Cups points to an overindulgence in life's sensual pleasures, such as eating too much or drinking too much; it indicates hedonism and the querent ignoring more pressing concerns by immersing themselves in activities that highlight fun but push reality away. Sometimes it suggests happiness and satisfaction as it would upright, but further suggests that the querent has a tendency to be too pleased with themselves and become smug, gloating and bragging rather than simply enjoying.

Keywords

Happiness, satisfaction, contentment, jollity, laughter, fun, welcome, host, wishes, delight, sensual pleasures, indulgence, overindulgence, smugness.

Ten of Cups, the Happily Ever After

"Once upon a time, there was a boy, the youngest of three sons. He went out into the world to find himself, and undertook many tasks and adventures on a quest for understanding and love. Isn't that the real reason for any quest, any adventure? If we know ourselves, everything else will follow. If we have run the full gamut of all human emotion, felt joy and happiness, grief and sadness, celebration and the call to turn inward, understood what it is to win and what it is to lose, then all the joys in life are made sweeter and all the failures are tempered by perspective. To understand truly is not to know the world out there, but to know the world in here, within oneself.

After many experiences, the young man found a reflection of his quest for understanding in another: a girl, the youngest of three daughters, who sought peace, happiness, and fulfilment. In each other they found love. Together they made the world brighter, the sorrows gentler, and the nights warmer. They faced many a test and obstacle, and each time they proved their honour, virtue, and love. They discovered that existence was both pure joy and pure sorrow, but that it was the celebration and acceptance of all that made them true lovers of the world.

Eventually, they were married, and in time they became parents to twins, a boy and a girl, who looked just like them, who one day would grow up to feel the same desire to understand, the same urge to look out to the world for happiness, and who would also come to the same conclusion and complete their quest by looking within. This is the way of our world, the way it has always been and the way it will be until the end of time: true bliss can only be found in the love one has for oneself and others, beauty shared and beauty created.

And ... they lived happily ever after."

Mars in Pisces / Malkuth in water

Illumination

The tens of each suit represent the fullness of their energy. This does not necessarily mean that they represent the *best* of their suit, but rather the culmination of all the energies of the previous cards trickling down through the suit until they finally come to rest in the ten. The feminine suits, the cups and the pentacles, catch the energies of the previous cards in their suit very well, being shaped and designed for the purpose of containing or supporting things, whereas the wands and the swords fare worse, as discussed previously.

In the Ten of Cups, we have the proverbial cup of kindness receiving all the emotions, love, bliss, happiness, and fullness of the preceding cards, and from this full cup we can drink deeply of the best things in life. The Ten of Cups is the achievement of happiness within ourselves, joy within our situation, and the deep love of others. As such, we are presented with a joyful, celebratory family scene that we should all hope to experience one day.

The family members in the card image are all wearing similar colours, blues and whites. This shows that they have the same dreams and goals; they work together as a unit, toward the same dream, driven by the same joy. Together they are sharing a moment of pure bliss and celebration, and dancing, which is one of the most primal and most human expressions of happiness. When we are extremely happy, we are said to be "dancing for joy." We dance at weddings, parties, and celebrations; we dance in groups especially to feel a connection. When we dance, we are all connected by the beat of the music, and we often feel it in similar ways. When we dance together, we are individuals moving together to the rhythm of music that unites us, just as the family members in the card image are wearing similar colours and supporting each other in their dance.

As in the Ten of Pentacles, the Ten of Cups is an image of the family unit at its happiest, and the various ways in which family members can express this joy together. The man holds his wife's arm, supporting her while he steps forward, symbolic of the desire to step forward into life and the world in unity. While his gaze is turned outward, hers is turned inward, signifying the need for recognising opportunities for happiness on both an external and internal level. The children are wrapped up in their own world, with the boy skipping and the girl walking with her arms outstretched in much the same way you would see a little girl pretending to be a fairy princess. The children themselves are symbolic of simple, innocent, carefree joy and happiness, unfettered from attachment and negativity, and free from desire for ambition or goals. They are enjoying the moment, and indeed we might look at them and be reminded of the two children from the Six of Cups, who brought us the simplest of life's pleasures. Children only appear in the tarot in the happiest of cards.

Unlike the Ten of Pentacles, the family in the Ten of Cups is not surrounded by wealth and possessions. There is a simple, unassuming home in the background, but they are not situated within in like the family in the Ten of Pentacles, showing that their stability and joy is not due to their accumulated wealth but instead their accumulated love. This family could be in a one-bedroom hut and they would still be dancing and smiling. Here, they are found in a green, lush landscape, their home sheltered in a valley, with plenty of space for them to grow and feel free.

Above them, we see a rainbow shining down from the heavens, within which is a shower of nine golden, jewelled cups. The final cup is held jointly by the man and woman, and all the cups have an ethereal glow around them in a similar colour to that which the family wears. It's as though the energies of this entire suit, which began with the ace in pure love, divine light, and bliss, have travelled all the way through the cards of the cups suit, and now rest in the Ten of Cups, the energy at its fullest expression. The cup resting in the couples' hands shows that the family is already benefiting from the blessings of love and happiness, and that these blessings are created from an emotional connection. The nine cups raining down on them show they still have much more goodness coming to them.

Rainbows are a symbol that evokes beauty and happiness. In the Bible, the rainbow was the sign that God sent to Noah and his family after the Great Flood as a sign of God's promise to mankind and the relationship they share with him. Rainbows are produced when light is refracted while shining through a droplet of water, which is then reflected inside and refracted again when leaving it. Rainbows are symbolic of the light of the divine being reflected in our emotions and therefore in the love we have for others and the happiness we feel. The various colours of the rainbow also remind us of the variety of happiness we can feel, all the different ways in which our joy expresses itself, and all the possible sources of that joy.

There is nothing wrong in this scene. Things really couldn't get better. In the background, we can see that the sky is starting to change to the pink-red glow of sunset, indicating completion and conclusion. The curtains close on the suit of cups, and we are left with a feeling of fulfilment and contentment. All is right with the world.

Revelation

When the Ten of Cups appears in a reading, the querent has good reason to be pleased—this is one of the most positive cards in the deck. Generally this card indicates successful completion and conclusion, as well as all the resulting joy, happiness, and bliss. The Ten of Cups indicates that the querent can look forward to a very happy future indeed. Everything they ever wanted is coming to them, though not necessarily in a material sense: this card does not mean they will win the lottery or marry the next in line to the throne of England!

If in a present position in the reading, it suggests that they are at a happy and contented stage of their life or their relationship: emotionally fulfilled, creatively active, and inspired. If it appears in a reading concerning work or business, the querent will find matters proceeding smoothly and achieving great results, and they might also discover that friends and loved ones can help them with their venture, or be helped by it. If the querent is uncertain what they want to do or where they are going in life, the Ten of Cups simply asks them, "What is it that you love the most? What makes life worth living?" It suggests that following their heart will lead them to the place they need to be. It often suggests, in any situation, following one's heart rather than second-guessing themselves or overthinking a situation. It can also indicate a harmonious workplace, and a work team that is like a second family to the querent.

In a relationship reading, this card indicates that the querent is (or will be, depending on its position in the spread) in a relationship that is fulfilling, happy, and content, in which they and their partner share their feelings with each other openly and have many reasons to celebrate. If they are in an established, long-term relationship, the Ten of Cups can point to the possibility of marriage or engagement, or considerations toward starting a family, whether through birth or adoption. This is an idyllic state, not necessarily because everything is perfect, but because, even despite any imperfections, true love exists and supports the people in the relationship.

Often the Ten of Cups talks about the sharing of love, so it suggests that the querent may need to take steps toward sharing their bliss and love with the world. This may take the form of creative pursuits or charitable work with others, but whatever its form, it makes the querent happy and makes others happy in turn. If the querent is going through a difficult time at the moment, the Ten of Cups suggests that one of the best ways to get through it is to simply look on the bright side: they have many reasons to be happy, and they have people around them whom they can be happy with. This card can sometimes show up in a reading to indicate the querent's family, as well as the family they have chosen to surround themselves with: their close friendship group. It may be time to focus on relations with them, to spend more quality time with them, and to get involved.

Reversed, the Ten of Cups doesn't take on any really negative connotations;

it is such a wonderful card that it requires other negative cards surrounding it in a reading to support a negative interpretation of it reversed. If this is the case, then it suggests obstacles or people getting in the way of a happy family or relationship, quarrels within a relationship or other harmonious situation, or physical or emotional distance between loved ones., It may also indicate that although some situation has turned out well, it will not last for long.

Keywords

Happiness, bliss, joy, completion, fulfilment, family, love, marriage, children, harmony, love shared, completion, conclusion, peace.

CHAPTER 26

The Suit of Pentacles

Ace of Pentacles, the Seed in the Garden

"Throughout the ages men have slandered me, calling me base and low, accusing me of distraction and debasement. In the black earth beneath their feet they located hell, in the dark caves of the world they located fear, and in the fertile wombs of women they located the origin of sin. For I am the world, and the daughter of the world; I am the garden and the seed planted therein. I am the origin of sin, for I am the origin of all things, the container of the manifold manifestations of spirit into matter. I am the lowest because I receive everything, and the highest because I birth everything anew. I am in you and all around you; I am the means by which you perceive me. You need me because I am your means of survival, but you love me because with me you cultivate beauty. You will find me in raw material, in the first seeds planted in the earth, in the furrows behind the plough, and in the knitting together of the child in the womb. You will display me in pride as jewels upon your breast, coins in your hand, and all of life's finest comforts. But never forget, when you have attained all your worldly desires and you sit upon thrones of gold and precious metals, that even the greatest things in life had the humblest of beginnings: a spark of almost-nothing, waiting in the seed in the garden."

No astrological associations for the aces / Kether in earth

Illumination

In this ace, we find the "lowest" of the elemental suits and the four aces. Being the element of earth, it represents manifestation, taking into it all the forces of the other elements. Perhaps this is why it is the only ace that does not contain Yods, as the divine light has now found a final resting place and need not travel any farther. The world around us is a complex formula of a vast array of chemicals and elements. Thus, the Ace of Pentacles contains not only all the other elemental forces of the aces but also all the other cards of the tarot deck so far. Whilst it is thus the "lowest" of the aces, being closest to the everyday world, it is also the highest, because it is so fertile that it gives birth to the world anew. It can do this simply because it has received all the other energies so far: a greater and more varied input makes a greater and more varied output. The Ace of Pentacles is therefore not only the first card in the suit of the everyday world, but also a representation of the colourful balance between the world of spirit and the world of matter.

We see this balance symbolically represented in the card image by the reflection of the pentacle in the river at the bottom of the card. We find rivers appearing in the Tarot Illuminati not only to illustrate the powers of the element of water, and therefore our emotions and connection to the divine, but also to illustrate a transition of some kind, usually on a spiritual level. The physical world of the suit of pentacles is deeply entwined with our spiritual and emotional worlds; the physical world is the lens through which we perceive the spiritual world, and the spiritual world informs our relationship with the physical world. Our daily life provides us with experiences through which we can grow spiritually, and the spiritual world provides us with support and guidance to engage effectively with the material world. This is important to remember, as in the tarot such things are always connected, and we cannot view the suit of pentacles as "only" the material world. We are reminded of a phrase essential to spiritual work, exemplified by the Alchemist (who uses the pentacle as a tool equally with the sword, wand, and cup), "As above, so below."

The symbol of the pentacle that illustrates this suit has a long history. As a five-pointed star, it represents the five senses of touch, taste, smell, sight, and hearing that are our gateways to perceiving and experiencing the world around us. The pentacle represents the body of mankind in Renaissance art, an example of which is Leonardo da Vinci's *Vitruvian Man*, created in 1487. This drawing was a study of the proportions of the male human body, but it has come to symbolize the essential symmetry of the human body, the universe, and our physical world.

We also find the pentacle in nature, in the cross-section of an apple when cut perpendicular to its core; this is also the part of the apple that contains the seeds. This reminds us that the Ace of Pentacles is, like the apple, a fruit that contains seeds from which future fruit will grow. It is the container of potential and the possibility of growth. It cannot be said to represent the material world as money or resources, but rather as the potential for such things, or perhaps the raw materials that have the potential to become these things. Aleister Crowley writes of the pentacle as a magical tool:

> *"The Pentacle is merely the material to be worked upon, gathered together and harmonized but not yet in operation, the parts of the engine arranged for use, or even put together, but not yet set in motion."*[23]

This reminds us of the saying, "From tiny acorns, great oak trees grow." All the greatness of the world is found here in the Ace of Pentacles, but it is still nascent, still in seed form. It has a long way to go before it will become the material world we know, the world of money, resources, jobs, work, great structures and works of art, power based on riches, businesses, wonderful food and home comforts, health, wealth, and prosperity.

The pentacle in the card image bears an inscription of the Theban alphabet, also called the Witches' Alphabet. This first appeared in the writings of Johannes Trithemius in the sixteenth century, and is likely to have been a cipher script designed to hide written secrets from others. Like any cipher, it hides the secrets in plain sight: others can still see them, but not understand them. Similarly, the powers of the Ace of Pentacles are hidden in plain sight: the powers of generation, resources, and growth hidden in a place too often taken for granted—the everyday world.

The setting of this card is one of cultivated natural beauty: a lush, rich garden that is well cared for and boasts an amazing array of flowers and plants. The flowers are in full bloom, as this is the height of beauty and fertility, as well as art in nature. The fact that the garden is well cultivated and cared for reminds us that although the seeds have been planted in the Ace of Pentacles, we have nine more cards in this suit before we reach fruition, and a lot of hard work, nurturing, and care is required to bring about a fruitful harvest or a garden displaying such beauty as this. In this garden there is also a stone bridge crossing the river, reminding us that the power of this suit is to provide stability and support throughout life, as well as creating a manifest interface

---

23. Aleister Crowley, *Magick: Book 4: Part 2* (York Beach, ME: Red Wheel/Weiser, 1994), page 111.

through which we can interact with the nonmaterial world. As with the other Aces, we see golden energy forming around the elemental tool of this card, but instead of bursting out or spiralling upward, the energy of the Ace of Pentacles flows down and outward like a peacock's tail, hinting at the beauty and success that will follow as we progress through the rest of this suit.

Revelation

When the Ace of Pentacles appears in a reading, it is often a sign of great things to come, but it is also a reminder that whatever the querent has planned is only in its most nascent stages. The seeds have been planted, but now the real work begins. The querent must now put their energies toward cultivating the seed and helping it grow, before they can expect to see any results. This means that if the querent is asking about a specific endeavour, they should not expect completion or a conclusion any time soon; it is likely to be a long time coming and the querent must also, therefore, cultivate patience! This card also appears to remind them that a journey of a thousand miles begins with a single step; in other words, actions, even little ones, have great effect, even if at the time it does not seem so. But if every little action goes toward a greater goal, then it is useful. This card can further indicate resources that the querent has that are not yet useful; they too must first be cultivated, processed, or developed before they can be applied to the situation.

It may also signify some sort of new beginning or fresh opportunity in the querent's daily life, their mundane world—their family, their home, or their work. Sometimes it can point to health concerns with the querent's body, especially if accompanied by other cards that related to the physical body, such as the Queen of Pentacles.

If the querent is concerned about money or work, the Ace of Pentacles advises them that although results will not be immediate, money will come and work will be offered. It suggests that they have already planted the seeds of their success, even if they don't realize it. This card also advises the querent not to ignore the material or physical world, or view it as less important in some way than other parts of their life; it is essential for them, and supports them and helps them grow. Without it, everything else is their life would suffer.

If the Ace of Pentacles appears reversed in a reading, the querent may be having trouble knowing how to cultivate certain aspects of their lives, or perhaps they lack the patience to do so. It might also suggest that the querent has neglected to lay the foundations or plant the seeds for some venture, and is now expecting results regardless. They should be advised that such results will not be forthcoming: output without input is not possible in this situation. If accompanied by cards that suggest similar, the reversed Ace of Pentacles may also indicate matters of ill health or lack of the raw materials required to start a project.

Keywords

Seed, growth, cultivation, nascent, fertility, garden, raw materials, foundation, patience, the environment, body, health, material world, material force, future results.

Two of Pentacles, Learning the Dance of Change

"When the weight of the world is first gifted to you and you hold your life in your hands, when you first set your feet upon the shores of life, you will discover that the earth beneath you is not solid. What you thought was rock is instead shifting shingle. What you thought was fertile earth is quicksand. Let yourself fall into the lie of certainty, believing yourself capable of holding on to everything forever, and you will soon discover your failure. The tree that bends in the breeze does not break, for it is flexible and adaptable to the winds of change and to the stresses placed upon it by the movement of the world. I invite you, student of the world, to join me in the dance of change. It's a dance you'll soon become familiar with and, before long, you will be able to execute it with ease and grace. It is a simple two-step, nothing more than a gentle shift of weight, a tilting of the hands, a change of gaze to a new focus. Sometimes it feels like being borne upon the waves—up and down, over the rolling sea—and when you find yourself on dry land once more, upon solid, immovable rock, your legs will protest and wish they were once again back upon the shifting, changing world-ocean, doing the dance of change."

Jupiter in Capricorn / Chockmah in earth

Illumination

In the Ace of Pentacles, we saw the unified world of material concern, the seed planted in the garden, the foundations laid. In the Two of Pentacles, we find duality within the material world, since the twos of the tarot bring with them the concept that if we conceive of "one," we automatically conceive of "not one"—duality is always born from unity. With the masculine twos (wands and swords), we see duality taking the form of splitting and further extension; with the feminine twos (cups and pentacles), duality takes the form of reciprocation and harmony. The Two of Pentacles shows us one of the greatest facts of life: that change is a constant in the universe. Change and the process thereof drives the world onward, keeps the cogs turning and the clock ticking, and keeps our bodies alive. One of the first skills we must learn for survival in the material world is how to adapt to change and be flexible in the face of obstacles; often, standing firm and still will see you fall, but dancing in the shifting energies will allow you to move forward and evolve.

Here we have an image of a young man, dressed in the clothes of a scholar or apprentice, holding two golden pentacles, one in each hand. He seems to be dancing, and his eyes are looking to the sky as he purses his lips in a whistle. To accompany his song, the winds pick up and blow his clothes and hair around, while behind him two ships set sail on a turbulent, undulating sea. His youth and his appearance tell us that he is in the process of learning the energies of the suit of pentacles. His material world has expanded from a single focus to one that requires divided attention and energy, yet it is a challenge that he is taking on readily and with ease. It seems that he is effortlessly juggling the two golden pentacles in his hands, and both are roughly equal in size and weight, showing that he is giving equal attention to each one. Yet his gaze is directed away from the pentacles toward the sky, indicating that he also has the capacity to focus on other things besides the material world, despite the demands for his time and energy.

Like any new scholar or apprentice, our young man is starting to move from a place of certain foundation, in the ace of the suit, to a position of broadening horizons. He is starting to play around with the energies of the suit, the tenets of his school of thought, the methods and practices of his area of study, yet he has not fully settled on anything. In the card image, we can see that he holds the pentacles loosely, rather than gripping them tightly, and holds them out away from his body instead of clutched to him (compare this to the Four of Pentacles!). He does not wish to tie himself down to anything, but instead wishes to explore all the opportunities available to him. This is to his credit and will ensure his survival as he continues along his path, as the Two of Pentacles tells us that the only constant and certain thing in life is change. The tighter we hold on, and the more we try to believe and act like things will always remain the same, the more chance we have of falling and failing when the foundations beneath us begin to shift.

In this light, the young man in the card image dances. It is not a dance of celebration like the Three of Cups or Ten of Cups, but instead a carefree, wistful dance that shows his nonattachment. He is not so attached to his golden pentacles, which represent his current projects, goals, or possessions, that he cannot allow them to shift and change, yet he still has a grasp of them; this dance allows him to balance himself beneath the shifting weight of these discs. The dance is also representative of an inherent playfulness in the card, a simple appreciation of the fun to be had in the everyday world, and how much more fun things can be when we don't worry about the fact that they might change tomorrow. There is also a reminder in this card that often we learn more effectively hands-on, when we are having fun with the subject, and when we are passionate about it.

The ships in the background highlight the ability to shift and rebalance according to changes in situation and circumstance. The waves that they sail upon are not gentle ones, but rather they are choppy and swelling. Ships can sail upon such waves simply because they are buoyant, bobbing up and down, rocking from side to side, as the ocean pushes and pulls them. They are carried by tides and currents, and pushed and directed by winds. If the ship were not so adaptable in response to such ever-changing masters, it would be dashed to pieces or overcome by the waves. The Two of Pentacles is telling us to emulate the way the ships move upon the waves in order to more effectively act in the everyday world—in other words, to go with the flow.

The change and movement being shown in this card is different from that shown in Death or the Six of Swords. This is not the passing of the old to make way for the new; this is simply change in and of itself. This is the change that occurs all around us every millisecond. This is the change of cells in our body dying to be replaced by new ones; it is the change that occurs in our lungs when we breathe in air made up of certain components in certain amounts, and then breathe out air made up of different amounts of these components. It's the change of the procession of the constellations and the burning of gas that fuels our sun. This is expressed beautifully by the golden thread of energy that links the two pentacles our young man is juggling: the thread forms a lemniscate, better known as the infinity symbol, representative of infinity and the endless dance of change. This symbol tells us that nothing in the universe is ever truly destroyed, only changes its state. The young man holds this mystery in his hands and is dancing with it, moving to its rhythm and understanding it. With this understanding, he can approach any changes in his life from a flexible and adaptable perspective.

Revelation

The Two of Pentacles often appears for a querent who is juggling many different aspects of their life or many different projects at once, with their time and attention constantly divided. This card indicates that they are managing their responsibilities and projects with ease, since they are being flexible and adaptable. It might also signify being given more projects or deadlines to work on, which will allow the querent to demonstrate their ability to multitask and rise to a challenge.

Often the Two of Pentacles shows up for a querent who is a working parent, or who is working more than one job, or working part-time to fund further studies. If accompanied by cards of care and compassion, such as the Queen of Cups, the Queen of Pentacles, or the Six of Pentacles, it can point to one who is juggling the responsibilities of caring for a disabled or elderly family member, as well as all of life's usual demands. Often, single parents are signified by this card, or other single guardians or caretakers with responsibility for another person's life in addition to their own.

In questions pertaining to future events, the Two of Pentacles points to an uncertain outcome. It suggests that there are too many factors involved, or factors that will change too radically, to be able to pinpoint the probable outcome. As such, it also says that the only way the querent will be assured of success and a positive outcome is through remaining flexible and adaptable, and able to respond to change quickly. They will retain their balance better in times to come, not through standing still and firm, but through moving with the flow of change.

In a relationship reading, the Two of Pentacles points to one person in the relationship doing most of the work and putting in most of the effort, or the querent being in a relationship where they find themselves very busy and having to stretch themselves between the relationship and other areas of their life. If surrounded by cards that indicate other projects, goals, and responsibilities, the Two of Pentacles might suggest that the querent is too busy to keep up with the demands of a relationship, and may find that the relationship has problems because of this. In a social situation the result is the same: the querent experiences more demands than he or she has time to satisfy.

At times this card can indicate the juggling of resources and skills to get the best fit for a venture. Often it signifies the juggling of money, such as account-keeping and budgeting. Very occasionally it points to travel or a change of lifestyle.

Reversed, the Two of Pentacles indicates that the querent is going to find themselves in a position or place where the demands upon them are shifting, and they are struggling to keep up. The goalposts are being moved, their responsibilities are being changed, and they are so accustomed to the current way of doing things that they are finding it difficult to make the necessary shifts to accommodate the new parameters. It can also point to trouble with budgets, trouble multitasking in a very busy lifestyle, or a precarious balance that the querent is almost exhausting themselves to maintain simply for survival. It may also be telling them that they have taken on too much, they are too busy to do anything else, and other areas of their life are likely to suffer.

Keywords

Multitasking, change, shifting, juggling, busy, changing lifestyle, shifting demands, juggling resources, budgeting, everyday survival, flexibility, adaptability, flow, flux.

Three of Pentacles, the Work of the Master

"In the realm of manifestation there is no room for waste, no room for talents being squandered and skills lying dormant. The true craftsman understands the need for structure and the sturdy support of life's scaffolding to enable him to work efficiently and productively on that which drives him forward. Passion, unstructured and unused, is wasted energy: it spills from us like the fabric of a robe that has been made too large by the unskilled tailor who has no pattern to follow. When we have structure, we also have guidance by which we can measure our progress. The master of his craft does not see potential, he only sees actualities: potential is uncertain and stands a chance of coming to naught. The best craftsman knows his skill and efficiency and therefore knows precisely what will become of it. My friend, let me tell you this: never try and tell a craftsman

what to do. It is his field of expertise, his speciality, but most importantly it is his passion made manifest. You will not be able to tell him how to work, yet you may add your passion to his; when more than one master unite toward a single goal, they are unstoppable, and their collective results will be astounding. Imagine the painter, the architect, and the builder working together, and what they will build as a result of their collaboration. Now imagine this: that the painter is your spirit, the architect is your mind, and the builder is your body. What wonders can you create when these three craftsmen work together within you? The true Work of the Master, therefore, is not to know everything about a given subject or skill, but to invest every part of himself into it—mind, body and spirit—that he might also become perfected."

Mars in Capricorn / Binah in earth

Illumination

After our brief foray into the balancing act of the Two of Pentacles, the three contributes necessary stability and solid footing—but it isn't so grounded that it keeps us from moving forward. All the threes have a sense of "doing" rather than "being," along with the first signs of manifestation and realization. The threes extend their exuberant energy outward into the world and toward others, so in the suit of pentacles this represents the act of structuring one's passion and skill into productive work.

Here in the suit of the material world in which we act and work, we see the finishing touches being put to a great work that is being undertaken. This is the work of the master craftsman. The Three of Pentacles is closely linked with the Eight of Pentacles, in which we see another craftsman at work. Whereas in the eight we see a craftsman working toward perfection through repetition and apprenticeship, through shaping and hammering, in the three we have a craftsman who represents the pinnacle of his craft, the height of his skill, putting his passion to work.

In the card image, we see a craftsman working on the embellishments for a building. He is pointing with one hand to a scroll that seems to contain instructions or a plan for his work, and with the other hand he points to the work itself. He appears to be working on an archway of gold filigree, with three golden pentacles set into it. These pentacles are repeated in the scroll. He kneels on a scaffold, and beneath the archway we can see more scaffolding. Two other figures feature in the card: one is a Tibetan monk wearing traditional yellow-orange robes and hat, and the other is a wealthy woman in delicate silk clothing.

It seems as though the craftsman has been hired for his skill and reputation to work for a religious or artistic institution, and is following a carefully delineated plan for the finished product. This would, theoretically, put him in a position of servitude beneath the monk and the woman, yet in the card image we can see that he is in the process of explaining something to the pair, while they listen. The woman's face seems to be acknowledging understanding or realization while the monk listens intently, trusting the craftsman to know his work. Perhaps the craftsman is making suggestions for changes, or simply demonstrating his progress. Either way, the traditional power structure is reversed, as the wise and great listen to the working man. The woman in the image wears six small golden pentacles as adornments in her hair, linking her to the acts of philanthropy in the Six of Pentacles and suggesting that she is the financial patron of the work being undertaken.

The very act of work being shown in this card represents putting skills, talents, and passions into practice and making them useful in the real world. There is an essential nature of productivity to the Three of Pentacles, in which we see work paying off and forming definite results, as well as gaining the attention of others. Yet the scaffolding in the card, and the fact that two patrons overlook the work, suggest that this card isn't just about any kind of work, or any means of using one's talents; this is skill, talent, and passion found within a structured framework or system, and those talents are being used to benefit the system. It suggests that when we direct our passion into a structured format, we achieve far more. The work that the craftsman is undertaking has the potential to become the work that he is remembered for, or the work that defines his style. It also reminds us that a *magnum opus* is rarely achieved through working on it haphazardly, and those who are truly productive understand how to structure their time and efforts most effectively.

The presence of three very different kinds of people in the card is highly symbolic. Firstly, they represent Mind, Body, and Spirit, with the craftsman as the body and the act of doing, the monk spirit and the act of being, and the woman mind and the act of thinking. This reminds us that in order to perform our greatest works, we must apply our whole self toward it—our action, our spirit, and our thoughts. These three people also have alchemical associations as the three prime elements used during the alchemical process to produce the Philosopher's Stone or the Great Work. These are Sulfur, indicated by the colour red in the clothing of the monk, which represents the omnipresent spirit of life; Mercury, indicated by the colour white in the woman's clothing, which represents the flow between heaven and earth; and Salt, the base matter itself, represented by the ordinary-looking craftsman. When these three prime alchemical elements are united in various processes, the Great Work of the alchemist is achieved, just as the great work of the craftsman is completed.

Revelation

In a reading, the Three of Pentacles often points to the work that the querent is currently undertaking, a project they are in the middle of, or any other ways in which they apply and use their skills and talents. If they are working on something specific, they can be assured that with this card in their reading, great things will come once the project is completed. It also suggests that what they are doing isn't just a job to pay the bills, but rather work that they love doing and that they want to make something of. It can signify any big projects the querent has at this time— for instance, a book they are writing, a symphony they are composing, a web design company they are starting up, or a tree house they are building for their children. Most importantly, the Three of Pentacles assures the querent that they have sufficient skill, talent, and knowledge to complete the work to a very high standard.

Sometimes this card appears in a reading to indicate praise and acclaim from others for the querent's work. They may find an increased reputation in their field coming soon, as well as more people hiring them for their work. Their project will find its target out in the world, and those people will be very interested. They may find offers of work coming to them, or increased projects in their current line of work. If this card is accompanied by the Eight of Pentacles and any cards suggesting business, such as the Two of Wands and the Three of Wands, then it points to starting up a business based on the querent's passion and talent.

If the querent is seeking advice, the Three of Pentacles tells them that they must structure their lives or their project more carefully in order to make the most of it, or put their talents to more effective use. This card suggests that they will only be able to truly engage with their passion if they find a way to work with it in a structured manner. It also recommends that the best way to approach anything is to do so with their body, mind, and spirit united to their purpose: no half measures will do for this card. It also says that the querent has reached a certain level of mastery in their particular field, with aptitude and skill that can serve as an example to others.

In a relationship reading, the Three of Pentacles can point to a relationship that has become firm in structure and foundation, but not in a negative fashion; the structure enables both partners to work toward their independent goals, while also remaining close emotionally. It may indicate that the romantic partners are working partners as well, or working together on a project.

Reversed, the Three of Pentacles suggests that the querent stands a risk of losing their work or not doing their talent justice through lack of structure. They may find structure difficult to deal with or feel that it stifles them, when in fact it is their ally in this situation. This card reversed can also indicate the querent finishing a project or piece of work and not receiving the positive feedback that they or the finished project deserves.

Keywords
Craft, talent, skill, work, structure, hiring, job, mastery, adept, aptitude, great work, magnum opus, projects, productivity.

Four of Pentacles, the Ownership of Power

"What better feeling is there in the world than being able to count your blessings? To know what you have because you can see it, hold, it, taste it, smell it... Not because you want to use it or spend it, or even enjoy it for what it can bring you, but because it's yours and nobody else's. You hold the power and it's not just any power but your *power. It is not for giving away! Give it away, put it toward some notion or fancy, and you will weaken yourself and show that weakness to others. Do not let them take you for a fool, nor for one who can be manipulated, used, or walked over. You are the strength and you are the power, and your proof lies in what you have to show for them. Look to your resources, look to what you have built, and it shall be your shield and armour against all who would see you fall. You and I are the same in this: we know that only through our strength and defences will we survive. Own your power, fellow castle-builder, and you shall truly be a ruler of your world."*

The Sun in Capricorn / Chesed in earth

Illumination

There couldn't be a more natural place for the number four to be expressed than in pentacles, the suit of the material world, money, and work. The fours are all cards of grounding and manifestation in some way, or of stillness and stagnation if taken to excess. Like the four walls of a house, the four corners of the Earth, and the four elements, they provide a stable foundation in their respective suit. In pentacles we see the foundation becoming a well-built and stable castle, within which we can store and grow our own power and strength. There are few cards in the tarot that are as earthy and grounded as this one.

In the card image, we see a richly dressed man, presumably a lord or a king, seated upon the parapets of a castle. Behind him are a vast number of walls and grand buildings, all built upon hills and mountains, and he clutches four golden pentacles to him: two beneath his feet, one at his chest, and one upon his head as a crown. This man does not smile, and has his back turned to the other buildings. It is clear that he has acquired a vast amount of worldly wealth, indicated by the pentacles, his fur coat, and his flowing robes. This shows us that he has money as a firm foundation beneath him, but also that he may use his wealth as a form of armour or defence from others, indicated by the pentacle being held close to his chest, or that the issue of money and finances is close to his heart. The pentacle upon his crown tells us that his thoughts are geared toward economics, finances, and the material world. This reminds us that the fours are about manifestation; here we have all the hard work and energy from the previous pentacles cards paying off and becoming real and accessible in the form of wealth and resources of all kinds. However, this card isn't just about wealth: it is also about power. The man in the card is clearly in a position of power, since he is seated in a high place, and his feet being positioned firmly on the two pentacles on the ground shows his control of his domain.

The man's stillness is telling. He has reached the point of manifestation, where his power and material wealth have reached an apex, but instead of showing us how he uses these things, we see him seated, taking no action and not moving anywhere. He is not moving backward, losing anything, but he is also not moving forward. He is at a point where he has his personal power and worldly power completely stored up, yet it doesn't look like he wants to use it for anything. This is unsurprising when we consider the nature of the fours and how they might manifest in this suit. Here we find that although there is immense power, stability, and manifestation, there is also a lack of desire to move or to change. This is a reminder as to why we need the fives in the tarot, despite the fact that they are all somewhat unpleasant: their disruption provides the catalyst to kick the stagnating fours out of their habitual ways and get them moving again, doing something with the results of the earlier, purer cards in their suit. As we will see, after the Five of Pentacles comes the six, in which the money, power, and resources start to flow out into the world, rather than being stored up.

It appears as though our lord or king in the card has built up his power for power's sake only, not to use it for anything tangible. Yet he has the potential to do so: let us not forget the immense potential contained within the element of earth and therefore the earthy number four. It is in the earth that we plant seeds and from the earth that we harvest our crops. Therefore the Four of Pentacles shows us a very specific point in the rise and growth of power in any form: this is the point at which the power reaches its peak and is still in a state of potential, waiting to be used toward a purpose.

There is also an element of this card that speaks of defence: the walls in the image are well-built, and all the buildings are situated on easily defendable ground. Although the worldly power they represent is easy to see and obvious, it would be difficult to take that power away. The castle is so strong that those attempting to attack it or capture it for themselves would inevitably fail.

Revelation

In a reading, the Four of Pentacles often indicates the successful manifestation of power, resources, and money in the querent's life, usually based on their previous work. It can point to a conservative and well-informed approach to their finances. The querent indicated by the Four of Pentacles will rarely be caught unawares by a sudden, unexpected expenditure and they are resourceful when it comes to money: they always get a bargain, are frugal, plan carefully for expenses, maximize the use of their money, and keep a savings account. It may also indicate that the querent is in a situation where they must keep to a tight budget.

Often the Four of Pentacles appears in a reading to advise the querent that they need to save money or start storing resources of some kind. They must take extreme care with their finances and make sure they can account for everything. This may be because they are currently not using their resources to their best ability. If the querent currently has a decision to make concerning spending, they are advised to think carefully about the matter before taking any action. Planning and organization will safeguard their resources.

The Four of Pentacles leaves no room for frivolity. It suggests that the querent may be so concerned with safeguarding their money that they are denying themselves things they probably deserve, like a nice holiday, eating out once in a while, or treating themselves to a new book. Others in their life might see them as a miser or skinflint. This card can also point to any stores of resources or bank accounts that the querent has, and can suggest that tapping those resources is the answer or solution to a current problem.

Sometimes this card indicates that money is at the heart of the matter that the reading is about. Money is the driving force, yet it is also the foundation that provides the querent with a stable point from which they can act. At times, the Four of Pentacles tells the querent that they can defend themselves or their position, or save something in the situation, with the correct application of money. Often this card raises issues of the querent's power: how they have gained it, how they maintain it, and what they do with it. It asks the question, "Where does your power lie?"

If the Four of Pentacles appears in a relationship reading, it can indicate that the relationship has a strong and firm foundation beneath it, or that it has shared wealth and resources. The relationship is strong, yet one or both partners may feel that it is too constricting, or perhaps there is a possessiveness issue between them. Certainly the querent does not want to change anything about the relationship, though this may not be due to the relationship's perfection, but rather a fear of loss. In a work or business reading, the Four of Pentacles is a good sign, indicating solid results and dependable work. Generally speaking, this card points to all forms of strong foundations, stores of resources, and stability rather than change.

The Four of Pentacles reversed often points to issues in a relationship concerning jealousy and possessiveness; it also brings a miserly tone to the reading. The querent is hoarding their money or resources, and keeping it from others with whom they should otherwise share it. This might also include their emotions and affection, as well as their time or energy. They may be on the defensive at this time and actively trying to keep people out of their lives, or trying to keep themselves uninvolved in a situation. This card reversed also indicates that the querent is putting up barriers and obstacles between themselves and their goal, or the fullest completion of their goal. They are afraid of loss and taking a risk, therefore instead of allowing themselves to change and move forward, they would rather stagnate and feel safe.

Keywords

Stability, results, manifestation, grounding, earth, defence, walls, power, hoarding, material wealth, kingdom, miser, resources, property, money, ownership, possession.

Five of Pentacles, the Outcast

"Have you ever wanted anything so much that you thought you would die without it? I don't mean figuratively, I mean actually... Have you ever known hunger, thirst, or what it is to sleep outside in the cold? Do you understand how it doesn't just break you physically, but also emotionally and spiritually? How you cannot do anything but worry and despair, and sooner or later you begin to convince yourself that this is the way things will always be. You're no good, you tell yourself, nobody wants you around, it might be better if you just disappeared ... at least then you wouldn't be a burden to anybody.

I know this attitude. I know it like the cold feeling that clings to your limbs and settles deep in your gut when you hear another refusal of help, another little piece of hope breaking off and falling away, like another light in the darkness flickering out. And what can I tell you? That things will get better? To look on the bright side? Tell that to the homeless man begging in the street next time you pass him and he asks you for a few coins. Tell it to the mother and child kicked out of their home with nowhere to go, when the sun starts to set and the chill air wraps around them. Tell it to those that your community has failed, and tell it to those that you have pushed out into the cold. No man is an island. Remember that, when you are in a position to help, and pray that you never have to remember it when you are the one asking for help. Yet all things change and shift beneath our feet, and you can never guarantee a fortune ... You can never guarantee the future."

Mercury in Taurus / Geburah in earth

Illumination

In the suit of pentacles, which represents our funds, our resources, our career or job, our health, and our everyday life, the energies of the fives do not sit well.

In fact, they do not sit at all—they do not stay or rest or find stability. In the Four of Pentacles, we saw stability taken to an extreme, with the earthiness and groundedness of the fours overemphasizing the stillness of the suit of pentacles, making for the hoarding of money and stagnation of resources through fear of loss. The five in this suit, as with the other fives, brings a solution to this stagnation, but through extreme measures: the imbalance expressed in these cards destroys economic stability, health, productivity, and stored resources. We can imagine that the grain stored up and guarded so jealously in the Four of Pentacles has been infiltrated by mice and they are making quick work of it. So here we are in the Five of Pentacles: out in the cold, outcast, injured, unemployed, and in need of aid.

The card image is poignant and evocative. The scene is set during a cold winter's night, when the snow is falling heavily and ice covers the ground. Two beggars wrap their ragged clothing tightly around themselves to try and keep out the cold. One is tall and thin, and wears the conical hat of a rural Chinese field worker. The other is old and hunched almost double, his arms resting heavily on a pair of crutches, obviously nursing his injured legs. Tattered rags or bandages trail behind him, and even his beard is frozen with ice. Behind them, a long set of stone steps ascends to a brightly lit pagoda that looks warm and inviting. Yet the beggars are walking away from it, toward a dense forest, and looking out of the card at us.

The snowy winter weather tells us immediately that this is a card of being left out in the cold, isolated, and in an extreme situation that threatens your material world and physical health. The icy ground underfoot makes for precarious and treacherous movement, showing that even from this low point, the figures in the card are in danger of becoming more injured and impoverished. It also reminds us of the instability of this card: at any point, material wealth and health can disappear from beneath you, and your firm foundations be pulled from under your feet.

It is unclear whether the beggars are moving away from the brightly lit pagoda without noticing its warm, inviting light, or if they have been turned away after having asked for help. Either situation is possible, however, the positioning of the tall man seems to suggest the latter. Perhaps the beggars had been wandering through the snowy streets looking for shelter, warmth, and a hot meal, when they came upon the welcoming-looking pagoda and struggled up the steps to the doors. It is sad to think that upon knocking and requesting help, they were turned away and thrown back onto the street for being poor and unwashed. This pagoda represents a society that has failed its most vulnerable members, as well as the spiritual community that surrounds them. It is probably a religious building, so the beggars being situated outside it symbolizes spiritual isolation. However, if we look at this card from the perspective of the beggars walking past the pagoda without seeing it, then it represents a failure to ask for help when it is needed, as well as a failure to see solutions to a problem.

The presence of a religious building filled with light in a scene of material lack tells us that when we have fallen on hard times, we are offered an opportunity to find comfort and solace in the nonmaterial world. The two beggars are shown together, and quite closely so, indicating some sort of bond between them; despite the lack of wealth and resources, they can turn to each other in friendship (or kinship; perhaps they are father and son) and appreciate each other's company. Often, times of hardship show in sharp relief what we have outside of material wealth.

With the Five of Pentacles comes not only the lack of material stability, but also the accompanying worry. Worry is a self-destructive behaviour that perpetuates the cycle of lack and loss. It keeps us firmly in the past or in the future, and never in the present: we rarely worry about this moment, right now; we only ever worry about something that has happened in the past or what may or may not happen in the future. As such, worry doesn't allow us to act properly in the present to take action. There are some things in life that can make us rich, and some things that keep us poor: worry does the latter.

When looking at the beggars in the card image, we are not just reminded of monetary poverty, but of any kind of poverty. Since the suit of pentacles concerns itself with our everyday world, it can also relate to any aspect of our life. Here we see poverty of wisdom, poverty of experience, poverty of friendship or love. Most importantly, we see poverty of options, for where do the beggars have to go? What can they do in their situation besides continue to ask for help? One of the blessings of this card coming after the Four of Pentacles is that the defensive walls we build around ourselves to keep people out have now been destroyed, and we are reminded of the importance of the support networks in our lives—our friends, family, community, or workplace. No person is an island, as indicated by the fact that we see two beggars here and not a lone one, and we must know when and how to be helped and to give help in return.

Revelation

The Five of Pentacles is an unhappy card to receive in a reading. It poverty, loneliness, and lack in the querent's life, as well as the potential for a radical shift in their material stability. It might suggest that the querent is at risk of losing their job, having to take a pay cut, or moving to a different job or career—although, if accompanied by positive cards, it suggests that the move will be good for them, even if the pay cut is difficult to adjust to. It can also point toward the querent losing money in some way, perhaps through a loss in stocks and shares, through poor investments, or through gambling.

If accompanied by cards that indicate the home, such as the Four of Wands, the Five of Pentacles can point to problems with the house, such as large repairs being needed or sudden damage being done to the property. It can also suggest instability in education or the system thereof, perhaps a lack of tuition or support from faculty, or through funding being lost for postgraduate research.

Sometimes the Five of Pentacles can indicate feelings of isolation in the querent's life, as though they are out in the cold and on the fringes of their community, family, or friendship group. This may have some truth to it: they may have undergone some experience that forced them away and out; however, it may also just be feelings caused through misinterpretation of people and events. Yet, once the querent starts to feel isolated, they will begin to act isolated, compounding their problem. Often, the Five of Pentacles brings with it emotional isolation: two people trapped in a bad situation together, both of whom want to get out, but neither of whom will take the action to improve things.

In matters of projects and plans for the future, the Five of Pentacles warns the querent that they lack the necessary resources and the required strong foundation to bring success to their venture. It may also point to a lack of productivity for some reason, or a waste of the resources the querent does have, perhaps even a misplacement or overestimation of them. Occasionally this card indicates the querent asking for help from others and being turned away: the request for a bank loan or small business subsidy turned down, funding cut, request for extra time to complete a project refused, or a request for help from friends ignored.

Since the suit of pentacles also deals with the body and health, the five of this suit can often point to health issues and problems with the body. It suggests that the querent's health is suffering, possibly due to money concerns or insecurity, and it is going to continue to get worse as time goes on unless the querent takes better care of themselves. This is a card of neglect of all kinds; the querent may be guilty of neglecting their health and diet, or overworking themselves and neglecting to take enough rest and refuelling time. It may also point to a lack of self-worth in the querent, creating a vicious cycle of self-neglect and isolation.

Reversed, the Five of Pentacles sees the querent in the process of overcoming financial instability and beginning to get back on their feet. They are working toward regaining their security, slowly building back up to where they were before. The effects of this card are still around, but they are not insurmountable, and the querent is facing the future with more hope than they may have done recently. On a less positive note, sometimes the Five of Pentacles reversed suggests that the querent has too much pride to ask for help, despite the fact that they need it.

Keywords
Financial insecurity, instability, loss, hardship, lack of resources, refusal of help, poverty, homelessness, isolation, outcast, health problems, worry, waste of resources, neglect, being out in the cold.

Six of Pentacles, the Success of the Philanthropist

"There is a careful balance in the world of men that must be held by those who know how. It is not a balance of equality, for no man is created equally, nor does he live equally, but rather a balance of giving where it is needed, receiving when it is given, and allowing one's resources and skills to flow where they are most needed. Do you think that I would, at this time of my life, rather be spending my money on more things to clutter up my home and my heart? No, that is for those that still do not understand that by owning such great things they are leading themselves to imbalance. What use is a beautiful house with acres of land if you are short of the money you need to eat? What benefit do all the jewels and fine art pieces give you if you do not have access to the financial resources that they represent? No, my fortune was never made for investment or to give me a symbol of wealth: it was made to benefit the world. Money is a strange creature.

We forget that it came from the earth, once upon a time, when it was still ore and unworked, and it passed on to the hands of men who worked it, people who worked for it … then where should it most rightly go at the end of its journey? Back to the people. One of the most beautiful things about our monetary system is that it is made to encourage and facilitate the flow of resources and energy between people. We work to earn money: this means that we exchange our time, energy and skills for coins that are symbolic of worth. We then exchange these symbols of worth for items of inherent worth, and thus our free time, free energy, and skills become, as if by magic, food and drink, a roof over our heads, means of entertainment, and funding for all our great adventures and endeavours. But money is not an end in itself. Its greatest purpose is to allow us to more freely exchange our skills and talents to build a better world.

So, I hear you are a seeker of such endeavours and ventures, and that you wish to seek aid for your future plans. Do not be ashamed in the asking; such great things are rarely funded by one person alone. It is my privilege to offer you, through my philanthropy, a means to an end. Ask and you shall receive."

The Moon in Taurus / Tiphereth in earth

Illumination

Things were starting to look bleak as we travelled through the Four of Pentacles and the Five of Pentacles. In the four we saw the hoarding of resources and a miserly perspective on the world, and the five brought us poverty, lack of resources, and isolation. The beggars in that card were not receiving the help they needed for their survival. However, here in the Six of Pentacles the request for aid is responded to, and the resources that were once stagnant or lost have been returned to a more harmonious, accessible state.

All the sixes of the tarot are generally pleasant. Like the Lovers card, which is numbered VI and represents the union of two forces toward a single purpose, they bring with them a harmonious energy and a reinstatement of balance after the instability and destruction of the fives. They are also "double threes," and the threes of the tarot all bear some form of manifestation energy, as well as being focused on the skills and talents we possess. As such, the Six of Pentacles brings harmony, rebalancing, and a gentle, flowing stability to the material world and our everyday lives. The sixes also bear the energy of love and inner light that shines out into the world, so the Six of Pentacles sees resources flowing out into the world as a means of expressing our inner light.

In the card image, we see an opulently dressed man, wearing the clothes of an accountant, holding in his left hand a set of golden scales suspended from a pentacle. These scales are currently empty, yet balanced, and from his right hand he gently lets coins fall into the cupped hands of a well-dressed young woman. In tarot symbolism, the left hand is often the receptive hand, receiving things or energy from the universe, and the right hand is the hand that acts and gives energy out into the universe. This positioning of the hands in the card shows us that the accountant has already received all the finances and resources, and is now letting them flow through him to others that need them. The smile on his face suggests that he is happy doing so, and his age shows his experience and wisdom. This reminds us that the act of giving to others comes from a place of wisdom, love, and life experience. His joy in the simple act of giving is also poignant, telling us that often we get greater joy from giving gifts to others than from receiving them ourselves.

The golden dragons emblazoned upon the man's clothing are a symbol of wealth and authority, and the fact that he is standing while the two younger people kneel before him suggests that he is in a position of power. As we saw in the Six of Wands, when we are in such a position it often, conversely, puts us in a position to serve others and to demonstrate duty and responsibility toward them. In the Six of Pentacles, this duty is to care for the financial well-being of others, and to ensure that resources are shared amongst those who need them.

We can see that the money in this card, representative of all our resources and our financial situation, is flowing rather than stuck or still. This represents resources that are accessible and easy to use, rather than money invested in property and equity that cannot be accessed for immediate use. The golden scales in the card image symbolize balance and therefore the rebalancing and harmony of the sixes, but they also bear the quality of judgment and discrimination, as well as the process of weighing things up, holding things in balance, and maintaining justice as well as executing it. These scales can also be found in the Justice card, in which they represent a careful balance being maintained through necessary adjustments. The young man and woman at the accountant's feet have been judged worthy to receive aid from him, and now he is acting upon his decision.

The lanterns lighting the scene are representative, as in the Hermit card, of an inner light that is being shone outwardly to the world so that others might be guided and aided by it. In a way, the accountant of the Six of Pentacles is a more material, mundane version of the Hermit, with a wealth and store of wisdom and experience, as well as a more human version of Justice. If the Justice card is concerned with the concept of universal balance, then the Six of Pentacles is concerned with human justice and balance in the material world. It is nice to imagine that the older man in the card image is a wealthy philanthropist or humanitarian, choosing to invest his worldly riches in the arts and sciences, and through gifts and charity. Perhaps the young man and woman are involved in charity work or the arts and have sought his patronage for future endeavours; certainly the woman looks like she may be an actress or a dancer, maybe even a geisha, and the young man could easily be her accompanying musician. They don't appear to be beggars who are asking for the money for survival, but they also are not rich enough to fund their endeavours and projects on a solo basis. Such funding and philanthropy would usually be undertaken as part of a contractual agreement between the older man and the younger people in the card—an understanding of what they would do with the money and what would be expected of them—resulting in a happy balance and mutual success.

Revelation

The Six of Pentacles in a tarot reading brings balance and harmony, love and stability. If it is accompanied by any other of the sixes (or the Lovers), the querent can be assured that great success and happiness is coming their way. If the querent has been undergoing a time of difficulty or imbalance, then the Six of Pentacles indicates that this will soon be righted, balanced restored, peace bought to the situation, and good results come from it.

If the card appears in a reading about an endeavour the querent has been undertaking or is considering for the future, it signifies great success and work that pays off with concrete results. Everything will run smoothly and be most satisfactory, with the querent being in a very strong position at the end of it. Often the Six of Pentacles suggests that the querent will need to ask for help from various areas or people to aid them in their endeavour; they might need to seek funding or financial help, not because they are in poverty (as in the Five of Pentacles) but rather because their goal requires more finances and resources than they, on their own, can provide.

Sometimes this card points to returns on the querent's efforts or investments. There is a strong suggestion that the querent will get their just rewards for their actions. This could manifest as hard work paying off soon (as opposed to the Seven of Pentacles, which sees hard work paying off over a long period of time), excellent exam results for a test the querent studied especially hard for, promotions at work for a job well done, or awards for their work in the community. However, if the Six of Pentacles appears with Justice, it can sometimes suggest court cases and legal matters between people, though it usually indicates a positive outcome for the querent.

The Six of Pentacles can sometimes show up in a reading to indicate a querent who works in a charity or for a humanitarian cause, or who often gives money to such causes. If it is accompanied by cards that indicate the querent is not in a position of power, however, such as the Five of Pentacles, Five of Cups, or Ten of Swords, then it indicates the querent being on the receiving end of charity or help. This card comes with the advice that the querent will receive help if they ask, whether it is financial help or support from family and friends in a time of difficulty. It can also indicate any form of social contract that the querent is involved in. Occasionally, and if surrounded by very lucky cards, such as the Star, the Sun, or the Wheel of Fortune, the Six of Pentacles can represent the querent receiving money unexpectedly.

Reversed, the Six of Pentacles retains its overall theme of reward, return, and balance, but indicates that the results will not be in the querent's favour. It may point out that the querent has not earned any reward, as their efforts were lacking or misdirected, or may simply suggest that they didn't put in enough work to ensure they would get any return for their effort. In a monetary reading, it may indicate that the querent will be in a position to give money to others, but that they should not expect anything in return.

Keywords

Success, return, reward, award, windfall, rebalance, philanthropy, humanitarian work, aid, charity, just rewards, gifts, social contracts.

Seven of Pentacles, the Waiting Game

"What better way to spend your time than in the beauty of your own garden, with the sun on your back and the cool earth beneath your feet? What could be more wonderful than finding yourself immersed in the diligent tending of your

crops and plants, paying attention to all their needs and stages of growth, and watching as they sprout from seed to bud to flower to fruit? Are we not similarly privileged if we can witness the growth of our lives from start to finish, at every step of the way? Pay close attention so that you do not miss any of the daily changes and movements. The real beauty is in the detail. Yes, the results may be a long time in coming but, oh, how sweet they are then! Do not spend your precious time worrying and bemoaning the lack of immediate results; be certain in the virtue and quality of your labour, be patient, and tread carefully. More haste, less speed, friend. It is not a race to the finish line. Here we are, in that peaceful, beautiful moment between first fruit and final harvest, watching with joy as our crops ripen in the sun, looking forward to the day we can taste them and enjoy them. This is a chance for reflection, to rest weary limbs and recuperate before the harvest. We are gestating now, safe in the womb of our own previous efforts, and all things will come in their own time."

Saturn in Taurus / Netzach in earth

Illumination

After the back-and-forth struggle between feast and famine found among the three preceding cards of this suit, we reach a card that is conversely one of changeability and movement, as well as manifestation and results. The sevens of the tarot bring with them the flux of their number, its fluidity and softening force, yet in the grounded and earthy suit of pentacles this results in a card of slow and steady movement, progress made step by careful step, and the patience to be able to move more slowly instead of rushing forward for an immediate reward.

The card image is a simple yet evocative one. We see a strong young man, dressed simply and practically, leaning gently on his hoe. He stands in a verdant garden featuring several archways of grapevines extending out behind him, and in the archway beneath which he stands we can see several golden pentacles accompanying bunches of full, succulent grapes. The young man is completely still, his gaze directed closely at the two pentacles nearest the ground. This tells us that he is concerned most with the immediate needs of his garden and the fruit he is growing; he has a down-to-earth perspective and realistic expectations of the results of his labour.

The garden as a symbol is first encountered in the Ace of Pentacles, in which we saw the seeds planted in the fertile earth of this suit. This suit is concerned primarily with the material world and our everyday life, and therefore the garden represents all of our physical reality, as well as any real-world results of our efforts and labours. The garden here is a project, venture, endeavour, or plan that was planted in nascent form in the ace; as the progression through the suit continued, it grew and began to bud and flower, and finally, in the Seven of Pentacles, to bear fruit. The young man, whose strong muscles tell us of the hard work and dedication he has already put into the garden, has spent a long time tending it, weeding it, fertilizing it, watering it, and watching it slowly blossom. Now he has seen the first fruits of his labour. However, not all the fruit has grown to full ripeness: the lower pentacles accompany either unripe bunches of grapes or smaller bunches, and in one case no cluster of grapes at all. Here we see the waiting game, the point between noticing the first hints of results and the ability to harvest and enjoy those results. We will not see the results being enjoyed until the Nine and Ten of Pentacles.

The agricultural tool that the man leans on is a hoe, one of the most ancient tools in archaeological record. It is used to move small amounts of soil, carefully, bit by bit. The way this tool is used reminds us of the slow progress and patient waiting game characteristic of the Seven of Pentacles: grand gestures mean nothing to it, but careful, diligent attention does. If we were to go about planting and tending our garden with a tool that could move soil faster and in greater quantity, but with less precision and attention to detail, we wouldn't be able to plant delicate seedlings and surround them gently with fertile soil, nor would we be able to remove the encroaching weeds without damaging our growing plants. The humble garden hoe is the most effective tool for tending the garden in the Seven of Pentacles.

We can see a few different types of grapes hanging from these vines: red grapes, black grapes, and green grapes. This showcases the multitude and variety of results promised by this card in the future, and the fecundity of the suit of pentacles in general. It reminds us that as long as we put in the hard work and effort, we will find our harvest is full and rewarding. Yet the results are still pending. The series of archways in the card image, each one going farther back to a stairway leading upward in the distance, shows us that there is still a way to go before the young gardener's harvest will be ready and ripe for picking. It also creates a womblike effect, with the gardener and his grapevines being in the womb still, gestating; beyond them we see the birth canal waiting and the eventual exit. This is the gestation period, the time for gathering strength before the final push of the harvest, but patience must be cultivated. To harvest too soon would be to have fruit that is undeveloped and bitter to the taste; to harvest too late would be to let the crop spoil; timing is key, and must be perfect.

This card brings to mind the sayings "More haste, less speed," and "Slow and steady wins the race." We are reminded of the fable of the hare and the tortoise that raced against each other, with the hare dashing off ahead and making good headway before deciding that since he was obviously going to win, he could afford to take a break and have a nap (after all, he was very tired!). Meanwhile, the tortoise, which had conserved its energy and took the entire racecourse at a steady pace, overtook the hare while he slept and reached the finish line first. The moral of the story is not only that slow and steady wins the race, but also that we must know how and when to expend our energy, how and when to conserve it, and especially how to recognize the perfect time to act.

Revelation

In a reading, the Seven of Pentacles generally indicates that good things are coming to the querent—but not just yet. Whilst they may begin to see hints of the results and the first small fruits of their labours, it will be a while yet before they can hold the full harvest in their hands.

Often, this card shows up in a reading to tell the querent that they need to develop patience in the current situation. In a relationship or social reading, it says that they should specifically develop patience with a particular person, and it might further suggest that the relationship or friendship in question will grow slowly and steadily over a long period of time, rather than being a fast-moving, all-consuming relationship. The Seven of Pentacles advises the querent that although this might not be the most romantic of outlooks, it provides great stability and certainty for a long-term relationship, and in the long run the relationship will bear many fruits for the couple to enjoy.

In a work or business-related reading, the Seven of Pentacles can signify investments or a new venture that will take a while to pay off and start earning back the money they originally cost the querent. They are reminded, however, that this venture will require a lot of hard work, time, energy, and effort from them in order to ensure it has the best start in life. This card often indicates some endeavour that will simply take a while, such as a long-term course of study, internship, or apprenticeship. In a similar fashion, it also indicates any project that will take immense amounts of hard work and time to fully flourish, like writing a book, creating a tarot deck, setting up a charity, or learning a new language. Generally, the Seven of Pentacles indicates all forms of delayed results, or completion that is held off for some reason.

As an advisory card, the Seven of Pentacles warns the querent that if they don't put in the necessary hard work, their results will be poor. They must be diligent and hard working, not shirking any responsibilities. They must not rush things or try and fast-track matters, since if they do, they will miss out on important foundational steps. They should take the long-term view in this situation rather than seeking immediate satisfaction, and they must pay close attention to details. The real magic is in the fine print, and the real transformation takes place at ground level.

Reversed, the Seven of Pentacles warns of a poor harvest and failure despite the efforts and hard work of the querent. It suggests that there may have been something missing in the past that has made success impossible in the present or future, like a missing step or a missing ingredient. It might also say that the querent has failed to lay down strong enough foundations or pay careful enough attention to their project, leaving it to its own devices instead of tending it regularly and checking its progress.

Keywords

Attention to detail, diligence, patience, delayed results, slow progress, care, tending, nurture, foundations, future harvest, hard work, effort, patience, waiting, gestation.

Eight of Pentacles,
in the Belly of the Blacksmith's Forge

"World-changing deeds, the conquering of new lands, and the obtaining of riches are not the only ways one can achieve greatness. Sometimes attaining perfection in your chosen field of expertise will make your name, although to others that field may be ignoble or lacking in glamour and grandeur. But if you dedicate your life to the devoted and demanding path of perfecting your chosen art, you are a true alchemist. When you undergo the rigours of reaching the height of your skill, you not only perfect your trade or your craft, but also your self. The finest

craftsman hones the strength of his arm, the steadiness of his mind, the skills of his hands, and in doing so hones the focus of his spirit. When I heat metal in my forge and hammer it while it is red-hot, then cool it and heat it again, over and over, until finally I have in my hands the shining example of my best work, I do the same to my soul. I put myself willingly into the belly of the forge, and let myself be heated and cooled, hammered out, and shaped in the fire. I am a work in progress, white-hot metal in my own hands to be melded. Though my muscles will scream in protest and the sweat pour down my back, I will not cease from my work, for it is not just work, but the Great Work, the road to perfection and the trial of fire that shapes the soul."

The Sun in Virgo / Hod in earth

Illumination

Numerologically, the eights of the tarot can be seen as "double fours," therefore double the strength that the fours provide, double the stability, and double the manifest qualities of their suit. Since the Eight of Pentacles is almost at the end of its suit, the conclusion of which is extremely positive, we can see that it represents approaching perfection, and the successful application of its energy in a real-world setting. What follows tells us just how successful this card will be: the Nine of Pentacles shows us gain and command of wealth, and the Ten of Pentacles shows us a wealthy, strong family in which fortune and prosperity aid everybody in the group.

The card image in the Eight of Pentacles shows us a blacksmith hard at work in his forge. Examples of his recent work hang from the rafters and rest against the stone upon which his anvil sits. He holds with implements a pot containing molten metal, which he carefully pours into a mould of a pentacle. His demeanour is attentive, focused, and careful, his muscles tense as he works. A fire burns behind him and about him we see a radiant glow. It is easy to imagine walking in on this scene and watching as he crafts his wares, completely engrossed in his task. He does not look out of the card at us but only at his work; if we tried to speak with him or engage with him, he would not reply or register our presence until he had finished his painstaking procedure.

Blacksmiths have a special and important role in history, which is also reflected in mythology. Historically speaking, blacksmiths created items of great practical application as well as beauty: agricultural tools, cooking utensils, fixtures, hardware, fencing, horseshoes, religious items, sculptures, and weapons. Blacksmiths and their products have been so important to the progress and growth of humankind that certain eras of history are referred to by the names of the metals that were most extensively worked in those periods, e.g. the Bronze Age, the Copper Age in certain parts of the world, and the Iron Age. (It must be noted that the dates for these ages are not global, but rather are different for each area of the world, as each culture discovered and used these techniques at different stages.) These were all preceded by the Stone Age, which was named for the material used most before any metals were worked. The ability to turn raw copper ore or iron ore into useable metal, which could then be fashioned into more durable tools and weapons, was a huge evolutionary leap forward for humankind. Our ability to use tools is often cited as one of the skills that sets us apart from other animals, so much so that when apes were observed using rudimentary tools, we were forced to rethink their capacity for abstract thought, planning, and application of skill, previously thought to be found only in humans.

In myth, there tends to be a blacksmith god or hero in nearly every pantheon of deities, reflecting the usefulness of this role to human societies. The Greeks had Hephaestus (the Roman equivalent was Vulcan) as the god of fire and smithing; he was lame because of an injury to his leg that would not heal, yet he was the husband of Aphrodite, the goddess of love and beauty. In some accounts, Hephaestus, who was also an inventor, crafted for himself supports so that he might walk. He also crafted items that were important to the other gods, including Hermes's winged helmet and sandals, Aphrodite's girdle, the armour of Achilles, Helios's chariot, and Eros's bow and arrows.

In Irish myth, the smith god is called Goibhniu, and in Welsh it is Gofannon, whose names both mean "smith." Both these gods were said to have magical abilities based on their skills in the forge. The ability to shape metal with fire into useful and beautiful objects is often given a magical, otherworldly connotation, and in later folk songs the blacksmith was often ascribed magical powers, particularly of shapeshifting, as if the shaping of metal corresponded directly to the shaping of the self. "The Two Magicians," a folk song from early nineteenth century England, speaks of a "coal-black smith" who desires a lady of higher stature and vows to deflower her, while the lady refuses and vows to retain her virginity. A chase ensues, with both of them shapeshifting into various animals and objects, until the lady finally shifts into a bed to hide from him in plain sight and the smith, seeing through her disguise, shifts into a bed cover and thus embraces her. This reminds us that the Eight of Pentacles is concerned with all forms of skill or talent being put to useful application, rather than just learned for their own sake.

The act of blacksmithing involves the heating and hammering or shaping of various metals with a range of tools (a hammer and anvil as bare minimum), and then the cooling and tempering of the working piece, over and over again until the smith is happy with the result. This act can be seen as a metaphor for our own evolution as individuals; the process of achieving perfection in a chosen skill is synonymous with perfecting an aspect of the self. Thus the Eight of Pentacles is a card of the perfectionist and the desire to achieve perfection, seeing the self and one's activities as works in progress, always with room for improvement. The fact that blacksmithing is a demanding task, requiring great strength, concentration, and perseverance, tells us that perfection must be worked for and strived for, and that we must be prepared to give it our all.

We can see in the card image that the pentacles the blacksmith has created and is currently creating are all the same, from the same mould. It is as if he is working on the same design over and over until he gets it just right; practice makes perfect. He is also working from a mould, which indicates he is incorporating what he has been taught by another; although he may be a master craftsman, he was once an apprentice, and perhaps he still has something to learn about his craft (perhaps he will never know everything about his craft!). The fires burn behind him and around him, telling us that there is a passion that spurs him into action and toward the perfecting of his work. In the same way, when we fuel our actions with passion, we are able to put ourselves metaphorically through the forge to achieve our goals and improve our selves. There is always room for improvement, always means by which we can perfect our skills and apply them to our lives.

Revelation

The Eight of Pentacles can be a hard taskmaster when it appears in a reading. It often shows up to tell the querent to work as hard as they possibly can toward their goal, and to put their all into the endeavour or situation (their "blood, sweat, and tears"). It reminds them that they will get back only what they put in: if they put in strength, their product will be strong; if they put in weakness, their product will be weak. The Eight of Pentacles usually speaks of the querent's work-life or career, or a skill and talent that they can put to use.

If they are currently in a state of uncertainty or looking for guidance, this card says that they must consider what they are good at and what skills they have. Sometimes it comes up in a reading to tell the querent that they are going to need to do the same task repeatedly until they get it right or until the task is done, and that practice makes perfect in this situation.

If the Eight of Pentacles appears in a relationship reading, it often indicates that the querent and/or their partner are working on the relationship—or that they need to. The relationship, like all relationships, may have its problems, but with the correct application of effort and skill it can easily be fixed or turned into something better. The same can apply to friendships or any other partnerships in the querent's life.

Sometimes this card suggests the querent will or should pursue the acquiring of a new skill, or take on an apprenticeship of some kind that will allow them to hone their skills or knowledge on the job, in a practical manner, rather than just learning on a theoretical level. The Eight of Pentacles speaks strongly against just reading books or learning a subject theoretically, safe behind closed doors where no risk is taken.

Often the Eight of Pentacles appears when a querent is considering starting up a business that uses their talents directly, such as a jewellery-making business, a counselling practice, a restaurant, or a tarot-reading enterprise. It blesses such a venture and tells the querent that this would be an exceptionally good move for them at this time; they should try and turn their skills that up until now have only been hobbies and pastimes into ways to make money or improve their livelihood. They have great talent, and it would be a shame to waste it. But they should be advised that what lies ahead will require hard work, dedication, long hours, and a keen eye for detail. This card can also appear in a reading simply to indicate the querent's place of work or the nature of their work, with the specifics being shown by surrounding cards.

If reversed, the work of the Eight of Pentacles becomes boring, repetitive, soul-crushing chores. It indicates a poor relationship between the querent and their job or their chosen line of work, long hours that take too much from their life, and tasks that affect them negatively. The reversed Eight of Pentacles is the querent being overqualified for their job, or working not because they love what they do but to pay the bills because there is nothing else available. It also says their skills and talents are being overlooked. At times, this card reversed suggests that perfection and the striving toward it becomes a dogmatic approach to their own work, and the querent is their own worst critic; nothing will ever be good enough for them, which is an unhealthy attitude.

Keywords

Practice, practical application, work, chores, career, job, talent, skill, shaping, livelihood, hard work, dedication, devotion, input, effort, perfection, perfectionist.

Nine of Pentacles, the Fullness of Independence in Gain

"There should be no surprise in seeing your efforts come to fruition. Why wonder at the natural ripening of the fruit on the vine when that is all it knows how to do? How can you be surprised when, after nine months of growth in its mother's womb, a child comes forth? When you have set in motion all the requirements for a particular goal and taken every step necessary to ascertain results, the gain of those results is assured. Rather, it would be better to be surprised if, from this stable and fruitful foundation of work, energy, skill, and time, growth did not occur! Thus, when you become the paragon of your path, filled with joy and at the height of your talent, when you stand out amongst the crowd for your efforts and abilities, do not hide your accomplishments away from the world, nor give them away out of guilt. Enjoy them. Revel in them. Let them be the roots grounding you as well as the wind beneath your wings of further, soaring ambition. Let your harvest give you certainty in your skill and the virtue of your path, and let it feed your independent soul. It is you who trod the weary path to this point; it is you who studied and learned and gathered your strength; it is you who applied yourself over and over again; and it is you who waited ever so patiently for the results. Here they are. And here you are. These are your firm foundations to stand upon in an uncertain world. This is your anchor in the swelling waters of the ocean. This is your testament to your own abilities so that you know you can trust yourself. This is your fierce stand of independence in the world. Here you are."

Venus in Virgo / Yesod in earth

Illumination

It has taken a lot of hard work, energy, time, and effort to get to this point, and at times it may have seemed like we would never reach a conclusion, but finally, in the Nine of Pentacles, we find the results of all our work coming to fruition so that we might now enjoy the fruits of our labours. All the nines of the tarot bear some sense of fullness and completion; nine is the last single-digit number, and therefore the last number that has meaning based solely on its own virtue (in numerology, the tens are actually ones, because $1 + 0 = 1$). Thus there is a sense of independence in the nines, and in the Nine of Pentacles this independence is found in the material world. We see financial and economic autonomy, with no need of aid from others, no need to rely on others at all.

As discussed previously, all the energies from the previous cards of the suit settle themselves in the nines for one final push into true completion and rebirth in the tens. In the Nine of Pentacles, this process is so earthy and grounded that it resembles a form of gestation; we are reminded of the nine months of gestation for human babies before they are born. Thus, the Nine of Pentacles sees the energies of manifestation and growth reaching their most perfect state of completion and fullness before they are delivered into the final stages of results. The waiting is over; results are inevitable.

In the card image, we find an opulent, beautiful scene of grace and elegance. A finely and elaborately dressed woman stands in a garden on a path that leads to a magnificent pagoda. Golden pentacles form stepping-stones across the verdant grass; they represent the preceding cards and all the energy that has come before this card. In the distance, the skies are blue with a couple of white clouds, green mountains and fields spread out in a vast expanse of openness, and around the woman we see grapevines in full growth. The headdress she wears to ornament her well-coiffed hair has jewelled fruit hanging from it, and upon her left arm, which is raised up, a falcon sits.

We can understand a lot about this card from looking at the woman herself. The colours she wears—red and gold—are the colours of wealth, fortune, luck, and prosperity. Her manner is regal and elegant, and she looks wealthy, yet her eyes are downcast slightly as if acknowledging our presence and giving a sign of respect. Her skirts fall down over her feet and flow over the ground slightly, and her sleeves are heavily embellished and hang down. This shows us that she does not have a need to perform any kind of manual labour; she is perhaps a lady of leisure, or she has reached a point in life where there is no need for that kind of work. This is in stark contrast to the preceding cards of this suit, the seven and eight, which show working men in practical clothing. The woman is not smiling, but she is not showing any negative emotion either; she is reserved, but not cold.

The opulence and sumptuousness of her costume tell us that this woman has no hesitation in benefiting from the material world. She embraces the gifts of the physical world and has no problems with enjoying her wealth and the results of her hard work. She knows what she deserves and knows what is due to her, yet she is not greedy and miserly like the man in the Four of Pentacles; in this card, the pentacles form a pathway and the foundation beneath her feet, and she doesn't feel the need to cling selfishly to them.

It would be nice to think that she has earned her wealth and independence through her own efforts. In the context of the culture represented by the card, her elaborate costume and the nuances of her makeup and her demeanour imply that she is the owner of a successful geisha house. In Japanese society, the world of the geisha is strictly ruled by women, run by women, and worked in by women. Until recent decades, it was the only field in which women could be financially independent and perform work outside of their marital home. It is a misconception that geisha are simply women hired for sexual pleasure; they are, in fact, highly skilled entertainers and hostesses. Guests at traditional tea houses will pay for the attendance of geisha at a party or evening event; the geisha's role is to introduce people to each other, to encourage social interaction and stimulate conversation, to sing and dance in traditional Japanese style, and to serve tea. She must remain in control of the social interaction at all times.

It is for the geisha's skill, talent, and reputation that she is hired and gains repeat clientèle, and it is for the reputation of a geisha house and the geisha who work from it that the house owner becomes wealthy. The house owner is likely to have worked as a geisha herself, and reached a stage of financial independence at which she could afford to set up her own house, becoming a business owner. In the Nine of Pentacles, we see the pinnacle of one's skill and talent, business acumen, and financial worth resulting in a comfortable, well-off life. The falcon on the woman's arm is another symbol representing her talent and skill, but this symbol speaks specifically of her keen sight, her rise to the top, her authority, and her acumen. Falconry is a pastime traditionally reserved for royalty or those that have a high standing in society. As such, this falcon shows the woman to be highly respected and in a position of authority. What does she have authority over? The pagoda behind her is her domain. From here she runs her business and has control over her life, finances, and situation.

The full and ripe bunches of grapes that are abundant on their vines remind us of the growth and ripening of skill and talent, as well as the outcome of hard work. They link this card to the Seven of Pentacles, where we see the grapes not yet ready for harvest, symbolizing the waiting period that has to occur while we wait for them to ripen on the vine. Here, however, the fruits are ready to be harvested and enjoyed, the grape being a fruit that is made into wine or eaten as it comes off the vine, symbolic of celebration and the joys of life.

Revelation

The Nine of Pentacles suggests that the querent has reached a delightful state of completion, in which they are able to truly enjoy the results of their hard work. If they have been waiting for results, they are assured of them now. Any plans or projects they have been working on for a while will very soon reach completion and fullness, and to great success! This is the kind of success that is a natural outgrowth of what has come before; the querent has set things out so that it would be unnatural for growth not to occur. If they are lucky enough to see this card accompanied by other cards of success, such as the Four of Wands or the Six of Wands, they can expect great things to come from the completion of their project.

Often this card appears in a reading to indicate an independent woman, particularly if accompanied by any of the queens, the Empress, or Strength. However, it can also indicate anybody who is in a position of financial and economic independence, or seeking it, particularly those who are self-employed or run their own business and employ others. Sometimes this card suggests that it is time for the querent to consider self-employment, or taking on employees to work in their business.

In a reading about work, finances, and business, there are few better cards to get than the Nine of Pentacles. Immense growth in the business is signified; a career that blossoms and gives the querent the opportunity to use their skills and talents to the best of their ability is also indicated. Any money they have put toward their ventures was well spent, as it will lead to stability and enjoyment.

In a relationship reading, the Nine of Pentacles shows who wears the trousers, since it is a fiercely independent card. If it represents the querent, it shows that they are the one who drives the relationship forward; it also indicates that the relationship is not codependent and the partners respect each other enough to allow each other to make decisions independently and to manage their own finances separately. However, if the reading is about perhaps opening up a joint bank account or putting all money from both partners into one source, it advises against this.

Sometimes the Nine of Pentacles suggests that the querent is going to be standing out from the crowd soon, in whatever area of life the reading is about. They might be noticed for their talents and skills, they might become the advocate in a social situation, or they might be noted for their elegance and flair. The querent should be assured that they have earned this, and are allowed to enjoy it. In any situation, the Nine of Pentacles asks the querent to keep firmly in their mind what results they are expecting, and to recognize them when they get them. Further, this card offers opportunities for the querent to gain something from the situation at hand—not in a manipulative or power-grabbing manner, but for their own use and achievement.

Reversed, the Nine of Pentacles indicates that the querent may be feeling that they lack independence, perhaps in the workplace or in their relationship. They may be finding that the results of their hard work are only fleeting: before long, the money has been spent, usually for the benefit of other people, and the querent is not enjoying the fruits of their labours. This card reversed also represents a querent who doesn't know how to cope with any position of authority they may be in, and has feelings of guilt associated with rewards and gain from their work.

Keywords
Gain, independence, growth, results, fruits, ripening, enjoyment, authority, business, self-employment, success.

Ten of Pentacles, the Wealth of Family
"I am very old, and the sounds of my bones cracking when I move is the sound of the earth shifting; the sound of my rasping breath is the sound of the wind in the mountains, and my fragile frame bends like the weeping willow over a river. But my wealth of experience is like the fountain of youth and my wisdom is like the elixir of immortality, for I offer it to those that have come after me, and I will live on in their joys and their achievements, their comforts and their challenges. I have worked all the days of my life and seen the wide world, and I have tales to tell that are truly wondrous. I may not be blessed with many more days, but what I have I will give wholeheartedly to my family, so they may know from whence they came, and what awaits them in life. May the best days of my life be their worst, and may they live to see as many seasons turn as I have. But

let them never forget their ancestors; let them always know that those who came before are smiling upon them... not because their spirits linger (we deserve rest after our long travels!) but because they leave a legacy upon earth that blesses their descendants. I did not always know the comfort in which I now rest, nor the luxury and wealth in which we now thrive; I began with little more than the ability to work hard and work well. It was the sweat of my brow and my tenacity of will, the hours I put in and the effort I expended, that raised me up in the world and in spirit and wisdom. My family now want for nothing, yet I wish for them to know the value of work, and this I will teach them before I am gone. Most importantly, I will show them what it means to be family, and what they will do for each other when called upon. My final legacy to my descendants shall be to teach them how to love one another unconditionally, how to respect one another and their elders, how to work well, how to celebrate joyously and frequently, and how to pick each other up when they fall. This they too will pass on to their grandchildren when the cracking of their bones is the sound of the shifting earth and the rasping of their breath is the sound of the wind in the mountains, and my days shall continue unto the end of my line."

Mercury in Virgo / Malkuth in earth

Illumination

When we reach the end of each of the four suits, the Ten of Cups and the Ten of Pentacles fare particularly well. All the energy of their suit has filtered down and manifested in many different ways, so that the tens benefit from that energy; here, the pentacles become platters upon which the fruits of the labours of this suit fall, ready to be enjoyed. This is therefore a card of great wealth, in which the results of all efforts are manifest and available; it is also a card of rest after hard work, but not the brief rest found in the Four of Swords or the Nine of Wands—a lasting rest, which shows that from now on worry and lack will be a stranger. It is the final result attained at the end of the arduous alchemical process, and therefore the Philosopher's Stone; lead has been transmuted into gold.

In the card image, we see a luxurious, golden, beautiful scene of familial comfort. A venerable grandfather is seated at the forefront of the card, a small child playing at his feet, holding onto his knees and engaging with him. Two dogs can also be seen at his feet, relaxed and attentive to their master, whilst in the mid-ground a couple—we can imagine that one is the old man's child and the other their spouse—embrace, and in the background two other figures are smiling and laughing. The children, robed in the blue of aspiration and new beginnings, are grandchildren and descendants, giving us a hint about the cyclical nature of the tens in the tarot. The tens are so full of the energy of their suit that they are pregnant with it, and they will therefore birth the ace once more.

The Ten of Pentacles relates to legacy and inheritance, with material wealth being passed down from one family member to another. The family are housed in a truly beautiful and magnificent home, testament to their joy in each other's company as well as the wealth they collectively possess. It is likely that it has been built and purchased by the grandfather, and has been passed down to his adult child to take care of whilst he enjoys it in comfort with his family around him. A dwelling such as this would be expensive, which reminds us just how much wealth has been gained and is now being enjoyed in the Ten of Pentacles. It also tells us about inheritance and the things that are passed down to us from our parents, grandparents, and ancestors. This can sometimes be physical wealth passed to us upon death, but it can also refer to traditions, customs, and family values. Most of us picked up our values from our parents and grandparents, and we will probably pass them on to our descendants. Traditions become entrenched quickly in families, without much history being required; if your mother has used the same Christmas cake recipe every year since before you were born, and she got it from her mother, then that annual baking of the cake is a tradition. If your father always takes you to play baseball around your birthday, and has done since you were old enough to swing the bat, then it is now tradition. These practices help instill within us a sense of continuity between ourselves, our parents, and those children and grandchildren that will come after us; they also serve to bind us closer emotionally to our family members.

The family scene in the card image asks us to think about the ways families interact with each other. We see the grandfather being given a place of honour, revering his wisdom and what he has done for the family in the past, while the relationship between him and his grandchild is one of teaching and playfulness. A second child clings to his father's clothing, illustrating a relationship of protection and shielding. The husband and wife seek solace in each other's arms, showing how family members can turn to each other in times of need and be completely themselves around each other, with genuine affection and love. In the background, the laughing figures represent the fun that we can have in families, the good times we create with each other, and the ways we can look back on the past with fondness or celebrate in times of good fortune. Families do not necessarily have to be made up of blood relatives, however, but by those who choose to spend their time closely with one another. In the modern age, we are just as likely to live in a shared household with close friends as we are with family members, and we often build families around us as we go through life, creating a network of love, respect, and support that exists outside of blood ties.

The presence of the two dogs in the card image further highlights the familial nature of the Ten of Pentacles, as the dog is the typical and traditional family pet. It is also symbolic of devotion, companionship, loyalty, and faithful affection, as the dog will always obey its master and loves unconditionally. The overall atmosphere of the card scene tells us that whilst it is good and wonderful to enjoy the fruits of one's labours and build an empire, it is much better to share those fruits with others. We cannot take our riches or experience with us, so why not pass it on to those who can use it after we are gone? The Ten of Pentacles, in the attitude of the grandfather, reminds us that comfort and happiness can be found when we know we have provided for those around us. Offering a legacy to the world that will survive after we are gone is its own brand of immortality.

Revelation

There are few cards in the tarot better than the Ten of Pentacles! Whenever it appears in a reading, the querent should expect truly wonderful outcomes to their endeavours. It can indicate a great amount of wealth coming to them, usually monetary wealth, but it can also be metaphorical, e.g., a wealth of knowledge or a wealth of experience. If the Ten of Pentacles is in a position in the spread that represents the present, the querent themselves, or a current situation, then it suggests that they are currently feeling like they have everything they have ever wanted and needed, and that they have seen the fruits of their labours and are now able to enjoy them. The querent has reached a stage where they have done well and achieved their ambition and goals. This card can therefore appear to indicate the end of one stage of life and the beginning of a new one.

This card brings with it life's finest luxuries and comforts, but it also has strong messages for the querent about family. Sometimes it appears in a reading to indicate their family in general, whether that family is their blood relatives or the family they have chosen to surround themselves with. Thus, if it is surrounded by negative cards, it can highlight any problems that might be occurring within or around the family unit; if surrounded by positive cards, it will point to strengths and successes in the family. It might also indicate that the querent needs to seek help from within their family in order to overcome a current obstacle or make the most of their current position.

If the querent is elderly, this card can point to their children or grandchildren; if the querent is young, it can point to their elderly relatives. It calls upon the querent to give respect to these family members, and suggests that they have a wealth of wisdom to offer them if they ask for it. It also suggests that the family ties they have are strong, loyal, and faithful.

Sometimes the Ten of Pentacles can appear in a reading to indicate inheritance coming to the querent, but also on a more metaphorical level: what have they inherited from their family that affects their current position? Any habits? Mores and values? Practices? We all have something about ourselves that we picked up from those who raised us, and the way we were raised.

If this card appears in a relationship reading, it indicates the relationship is being built on a strong foundation and will grow in strength and love as time goes on, eventually reaching a stage of true happiness. If the relationship is still in a nascent stage, and this card is supported by other cards such as the Four of Wands, the Two of Cups, the Ten of Cups, or the Lovers, it can indicate a marriage or civil partnership, and a long, happy, committed relationship together. This partnership is faithful, true, and steadfast. The Ten of Pentacles is just as positive for business or work-related questions, indicating that the outcome will be very good and the querent will find themselves earning quite a lot of money from their business or work. They might also wish to consider investment and savings. Sometimes the Ten of Pentacles points to the querent taking retirement.

If this card is reversed, the inheritance from the family becomes a burden for the querent, one that they wish (or need) to shake off. Perhaps they are feeling weighted down and unable to progress because of their family issues or the needs of another family member overriding their own. The Ten of Pentacles reversed sometimes indicates that a member of the querent's family is in need of help; it is time for the querent to repay the support that they have received in the past. In terms of business and work, a reversed Ten of

Pentacles sees a delay in outcome or assets that the querent cannot get access to for some reason.

Keywords

Inheritance, wealth, family, home, completion, fulfilment, faithfulness, loyalty, companionship, commitment, experience, legacy.

PART 3:

The Court Cards: Stars on Earth

If the major arcana cards are the big themes of our lives, and the minor arcana cards the detail and everyday activity, then the court cards are the people that populate our lives, as well as our own character traits, tendencies, and perspectives. As such, they are given titles that indicate they are people—princess, prince, queen and king—and they all have different roles to play in their suit.

It is important to note that although the titles given to the court cards are gendered, they do not necessarily represent a person of that same gender. Each court card can be a person of any age or gender; they generally indicate personality types and tendencies rather than physical attributes. You may also find that court cards represent ways of approaching a situation, strengths and weaknesses, and occasionally events. As such, they can often be the most difficult cards to read in a spread, although practice will help, and listening to your intuitive response in the context of the reading is useful.

Court Card Essences and the Elements

As with the cards of the minor arcana, each type of court card shares an essence. Where, for instance, the aces share an essence, so do the princesses. They are also associated with one of the four elements.

Princess/Earth: Awakening, nascent power, the fertile womb, seeds, foundations.

Prince/Air: Expansion, seeking or questing, discovering, planning, movement.

Queen/Water: Flow and flux, nurturing and care, channelling and process, reflection.

King/Fire: Peak and pinnacle, mastery, action, achievement, consumption.

Since each of the four suits is also associated with the four elements, the sixteen court cards form sixteen different ways of those elements interacting. The Princess of Wands, for instance, is earth (princess) and fire (wands), but specifically it is the earthy aspect of fire.

Princess of Pentacles: Earth of Earth; **Princess of Swords:** Earth of Air; **Princess of Cups:** Earth of Water; **Princess of Wands:** Earth of Fire

Prince of Pentacles: Air of Earth; **Prince of Swords:** Air of Air; **Prince of Cups:** Air of Water; **Prince of Wands:** Air of Fire

Queen of Pentacles: Water of Earth; **Queen of Swords:** Water of Air; **Queen of Cups:** Water of Water; **Queen of Wands:** Water of Fire

King of Pentacles: Fire of Earth; **King of Swords:** Fire of Air; **King of Cups:** Fire of Water; **King of Wands:** Fire of Fire.

We could also say that, for instance, the Queens of Cups is the nurturer (queen) of emotions (water), the Prince of Pentacles is the expansion (prince) of finances (pentacles), and the King of Wands is the mastery (king) of the self (wands). Further examples include "the Depth of Water" (Queen of Cups), "the Sudden Flash of Light" (King of Wands), and "Steady as a Rock" (Prince of Pentacles). There are many permutations of this style of interpretation for each court card, since each suit concerns itself with a number of aspects of everyday life, and the four court cards may manifest their qualities in many different ways.

Making Light Work 5

For each court card, create a few sentences that are short expressions of the card's essence mixed with the elemental association of its suit, as discussed above. You could start with:

1. Queen of Swords (Water of Air)
2. Prince of Wands (Air of Fire)
3. Princess of Cups (Earth of Water)
4. King of Pentacles (Fire of Earth)

Making Light Work 6

The elemental interactions in the court cards create sixteen sub-elements, which can be found all around us in the natural world. For instance, the Queen of Cups, water of water, is the deepest expression of the receptivity of water, like the depths of the ocean. The Princess of Wands, earth of fire, could be considered the fuel for a fire. Try to think of a natural occurrence for each of the court cards.

Astrology in the Court Cards

Astrology is everywhere in the tarot, like the silver thread that ties all the cards together. In the court cards, the twelve zodiac signs and their associated character types are attributed to the princes, queens, and kings, with the princesses being viewed as the "thrones" for the rest of the court cards to sit in—in other words, as being representative of the primal nature of that element.

Luckily, the astrological associations of these cards are simpler than those of the minor arcana. The three fire signs are given to the suit of wands, the three water signs to cups, the three earth signs to pentacles, and the three air signs to swords. Further, the kings are given the fixed signs, the queens the cardinal signs, and the princes the mutable signs. You will see throughout the court cards that these signs are referenced symbolically in the card images, such as the lion throne upon which the King of Wands is seated, or the goats carved onto the Queen of Pentacles' throne.

	Wands	Cups	Swords	Pentacles
King	Leo	Scorpio	Aquarius	Taurus
Queen	Aries	Cancer	Libra	Capricorn
Prince	Sagittarius	Pisces	Gemini	Virgo

Making Light Work 7

You probably know at least a little about some of the zodiac signs, perhaps because you know your own sign and your partner's, or your parents', or your best friend's. For each one that you know something about, try and think about what qualities are typically associated with that sign's personality, both their good points and their bad points. How might those qualities be reflected in the corresponding court card? Next, do a little bit of research online about the zodiac signs and come up with one or two keywords that apply to each court card.

CHAPTER 27

The Princesses

Princess of Wands, the Fuel of the Fire

"Before the fire is even a spark, when it is merely an idea in the mind and the desire for light and heat, there must be fuel. Just as fire feeds on wood, every act must feed on energy, and continue to be fed and fuelled for its continued existence. In the same way, no creative act occurs without inspiration, without a foundation, without grounding in the reality of action. Although I am the lowest child of my element, I am the most necessary for its birth and growth: without me, the fuel and the foundation, the element of fire is nothing. I am the ground into which creative impulses are seeded, the waiting womb in which the first fiery burst of inspiration is planted and rooted, the sating of desire when impulse becomes action and, in turn, the result of that action. I am on fire with divine inspiration, the flames of passion that drive us forward, and it is in the girding of my loins that I bring forth more fire. Passion feeds passion, and desire feeds desire, just as inspiration leads to further inspiration. Within the seed is already contained the final result in potential form, just as the womb is the vehicle of desire and also produces its result. Yet, with my birthing into actuality of the first spark of inspiration, I also become the boundaries within which desire and passion function. I am the container of fire—the lamp, the torch, the hearth—and I am the vessel of creative thought and passionate impulse—the finished masterpiece, the spark of inspiration made manifest."

Earthy part of fire / No astrological attribution

Illumination

The princesses are the "youngest" court cards in their respective suits, and often considered the lowest. They are associated elementally with earth, also the lowest of the four elements, being the element of physical manifestation and reality, the one upon which we walk, and which constitutes our body, the Earth, and our sustenance. Whilst the princesses and earth are considered the lowest, therefore they are also the vital foundation of their suit, as well as the fertile growth of their suit. As the earthy part of fire (the suit of wands), this princess is the foundation and growth of everything fire represents: inspiration, creativity, passion, desire, impulse, sexual drive, ambition, courage, the self, personality, and ego. As earth, she is also the fuel for these things, the awakening of them, and the container of them.

In the card image, we see a young woman with thick, long black hair flowing down her back. Although her hair is wild and starting to break free from its bindings, it is still contained and held back, just as the princess contains the unruly fire. The blackness and thickness of her hair reminds us of her earthy nature. The staff that she holds—the staff that is found throughout the rest of this suit, with life flowering from its apex—seems to have a golden, flaming energy rising up around its tip, as if she holds a fiery torch in her hands, the flame-bearing priestess of her suit. She holds the staff tenderly, almost caressing it, and her hands are such that she might be encouraging the fire to rise up the staff, raising the energy higher and higher, feeding the flames with the fuel of her own passion. The colours that she wears upon her body—green, gold, and orange—are those of life, sunlight, and the flowering earth, showing us that not only is she a priestess of the flaming torch, but also a priestess of the rising of life itself. Fire is essential for our continued existence as well as the spark of our existence: as the sun, it gives us the light and heat that we rely upon, and as flames it gives us the ability to see in the dark, protect ourselves from predators, signal others, cook raw food, and process other raw ingredients into useful compounds. When we see the Princess of Wands stroking the shaft of the staff, and the flames licking the enlivened tip, we know that she is containing, fuelling, and providing a foundation for the energies of life itself.

Even the billowing cloak that the Princess of Wands wears is fiery in appearance. From her headdress, a white and gold veil is whipped upward by the wind, and from her shoulders a red and gold cloak flies in the same direction. It is almost as if she herself is on fire, ignited with the energies of life, with the white-hot flame at her head and the red-hot flame around it. Once again, this princess is the earthy fuel upon which the fire can feed, and with her presence the flames burn hotter.

In many ancient cultures, fire was sacred. In Rome, the sacred fire of Vesta, the goddess of hearth and home, was tended by the Vestal Virgins, priestesses who vowed to remain chaste. The safety and sanctity of the city was believed to depend on the purity of these priestesses, and if anything dire befell the city, the accusing eyes would turn upon them. In Kildare, Ireland, a group of nineteen priestesses tended the sacred fires of Brighid, the goddess of healing, the forge, and inspiration. Later, a Christian church was founded at the site and nuns lived there, yet they watched over the sacred spring of St. Brigid and continued to guard her sacred fires. The chastity of such priestesses is symbolic of the purity of the container and fuel for the flames. If we feed the flames of a fire with impure fuel, we get a flame that is discoloured, with rank smoke or a bad smell from the fumes. Symbolically, this tells us that if the fuel of our inspiration, our energy, or our personality is full of impurities, the resulting flame will not burn in a wholesome way. Although to many of us this vowed chastity seems like a limitation, the earthy nature of the Princess of Wands reminds us that limitation of some kind—a container, a form—is necessary for inspiration and creativity to become manifest in reality. For us to create, say, a work of art, we must limit the first fiery thrust of ambition and inspiration into a plan and a resulting image. Yet this limitation can also be a relief, as anybody who creates on a regular basis will tell you, as it allows the resulting expression and actualization of something that has, until now, been burning away inside the creator, without a means of expression. It is like sexual desire that arises yet has no way of being expressed or relieved. It is potential without a direction, without a foundation for growth. The limitations and boundaries of earth are essential for potential to become actuality in all the princesses of the tarot, but much more so in the Princess of Wands, whose element of fire is so far removed from earth and so unmanifest that it requires such grounding much more than the other elements.

As such, the Princess of Wands is both the instigator of desire and passion, and that which is attained as a result of it. The flowers that spread over the green earth all about her in the card image represent the first awakening of the element of the suit, the opening of the bud to become a flower; yet they are also symbolic of results, being objects of beauty in themselves. Just as we all come from the earth in the beginning and return to the earth at the end, the Princess of Wands gives us the first sparks and awakening of fire as well as the contained result of it.

Revelation

As with all the court cards, the Princess of Wands can appear in a reading to indicate a person in the querent's life or the querent themselves, as well as various personality traits (both positive and negative) of that person or the querent. It can also point to a general theme in the querent's life, an approach the querent is advised to take, or an event. Surrounding cards and the context of the question can help the reader decide what aspect the court card is taking.

As the earthy aspect of fire, the Princess of Wands often appears in a reading to indicate the first awakenings of desire, passion, or drive. As such, it can point to the querent's initial idea, or their passion for a newly discovered subject or project. This is the card of the enthusiastic youth, discovering something that makes them passionate and getting very excited about it, eager to delve deeper and explore it (however, the exploration itself is usually indicated by a prince). This could translate to the young student who has just discovered their passion for a certain subject, which they wish to study at a higher level, the person who has found a desire to create music or art awakening within them, the person who has an initial idea for a possible business, or the person who has instigated a plan to further a burning inspiration they have had. It can also represent the spark of an idea, still tiny and nascent, yet with plenty of fuel behind it and a suggestion of direction starting to develop. As such, the Princess of Wands as an event usually indicates the querent's first steps toward the turning inspiration into results.

Since all the princesses represent an awakening of some kind, this card can often point to an awakening of the self, particularly in relation to sexuality. As such, it can appear in a reading for a querent who has previously been confused about their sexuality, someone who is just starting to come to grips with the idea of themselves as a sexual being, or a newly realized sexual orientation. It can also point to a sudden new desire for a certain person.

This also goes for awakenings of new aspects of the self, in which the querent discovers a part of their personality that has lain dormant until now, which is currently coming to the foreground of their life. This may, for instance, be the awakening of new confidence in the querent, new optimism, new courage, a more passionate way of approaching life, or a more inspired way of living.

Conversely, the Princess of Wands also can indicate the results of these awakenings and first sparks. As such, if she appears in an outcome position of a spread, she points to the attainment of a goal into which the querent has been putting all their desire and passion. This card is the actuality and manifestation of the querent's passion and ambition, and often says that from this result, the querent will find further inspiration.

In a relationship reading, this card can signify a sudden new burst of passion and desire, perhaps a relationship that burns brightly for a short time and then fizzles out if it is not fed and fuelled properly. In a reading about work or career, the Princess of Wands suggests that the querent needs to bring more passion and ambition to their work; without it, success is not possible. This card also speaks of the need for more enthusiasm and optimism in all areas of life, so it can appear in a reading to suggest that the querent try and liven up the otherwise boring parts of their usual routine.

A person represented by the Princess of Wands is passionate and filled with enthusiasm for life, but often appears childlike or childish, great at starting things and great at knowing what to do with the end result, but not so good at the bits in between. They are also mischievous, a trickster at times like their older brother the Prince of Wands, and they are known to do things just for the fun of it. They are often creative and inspired, and get very passionate about whatever it is they are currently working on. However, they can often get their fingers burned by playing with fire; their passion pushes them forward without caution or thought.

Reversed, the earthy aspect of the Princess of Wands does not act as a fuel for the fires of inspiration, passion, and ambition, but instead smothers those flames. It can point to a lack of fuel for inspiration, or a foundation so sturdy and firm that it is unbending, resulting in inspiration being lost in the rules or politics of the situation. This card reversed can also indicate confusion about self-image or other difficulties that the querent is having with their personality and ego.

Keywords

Passion, instigation, inspiration, spark, enthusiasm, awakening, ego, self, new ideas, new awareness, foundations, results, manifestation.

Princess of Swords, the Fixing of New Ideas

"It is a mistake to believe that thoughts are mere wisps of ideas, children of pure air and flitting creatures that are separate from earth and reality. In truth,

thoughts are the children of two parents: the world of experience is the mother, and the ability to perceive and conceive in the mind is the father. There is no simple dichotomy to be found here, only the matter of how the resulting child-thought is applied. I came into the world with little: no great wealth nor beauty, no high-born parents, and no destiny. But I had the greatest gift of all: a sharp, keen mind, and the capacity to ground it in action. Your mind is a tool to be used to solve the puzzles of the world, and to learn how to take it apart and piece it back together. Do not be afraid to be an inventor and architect of your own life, and do not fear rebellious thought: let it not be bound in a prison of preconception and acceptance, but rather let it fly free and high. Dare to think independently and establish for yourself the rules and parameters of your life. Dare to be your dreams, to bring all your ideas down into existence and to create all you wish to be. Build foundations beneath your castles in the sky and never let establishment or kingdom, ruler or acceptance, govern your mind except through their own virtue and merit. Foundations of thought are two-edged like the sword: they can support and hold you up, yet they can bind and hold you down. Know how to discern the difference, and you will truly be a free thinker."

Earthy part of air / No astrological attribution

Illumination

Elementally, the Princess of Swords is the earthy aspect of air, the foundation, materialization, and fixation of everything this element and suit represent. As the princess, she is symbolically the youngest of the court cards, which also means that she is the nascent awakening of the suit of swords. Since this suit is primarily concerned with the mind, thought, and ideas, we can easily see that the Princess of Swords represents the grounding of thoughts and ideas into reality through application and invention, as well as the breaking down of the established and accepted rules with a fresh perspective and new, revolutionary ideas. If the Princess of Swords is anything, she is firstly the power of invention, and secondly of revolution.

The image of this card shows a young woman with long, flowing red hair standing firm upon a windswept hillside. She raises a glowing sword with both of her hands, high into a stormy sky in which seagulls fly and cry out. Behind her are the rugged rocks of Britain. Her costume is Elizabethan, and she is inspired by the young Queen Elizabeth I of England, who was put upon the throne after first being declared illegitimate by her father, King Henry VIII, after her mother's execution, after being cut out of the monarchy by her half-brother Edward VI, and after being imprisoned for a year of her half-sister Mary I's bloody reign. This time in British history marked great religious upheaval and turmoil, during which Catholicism and Protestantism fought for control. Henry VIII bought Protestantism into political power during his reign, as did Edward VI, but upon Mary I's succession Catholicism was reinstated, and the young Princess Elizabeth was imprisoned under suspicion of secretly supporting Protestant rebels. During Mary's reign nearly three hundred religious dissenters who spoke out against the enforcement of Catholicism were burned at the stake under Mary's orders, and Elizabeth quickly became a focus of Protestant opposition. She had been educated thoroughly in the Protestant tradition, and before Mary's reign had practised it outwardly. In this sense, the young Elizabeth I as the Princess of Swords represents rebellion, breaking away from oppressive forms of thought, and a focus point for new ideas and fresh perspectives to take root.

The young Elizabeth was also highly educated, and by the end of her formal education at age seventeen, she was one of the best-educated women of her time. She could speak several languages, many of them fluently and as well as a native speaker (according to reports), including Welsh, Cornish, Italian, Flemish, Spanish, French, Scottish, and Irish. In addition, she could read and write English, Latin, and Italian. Her surviving speeches and writings tell us that she was extremely well-spoken and eloquent, a trait born from both her education and the sharpness of her mind. Our Princess of Swords shares this sharp mind, but it is always focused on matters of learning that are useful, rather than merely abstract: philosophy and lofty thought is of far less concern to her than languages and skills.

Despite being raised Protestant and more closely sympathizing with Protestantism than Catholicism, Elizabeth very quickly put into place several religious reforms that offered room for Catholic feeling whilst siding with Protestantism. This included retaining various Catholic elements within the church, such as priestly vestments and the crucifix. This demonstrates the dual ability of the Princess of Swords to respect well-founded traditions whilst not being afraid to overturn those that are no longer useful. There is a pragmatism in the Princess of Swords' approach, in which rebellion is not done for its own sake but as a means to a more effective and useful end.

There is much more to Elizabeth I's reign, and we will meet her again in her later years in the Queen of Swords.

The Princess of Swords is notable for being the only female court card to have completely free-flowing, unadorned hair. This indicates her fierce love of freedom in thought, since the hair is connected to the head and therefore the mind; it flows free like her thoughts and ideas, and is also free from pretension, unnecessary jewels, impractical headdresses, and heavy crowns. The thought processes represented in this card are not those used for social manipulation or power for its own sake, nor are they used as simple adornment in their own right; they must have practical application and use. They are also intensely independent and not afraid to fly in the face of established ideas if necessary. The rocky hillside that provides the setting and foundation for the card represents the manifestation of ideas and thoughts to build structures—though they are not smooth and easy to walk upon, just as the Princess of Swords sometimes creates a challenge through her rebellious and independent thought. Her costume is in the light blues and whites of the element of air and the clear sky, with touches of yellow to represent light; the seagulls above her are well known for their loud cries that echo through the sky, unpleasant, yet clear.

Revelation

The Princess of Swords often appears in a reading to indicate a person, although it does not necessarily indicate that the person is female nor that they are young, but rather it relates to personality traits and character. It also points to processes of thought and actions in the querent's life, and very occasionally indicates related events.

As a person, the Princess of Swords is an independent thinker, courageous in thought and often rebellious, viewing ideas as tools for change that can overcome obstacles and overthrow dogma and institutions. They believe that ideas should have a practical application, rather than being abstract exercises, and they eschew those that merely talk about ideas rather than taking action on them. As such, the Princess of Swords is often an inventor, political protester, writer, architect, or scientist. They do not ask "Why?" but rather they ask "How?" How does this work? How can this be improved? How can we embrace reform? How can we encourage understanding?

As the earthy aspect of air, the Princess of Swords can represent the ways in which the querent creates reality from their ideas. It brings to a reading the establishment in a real, everyday form of an idea or thought that the querent is having. This might manifest as writing, since thought made manifest is initially put into written form. It might also manifest as the beginning stages of an intellectual project, plan, blueprints, or outline. It can indicate the beginnings of communication between people, particularly if it appears in a relationship or social reading. In such a spread, the Princess of Swords blesses the querent with clear communication that is free from pointless debate, argument, or abstract thought, but which instead deals with practical measures. If the querent is having difficulties at work or in a relationship, the Princess of Swords advises that any discussion to solve the problem should focus on its practical, everyday aspects.

The Princess of Swords is sometimes a student, particularly in higher education, or one who is embracing the beginning of a journey of learning and discovery. This card relates to exploration and new intellectual horizons, and advises the querent not to be afraid to consider new ideas and possibilities. It also represents the organizational capacity of the mind, giving order to unformed and chaotic thoughts, so it can often indicate the querent making plans, or the plans they have already made.

Reversed, the Princess of Swords is an iconoclast, rebelling against established ideas simply because they are established. This card reversed can also represent the mind becoming bogged down and rigid, staid and conformist, rather than maintaining the ability to think creatively or independently. The querent clings to the familiar out of fear rather than developing solutions that are new and unique, and probably more useful and practical in the situation.

Keywords

Student, studies, new ideas, plans, revolution, rebellion, rebel, practical ideas, invention, architect, iconoclast, problem solving, solutions, independent thought, freedom, liberation of the mind, materialization, manifestation.

Princess of Cups, the Muse Within the Dream

"Dreams have power. In the dreaming state we are receptive, open to receiving messages from the universe and our higher self, and it is in this state that we also find inspiration and creative impulse. Do you know what it feels like to have the tingling sensation of some message, some realization, some vision trying to

find its way into your subconscious? Have you ever stood before a blank canvas with brush in hand, or sat with ink and paper, knowing that you have a well of artistry, creativity, and beauty inside you waiting to be expressed in the world, yet not knowing how to form it? I am that which you seek. I am the muse every artist and poet, every dancer and writer, every lover and musician awaits. I am both the inspiration and the goal, for in truth the artist does not desire anything beyond the inspiration taking root and forming. Thus, the lover awaits his muse, and when he meets her, he is in love and has also found the destination of his love; the artist finds his muse and paints her as goddess, nymph, dryad, or mermaid, naked and voluptuous… I bring you this vision and the nascent thrill of love, the intuitive state in which you might crystallize beauty, fantasy, and imagination that knows no bounds yet forms the kingdom and throne of your creative yearning. But seek me not in action, nor in learning or words, but only in the depths of your own soul and heart, in your half-remembered dreams and waking dreams and the countless dreams of your night-time mind."

Earthy part of water / No astrological attribution

Illumination

The beautiful Princess of Cups has the elemental associations of the earthy aspect of water. As a princess, she is also the "youngest" of the court cards, and thus corresponds to the faculties of awakening, blossoming, nascent formation, and potential within the suit of cups, which relates to emotions, feeling, spirituality, the inner self, and creativity. As earth in the suit of water, she performs the function of crystallization, in which emotions and creative impulse, dreams and imagination, take on a solid form through the creative act. Thus the Princess of Cups is also intimately connected with the process by which we attach our emotions to an object, a state of being, or a person. Further, since she is the potential found in earth to grow things within it, the Princess of Cups not only provides a foundation for the emotions and creative, inner self, but also the source and wellspring of them. She is therefore both the inspiration *and* the inspired person, as well as the finished product of the creative endeavour.

In the card image, we see a young, white-haired woman dressed in vivid blue, the breeze gently picking up wisps of her hair and blowing her white veil back from her face. She is seated on the steps of what might be an ancient temple, with its steps descending directly into the beautiful blue ocean, upon which the sunlight dances. Upon the rocks by her side sits a golden cup, from which a tropical fish leaps. The woman raises a hand to her chest as if in surprise and stares intently at the vision. It is easy to imagine her as a priestess or oracle of her temple, scrying the future in the ocean's waters.

The colours that the princess wears immediately tells us the realm in which she moves: she is firmly rooted in the subconscious mind. Since the blue she wears matches the colour of ocean, we know that she is found in the intense depths of emotion, love, and beauty that the sea represents. This is not the grey-blue of sadness, nor the royal blue of maturity, but instead a playful blue that indicates youth, naivety, and a carefree nature. The Princess of Cups is immersed in the joy of life, with the foundation of her personality being a love of all the fun that the world has to offer. Yet it is not the kind of fun found, for example, in the Prince of Wands, who revels in fun out of a desire to experience everything, but instead a fun that celebrates the beauty of life. This can be further seen in the way the sunlight plays upon the water in the card image. There are two main ways in which the ocean acts as a symbol in the Tarot Illuminati: it can appear as a dark, deep, foreboding body of water, representing raw power and fear of the unknown; or it can be the brightly lit ocean of warmer climes, decorated by sunlight, in which we are invited to frolic and appreciate beauty.

The white veil that she wears, which is being blown from her face, indicates her youth and inexperience yet also places her in the role of priestess, the keeper of mystery; with the veil being blown back, she herself is being shown one mystery. This dichotomy of the youthful wise-woman is found regularly in the tarot, most particularly in the High Priestess and the Star, with whom the Princess of Cups shares a kinship. It is found in each of the princesses, since they are both the youngest of the court cards and the ones that contain the most potential, being elemental earth. This shows us that the Princess of Cups not only represents the blossoming of mystery and revelation, but the potential for deeper understanding.

Leaping forth from the golden cup in front of her is the tropical fish, which also has a sense of playfulness about it. It is not just any fish, but a colourful and unusual one, just as the vision it represents is unique. It comes from the cup, which represents the inner self and emotions, suggesting that whatever the fish represents is being brought forth, outwardly into the external world, from the princess's inner world. This fish can therefore represent a myriad of things associated with this suit: creative impulse, imagination, wonder, love, romance, friendship, understanding, expression, intuition, psychic ability, artistic ability, or fantasy. As such, we find that the Princess of Cups represents the awakening of love and mystery, the first spark of artistic or creative endeavour or ability, and the manifestation of all those things. Thus she is the muse that inspires the artist, or the ways in which we manifest love and romance. In essence, she brings into reality those abstract concepts that otherwise would only be felt on an inward level.

The fish leaping from the cup also has another level of symbolism: it is the vision and revelation of mystery. Such epiphanies may happen without expectation, surprising us, or they may be sought actively. As such, the Princess of Cups represents the process by which we enter into an intuitive state of mind that can engender these visions and realizations, including all forms of divination such as the tarot, mediumship, and spirit contact. The Princess of Cups grounds the messages of the divine, expressing divine light into the everyday world.

Revelation

In a reading, the Princess of Cups most commonly represents a person, but it is also likely to indicate events or themes running through the querent's life. It is best to assess the surrounding cards and the context of the question to decide which aspect the card is taking.

As a person, the Princess of Cups can represent a person of either gender who is naïve, innocent, and gentle—someone who acts young, though they may not be young physically. They feel emotions intensely and deeply, though they may not fully understand them or the source of them. Often this person is still coming to terms with themselves as an emotional being, trying to understand how their feelings manifest in the world around them and how they can best express them. As such, the Princess of Cups can be a person who is often falling in love or engaging in a nascent romance.

The Princess of Cups often shows up in a reading to indicate an artist or other person involved in the arts. Actors, performers, writers, and musicians are all found in this card, particularly those who are just beginning in these fields, or those who have recently found their footing in those areas and wish to create a more stable career or further their skills.

Often this beautiful card indicates the beginnings of a new relationship, the blossoming of new feelings in an old relationship, or the manifestation of love between two people. It not only suggests that love will grow and feelings will blossom into something intense and deep, but also that there is a strong foundation already present upon which the relationship can be built. This relationship has immense potential, and the partners within it will find that they are able to express their feelings fully and explore their emotions in a playful manner, discovering new or unknown aspects of their emotional selves through the relationship.

In a work, career, or project-related reading, the Princess of Cups suggests the need for more creativity and imagination, particularly on a personal level, rather than applying logic to the situation. Others will be looking for somebody who can bring an artistic flair to the project or workplace, or liven up a situation with creative ability and a bit of imagination. Others may also be looking to the querent for inspiration or creative suggestions, seeking advice from them as to how they can express their own creative thoughts and imagination.

Occasionally the Princess of Cups appears in a reading to indicate a creative project the querent is currently working on, such as a painting or a piece of music. It suggests that the querent needs to focus intently on this project, because it contains the potential for a greater understanding of the world or themselves, and will reveal the answers the querent is looking for. Often, the Princess of Cups points to this need to find deeper answers or meaning, particularly a querent who is "looking for a sign," and it can suggest that such signs will be forthcoming. Depending on the question, the Princess of Cups might even be the sign itself!

Reversed, the Princess of Cups indicates naivety in the querent's personality that is holding them back or causing them to misinterpret a situation, as well as a lack of inspiration or difficulty in finding their muse that is preventing them from following their creative and imaginative impulses. It might also indicate that a relationship the querent is considering, or which has recently begun, may not progress beyond its nascent stages, failing or fizzling out after a short time. Sometimes, the Princess of Cups also advises the querent to look deeper within themselves for the answers, rather than looking to others or the world around them. They already know the answer; they just need to realize it.

Keywords

Vision, blossoming romance, new love, muse, artistic capability, flair, imagination, vision, psychic ability, divination, crystallization, naivety, fantasy, expressing creativity.

Princess of Pentacles, the Womb of the World

"My sisters are often given the glamour and wonder, the acclaim and mystery, and I am relegated to the background, a mere prop or scenery for the grander design. I am the youngest of the young, the lowest of the low, made up of dirt and earth and bedrock. Yet do not make the mistake of passing me over and thinking me naught, for within my lowness I contain the complete potential for all the highest things in the universe. I am the fertile earth that is always beneath us, yet which houses seed and life, blood and bloom. I am the rising of the sun from behind the hills, born anew from the world below with each dawn, the light of illumination being brought to our minds and hearts through the simple act of birth. I may look young, yet I am pregnant with the fullness of the universe, ready and bursting to bring it forth and offer it to you as a gift. This is the truth of harvest: it can only come from the first awakening and blossoming of the earth, and endings and beginnings are intimately entwined. Mother is daughter, and daughter is mother. It is for this reason that I tend to the fields and the harvest, give thanks to the Earth Mother, and follow the turning seasons: she sacrifices herself for us, and we must in turn give back to her. One day, you will return to her belly, and she will be both mother and destroyer of you, and that shall be your ultimate sacrifice in gratitude. Until then, however, your body is a reflection of the earth's beauty and mystery, every moment within it a testament to the potential of the earth to create completion. As a physical being, born of earth, you are both the lowest point of creation and the height of its wonder."

Earthy part of earth / No astrological attribution

Illumination

The Princess of Pentacles is given the elemental association of the earthy aspect of earth. As such, she is not only quintessentially earth, but also the foundational and manifesting aspects of earth: the role of earth as foundation beneath us and kingdom around us. All of the princesses share the common theme of awakening and blossoming, but none exemplifies it more so than the Princess of Pentacles, as she is found in the suit of the everyday world in which we are born, grow, live, and die. All the princesses also share the attribute of being the recipients of new knowledge, apprentices and students in their suit, bringing with them the first foundations of future success in each area of life. In the case of the Princess of Pentacles, these foundations are to be found in the everyday world, the world of work, study, money, and health.

Earth, being the lowest and most manifest of the four elements, may at times be seen as less important or disconnected from the spiritual plane, and thus the Princess of Pentacles may also seem like the lowest manifestation of energy in the tarot. However, earth is fertile and fruitful, it provides us with all of our sustenance, a foundation for our lives, and it is on the earth plane that we grow. Thus, although the Princess of Pentacles is, indeed, the lowest of the court cards of the tarot, she is also the most fertile. All the energy of manifestation has fallen into this card, and now it lies within the belly of the princess, who will bring it to birth. Essentially, in this card we find rebirth for the tarot itself, as we can imagine that each card is contained within the princess's womb, just as all the seeds of life are contained within the earth.

We can see this rebirth aspect of the card, and the potential for growth and birth that the card represents, in the symbol of the rising sun that splashes its golden rays across the sky in the image. This sun brings dawn with it, and it has been reborn from the underworld of night, seemingly from within the earth. The sunlight is synonymous with illumination and the divine light found in the universe and within ourselves, and thus it represents the awakening of illumination in the everyday world. This also reminds us of the connection between the mundane world and the world of spirit, a connection which can be found repeatedly in the suit of pentacles.

The hill from behind which the sun is reborn has a white road snaking over it, winding gently along its green contours. This tells us that the Princess of Pentacles represents a stable pathway in the everyday world, a guide and map which we can follow as we begin a new journey or project. The path through the hills is clear and easy to follow, and the Princess of Pentacles is simple and uncomplicated, a refreshing change from many of the other cards in the tarot! Around her, amongst the hills, are cherry trees in blossom and blood-red poppies. The cherry tree symbolizes the act of blossoming, life awakening, and new beginnings. It is fitting to find her card so full of flowers, nature's sign of fertility and the stage in plants that occurs before the fruiting. These flowering trees therefore show us the potential for harvest and results, rather than results themselves. Poppies are a symbol of sacrifice, their colour mimicking blood; in the Western world, the poppy itself is worn to remember those that gave their lives in the two world wars. They remind us that our blood will one day feed the earth when we pass on, and that the foundation of earth beneath our feet is made up of the blood and bones of our ancestors and all the creatures that have come before us. The poppies ask us to be prepared to make sacrifices in order to build strong foundations beneath us, in all our endeavours.

In her left hand, the Princess of Pentacles holds up a sheaf of golden wheat, representative of the harvest and the promise of future results coming to fruition through hard work, effort, and sacrifice. Yet we do not see golden fields in this card, and therefore these few sheaves are merely a hint at the harvest. This card does not represent that harvest itself, but the potential for it. The way in which this beautifully adorned young woman holds the sheaves aloft and gently supports the weight of the golden pentacle in her hand as she wanders across the flowered hills at dawn is suggestive of a sunrise ritual welcoming the sun back to the world after the night. Our Princess of Pentacles might be a priestess, like her sister the Princess of Cups, but whereas the Princess of Cups was an oracle and sibyl in her temple, the Princess of Pentacles is a handmaiden of Mother Earth. Her concerns are with the turning of the seasons and the world that sustains us. She heralds in the dawn because this card also heralds in new beginnings of all kinds. This is a new day, a new dawn, a new life, and a new opportunity.

Revelation

In a reading, the Princess of Pentacles can represent a person in the querent's life, or the querent themselves. It is also likely to indicate an event, theme, or state of being in which the querent finds themselves. The surrounding cards and the context of the question will indicate which aspect the card is taking.

When the Princess of Pentacles appears in a reading, she brings with her much raw potential, suggesting new beginnings with a good chance of success because of their firm foundations. The querent may be in the initial stages of a project and working on the first steps, moving logically and carefully forward. It is likely that whatever venture the querent is beginning represents something entirely new for them, something they have not explored before, and which therefore contains great life-changing potential for them. This is new ground for the querent, and they are likely to be excited about it. The seeds are sown and the querent has the chance to bring them to fruition.

Most often this card signifies new beginnings or the start of a new project in the areas of money, work, skills, talents, or the family. The querent may be picking up a new hobby, craft, or trade, learning a new skill, or applying themselves to studying something practical and hands-on. The Princess of

Pentacles does not often deal with abstract and intellectual subjects, but instead is pragmatic, realistic, and down-to-earth with the skills she chooses to learn and apply. This card advises the querent that they must be realistic about their goals and the returns they expect to see from their efforts; there is a suggestion of harvest and eventual outcome, but it is not certain. Only their hard work and dedication, action and manifestation can bring about results. As such, the Princess of Pentacles also suggests that the situation or problem the querent is currently involved in will be best approached or rectified through dedication and a clear understanding of what is required of them, the hard work they need to put in, and a willingness to give everything they've got.

The Princess of Pentacles can sometimes represent a student or apprentice, but most often the act of learning something through doing rather than reading or thinking about it. As such, it can indicate any practical study of life skills, including budgeting, cooking, handicrafts, or gardening. It often points to activities involving the outdoors or nature, such as growing vegetables, taking care of a plot of land, and ecology or conservation work. This card can also represent a new savings account or investment, the nascent idea for a business, or the first steps on a career. Occasionally, the Princess of Pentacles, particularly if accompanied by the Empress and the Queen of Pentacles, can represent pregnancy.

As a person, the Princess of Pentacles is practical and pragmatic, realistic and studious. Though probably young in personality (though not necessarily in age), they are no stranger to dedication and commitment. They are often a student, apprentice, or somebody who is just starting to climb the ladder of their chosen career. The person indicated by the Princess of Pentacles contains great potential within them, and they have immense skill and talent, and the desire to build something with those things.

Reversed, this card brings a focus on the everyday world that ignores all other aspects of life, such as the emotions or spiritual matters. It can point to daily life becoming so rigid that it holds the querent back, or foundations that they are either afraid to move away from or unable to move away from, halting their progress and creating obstacles. Sometimes, this card reversed indicates somebody who initially provided the querent with help on a project, but who is now creating a hindrance for them.

Keywords

Potential, new beginnings, awakening, blossoming, foundation, kingdom, the everyday world, Mother Earth, cultivation, pregnancy, pragmatism, seeds, future results, dedication, commitment, new investments, new projects.

CHAPTER 28

The Princes

Prince of Wands, the Adventurer of Passion

"Life is a colourful tapestry, rich and vibrant, there for the taking and offering itself up like a youth in first love. How can you not take it every which way you can? How can you not immerse yourself completely in it, lose yourself in it, and embark on any adventure that calls you? You must be able to feel it, like a fire coursing in your bloodstream, burning from the inside out. It makes you want to rush forward, thrust your way into life, throw yourself headfirst and experience everything, take any risk, climb any mountain. Oh, for the thrill of the chase and the challenge of a lifetime! For the chance to prove yourself! Some say it is best to take life as it comes, to saunter gently by while enjoying the scenery. I say no. Everything is imperative. Everything must be done now, in the moment, before life gets away from you. Seize the day, give time a run for its money, and never become a passive participant in the magic that is your life. Think of all the foreign lands and cultures out there, all the languages you don't yet speak, cuisine you have yet to taste, sights yet to be seen and people yet to meet. How could you pass up any opportunity that might lead to new horizons? If it is new, unusual, novel, it is good. Don't allow yourself to be tied down to one place, rooted to anywhere or anyone—one thing is never enough. Your actions are a direct reflection of your personality, and they are on display for all to see, so make them count. Be the adventure, be the passion, and go out and grab life in both hands."

Airy part of fire / Sagittarius

Illumination

All of the princes are bound to take your breath away in their own unique fashion: the Prince of Cups with his romance and desire, the Prince of Pentacles with his loyalty and intensity, and the Prince of Swords with his heroism and impulsiveness. Yet it is the Prince of Wands that is perhaps the most dashing and awe-inspiring of them all, yet the least predictable and the most likely to bring danger in his wake. He shares an essential masculine quality with his brother the Prince of Swords; he is associated with the element of air because he is a prince and with the element of fire because he is in the suit of wands. Like all his airy brothers, this prince seeks expansion, exploration, discovery, and opportunity. He is a seeker within his suit, venturing out to come to grips with the nature of his suit. In the context of the wands, this makes him a seeker after the self, the ego, personality, passion, ambition, opportunity, drive, sexuality, and fun. He is extremely driven, a force to be reckoned with, and he shares the rushing, impetuous nature of the Prince of Swords. Further, he is impulsive and explosive, being a combination of the air that feeds the fire, plus the fuel of the wood that each wand is made of.

Air and fire acting in conjunction in this card can be seen as the act of fanning the flames, making the fire bigger and therefore also more dangerous. Anybody that has watched fires being set and then seen them take hold, seen them burn and consume their fuel, and watched them grow bigger, knows that they are hypnotic and beautiful to look at, but also require containment. Whereas the Princess of Wands, the earthy part of air, is both the fuel of the fire and its container, the Prince of Wands is the further feeding of the fire without any containment. It is a card, therefore, of going out of control, a force taking over so rapidly that it cannot be stopped, and a continuous desire for more of everything. The Prince of Wands must constantly be stimulated, and his airy nature means that he must also continually encounter new experiences and make new discoveries. Like the fire given endless fuel and no containment, he never stops, and he has the passion, drive, and ambition to back him up, unlike his brother in the suit of swords who has momentum and the need for a cause, yet no drive, no reason, and no plan beyond the moment.

In the card image, we see that the prince's horse is rearing up dangerously, showing us the rash and impetuous nature of this prince, as well as his tendency to get into trouble. The beautiful white castle in the background, complete with grand towers and domes, and the fact that our prince is situated at a height in the mountains, represents his desire to always make a good impression; reputation and fame are two things that he desires greatly, much like the queen and king of this suit.

So the Prince of Wands brings with him a desire for adventure, passion and burning instinct, and the ability to follow through. If we all had the drive and willpower of the Prince of Wands, we would all be successful and lucky. However, we must remember that he is still only the prince of his suit, not the king, and therefore has a lot to learn yet. He is still exploring and discovering his suit and all it represents, and therefore he is like a teenager: he thinks he knows everything and acts as if he does, yet often gets into trouble because of his lack of knowledge. As an air card, he is fond of talking about himself and his achievements, his skills and strength, yet there is a strong suggestion that he is "all talk and no trousers," a braggart or boast who would be unable to prove himself if he were challenged. There is an essence of trickster about him too, since his intelligence, wit, and charisma allow him to impress people, to convince and persuade them, and if he chose to, he could use this to his advantage (and their disadvantage) quite easily. Thus, the Prince of Wands is often a charlatan, only in it for what he can get. He is also, being in the suit of fire, ego-driven and self-centred, and whilst this can be a positive thing, bringing with it confidence and a can-do attitude, it can also lead to the prince being a manipulator of those weaker than him. However, sometimes the prince does not do this deliberately; he can often be well-intentioned, embarking on what to others are hair-brained schemes and idle quests, but which he believes will gain him fame, renown, riches, and so on, which also end up getting those around him into trouble somehow. Although he may be an adventurer and an explorer, he is an inexperienced one, making him the most likely of all the court cards to end up in a sticky situation.

Because of his airy desire to explore and expand, and his fiery way of moving from one fuel to the next, the Prince of Wands is the quintessential jack-of-all-trades, yet master of none. He knows a little about a vast number of things, usually just enough to get by and to give the impression that he knows a lot, but actually not enough to do anything with. He's great at a party because of this—he can converse about any subject that comes up, but not in-depth, and after a while, anybody who has a reasonable level of knowledge on that subject will quickly see the Prince of Wands for what he is. Yet this does not stop the Prince of Wands being a braggart and a boast, happy to tell anybody who will listen about his exploits and skills, often exaggerating his character and achievements.

However, whilst the Prince of Wands is being painted in a somewhat negative light above, we must remember that he represents something very vital within our lives, which many people lose as they grow older, but which at some point we have all experienced. He is the need to seize the day, to seize every moment and grab every opportunity with both hands, to squeeze the most out of life and to see the world while we are able. In this card can be found all the hopes and ambitions of our younger selves: when we wanted to rule the world, make exciting new discoveries, travel to all manner of exotic places, make ourselves rich, and do all manner of crazy things. It is the Prince of Wands within us all that makes us skydive, bungee jump, walk on fire, swim with sharks, climb mountains, take a gap year to go backpacking across Asia, sell everything we own to buy a camper van and become a traveller, or get a tattoo. The Prince of Wands is youth at its best (and its worst), and a constant reminder in the tarot that youth is not dependent upon age but upon mindset.

Revelation

As with all the court cards, the Prince of Wands in a reading can indicate a person in the querent's life or the querent themselves; it can also indicate a character trait or aspect of the querent's personality that is relevant at this time. Further, it can point to a theme in the querent's life or an event. Surrounding cards and the context of the question can help the reader decide what form this court card is taking in the reading.

Most often, the Prince of Wands blazes into the querent's reading to indicate opportunities for adventure. If the querent has been considering trying something new, making a big change, or doing something that might be considered risky, the Prince of Wands is the card that advises them to do it wholeheartedly. For instance, the querent may be thinking about selling everything and moving abroad, away from everything and everyone they know; they may be thinking about taking a risk financially on an investment, or dropping out of college to pursue a different path, or perhaps taking up a project that may seem like it would never be worth the time and effort; the Prince of Wands says that such a venture is indeed risky, but it is a risk worth taking. However, he does not assure success; instead, the Prince of Wands assures the querent that their risk-taking will lead to greater experience, passion, and ambition. Failure may still occur, but the querent will be better off afterward, regardless. The Prince of Wands is all about the journey rather than the destination, and he'd much rather see a colourful, fun, and vibrant endeavour fail than a boring, dull, and monotonous endeavour succeed. He often appears in a reading for a querent who feels deep down that it is time to do something completely different, something that challenges them and offers them adventure and excitement, but they don't know how to manifest it. Surrounding cards may help answer this question.

The Prince of Wands often shows up in a reading to indicate young people, particularly students in higher education, who are just venturing out into the world on their own and busy exploring everything it has to offer. As a person, the Prince of Wands is a "try-sexual"—he (or she) will try anything once. He is often taking risks and getting into trouble, but also having amazing adventures and a lot of fun. This card therefore indicates fun times, parties, and opportunities for the querent to shine socially and to explore their own personalities and selves through interaction with others. It's also a time in the querent's life for discovering what drives them and makes them passionate, which is likely to require dabbling in a great number of different things to find out what they are like before settling on one. This also goes for romantic relationships: the querent is likely to be in a position where they have the desire and/or opportunity to have many and varied dalliances and flirtations rather than one serious, committed relationship. If the querent is looking for a more long-term romance and the Prince of Wands appears, they should be advised that their next love interest is likely to only want something short-term, just for fun, with no strings attached.

Career and work-wise, the Prince of Wands suggests to the querent that it may be time for a radical change, something completely new. This may involve taking a risk, such as quitting a job before the next is lined up, or taking a pay cut to pursue a more desirable role. Socially, the Prince of Wands can be a very positive card of fun, frolics, parties, and adventures with friends, but it can also suggest that the querent's social circle lacks depth and dedication, and may be easily split up or dispersed.

Reversed, the Prince of Wands warns the querent that they may be taking too many risks, or rushing in without thinking. They may also need to be certain that they can back up any claims they make, or else they are likely to be called out by those in the know. This card reversed can also point to charlatans and tricksters who may wish to manipulate or use the querent in some way, or a love interest that is going to turn out to be a big mistake.

Keywords

Adventure, excitement, challenge, fun, risk-taking, opportunity, charlatan, jack-of-all-trades, trickster, braggart, boast, dalliance, youth, impetuousness, danger, exaggeration, passion, ambition.

Prince of Swords, Charging into the Fray

"Breathe in. Let the cold air fill your lungs to bursting. Feel it all around you, that rush of wind and the gust of the storm rising; feel the energy palpable in the air, tingling and stimulating, picking up your hair and whipping it across your face. Let it push you forward, giving you momentum as you rush headlong into the fray. Relish the battle for its own sake, not for what it might bring you or for your chosen cause. Do you even remember what you're fighting for? When you're caught up in that exciting whirlwind of force, what is there except to keep moving? Talking is done and planning is brief; strategy is a fine thing to hide behind for those that lack courage. Be bold, for fortune favours the brave! Let me lead you into the battle, let us raise our swords together, and let the air that fills our lungs become a war cry to shake the very mountains! Let us prove our worth and take up the sword for any cause, and let our desire for the soaring rush never let us tarry, but always take us onward to other horizons."

Airy part of air / Gemini

Illumination

The Prince of Swords charges his way into the court cards of the tarot, blustering and bold, impetuous and arrogant, his war cry loud and shattering. He brings with him a mighty storm with rushing winds, and all around us we can hear the howling and shrieking air. Since all the princes of the tarot are associated with the element of air, and this prince finds himself in the suit of swords, also associated with air, he represents that element at its most quintessential. As such, he is the rushing forth of ideas, thoughts and words being carried forward, immense intelligence and desire for exploration, discovery, and expansion, but also the inability of those ideas to take form or find a foundation. Air is one of the least manifest elements; it is invisible, wispy and barely formed. Without the addition of other elements, such as earth to provide stability, fire to provide desire, or water to provide expression, our thoughts and ideas are unformed and flighty. They are merely inclinations, streams of consciousness, sudden intellectual inspirations, flights of fancy, abstract ideologies, and thoughts raised up onto pedestals conveniently out of reach. As such, the Prince of Swords is a champion of any and every ideal and belief, thought and cause, a proponent of any new idea, an eternal explorer, always curious and rushing into situations, and perhaps too impetuous and foolhardy for his own good, as he is carried forth on the spur of the moment. In this sense, the Prince of Swords has a lot in common with the Fool card's more negative qualities: as the saying goes, "Fools rush in where angels fear to tread."

In the card image, we see our prince bravely leading the head of a battle charge. His face is set and determined as his red hair whips about him, picked up by the brewing storm. In his left hand, he carries an overly large sword, and it seems that this sword is more for show than for use: it is ornate, clean, unscarred, and if we assume that a greater number of people are right- handed, it is also held in the wrong hand. Even his armour appears more decorative than functional, being fashioned in gold, a very soft metal. Even his horse is dressed in gold armour, with butterfly motifs repeating on both the horse and the prince, to further express the link to the element of air and its more unstable qualities. It is clear that although our prince is brave and valiant, unafraid to be the first into battle, he is also untested, untried, and inexperienced; there is the suggestion that he is going into battle more for the sake of going into battle than for any cause or potential result. He is like the young men throughout history who have lied about their age to sign up for the army and march off to war, unaware of the horrors that they will experience, driven only by the need to prove themselves or seek new horizons, to test themselves or to follow a half-formed idea or desire.

We can see that the army the prince leads is a vast one, and it is now running behind him at full speed in a charge toward the enemy. He leads an unstoppable and fearsome force, but the fact that he is at the front of it, on a horse, with shining armour, shows that he represents the idea itself that the men behind him are fighting for. The Prince of Swords not only rushes forth with an idea or thought, he also personifies that idea or thought held aloft as the highest good: a cause to fight for, an ideology to push forward, an untamed idea that is being sent out into the world to find its way.

As the element of air in the suit of air, the Prince of Swords is the expansion of new ideas into the world, the principle of exploration and discovery. He is therefore not just the leader of a battle charge; he would not be out of place in a scientific laboratory, an observatory, or a library, seated in front of reams of paper covered in scribbled calculations and mathematical formulae. He is the scientist, researcher, and genius, the Einstein of his age. He is eager to stretch the capabilities of the mind to their greatest extent, pushing the boundaries of his field of research, testing new theories, and creating new hypotheses. But as with so many new hypotheses, the Prince of Swords does not move beyond the theoretical stage. Often this is because, upon closer inspection or testing, the hypotheses are disproven, but with the Prince of Swords it may also be because he gets easily distracted and very quickly goes off on a tangent in his research.

The mind of the Prince of Swords is not completely mature, in that he finds it difficult to dedicate himself and commit to an idea, philosophy, or plan. He does not, in fact, make plans at all, but prefers to improvise, play things by ear, and respond to events rather than acting based on a strategy. The Prince of Swords is very "teenage" in this manner. Like an impetuous youngster, he is prone to picking up an idea or philosophy, dabbling with it for a while, and then moving on to the next thing quickly, before he has thoroughly explored this one or taken any action on it. He might, for instance, decide that learning a new language would be interesting, so he starts doing so, but quickly gets bored and drops it after a few weeks in favour of white-water rafting or learning to play guitar. For the Prince of Swords, whose mind is always on the go, there are so many amazing things in the universe to learn, it is impossible to stick to just a few. Is therefore the ultimate jack-of-all-trades, yet master of none. However, don't let this disenchant you of him: he is brave and courageous, enthusiastic and intelligent. If he has a cause to fight for, he will be an unstoppable force carrying it forward and expanding it, but he will require commitment and dedication from others to stabilize his ideas.

Revelation

In a reading, the Prince of Swords often represents a person in the querent's life or the querent themselves, or perhaps an aspect of the querent's personality, a role they need to play in their life, or an approach to a situation that they should take to elicit the best results or solve a problem. Court cards can also represent events, so be aware of other cards in the reading, the context of the question, and your intuition to help decide what form they are taking.

When the Prince of Swords breezes into a spread, he indicates sudden changes and upheavals, uncertainties and possibilities. If the querent's question was regarding the success of a project, the Prince of Swords is not the best card to receive: he does not deal in certainties and suggests that results are not guaranteed; everything is still "up in the air," and there are more possibilities than the querent is perhaps aware of. He also suggests that the querent may not have laid the foundations yet, or put in enough effort or work, to create anything solid in the situation. Although the querent may be blazing ahead and very enthusiastic, tackling the situation head-on, they may also be so caught up in doing so that they may not realize that success and victory are uncertain. However, the beauty of the Prince of Swords is that it represents a time when the querent is so caught up in the rush of something new, or taken up with an idea, that they can enjoy it for what it is, in the moment, rather than only enjoying it for the results it can bring. This card therefore also represents the querent living in the moment, particularly on an intellectual level.

Sometimes this card represents new discoveries and horizons for the querent intellectually, new philosophies for them to explore, and new ideologies and ways of thinking that are opening up to them. The Prince of Swords advises the querent not to be afraid to entertain these new ideas and to dabble in ideologies; although some may frown upon dabbling, seeing it as not providing enough certainty or experience to be of any use, it will benefit the querent who will be able to test things out and then later commit to a path. Like his fiery counterpart the Prince of Wands, the Prince of Swords will try anything once, just to see if it is suitable, and he has the momentum to move on quickly if it is not, something that his more down-to-earth brothers—the Prince of Cups and the Prince of Pentacles—find difficult.

If the Prince of Swords appears in a reading regarding relationships and romance, it usually doesn't indicate an established relationship at all, but rather a fleeting dalliance, most often a suitor who quickly breezes into the querent's life and just as quickly breezes out again after a short period of time. It may also signify a possible relationship option for the querent to consider. If the Prince of Swords represents a partner in an established relationship, the querent needs to be aware that this partner is prone to running away when commitment is required; they are easily distracted by other options and opportunities.

As a card showing up in career or workplace readings, the Prince of Swords suggests the querent becoming champion of an idea, trying to promote a new method or theory, and being the spokesperson for it. This card is particularly well-suited for intellectual pursuits, studies, and projects that require a lot of mental activity. It indicates an active mind well-disposed to research and exploration, yet the querent is advised to cast their intellectual net widely rather than focusing too much.

As a general advice card, the Prince of Swords says that fortune favours the bold. If the querent is in any way concerned about a course of action, this card says: *do it*. As a person, the Prince of Swords is impetuous, foolhardy yet brave, always on the go, eager to explore everything the world has to offer, and extremely intelligent, with strokes of genius happening frequently. This person flits from one thing to another quickly, finds commitment or dedication difficult, and will happily champion any cause that he picks up.

Reversed, the Prince of Swords indicates foolishness and impetuous action that can lead the querent into danger or difficult situations, as well as an iconoclast who champions rebellious causes for the sake of being rebellious, rather than for any goal. Reversed, this card can indicate that the querent is so disorganized, and so eager to try as many things as possible, that they are missing out on a lot that life has to offer. They are in danger of never learning anything of substance, and never training their mind to focus on a purpose. It also indicates that the querent may be rushing into a situation or project without suitable planning or preparation, and that this might cause them problems.

Keywords

Rushing, impetuousness, foolishness, disorganization, exploration, research, discovery, champion, cause, philosophy, novelty, instability, new ideas, uncertainty.

Prince of Cups, the Saviour and Grail Seeker

"Do you know what it is to love? Do you understand the force that urges you ever onward toward union, and creates an all-pervasive, overwhelming tidal wave of emotion that pushes you toward your desire? Oh yes, every human has known love and affection, and has felt emotions stirring within them, but it takes a particular kind of person to truly know love… the kind of love that is tragic and beautiful, the kind written about by bards of old and captured in the finest of poetry, the most passionate of spiritual writings, and the most well-known tales. This is the love of Lancelot, Romeo, Psyche, and every mystic treading the path to union. This is the yearning for the divine, the beloved, the Holy Grail and ultimate understanding. Yet even upon union, with the object of desire firmly

in your grasp, the quest will not be complete. It never can be. The heart always wants more, always needs to move, seek, and yearn. And so, the Grail Quest is lifelong and for most is never completed; only the purest achieve the vision of the Grail, and they are the unlucky ones. For what can one do when the yearned-for desire is achieved? What comes next? They say that when Alexander the Great looked out over his empire he wept, for there was nothing left to conquer. How sad and lonely it must be to finally get what you want. Is it not better to always be in a state of yearning? Poor Romeo… he got the lady after whom he lusted, and in the end death was sweet release. And Lancelot, that knight of renown so favoured by the lady Guinevere? What joy for him to never have to sully his love of that goddess with reality! In truth, can there be any difference between one's love of a woman and one's love of that divine Grail? No. The heart must always love and seek, yet the object of its desire takes many forms."

Airy part of water / Pisces

Illumination

It should come as no surprise to find many readers swooning and slightly out of breath when faced with the image of the stunning Prince of Cups. Arrayed in silver armour and flowing blue silk robes, his long platinum-blond hair flowing gently in the breeze, with a pair of angel wings upon his back, this prince is the quintessential "knight in shining armour" of many teenage fantasies. Here, astride the whitest and most elegant of horses, is Prince Charming as our willing lover, a dashing beauty who desires us and yearns for us, whose passion is almost overwhelming in its intensity.

The personality of the Prince of Cups is evocatively portrayed in the card image. Everything about him seems pure, noble, gentle, and peaceful. His horse is moving gently, not rushing forward like its brother in the Prince of Swords, not rearing up as in the Prince of Wands, yet not static as in the Prince of Pentacles. This indicates that the Prince of Cups enjoys movement and progress, but is thoughtful about his choices and actions, not rushing in or making hasty decisions. The horse being white tells us of the purity of the prince's intentions and choices, and the angelic wings the prince bears indicate his desire to help others and to perform acts of goodness and kindness, often in the role of saviour to others, rushing in to pull them out of trouble, or to inspire goodness in them. Yet in his arms we can see a bouquet of peacock feathers, this plumage being symbolic of vanity, pretentiousness, and rivalry in matters of love.

The Prince of Cups, elementally, is the airy part of water, sharing the qualities of air with his brother princes, and existing in the suit of water. As with his brothers, he seeks to expand, move forward, learn, and explore, but in the suit of cups these qualities manifest as a continual seeking of love and affection, yearning toward an object of emotional desire, and moving quickly from one state of love to another. This makes the Prince of Cups the eternal lover, the figure upon which characters such as Romeo and Lancelot were based— but also the most fickle of lovers. Here we find a strange dichotomy in the prince of this suit: whilst he is committed to the journey of desire, he is not necessarily committed to the *object* of desire. Attachment does not come easily to any of the princes, and the watery part of this prince's nature means that not only is he always moving, but he is also always in flux, changeable and reflective. As such, when he achieves union with his object of desire, he very quickly gets bored and moves on, finding something new to yearn for. The Prince of Cups is more in love with the quest for love than he is with anything or anyone.

However, as the typical "knight in shining armour," the Prince of Cups is a force for good, a champion of all things right, and a loyal servant of whatever it is he currently loves. He acts with purity of intention and heart, and those that see this seek to emulate him. It therefore makes sense that throughout the age of film, the greatest and best-loved characters have been dashing, valiant young lovers, swept away by the intensity of their feelings, yearning for (usually) another person's love, and eventually receiving it. Yet these same films do not often show us what happens after the attainment. The lovers are united, the guy gets the girl or the girl gets the guy, and then the film ends, as if that is the furthest conclusion. Yet in reality we know that this is merely the beginning of a relationship, which takes commitment, work, understanding, and compromise. The Prince of Cups is not about the reality of a relationship, but rather the desire for one, the idealistic dream of love rather than its truth and actuality.

The Prince of Cups is similar to the love-struck poet found in much folklore and myth, or the mystical seeker yearning for divine love rather than human love. The emotional exploration of the Prince of Cups does not necessarily take place through desire for another; it can also take place on a spiritual level, with the prince being the one that searches for meaning or understanding. We find this motif throughout mythology, in deities, and in heroes and heroines who have undertaken grand quests—not for glory or vanity, but to achieve understanding and divine union. Psyche, the Greek goddess of the soul, is a perfect example of this. Her particular quest had as its goal Eros himself, a personification of erotic love and passion, and in uniting with him, Psyche also achieved immortality as a goddess.

Although the Prince of Cups often represents a romantic interest or lover, it also represents the act of looking for emotional fulfilment in some form. Of course, since emotions and people are extremely varied and individual, this can manifest in many ways. The journey upon which the Prince of Cups treads is a universal motif of longing, yet the details of it are always different. Luckily, however, being a card of air as much as water, he represents progress in the concerns of this suit, movement forward and ever onward, even though the goal may prove to be unattainable. Yet since the element of air relates to the mind and thoughts, and the suit of cups to love, emotions, and the social world, our prince can devolve rapidly from heroic, gallant lover to obsessed creep. When all of one's thoughts and mind are focused on an object of desire, it is all too easy to lose one's perspective.

Revelation

As with all court cards, in a reading the Prince of Cups often indicates a person in the querent's life, or the querent themselves, yet it can also be more symbolic. It can, for instance, represent aspects of the querent's personality, certain character traits that are required in the current situation or becoming prevalent in their life. It can also indicate an approach that is required, an overall theme or feeling, as well as an event. The reader's intuitive response, the context of the question, and the surrounding cards can clarify what form this court card takes.

As a person, the Prince of Cups usually indicates a lover or love interest of either gender, and the prospect of a relationship with that person. It can also represent the querent looking for love or a relationship. The Prince of Cups is often in love repeatedly, a serial monogamist, enjoying more the act of falling in love than perhaps the actual relationship that results from it. He or she is always getting distracted by the next prettiest thing or the shiniest new fad, but they are just as committed to this new object of desire as they were the last. Although they can be vain or fickle, they do not lack dedication and commitment. The Prince of Cups is a romantic at heart, who prizes beauty highly, as well as goodness and kindness; as a lover they are considerate and deeply emotional, intense and giving. They feel everything acutely and get easily drawn into a relationship. However, they can also be an idealist, and often fail to see the reality of a situation or relationship, instead seeing what they want it to be, or creating an ideal future that they feel they can attain. The Prince of Cups as a person is also poetic, often expressing their emotions through writing poetry or fiction, or following other creative pursuits; many of these pursuits are never shown to others. They enjoy helping those in need and often "ride in" to save the day.

If the querent is the Prince of Cups, this card suggests that he or she may be so in love with their ideal picture of the future in their current relationship that they are missing the truth of the relationship. For instance, they may be so caught up with planning their wedding that they are blind to the parts of their relationship that they hate.

As an event, the Prince of Cups represents the act of being swept off one's feet. It is that rushing feeling of love, desire, and attraction that we often feel at the start of a relationship. It can also indicate a flirtation or courtship that the querent is beginning with another person, or even an infatuation with a new way of being. It might also put the querent into the role of saviour, requiring them to face the current situation with kindness and show that kindness to another person in their life.

In a career or work-related reading, the Prince of Cups can sometimes indicate a dalliance in the workplace, but it can also suggest that the querent is not entirely happy in their current position and is seeking to move into an area that they are more connected to emotionally. In a reading about spiritual matters, this card points to the searching for mystical union, understanding, and spiritual wisdom. In this sense, the Prince of Cups might indicate that the querent is a mystic or spiritual seeker, on some kind of personal Grail Quest.

Reversed, the Prince of Cups can represent obsession, either by the querent, by somebody else, or directed toward the querent. It can indicate that the querent is ignoring the reality of a relationship and preferring to only see their idealized version, or that they are more in love with the idea of being in love than with the person they are supposedly in love with. Sometimes this card reversed can represent a relationship that has become dull and boring, or which feels oppressive and over-the-top. At times, the Prince of Cups reversed also says that the querent or a partner might feel overwhelmed by their feelings and therefore is trying to run away.

Keywords

Love, lover, relationship, courtship, romance, poetry, idealism, knight in shining armour, saviour, kindness, goodness, partner, yearning, desire, mystical quest, flirtation, obsession.

Prince of Pentacles, the Stone Guardian

"Some chase after noble causes, the hands of fair lovers, renown and fame, adventure and excitement, but only a fool does so before he has first established a stable and solid foundation. How can any of these things truly be obtained without first having the practical means to pursue them? How can they offer anything but fleeting possibilities, never realized? They say youth is wasted on the young and perhaps I am guilty of losing my years to slow and steady movement, rather than rushing into life, headstrong and reckless. Yet I will learn from history and the past mistakes of others, and I refuse to be doomed to pitfalls that can be so easily avoided. Caution is the best way to advance; slow and careful movement will assure future success. Before crops can grow in a field, it must be carefully ploughed, tilled, sown, and cared for; it must be watched over, protected from creatures that would eat away at the seeds or buds. Before any plans can reach fruition, one's future investments must be protected, considered, watched over, and cared for. How unwise to go rushing off to something new, leaving your efforts to waste away due to lack of attention! How ignorant to think that speed is the only means of measuring success! One day, we all will be in need of the stability I can offer; I am the loyal stone guardian and the reliable friend, the companion, and the rock upon which you can lean. I am the mind at its most stable, the careful plan and the slow progress toward actuality."

Airy part of earth / Virgo

Illumination

All the princes in the Tarot Illuminati share the element of air, associated with the mind, questing, seeking, movement, and exploration; the Prince of Pentacles is also represented by the element of earth. The princes themselves are expansive in nature, since they are not yet kings in their realm but aspire to such; they are the youthful desire to go out into the world and explore. After the princesses, who represent the first awakenings of the elemental powers of their suit, the princes represent the exploration and expansion of their suit. As such, the earthy Prince of Pentacles seeks to explore, expand, and make progress in areas of finances, investments, security, home, family, the environment, health, wealth, and prosperity. Princes are known in the tarot also to be guardians and defenders of their suit, and thus the Prince of Pentacles is the most stalwart defender of those practical matters in his realm.

In the card image, the prince's gaze is focused intently on the golden coin in his hand: he is carefully considering the current state of affairs, rather than rushing onward to create a new one. This prince is clearly paying attention to the task at hand and would put a lot of store in the saying, "A bird in the hand is worth two in the bush." His horse is black, like the richest of soil, indicating the practicality and earthiness of the Prince of Pentacles, and it is the kind of horse that would not look out of place pulling a plough. This is a working horse, well cared for and strong, showing us that the priorities of this prince are protecting what he has and ensuring prosperity, longevity, and success in the future. Whereas the princes of the other suits are riding horses that are moving, rearing up, or charging forth, this horse is at a standstill, merely raising one hoof perhaps as a sign of impatience. It might, at first, seem that the richness of the prince's costume and armour is at odds with the practical nature of the card, but this prince is the richest of all of them because he has created an investment and is guarding it, watching it grow, instead of rushing off to the next distracting adventure. Thus he is situated by the ploughed fields that are pushing forth crops. Although his progress may be slower than that of his brothers—as slow, in fact, as the progress of crop growth, which cannot be hurried—his success is almost certainly assured. If he loses his investment, it won't be for want of trying, but through unforeseen circumstances or unfortunate accident.

Since air is associated with the mind, thoughts, and communication, the Prince of Pentacles shows us the mind when it is at its most stable and down-to-earth, practical and applied to the real world. Instead of rushing off in flights of fancy like the Prince of Cups, or getting easily distracted like the Prince of Swords, or trying to master everything by briefly dabbling as in the Prince of Wands, the mind of the Prince of Pentacles is dedicated, devoted, and calm. He knows his task and keeps at it until completion, paying careful attention to detail and applying hard work to back it up as a firm foundation. This does not mean, however, that the Prince of Pentacles is necessarily intelligent or clever; out of all the princes he is perhaps the least witty, least clever, and certainly the slowest to come to a conclusion. However, where one of his brothers might have a quick and risky idea that occasionally comes to fruition and proves useful through sheer genius, the Prince of Pentacles has fewer ideas, but nearly all are guaranteed to reach fruition simply because he considers all practicalities, requirements, possibilities, and uses. As far as the Prince of Pentacles is concerned, if an idea does not have an almost-certain chance of succeeding, he will not waste his time with it, and if an idea has no practical use, it is not worth the effort. This card does represent progress, though of a slow and steady kind.

You can be certain, therefore, that when the Prince of Pentacles attempts something or finds a cause to stand for, he is the most reliable and stalwart of all the princes as its defender and champion. He is known as a good friend or companion, the kind of down-to-earth and steadfast person you could trust with anything precious to you. His word is his bond and his promises are always kept. He is trustworthy to a fault. Because of this, he is also easy to read, and many people try to take advantage of him.

As an explorer in his suit, the Prince of Pentacles is the part of the self that seeks security and stability, the part searching for a strong foundation and a place to call home. It is our desire for a family and a stable environment, something we can place our trust in and rely on as our foundation. Without such a stable foundation, most of us feel disoriented, lost, and out in the cold. There is also an aspect to the Prince of Pentacles that represents the need to seek money and riches, which, in our culture, usually go toward buying security and stability, or looks for ways in which to gain employment or usefulness of some kind.

Revelation

As with all the court cards, the way in which the Prince of Pentacles can be read when it appears in a reading is varied depending on the context of the spread and question. Most often, he will indicate a person in the querent's life or the querent themselves, or perhaps an aspect of the querent's personality. It can also point to themes and events in the querent's life, however, so the reader should examine the entire reading to decide which aspect of the Prince of Pentacles is relevant.

As a person, the Prince of Pentacles is extremely practical, down-to-earth, and pragmatic. Rather than looking to move on quickly, he or she prefers to focus on the present and ensure that everything in the current situation is concluded completely before moving on. This person is cautious, and therefore sometimes misses an opportunity when it presents itself due to a delay in reaction. However, they know how to safeguard their investments and the status quo, and see no point in wishful thinking or speculation. They are devoted, dedicated, and loyal friends, the kind of friend that others describe as their "rock"—stalwart, true, and trustworthy. However, the Prince of Pentacles is not the brightest spark and can sometimes be slow to pick up on an idea; they take their time with everything, sometimes through perfectionism but sometimes because want to understand every aspect of the situation and take longer than others to come to terms with it. But the Prince of Pentacles always reaches a conclusion eventually, and slow and steady often wins the race.

When the Prince of Pentacles appears in a reading, he is often giving advice to the querent: more haste, less speed. The querent should not worry that progress is too slow, because the gradual pace allows them plenty of time to fully assess the situation or plan, get a handle on it, understand it, and ensure that it does not fail. If the querent rushes ahead without careful planning, or gets distracted from the current situation, whatever they are working on will almost certainly fail. The querent is also advised to stick to one thing or one approach, rather than trying others or dabbling, since dedication and standing firm will set them in good stead. This approach works for people in the querent's life too, whether those people are in their social sphere, romantic sphere, or workplace: if the querent shows to others that they can be trusted to stick around, they will find that their situation will improve. This also suggests that perhaps one of the reasons for difficulty at this time is caused by the uncertainty of others that the querent can be trusted.

If this card appears in the reading accompanied by other cards of slow movement, such as the Seven of Pentacles, the Three of Pentacles, or the Four of Pentacles, the querent should be aware that whatever they are hoping for in the future is going to take a longer time coming than they think, and will require more patience and hard work than at first they expect. It is time for the querent to manage their expectations and be realistic about timing and returns. They are also advised to focus on what they already have, to count their blessings, and to realize just how much they already have. Mending, rather than throwing away and obtaining something new, is also a good response at this time.

Sometimes the Prince of Pentacles shows up in a reading simply to indicate the querent's closest friend, somebody they can turn to for help at this time. It can also point to a coworker, but only if the querent is close with that person. Often, it appears to show the querent's desire for stability and security in life; a search for employment, a new job, or ways to make money; or perhaps even a search for a home to live in. If accompanied by cards such as the Ten of Pentacles or the Ten of Cups, it may point to the querent's desire for a family.

Reversed, the Prince of Pentacles suggests that progress may be too slow, and that the querent is spending so much time on details and perfection than they are failing to reach the finish line, or missing out on another opportunity. This card reversed can also point to an inability to accept new ideas or points of view, old-fashioned ways of thinking that hold the querent back, dogma, fundamentalism, and a refusal to accept a new turn of events.

Keywords

Stability, friend, loyal, trustworthy, practicality, pragmatism, search for work or employment, seeking security, slow progress, protection, guarding, investments, growth, mending, support.

CHAPTER 29

The Queens

Queen of Wands, the Flowing Beauty of Fire

"Set a fire and watch it burn. Stare deep into the flames and embers and listen to the crackling, popping, and hissing. See how the flames move and dance, the colours alive and beautiful, the shapes they form enticing and hypnotic. Can you turn your gaze away? Can you stop marvelling at the amazing miracle before you, the miracle of fire that gives you life and warmth and light? It is this very same fire that you see in the most brightly shining of souls: it radiates out from them, flowing into the world around them, and it is so enticing and hypnotic that everybody is in awe of them. Their movements, their words, their very being is as beautiful as the dancing flames. So look into the flames and see me there. See my dance of beauty, see my hands and smile beckoning you to me, see the magic in my eyes as I draw you closer, bringing you into me. I love you, I yearn for you … I want so much in life and I always get what I want, but not because I am stubborn, or spoiled, or cunning, but because I am beautiful, filled with light and life. When your words are sweet, sweet things come to you; when your heart is joyful, happiness comes to you. When you show beauty and welcome to all those around you, they welcome you into their hearts and homes. Some think me a seducer, a witch, wearing many masks, each one more beautiful than the next … yet this laughter and light, this love and liberty I wear upon my lips and which shines in my eyes comes from my innermost being, true and bright as the sun and the flames. But most cannot appreciate my honesty: they are fearful when they feel out of control; they are angry when they think another person so much more powerful and beautiful than themselves. I cannot help the jealousy of others, just as I cannot help being a shining beacon of light, radiating optimism and confidence. This is my blessing, but I share it freely with all those who are willing to receive it."

Watery part of fire / Aries

Illumination

Of the queens in the tarot, the Queen of Wands is perhaps the most beautiful, enticing, and awe-inspiring of them all. She, like the King of Cups, combines the two opposing elements of water and fire, thus she is a perfect unity of both receptive flow and active dynamism. Whereas the King of Cups is the fiery (dynamic) part of water, the Queen of Wands is the watery (flowing) part of fire, being in the suit of wands. She is the movement, beauty, and colour of fire, the way it dances and flows, the aspect of fire that entices and hypnotizes us when we stare into flames. If you've ever sat around an open fire with a group of people, you'll have experienced the pull of the fire's beauty and therefore that of the Queen of Wands: at a certain point, regardless of how exciting and stimulating the company or conversation is, everybody will turn to stare at the fire, and their gazes will get lost in the movement of the flames. Suddenly, despite the fact that most people would otherwise find silence in a group uncomfortable, everybody falls quiet and simply stares. They are all lost, together, in appreciating the light and warmth that unites them. Fire brings people together in harmony, whether in a social group or a family, and it provides us with warmth and a focal point for our gatherings where we share stories and laughter. The ancient Greeks gave to Eros both the power of fire, as well as sexual attraction and love, because it was through the light of a fire that lovers could see each other in the darkness and unite. The social aspects of fire are all found in the Queen of Wands. She brings people together, and because she herself is so bright, so warm and welcoming—just like a communal fire—she provides a united focus for groups and communities. Although she is often at the centre of attention and in a leadership position due to her fiery and passionate nature, it is not because she wants to build up her own ego, but because she knows that she is the kind of person around whom others can rally. As a watery card, she possesses the power of flow and channelling as well as nurturing, and thus she provides a mode of expression and natural flow for everything the suit of wands represents: passion, desire, ambition, creativity, sexuality, sensuality, ego, self, and personality.

In the card image, we are met with a clearly powerful woman. Her gaze is directed at us and is not humble or gentle, indirect or questioning; it is in control, passionate and somewhat seductive. Although she does not smile, she still seems warm and inviting, and the colours she wears are glowing with life:

the yellows and oranges of the sun, and the greens of burgeoning nature. Even the patterns on the material of her dress are of leaves and swirling flowers. On her lap is a black cat with an orange collar, tame and comfortable, its eyes like those of its mistress (try having a staring contest with a cat!). This queen wears golden jewellery on her hands and at her throat, and a low-cut neckline revealing impressive cleavage, obviously designed to entice. She is seated upon a throne carved with lions and embellished with embroidered sunflowers, and behind her is a sea of sunflowers, all turning their heads toward her.

Sunflowers are given their name not only for their appearance but also due to the fact that their heads turn to follow the path of the sun throughout the day, to maximise the amount of light they receive. This is the effect the Queen of Wands has on everybody around her: they all turn to look at her, basking in her light and warmth. Note also that we find these flowers in another card of the Tarot Illuminati: the Sun. This is because the Queen of Wands, as the watery aspect of fire and therefore the channel for nurturing fiery energy in our lives, represents a more earthly form of the sun's life-giving rays, in which we bask on sunny days and look forward to all winter. This queen also shares a link with another of the major arcana: Strength. In that card, we saw a maiden in white taming a lion; here, we have a woman in gold with a domestic cat. The Queen of Wands is a tamer, more domestic form of the raw power of Strength; she is the untamed fiery power of Leo (ruled by the sun), tempered by the element of water. Thus, the Queen of Wands possesses inner strength and tamed power that she can use to bring her desires and passions into reality, and which she can use to help others do the same.

The black cat has many layers of symbolism in the context of the Queen of Wands. Traditionally, the black cat is associated with witchcraft, and traditionally so is this queen. This is because, being found in the suit of wands, she is linked to power of all kinds, but mostly inner power, and as the flowing, watery aspect of the suit, she channels power and raises it up. Witchcraft is the channelling of power toward a desired goal, traditionally practised by strong, independent women, and stereotypically for seductive purposes. Far from being the old hag of nursery rhymes, the Queen of Wands' kind of witch is the beautiful temptress, using her inner power in every way she knows how, whether it is through getting a job done, through her knowledge, or in this case, through seduction.

Further, the biology of cats shows them to be innately sexual creatures.

Unneutered female cats are called queens, fitting for this card, and are well known for their overtly sexual pre-mating behaviour. A female cat calling for a male will make her desire known through yowling loudly, presenting her behind, rubbing herself against people and things, and trying to get outside. Even cat mating is loud, and a female cat will mate with many males in one evening, often meaning that one litter of kittens will have more than one father (due to post-coital ovulation in feline anatomy). In the same way, the Queen of Wands is vocal about her desire, often overtly sexual in nature, and dresses herself up to seem enticing. She is not known for being shy about her sexual nature and is confident in herself. She often has many suitors and in turn is attracted to many different people. This makes her, like the flames of a fire, fickle in matters of love, as her desires burn quickly.

Since the element of water not only acts as a channel but also as a nurturer of life, the Queen of Wands not only channels her own power and energy into the world, but also nurtures power and energy in others. Thus, like the rising flames that are symbolic of our own rising energy, the Queen of Wands brings out the desires of others, causing the awakening within them of passion, desire, or lust. Her very being can instigate a powerful transformation in others once they realize and begin to channel and direct their rising desire and sexual energy. As such, the Queen of Wands often appears as an object of desire, but not in a receptive, powerless way; she is very much in control and powerful, not over others but over herself. Since water flows around things, this queen's power flows around others, accommodating them and their needs; she is the perfect hostess and actively encourages the best qualities in others. There is also a quintessentially social aspect to this queen: she is the life and soul of any party, a social butterfly who thrives on the company of others. To some she seems like an attention seeker, but really she cannot help being the centre of attention—her light is too bright to be ignored.

Revelation

As with all court cards, in a reading the Queen of Wands often represents the querent or another person in the querent's life; it can also point to certain personality or character traits of the querent that may be possible solutions to a current problem, or which are coming to the fore in a current situation; sometimes a court card can also indicate an event or theme in the querent's life. Assessment of the spread in context will aid the reader in discovering which aspect of the Queen of Wands is most relevant.

As a person, the Queen of Wands is truly a wonder to behold. She (or he) is beautiful, fabulous, outgoing, charismatic, confident, filled with laughter and a love of life, with an inherent sense of fun and welcome. She loves being a social butterfly, and can often be found as the hostess of a party, charity function, or other social event; even when she is not the organizer or hostess, the party doesn't really kick off until she arrives as a guest. She's the kind of person everybody wants at an event because she breaks the ice, draws people together, makes great introductions, brings shy people gently out of their shell, and encourages fun. She nurtures an environment of sharing, laughter, and joy, yet at the same time she is strong and powerful, and knows who she is and what she wants. She will not be afraid of standing up to anybody, or standing up for something she cares deeply about, as her own passions run deep and true. She is also intensely sexual and sensual, and enjoys everything beautiful in life, thus appearance is important to her; she also knows that beauty comes from within and shines like a light out into the world. If the Queen of Wands represents a person in the querent's life, she can be a woman in a position of power, or the querent's female employer; this card occasionally represents a love rival or somebody on the lookout for a new partner.

Often the Queen of Wands appears in a reading to point to an increase in sexual activity, or the desire to attract a partner—sometimes a specific person, sometimes in general. It can also represent the desired partner in the reading. It points to the querent having come to terms with their sexual nature and energy, as well as their sense of self and personality, so that they might be in a better position to bring a partner into their lives. Sometimes the querent may be in the position of the Queen of Wands, encouraging another person to do this and nurturing their burgeoning awareness of themselves. This card can also point to activities that lead to a sexual awakening in the querent, such as kundalini yoga, sex magic, couples' sex therapy, positive affirmations, and more.

In work and career-related spreads, the Queen of Wands points to the querent being in control of this area of their life, bringing a sense of self, power, and personal direction to their workplace, being certain of their career goals, and being able to nurture them and flow around any obstacles. The Queen of Wands also reminds the querent, especially one looking for work, that they have a certain inner quality that shines through so strongly that others, such as potential employers, are bound to see it.

As advice, the Queen of Wands commands the querent to go out there and be fabulous! Be the life and soul of the party, the centre of attention. It is time for them to let their powerful inner light and uplifting energy shine through for others to see, as by doing so they will be able to build a stronger community around themselves, and also help others. It's also time for the querent to stop denying their sexual nature, or any power they have, and instead learn to channel it and let it flow in the right direction.

Reversed, the Queen of Wands is a powerful rival, often female, in any area of the querent's life; she can also represent the querent's worst self: the selfish, attention-seeking, fickle person with little care for anybody but themselves, who only wants glamour, fame, and praise from others for its own sake. The Queen of Wands reversed is a social manipulator who wears many masks and who will use others as means to an end. She is often a spoiled brat, and therefore can also indicate problems arising from the querent not getting what they want.

Keywords

Beauty, hypnotism, enticement, entrancement, social butterfly, confidence, inner strength, inner power, sexuality channelled, centre of attention, centre of community, inner light shining forth, witchcraft, seduction, optimism.

Queen of Swords, the Cold Teacher of Wisdom

"Some think me cold, hard, uncaring, and unloving. Some call me a widow, a spinster, an old maid turned sour through lack of feeling. These people are fools, blinded by their own ignorance and moulded by the false idea that I am defined by my gender. There is more to the feminine than what lies between the thighs, or sweetened words on honeyed lips; the receptivity and passivity that embodies flow can be found even in the sharpest of minds, the keenest of perceptions, and the coldest of tongues. For what is the mind without a means of expression? What are thoughts without the words to speak them? Where would be the wisest men of the world if there were no teachers, no communicators, no imparters of wisdom? The mind must have a guide, a channel into which it may flow, and it must be nurtured and moulded. Yet my teaching is not of the gentle kind, coaxing and coddling you to an understanding; I have no patience for ignorance,

foolishness, and incorrectness. Under my tutelage you will hone your skills and wisdom to the finest precision, you will learn to be right, and you will learn to think independently. Love wisdom, and dare to know more about the world than others think you should. Listen to my words of truth—for I speak nothing else—and you will become a true lover of wisdom. Ignore my words and I will give you no quarter, no second chance. Anybody as foolish as that does not deserve a second chance. I am a queen, not your mother, nor your lover or mistress, nor a lofty idea of a goddess. You must learn to need nobody but yourself, to rely on nobody but yourself, and to think for nobody but yourself. Realize that you are the only person responsible for your thoughts, ideas, perceptions, and responses, and do not blame me if you have not learned your lessons thoroughly enough."

Watery part of air / Libra

Illumination

We met the young Queen Elizabeth I in the Princess of Swords, and we meet her again, years later, in the Queen of Swords. She is older, wiser, colder, and sharper, her youthful innocence gone, her road of learning travelled; now she is in the role of advisor, mediator, communicator, and teacher. Elementally, she is the watery aspect of air, the flow of everything the suit of swords represents: thoughts and words, ideas and expressions, as well as the nurturing of them and the channelling of them toward a direction. As such, the Queen of Swords does not necessarily rule this element, but instead passes it on to others so that they may reap its benefits.

The Queen of Swords in our card image does not smile, and her face is painted white, as was the custom for noble ladies of the Elizabethan era (this makeup was actually created from lead, a poisonous substance that often caused lead poisoning after a time). She appears cold, distant, and intense. We can tell from looking at her that she will brook no argument and offer no second chances; her dealings will be straightforward, precise, and to the point. The butterflies in the card image tell of her rulership over communication, as the butterflies are colourful, like ideas and thoughts, and flit about through the air just like words. They may be light and easily lost, but they are also unmistakable and bright. A parrot also flies above the Queen of Swords, symbolic of the talking she is so good at. Parrots are renowned as birds that can speak, and even when they are unable to mimic human words, they are noisy avians! On her throne are carved more winged creatures, this time angels, representative of the application of her thought and communication toward human concerns.

The Queen of Swords wears an ice-blue dress that is in stark contrast to her red hair and orange-gold bodice. This ice blue reminds us of the coolness and distance of her form of thought and communication, as well as her subtlety and reserve, yet the hints of red and orange tell us of her hidden passion for her favoured subject matter or area of knowledge. The red roses scattered around the card are also symbolic of this passion; however, they are all in bud rather than full bloom, showing that perhaps her passion is not fully acknowledged or tended to by our queen, who is far too busy with her thoughts, teaching, and rulership to give any time or energy to her own feelings or desires.

In government, Queen Elizabeth I was well known for her motto *video et taceo*—"I see, and say nothing." She, like the Queen of Swords, understood the necessity and wisdom of sitting back and taking in all the information available, rather than trying to manipulate or control or take more of an active role. This demonstrates the Queen of Swords' dual nature: she is passive and receptive due to her watery nature as a queen, and thus takes in information, yet she is active due to her presence in the suit of swords, and therefore her realm is that of the active mind. She not only learns and perceives, but also teaches and advises others. In the same way, Elizabeth I stated that she would rule through "good advice and counsel," yet she was not afraid to make clear and well defined decisions while also remaining fair and magnanimous to all involved. Her policies on religion were more tolerant than her predecessors, her military strategy was mostly defensive and protected her realm without unnecessary loss of life in the name of "glory," and her international dealings were often careful, reserving something for later.

The Queen of Swords is perhaps the least "feminine" of all the queens, and indeed Elizabeth was well known as the so-called "Virgin Queen" because of her refusal to marry. She once stated that it would be preferable to her to be a "beggar-woman and single" than "queen and married," although this didn't hold her back from using courtship and the offer of marriage in her international political dealings, as she negotiated with several different suitors, sometimes for years at a time. This is not unusual throughout history; there are a number of examples of strong female leaders and thinkers remaining unmarried and uninterested in taking lovers, such as Hypatia, the renowned Greek philosopher who once abruptly pulled one of her students out of his romantic reveries of her in class by throwing her used menstrual cloth at him to show him the reality of her womanhood. The Queen of Swords expects her students to deal in reality and not fantasy, to think clearly and concisely, and to focus on facts, not daydreams or imaginings. She teaches them to think, even if she does not teach them the actual facts.

Elizabeth's reactions to hostility were both fair and forceful, depending on need. The Queen of Swords only does what is necessary; she is a pragmatist by nature. Thus, when dealing with the Irish rebellion, Elizabeth advised that the Irish be treated well, yet did not try to prevent the scorched-earth tactics used against the rebels. One of her most famous speeches, delivered to her troops before their defeat of the Spanish Armada, during which she worse breastplate armour over a white dress, epitomises the Queen of Swords' more masculine nature:

> *"I know I have the body but of a weak and feeble woman, but I*
> *have the heart and stomach of a king, and of a King of England too,*
> *and think foul scorn that Parma or Spain, or any Prince of Europe*
> *should dare to invade the borders of my realm."* [24]

As such, the Queen of Swords is harsh and unforgiving, yet she desires nothing more than fairness, liberty, and willing students to whom she can pass on her knowledge and wisdom. Thus she is not only a victorious battle goddess, but also a teacher, her words of wisdom and her wealth of knowledge being the elixir of life for those who drink of it.

Revelation

The Queen of Swords can appear in a reading to indicate a person in the querent's life, the querent themselves, an aspect of their personality or an approach to a situation, and sometimes even an event. Out of all the queens, the Queen of Swords is possibly the least lovable, yet certainly this does not weaken her in any way. She an extremely powerful and her strength will shine through in any reading.

Often, this card represents a teacher or communicator, somebody involved in expressing knowledge, wisdom, facts, and ideas to others. It can be a man or a woman of any age, despite the gender depicted in the card, although if the

---

24. Anne Somerset, *Elizabeth I* (London: Anchor Books, 2003), page 591.

person indicated is young in years, they may appear older due to their wisdom and intelligence. Often the Queen of Swords can be found in advocates—those who speak on behalf of others—librarians, research supervisors, translators, and interpreters. They value truth and justice as well as knowledge and open lines of communication, and loathe those that would deliberately distort or misrepresent the truth, or block and oppress the communication or ideas of others. For the Queen of Swords, ideas and thoughts must be given the liberty to flow and be nurtured, and thus this card encourages the querent to find means to influence the growth of their ideas and the direction of their communication.

The Queen of Swords asks the querent to consider the manner in which they communicate. How clear is their communication with others? Are they good at speaking and expressing their thoughts and ideas? How do they perceive and develop ideas? Do they let emotions influence their intellect too much? What is the main source of their intellectual inspiration? Often, if the Queen of Swords appears in a reading to pose a solution to a problem, it advises clear communication, an open exchange of ideas, and knowledge of one's strengths and weaknesses on an intellectual level.

In a relationship reading, the Queen of Swords can sometimes represent communication between the couple, but often indicates difficulties in a relationship due to unrealistic expectations or differences of opinions, or perhaps two strong personalities that are beginning to clash. As such, this card also indicates the need for self-reliance and independence, both in life and in thought, rather than copying the ideas of others or relying on others for answers. The Queen of Swords does everything for herself; if you want something done, do it yourself, or if you want something done, give it to a busy person. The Queen of Swords is always busy, moving quickly between tasks, multitasking easily and seemingly effortlessly. Her mind is always active, never stopping and always one step ahead of everybody else.

Reversed, the Queen of Swords signifies loneliness, separation between couples, misrepresentation of the truth, and gossip. It might also suggest that the querent is stuck in their situation due to a lack of clarity in thought or poor communication between the people involved, and it can point to rumour being the cause of the problems the querent is facing. Sometimes the Queen of Swords reversed is a person that the querent fears because they are so cold and unyielding, possibly intimidating the querent with their keen intellect and demanding precision.

Keywords

Teacher, advocate, communicator, expression of ideas, talking, separation, coldness, harsh, busy mind, multitasking, strong personality, tough love, nurturing, truth.

Queen of Cups, the Depths of the Subconscious

"People say that a sailor's mistress is the sea, and that he sails upon the waves through his love of the ocean in all its beauty, glory, terror, and depth. They also say that a true sailor will not learn how to swim, so that if his ship is lost to the storm and his body given to the waves, he will fall into his mistress's arms quickly and easily, without struggle. The connection that the sailor feels for the ocean is found deep in his soul, coursing through his veins with every pump of his heart; it is a pull that he feels in his gut, which he cannot ignore. I am that pull, that siren song drawing men into the depths where they either swim or drown. I am the enticement, the beauty offered, the mystery half-concealed and flirtatiously half-revealed to draw you in. I am the mermaid playing in the sunlit waves, tail flicking and hair flowing, laughing as you come closer. I am the mermaid's arms and wet lips that surround you as the sunlit surface is replaced by airless depths and you are dragged by a kiss to the lightless abyss. In my depths there is wonder and danger, the choice of which is yours alone. Will you swim in the waters of your emotions and your subconscious? Will you dance with the sunlit waves like the mermaid? Or will you drown in the depths, crying and lonely like the whale in the darker sea? The mermaid and the whale are sisters of the ocean, and you can love them both equally, swim with them both side by side, and this way you will learn not to drown. But fear not the depths, for in the concealment of the darkness lies wisdom and profound mystery, and the pearls are treasure to be found within the dullness of each oyster."

Watery part of water / Cancer

Illumination

In the enigmatic and beautiful Queen of Cups, we have quintessential water: all the queens of the tarot are given the element of water, and the suit of cups is ruled by it also. As such, she is the depths of the greatest body of water, the ocean, teeming with life and beauty, mystery and the unknown. When it comes to the extent of our human knowledge, we have barely begun to discover what mysteries Earth's oceans hold. Thus in the tarot the ocean as a symbol is twofold: firstly, there are the sunlit, dancing waves upon the surface of the ocean and all the brightly coloured creatures that we see often, the water in which we swim, play, and fish, the water that carries us to new lands. But secondly there are the darkest depths of the murky deep, the heart of the ocean we rarely see because its coldness and pressure would kill us, the place in which some of the planet's strangest creatures thrive. Many of these creatures are monstrous, like something out of our nightmares. Yet they live beneath the beautiful, shining surface of the sea that we know and love. The ocean, and therefore the Queen of Cups, is an evocative symbol for the subconscious mind, as well as the human heart, emotions, and imagination.

The Queen of Cups in the Tarot Illuminati exists in a mythical landscape, surrounded by glowing crystal dragonflies that could also be seen as fairies. Her throne is decorated with mermaids, and behind her rises the white towers of a fairytale castle; the curtain of a beautiful waterfall thunders in the background. Everything glows and shimmers, but it is her gaze that we are drawn to... enticing and beckoning, as if she is holding us in a glamour, calling us ever-onward toward her. She holds out a golden cup to us, yet this is not the same cup as we have seen throughout the suit: this cup is covered, its contents sealed firmly within and completely unknown to us.

This sealed cup is the key to the Queen of Cups. She deals with mystery and the unknown, the depths and the deep. Whilst around her we can see light and illumination, just like the sun on the dancing waves, the focus of her offering is representative of the dark mystery in the depths of the ocean. With her beauty, glamour, and enticement, she leads us deeper into our psyche, deeper into our selves, deeper into our emotions, deeper into our subconscious. What will we find there? We cannot know until we reach it. We cannot know what is contained within the sealed cup until we unseal it. This cup is therefore also the Holy Grail, symbolic of deep spiritual unity, as well as the mythical Cauldron of Rebirth in which we might drown and be reborn anew. It is also the womb from which we all came, out of darkness and into light, out of potential into actuality, and of course it is the original womb of the ocean from which all life on Earth originally came. It is being offered to us by this watery goddess herself: what magic awaits us? What transformation?

We already know that this queen has a quality of psychic ability and intuition about her, as she shares the same colours as the High Priestess. The depths of the subconscious are the training ground for intuitive and psychic gifts, but the Queen of Cups shares another quality of the High Priestess: receptivity. As the watery aspect of water, she is the most receptive of all the court cards, taking in everything around her. She soaks up energy like a sponge soaks up water, but she retains it rather than letting it go. As a supremely watery figure, the Queen of Cups is also flux and changeability, and she might as well be a shapeshifter! Since she absorbs everything around her, she often changes to reflect that. The deepest water runs the stillest, and becomes like a mirror, and like a mirror the Queen of Cups never really expresses her true self, but only a reflection of others around her and what they want her to be. She is, because of this, the ultimate desired beauty of the tarot: she can be anything and everything you want her to be.

The mermaids upon her throne are symbolic of this side of her nature. They are creatures of water, human in their feelings yet oceanic in environment. They are well known in mythology and folklore throughout the world, and in many traditions they appear to sailors or fishermen as beautiful women, usually naked, often combing their long hair and singing sweetly. In some cases, they lure men out to sea using their enticing beauty and hypnotic song, and then drown them; in others, they actually fall in love with land dwellers, and when the feelings are reciprocated and the couple entwined in passion, the mermaid forgets that her human lover cannot survive beneath the waves, and thus the human drowns in the arms of his beloved. Mermaids are symbolic not only of humanity's relationship with water, but also the deep love that those who live and work upon the sea are said to have for it. It is often said that the mistress of a sailor is the sea, and he learns her ways so that he might sail upon her just as a husband might learn his wife's ways so that he might live with her in peace. It is also said that a true sailor in times past would not learn how to swim, so that if the ship were lost at sea, he would sink quickly into the arms of the ocean. This we also find in the Queen of Cups: enticing beauty, deep love, obsession—and the very real possibility of drowning. We can drown in our feelings, our romances and relationships, our subconscious, our sensitivities... and in a positive way we can also drown in the arms of our lover, carried off on the rocking waves of bliss.

The Queen of Cups is a creature of fantasy herself, not quite real but instead reflecting the desires of others. As such, she herself can drown; as a card, she represents all the negative as well as positive ways in which we do so. She is the person suffering from depression, drowning in their feelings; the alcoholic pushed by their deepest fears to drink, the addict chained to their chosen obsession to escape depth of feeling or, conversely, to escape numbness. She is the person so afraid of losing a loved one that they smother them, removing their freedom and ultimately driving them away by doing so. She is all the ways in which our mind can become clouded and uncertain, in flux and afraid of the unknown, and she can also be the madness of the mystic faced with great depth of spiritual feeling.

Revelation

In a reading, the Queen of Cups often indicates a person, or perhaps the querent themselves, though it can also indicate a personality trait of the querent, an approach they need to take to a situation, a role they need to play, or an event in their life. Surrounding cards, intuitive response, and the context of the question will help you assess what form the court card is taking in the reading.

As the watery aspect of water, the Queen of Cups relates to all modes of receptivity in the querent's life, every way in which they receive information, love, or emotions. Since this card is so fluctuating and changeable, it also points to the ways the querent changes to reflect the needs, desires, perceptions, and expectations of others. At best, this may suggest that the querent's strength in the current situation lies in being flexible and moulding themselves to fit the state of things and those around them. It may be that others need them to be something, and the Queen of Cups enables them to be this thing with ease. This also means that the Queen of Cups is excellent at picking up on the feelings of others, seeming psychic to others when in fact she is highly sensitive to emotions and energies. As such, the Queen of Cups suggests that the querent is an excellent listener, and the kind of person that often ends up with people confiding in them, or looking to them for emotional support.

This card can also represent the querent finding their way deeper into their own emotions or psyche, perhaps on a spiritual or magical journey, or through therapy, counselling, meditation, or even a deep, loving relationship with another person. In the depths of the querent's self they will find great treasure, just as there are many sunken treasure ships to be found in the ocean. When the Queen of Cups appears in a reading, the querent should expect an intense emotional journey or a call to deeper awareness.

In a relationship reading, the Queen of Cups indicates an intense depth of feeling that is shared between the couple, as well as love in its most profound, yet sometimes overwhelming, form. However, the Queen of Cups does not always "fit" with another court card, so if she appears as an indicator for one partner, the reader should always look further to see if a second court card represents the other. Since the Queen of Cups is so watery and emotional, she would not fit well with the King of Swords, who is sharp and cold, disdaining emotion and holding pure logic as the highest truth. The King of Wands might be a good partner for her, since he is the fire to her water, the activity to her receptivity. The King of Pentacles might also be suitable, since he would provide a stabilizing influence.

The Queen of Cups can also represent a mother, so there may be children involved in the relationship, perhaps from a previous relationship, or perhaps the querent may be looking to start a family. Where the Queen of Pentacles is earthy and therefore a mother in the physical world, caring for the body, the Queen of Cups is more likely to be a mother in the emotional world, looking after the heart and soul. The former fixes the skinned knee, the latter fixes the broken heart.

Sometimes the Queen of Cups can represent beauty, art, and any creative goal; it also represents fantasy and imagination. It suggests that not only does the querent have a great deal of inspiration contained within their psyche, as well as the desire to create beauty, but also that they are prone to living in a dream world rather than reality.

Reversed, the Queen of Cups suggests that the querent is so changeable and prone to reflecting the feelings of others that their actual personality is almost nonexistent, and they find themselves being moulded too easily by others. This can also manifest as the querent soaking up all energies from their environment and people around them, negative energies in particular, and thus they are easily affected by the emotional upheavals of others. The Queen of Cups reversed may also suggest that the querent is in danger of drowning in the present situation, probably because of their intense emotions. This card at its worst can indicate addiction, particularly alcoholism, depression, and emotional numbness. The querent should also be warned that if something or somebody looks too good to be true, it probably is, and they should avoid being enticed in too deep.

Keywords

Beauty, fantasy, imagination, enticement, depth, siren, changeability, flux, fluctuation, reflection, intuition, psychic ability, receptivity, motherhood, care, psyche, confidante.

Queen of Pentacles, the Nurturing Mother Earth

"When the richness of the earth reaches fullness and its abundance is nurtured to fruition, it gives of itself willingly so that everything within it and upon it might be sustained. Thus, the deepest love of the mother for her child is to sacrifice all for its survival, and the deepest secrets of the earth flow only in one direction: life. Life will always find a way… it will flow through and around all obstacles, it will mould itself into any form, and it will perpetuate itself. Never underestimate the desire of nature to grow and sustain; the mother bear protecting her cub and the lioness protecting her young are unstoppable. When life is at stake, everything must be done to protect it and nurture it, care for it and see it grow. Think of your own body and the power contained therein. Know that your body rebuilds itself and knows how to nurture itself, how to grow from the tiniest seed. Think how the entirety of the Earth and the global ecosystem you inhabit feeds itself, one part of it sustaining and supporting the other, one big flow of life in a precious cycle of birth, growth, death, rebirth, and transformation. I am the Mother of Earth, and I am the cycle that holds life up; I am the giver of life and the taker of life, and the continual flow between states. When your body returns to the earth, I am the process through which you in turn feed it, as it once fed you. There is no end to my bounty, for I am the eternal harvest and renewal. Through me, fertility springs forth and all things are born; I gestate the seed and nurture it, bring it to the light mewling and crying. I kneel in the mud and the blood and the flowing rivers, my body of clay and my heart bursting with love to bring forth life. I am the great opening of the womb and the gushing forth of the waters of the abyssal sea from therein. Only in my birthing cries, only in the blood and the red earth from which you came does the sacrifice that created life become clear. They say the first of the harvest is always for the gods, but it should also be the last of the harvest that goes to them: not in thanksgiving, but to ensure that a seed of the old replenishes and feeds the seed of the new. Therefore recognize your body as the miracle it is, and bear witness all around you, in every moment, to that perfect self-perpetuating cycle that sustains you."

Watery part of earth / Capricorn

Illumination

When the watery association of the queens unites with the earth association of the suit of pentacles, we find ourselves with the most fecund, abundant, nurturing, and nourishing of all the court cards. The Queen of Pentacles is the flow and cycle of everything that sustains and supports us on a physical survival level; she is the nurturer of everything in our daily lives and all aspects of our bodily selves. This is Mother Earth, Mother Nature, at her most giving, most abundant, and most fertile. As such, the Queen of Pentacles has many layers of meaning: she can represent the greatest and most complex of nature's cycles, fertility and harvest, the concepts of nurturing and sustenance, as well as the everyday aspects of health, diet, exercise, and the body.

The Queen of Cups and the Queen of Pentacles share motherhood in common; however, their styles of nurturing are very different. Whereas the Queen of Cups is more likely to nurture the emotional world and fix a broken heart, the Queen of Pentacles is better suited to nurture the mundane world and fix broken limbs. We might turn to the Queen of Cups to cry on her shoulder and be soothed, but it is the Queen of Pentacles that we turn to for our very survival. She is the mother feeding her newborn child from her own breast, the mother's milk being an apt symbol for this card of both earth and water. As such, she also carries connotations of harvest and abundance, since water, as a channel, carries earth's fruition and manifestation into our lives.

In the card image, we see a black-haired woman in ornate and luxurious golden robes, seated upon a stone throne that is swathed in blood-red material and decorated with two winged goats. Her headdress is spectacular, probably the most detailed and complex of all the ladies in the court cards, showing her richness and abundance. There is nothing in this card that suggests any sort of lack whatsoever, yet the richness around her is more of the natural world than manmade objects: at her feet is an overflowing cornucopia of harvested fruit and the forest floor is a sea of colourful flowers in full bloom. A small rabbit sits by her and looks attentive, signifying her fertility as well as being an archetypal symbol of femininity, with its worldwide association with the lunar cycle (this is due to the fact that many cultures see the patterns upon the moon as a rabbit or hare). In her hands, the Queen of Pentacles holds a large bunch of grapes, another symbol of abundance as well as the joy of life, and a golden pear. This golden pear is found in Chinese symbolism and mythology to represent immortality as well as riches and prosperity. In Greek and Roman myth, the pear is sacred to Hera, mother of the gods; Aphrodite, the goddess of love; and Pomona, also the goddess of apples. The pear, upside down, is shaped much like the human uterus, and is therefore a quintessential symbol of the female body and motherhood. Behind the queen are fruiting apple trees, another symbol of fertility and abundance, as well as signifying a time for harvest and a focus on nutrition and the natural world. To the queen's left is a small nature spirit, a faun, creating wild energy with his song and dance. This faun, like his mythological father, Pan, signifies the raw power of the earth and nature; in art and mythology, these creatures were often depicted not only in the wilder parts of the natural world but also in pastoral scenes.

Other ancient goddesses are referenced in this card through the symbol of the cornucopia. In Greek myth, the origin of this horn of plenty can be found in the childhood of Zeus, who was hidden from his murderous father in a cave on Mount Ida in Crete, and suckled by the goat Amalthea. Zeus, being endowed with godlike strength, accidentally broke off one of Amalthea's horns while he was suckling from her, and this horn retained some divinity, having the power to provide endless nourishment. It is also found in depictions of Gaia (the personification of the Earth), Fortuna, Abundantia (Roman goddess of abundance personified), and Annona (the goddess who oversaw the grain supply in ancient Rome). This reminds us that the Queen of Pentacles nurtures and cares for our bodies, providing us with sustenance and nourishment, and that if we live in a respectful and symbiotic manner with the Earth and our environment, we can have an endless supply of that nourishment. Yet the flowing nature of all the queens says that if we expect this sustenance to be a one-way street, we will eventually fail.

There is an element of sacrifice to the Queen of Pentacles. As any mother will know, some sacrifices are necessary but accepted, since they serve to nourish our children. The Queen of Pentacles represents the effort, the strain, and sometimes the pain that we go through when we bring something to birth, whether this is an actual child, a creative work, or a project. Everything that we create gives us labour pains, we toil and strain to push the finished product to completion, and often we gestate it within ourselves until it is ready. The blood-red material upon the queen's throne reminds us of the sacrifices we make to bring in our harvest when it is ready, and the fruiting trees remind us that only when the harvest is fully ripe can it be brought in.

As the watery aspect of earth, the Queen of Pentacles can be seen as the ways in which resources flow in and out of our lives, and also how we manage those resources. It reminds us that every part of our daily lives is a constant flux of resources, and the transmutation of one resource into another. Time and skill, for instance, are transmuted into money, which is transmuted into food, which is transmuted into energy, with which further actions can be performed. Or, time and skill are transmuted into money, which is eventually transmuted into a home, which provides a stable environment for a family. This also gives the Queen of Pentacles a deeply practical focus: she is hands-on and doesn't mind hard work. She is the kind of person that can happily get down in the dirt and get a job done. Like the other pentacles court cards, the queen would much prefer doing rather than thinking, and abstract theories are not her stock in trade. She deals with realities, absolutes, and manifested results, and she ensures that they go in the right direction and are used where they are needed. She brings with her not just care and sustenance, but practical, real, and necessary care and sustenance … just like Mother used to make.

Revelation

As with all the court cards, the Queen of Pentacles has many possible interpretations in a reading. Most often she will represent a person in the querent's life or the querent themselves, or perhaps a character trait of the querent's that is becoming prominent in the situation or at this time. Sometimes a court card can point to events or themes, and often they give advice on how the querent can respond to the situation.

Most often, the Queen of Pentacles indicates a practical, down-to-earth, caring, and motherly person (of either gender), who has a strong focus on health, diet, nutrition, exercise, and the body. They will have an interest in bodily maintenance, both traditional and alternative, including standard exercise, yoga, massage, physical therapy and breastfeeding, as well as an interest in cookery, power foods, or multicultural cuisine. If the querent has asked about health in their reading, then the Queen of Pentacles advises them to watch their weight, assess their diet, and perhaps stick to an exercise plan. This card views health as the highest good, knowing that when we get old it will be the thing we miss the most.

The Queen of Pentacles can also indicate the querent's biological mother, or motherhood in the querent's life. If accompanied by the Empress or the Ace of Wands, it can point to the possibility of pregnancy, and often raises points concerning the querent's fertility or virility. Sometimes it suggests that now, or the near future, is a good time for the querent to start trying for a pregnancy or starting a family. It can also indicate that the querent might need to be in the position of caretaker for another person, particularly on a physical, everyday level.

Often the Queen of Pentacles appears in a reading to reassure the querent that life is providing them with an abundance of nourishing goodness and richness, as well as a great many resources that they have control of, and can use as they see fit or transmute into other resources. This card reminds the querent that sometimes, when a resource seems missing or difficult to obtain, it can be created from another source.

If this card appears in a reading about a relationship, it can indicate the everyday realities of that relationship: the home environment in which the couple exists, the daily lives of the people involved, and how their resources interact. It particularly suggests issues of money and budgeting, and reminds the querent that the relationship must necessarily have some grounding in the everyday world, instead of just being a romantic breeze of love. Some practicality may be required for any future relationship decisions. If the Queen of Pentacles appears in a work or career reading, it is a very positive card, indicating abundance of results and a rich harvest due to the querent's hard work and efforts. Whilst it may not indicate promotion or recognition for hard work, it instead rewards the querent with very real results in the form of resources that they can use.

Reversed, the Queen of Pentacles can indicate a lack of abundance in the querent's life, as well as a lack of practicality and realism about the current situation. The querent may be shirking hard work or trying to find an easier way around something; her advice is that there is no easier way, and they just need to accept that they are going to get their hands dirty. This card reversed can also point to sacrifices that need to be made in the querent's life, or problems with the querent's health and diet.

Keywords

Health, nutrition, sustenance, physical care, environment, abundance, sacrifice, hard work, motherhood, flow of resources, everyday routine.

CHAPTER 30

The Kings

King of Wands, the Centre of the Sun

"The strongest wills burn most brightly, the strongest desires burn with the most heat, and heat always rises. I am the height of my very self, the pinnacle of all that is possible, the achievement of all things. I am everything that I ever wanted to be and more, and I am master of it all. The four worlds are at my fingertips, all skills are in my knowledge; I have seen the world, and I have heard all its songs, met all its people, loved fiercely and deeply, adventured beyond the limits of my perception. There is nothing I cannot do, nothing I do not want to do, and I will experience everything, consuming it as others would water, or food. I live on it, I thrive on it. Goals are only there to be achieved and then surpassed, the will is only there to serve you, and desire is there to drive you ever onward to yet more desire. Thus you should not be surprised that I am the King of Kings; I am God incarnate, seated upon a sunlit throne, the centre not only of the universe but the very centre of that centre itself. I burn as brightly as the midday sun, and once you have beheld me, you will never forget me. I am your strongest, most passionate desires, your need to consume experiences and adventure, the very heights of your self. I am you at your best and finest. I am here to tell you, beyond a shadow of a doubt (for shadows do not exist where I am) that you are capable of more than you ever dreamed of. You are in control of everything you are, have been, and will be, and thus you are in control of the universe around you. Every single person is the centre of their own universe, their own personal sun, and their actions are like solar rays reaching out beyond themselves. You are—as I am—to be worshipped and praised, loved and admired, respected and adored, for what is there that you cannot achieve when your desire, will, passion, and energy are all driven toward the same goal? If you choose to forget all other things, remember only this and you will never fail: you are awesome, in the most total sense of the word. And so am I."

371

Fiery part of fire / Leo

Illumination

The King of Wands could be otherwise called the King of Kings, since as a king he represents the element of fire, and he is found in the suit of wands, also associated with fire. He is therefore the fiery aspect of fire, and since fire is seen as the highest of the four elements and closest to spirit, he is the highest of the high in the court cards. Conversely, this also makes him the least manifest of all the court cards, just as the Princess of Pentacles is the most manifest, and, like the Princess of Pentacles, he contains potential in immense form. Whereas the Princess of Pentacles (earth of earth) contains within her the seeds of the universe waiting in the womb, the King of Wands (fire of fire) represents unmanifest potentiality, awaiting manifestation through the lower elements. As such, he represents not only the highest goals and desires we can think of, but also their achievement; he brings with him a strong message that we can get whatever we want, if we desire it strongly enough. All dreams are possible, and all ambitions viable. Since he is also the king of the suit that concerns itself most with the will, personality, self, desire, passion, and drive, he reminds us that everything rests entirely on the self. If we fail, it is because of the limits we have put upon ourselves; if we succeed, it is because we allowed ourselves to. As fire of fire, the King of Wands is also a solar, phallic god within the tarot, the sun itself blazing hot and bright, reminding us that we are the centres of our own universes.

The card image is bright and vivid, as might be expected for the king of fire. A powerful-looking king sits proudly upon a throne carved with lions and decorated with sunflowers. He wears golden and red robes, and a fitted breastplate and tassets made from gold. Over his crotch we can see what might be dragon-scale armour for added protection, and this same golden armour covers his head and neck in the form of chainmail. Atop this is a red turban crowned with gold flames and finished with large white feathers. The whole effect is of the Sun King, blessed and armoured with light, himself glowing and emanating that light and heat for all to see. There is no chance of missing this bright figure! His stance is one of openness yet control: as with many other masculine figures, he is seated with his legs far apart, the red on his robes streaking downward between them. This, along with the dragon-scale armour that protects that area, shows that the King of Wands is intensely sexual in nature, extremely masculine, and passionate. The wand and the phallus are synonymous symbolically, and this king holds his large golden staff out for everybody to see, with a strong arm and a powerful grip, supremely confident.

The headdress that he wears is the only part of the card that is white. It resembles white-hot flames, and white-hot flames burn far hotter than red-hot ones. Since it is situated around his head, it symbolizes the hot-headedness of this king, as well as the fact that his mind, the seat of his knowledge, is the highest of all the heated parts of him. It is here that he keeps his wisdom and experience, since our King of Wands is a jack-of-all-trades. Unlike his younger counterpart, the Prince of Wands, he is also a master of all those trades. He is the kind of person that has developed a great number of skills over their lifetime, has undertaken many wonderful adventures, and done things that most of us would never even consider. He might be a violin virtuoso, a playwright, a novelist, a stage magician, a published academic, a trained nurse, a psychotherapist, a carpenter, an astrologer, an athlete … all at once. He is a wonderchild grown up, a boy genius turned man.

We can see the sunflower emblem of the Queen of Wands gracing the king's throne back, not only highlighting the relationship between these two court cards, but also reminding us of the optimism and brightness of the court cards of this suit. Like the queen, the king is the centre of everybody's attention, and their faces turn toward his light just as the faces of the sunflowers turn toward the sun. He is the leader that everybody looks to for inspiration, guidance, reassurance, and decisions, and they take their cues from him. This makes him a fitting partner for the Queen of Wands; together, they are so dynamic and charismatic that they are virtually unstoppable. In fact, together they could rule the world.

The lions that appear in the card image link the King of Wands to the astrological sign of Leo, associated with confidence, ego, fame, sunny dispositions, outspoken and outgoing personalities, being the centre of attention. Leos are also well known for their stubborn pride in themselves and their achievements, and their need to make everything about themselves. The King of Wands is not very good at putting others before himself because he sees himself as the centre of the universe, and expects others to also see themselves as such. He cannot understand people who rely overmuch on others, or require others to make things happen for them. He also lacks patience with failure in others, or weakness, or anything less than brilliance. This might make him seem like a difficult person to know, yet the opposite is the case: he is a joy to know socially, since he always boosts the confidence of others around him, brings joy and laughter wherever he goes, and leads by example. However, at his worst he can be a braggart, boasting about his achievements, ignoring the accomplishments of others, and considering everybody else to be less than him in some way. To others it might sometimes seem that the ego of the King of Wands is the size of a small planet. Another animal companion can be seen by his left foot: the salamander, a desert creature and symbol of elemental fire.

Behind the King of Wands is a hot, red desert, with wavy, flamelike patterns etched into it by the wind. No water or other living creatures grace this parched earth; it is the result of too much heat and not enough moisture. Deserts are teeming with life that usually comes out at nighttime, when temperatures are cooler, but it is still an unforgiving and harsh environment for survival. This shows us that the King of Wands can be harsh and unforgiving toward others, with a high set of standards for himself that he also expects others to live up to. He is at his best when partnered with a more watery personality, such as any of the cups court cards, as they can show him gentleness and calm his pride.

Revelation

The King of Wands can appear in a reading to indicate a person in the querent's life, or the querent themselves, as well as personality traits that might be required at this time, or coming to the fore of the querent's life. Sometimes it can represent themes or events, and often it brings advice on the best course of action or perspectives for the querent to take in the current situation. The reader should examine surrounding cards and use their intuitive responses to assess which aspect this card is taking on in the context of the question.

Usually the King of Wands represents a charismatic leader or a person in authority who is well known to the querent. Once seen, never forgotten, the King of Wands is like a blazing comet streaking through the sky, expecting everybody to watch and admire him (or her). He is a highly skilled and experienced person, with a great number of interesting tales and character traits, and a vast knowledge of many things. Any kind of virtuoso or expert can be represented by the King of Wands, but he is often an expert in more than one area. He is also deeply passionate about life and its many aspects, and lives fast. The phrase "it is better to burn out than fade away," made famous by Kurt Cobain, would be applicable to this character, who would rather become burnt out through doing too much and living life to the fullest, than conserve energy through doing less. He is always on the go, never stops, and seems to have an unending amount of energy and enthusiasm, and this leads others around him to live similarly. He often has great power and influence in many different social circles or communities, and his confidence and self-admiration shines strongly. He can be very egotistical, however, extremely prideful, and does not like being spoken against or disagreed with. He can become angry quickly, with a hot temper that flashes up without warning, yet it usually disappears just as suddenly to be replaced by his usual friendly, sociable, optimistic demeanour. The King of Wands works best when surrounded by other people—preferably people who will admire him, praise him, listen to his stories about his exploits, and tolerate his ego. He is also extremely sexual in nature, and often the recipient of the attention of many admirers.

If the King of Wands appears in a career or work-related reading, he represents brilliant opportunities for advancement: the querent's work and actions, particularly their leadership qualities, have been noticed by those in authority and are soon to be rewarded. Although the querent is not promised any great wealth or monetary security by this card, they will have enough money to do everything that they want to, and shouldn't feel they have to cancel social engagements or adventures for fear of not having enough money to fund them.

In a reading about relationships or love, the King of Wands usually represents a love interest, particularly somebody with whom the querent may be infatuated, or somebody whom they think is out of their league. The King of Wands advises them to take action immediately, embrace passion and new romantic adventures, and not be afraid of something completely different. He usually ensures success as well.

Reversed, the King of Wands suggests that the querent is being too prideful or egotistical to be able to act correctly in the situation, and they are thinking of themselves when, in fact, they would do better to put others first at this time. Sometimes it can point to an issue with the ego, or a false belief that a thing cannot be done, a negative attitude that puts obstacles in the way of success. It can also indicate that the querent, conversely, is being too heated about something, or being led by a sexual urge rather than logic.

Keywords

Achievement, accomplishment, genius, sexual urges paramount, hot temperament, high standards, fast pace, activity, confidence, admiration, leadership.

King of Swords, Strategy in Action

"You do not have to like me. I am not here to be your friend, your partner, your confidante. In truth, I care little for your petty concerns and worries. They are minor trifles in the face of the bigger picture, and I see that picture in its entirety. Before me is the world, a great puzzle to be solved, a machine that must be kept working and powered by new discoveries. Behind me is a carefully constructed strategic plan, and every single action—no matter how small, no matter how detailed—has been intentional and directed toward my goal. The strategy, the plan, the action toward the clearest and most logical goal is paramount. Be a part of my plan, share my vision, understand my logic, and you may be of use to me, and I to you. Stand in the way of my strategy and I shall not hesitate to exert all of my strength of will to cut you from my world. As I said, you do not have to like me, but I do know best."

Fiery part of air / Aquarius

Illumination

The King of Swords may not appeal to everyone: he is a stern-faced man, his arms crossed over his chest, keeping us at a safe distance. His brows are heavy and his eyes small, and they stare at us intently, like he is puzzling us out and trying to use the information he gains to plan one step ahead of us. At the same time, his legs are wide apart in what would usually be a vulnerable position, yet on our king it shows his power and authority, as well as expressing his fiery nature.

Elementally, all the kings of the tarot are given to the element of fire, and the suit of swords to the element of air; therefore, the King of Swords is the fiery aspect of air, thoughts and ideas taken action upon and used to further goals and plans, the ego and the needs of the personality. He is the mind at its most active and applied, but also its most aggressive. Whereas the Princess of Swords saw the mind applied to the everyday world, the Prince of Swords desired to send the mind off to discover and explore, and the Queen of Swords showed us the mind as teacher and communicator, the King of Swords is the strategy behind them all and the most forceful abilities of the mind. He is the tactician, the planner, the organizer, the one who always has a cunning plan and knows how to manipulate others using clever words. He approaches discussion and conversation as debate or battle, desiring to demonstrate his intellectual superiority over others.

We can see this active, aggressive nature in the fiery red cloak that the King of Swords wears, accompanying the blue and gold associated with his suit. Despite the fact that he wears no armour, he is intensely martial and military, with a mind built for fighting battles and winning them. When he sets his mind to a task, he is an unstoppable force. This puts him in the same league as some of the greatest military leaders and tacticians ever to have lived, such as Alexander the Great, Marcus Claudius Marcellus, Hannibal, Genghis Khan, and Napoleon Bonaparte. However, unlike most of these leaders, the King of Swords himself will not be going into battle, but simply using his mind and insight to direct others. This does not make him a coward, though, as such a great mind should not be risked, instead continuing to be used to further ends. Thus, we can imagine our King of Swords seated before a world map, littered with pieces representing armies, ships, and military commanders, positioning them and deciding on the best plan of action to respond to each possible move the enemy might make. This is how the King of Swords functions: he considers every single possibility thoroughly and makes a suitable plan for each. He is never surprised, never shocked, never caught unawares. With a mind like his, filled with complexities and twists and turns, it is no wonder nobody can get one step ahead of him! As such, he seems inscrutable, hard to read, cold and distant. This is exactly the way he likes it. We can see from the card image that he does not invite familiarity or warmth; in fact, he seems to be a perfect match for the Queen of Swords, cold and pale and exacting.

The King of Swords is a large man, built robustly to symbolize his larger than life nature, his forceful personality, and his ability to stand in the way of those who would cross him or not serve his interests. He is most definitely the boss, the one in charge, the one with authority, and he has gained his position through experience and wisdom. Despite his flaws, we cannot deny that he sits in his throne through the virtue of truth and fairness. Since the suit of swords often deals with concerns of law, rights, contracts, and promises between people, we can be certain that the King of Swords holds himself as much beholden to the principles of truth and honour as any of his subjects. He means what he says and says what he means, even if sometimes the truths he speaks are harsh and unkind. In his mind, only truth matters; emotions simply confuse the issue. He would rather seem callous and cause somebody pain through revealing the truth than hide the truth and leave the person in blissful ignorance.

This makes the King of Swords seem extremely aggressive to those not inclined toward his methods. Since he is willing to fight to the death for his principles, to defend an idea, or to stand up for the truth, he is stubborn to a fault and often pushes people away. If he holds a certain viewpoint that is in opposition to another's viewpoint, he will happily engage in debate with them, although rather than seeking to learn from his opponent he is more likely to try and force his view on them, seeing it more as a triumph in battle than a sharing of ideas.

Revelation

In a reading, the King of Swords can represent a person in the querent's life, the querent themselves, an aspect of the querent's personality, or a role that the querent plays. It can also relate to an approach to the situation, or even an event. It can often be difficult to work out which aspect of a court card is appearing, so let the surrounding cards, your intuitive response, and the context of the question guide you.

Most often, the King of Swords indicates somebody in a position of power or authority over the querent, usually a boss or manager at work, or a higher-ranking person in their workplace or area of expertise. It can also signify somebody in power in the area of law, contracts, and oaths, like a lawyer, barrister, investment broker, or somebody who pitches ideas. Further, it can point to military people as well as those involved with the armed forces in any way, whether they are front-line fighters, radio communicators, or military intelligence.

As a person, the King of Swords is cold, harsh, sometimes cruel, and extremely intelligent. He is so clever, witty, wise, and knowledgeable that he intimidates most people (although remember—this card does not necessarily indicate a man, despite the use of the term "he"; it can also indicate a woman). For the King of Swords, knowledge is power, and it is only through his immense learning and the application of his intelligence that he has reached the position he is in today, and it is only through these things that he maintains it. He loves knowledge more than perhaps anything else, and values truth more than any other virtue. However, the King of Swords does not simply sit and think about things: he applies his thought in action. He always has a plan, strategy, or tactic, and always knows how to approach any situation. Often this card will appear in a reading to specifically indicate not only the King of Swords himself, but also the fact that his plan is now being put into action—for better or worse for the querent.

It can sometimes be the case that the King of Swords appears in a reading to bring up any contracts, promises, or oaths the querent has made, and therefore any issues or requirements concerning them. Sometimes it simply suggests that the client look over the small print more carefully, as there may be a solution to their problem hidden there, or that they use a contract or written agreement of some kind between themselves and another person to prevent any potential future difficulties. If possible, the querent is advised to put everything in writing, preferably in duplicate or triplicate! They must prepare for every possible eventuality or result, so that they are not caught unaware in the future. In fact, this advice holds true for the King of Swords whenever he appears in any situation, whether it is love, money, friendship, travel, further education, or creative pursuits.

Often, the King of Swords shows up like a stern father in a reading, crossing his arms across his chest and staring intently at the querent while asking them what their plans are for the future, what provisions they are making for their old age, what intentions they have toward his daughter…The querent should ensure they have well thought-out plans, rather than flowing through life without a goal or direction.

In any reading about intellectual pursuits, the King of Swords is a blessing. He indicates that the querent will enjoy wide success in their area of expertise, possibly becoming a well-known expert in that field, or that they will rise in the ranks and gain promotion through their plans, ideas, or intelligence. If the querent has a good idea that they think will make things in their workplace or community run more smoothly and efficiently, they should not be afraid to express it and also to start to take action upon it. The King of Swords reminds the querent that just to have ideas is nothing great, but to have the courage to implement them is.

Reversed, the King of Swords is not a friendly face at all. He becomes an oppressive boss, employer, or father figure who is too forceful and aggressive with his views and thoughts, and who expects everybody to conform to his way of thinking. He can be a fundamentalist, trying to convert others to his views and ideologies, or he can be an iconoclast, intent on destroying anything and everything that is not completely based on logic. All emotion, romance, and friendship is seen as weakness and cut away, because it cannot be proven, nor is it logical. Reversed, this card may suggest that the querent has a mental block, a mind at war with itself, or that they lack a plan of action.

Keywords

Intellect, plans, strategy, tactics, cunning, guile, wit, cleverness, knowledge, wisdom, boss, authority, law, military, promises, oaths, contracts, fine print, challenge, debate, argument.

King of Cups, Healing with Active Compassion

"Some mistake the powers of water for gentleness, for weakness, for slow movement, bending and reflecting rather than holding its own qualities. Yet do not be mistaken: there is no weakness in my character, no desire to bend to the will of another, nor the need to merely reflect and act as a mirror for others. I bring activity and mastery to the waves, and I also stir them up and create their turbulence; I cause the rain to hammer down and springs to become heated; I allow water to boil and be purified, and steam to rise up. It is through activity, not passivity, that water attains its most powerful qualities: healing and compassion. When emotion is passive, it cannot go out into the world to do any good; it cannot influence anything or anybody. When water is passive, it merely reflects from a still surface. Yet when both water and emotion become active, emotions can be shared, and so the tears of the bodhisattva become the desire to aid another, and then become the act of stepping down from isolation into the world of suffering to do so. Mine is the power of active compassion, the power to see pain and suffering and heal it, to purify the wounded and injured, and to guide the lost soul in times of trouble. I travel upon the ocean, because to swim in it would be to let it overcome me; I rule my emotions, not the other way round, and it is this which allows me to heal the wounded feelings and souls of others. I have attained the Holy Grail, mastered all aspects of the emotional world, and have nothing left but to give to others."

Fiery part of water / Scorpio

Illumination

As the fiery aspect of water, the King of Cups brings together two seemingly opposite elements, since all the kings of the tarot are associated with fire, and the suit of cups is associated with water (compare him with the Queen of Wands, who represents the watery aspect of fire and also unites these two opposing elements). Water is considered passive, receptive, and feminine, whilst fire is considered aggressive, active, and masculine. The suit of cups is all about emotion, the inner self, spirituality, romance, love, and the social realm, and as such the King of

Cups can be seen as the most active form of these associations, as well as the mastery of them, since his position as king puts him in a position of power in his suit. Emotions are usually viewed in the tarot as receptive, but the King of Cups exemplifies all the ways in which emotions can be used outwardly, or in which they take an active role in our lives. As such, he is the king of compassion and healing, using his mastery of his suit to help others.

The card image shows us an older man with grey-white hair, tenting his fingers in thought as he looks directly at us. He wears flowing robes of his elemental colours, blues and whites, and grey-white armour of similar colour to his hair and beard. His crown, signifying his rulership of this element, is fashioned into tiers, much like that of the Hierophant whose wisdom and spiritual authority is unquestionable. This shows us immediately that the King of Cups bears great wisdom within him from experience. His beard is grey-white to show his age, and with age comes this wisdom and knowledge of life, with all its ups and downs. The King of Cups has mastered his element and can help others to do so too, because he has experienced everything it has to offer. We could say that, as the representative of fire in his suit, he has consumed everything cups has to offer as fuel for his flames. His resemblance to the Hierophant also puts him in the role of spiritual leader and advisor, rather than political leader, social leader, or boss, as his brother kings are.

We can see a boat sailing behind the King of Cups in the card image. This boat tells us not only that he is master of the waves, but also that he rises above the mire of turbulent emotions to use them as a strong foundation for all his ventures. A true master of emotions does not allow himself to drown in them, although he may be immersed in them, and to sail above them does not mean that one does not feel at all, but instead that feelings are used to buoy one up and bear one's weight, supporting rather than holding down. The King of Cups has power over his emotions, but is not held enthralled by them or at their mercy. Similarly, whilst he is open and does not hide his emotions, he also does not wear his heart on his sleeve (like the Prince of Cups). This is further symbolized in the image by the fact that although he is seated in the middle of the ocean, the King of Cups' throne is situated upon a rock that is entirely out of the ocean, barely kissed by the waves. He is in the middle of the emotional world and surrounded by it, yet it is on his own terms and he maintains control over his relationship with it.

As the active aspect of water, the King of Cups is the showing of compassion and kindness toward others, and the power to heal others and their emotional wounds. In the card image, we can see that whilst only one of his feet is visible, it is stepping forward off the stone base of his throne and touching the water. This reminds us of the various Taras in Buddhism, the bodhisattvas of compassion and embodiments of the saviour in female form. Some of these Taras, given colours such as green, white, black, and red to signify their various qualities, can be seen seated, yet with one foot stepping off their throne and into the world, so as to take action to alleviate the suffering of the world. In Buddhist thought, the bodhisattva is somebody who has attained freedom from the cycle of suffering in reincarnation, but who chooses to reincarnate to help relieve the pain of those still trapped in the cycle. The King of Cups can be seen as the bodhisattva of the tarot, since he has been given mastery over the turbulent waves of emotions, the ability to rise above emotions and control them, yet chooses to go back down into them in order to help others. As a king of the ocean, we can imagine him having the ability to save people from drowning in the sea, symbolic of his ability to save people from being so wounded emotionally that they are unable to move forward.

We must also remember that as the fiery part of water, the King of Cups heats water, makes it boil, and turns it into steam. In the natural world, he can be found in hot springs, in which people around the world have bathed to soothe aching muscles, seek solitude and relaxation, and cleanse themselves. As boiled water, the King of Cups offers the property of sterility; boiled water can safely be used to clean wounds, or to drink. He is a healer, using his vast experience and wisdom of the emotional world and everything he has been through to help others; he offers counsel and advice when the waves of our inner world are at their most turbulent, and he helps us steer a course when we are uncertain. He is almost a fatherly figure, but he does have a negative side: since he is the fiery aspect of the emotional world, he can embody the more aggressive emotions such as rage, anger, frustration, jealousy, and hatred.

Revelation

In a reading, the King of Cups can appear (like every other court card) as a person in the querent's life or the querent themselves, or a character trait in the querent or another person. It can also indicate events, themes, feelings, or approaches that might be necessary in the current situation. It can be difficult to tell which aspect the court cards are taking on in a reading, so intuition, the context of the question, and the surrounding cards should be looked to for guidance.

As a person, the King of Cups is wise and experienced, emotionally balanced and kind, caring toward others, patient, and seems to have a deep understanding of the human heart and soul. He (or she) has a calling to heal others and help them, and is often involved in compassionate work or charity—but they usually give their time and energy as a volunteer, instead of simply donating money.

The King of Cups often appears in a reading to indicate the querent's father or somebody who acts like a father in their life, somebody they consider wise and experienced who lends them a helping hand and provides support for them in their time of need. The King of Cups also indicates somebody who offers the querent advice and counsel, or perhaps the querent themselves being in that role for another person. It can point to the querent being in a fatherly role specifically. Sometimes the King of Cups can indicate a counsellor, psychotherapist, or spiritual healer, perhaps one that the querent is already visiting, or perhaps suggesting that a possible solution to a problem would be to seek one out.

This card often shows that the querent is in a position of mastery and control over their feelings in the current situation. If it appears in a relationship reading, it puts the querent in control of the direction and movement of the relationship, and shows that they are the dynamic force making the relationship happen and progress. If the querent is undergoing a time of emotional difficulty, they should be advised to try and rise above it, not letting their emotions control them but instead learning to use their emotions to buoy them up, support themselves, and teach them what they need to know about the situation. The King of Cups also suggests to the querent that in this situation they may be their own best healer, rather than looking to others for aid.

Sometimes this card appears in a reading regarding health to point to emotional difficulties that are causing physical ailments, such as stress caused by a relationship negatively affecting the querent's health. Since the King of Cups is the emotions in action, it reminds us that our feelings are not just passive components of our personality but rather active influences upon us in all areas of life. To prevent the querent from becoming more ill or negatively affected by their emotions, they need to learn to overcome the feeling of drowning in them; they must begin making things happen in their emotional world, rather than letting things happen to them.

The King of Cups can also indicate all the ways in which the emotions affect the querent's daily life. In a work or career reading, for instance, it can indicate feelings coming to the forefront in the workplace, or a job that is based on the querent's strong feelings about something. Socially, the King of Cups can put the querent in the role of counsellor and advisor to their friends.

Reversed, the King of Cups indicates strong negative emotions that can affect the querent and the situation. Anger, aggression, jealousy, hatred, and distrust can all be suggested by this card, with strong negative feelings causing the situation to escalate. This card reversed can indicate particularly rough and turbulent emotional situations for the querent, with the querent feeling like they are lost at sea without a guide. It can also indicate a request for aid or healing being refused.

Keywords

Healer, aid, counsellor, advisor, father, emotional control, compassion, active emotions, feeling, volunteer work, care, spiritual wisdom, emotional experience.

King of Pentacles, the Master of the World

"They say that when the great Alexander looked out over the vast lands of his empire, he wept, for he knew that there was nothing left to conquer. I say that this is weakness, for one does not rule for the thrill of it, not for the act of conquering and taking possession, but rather for the security, the status, and all the resulting effects of ownership. To conquer should never be an end in itself, and to possess something should never be the final goal, but simply a means to an end. I have worked and toiled to find a place in the world where I can be master of all I survey. I have conquered a great many things, owned a great number of objects, and amassed a great deal of fortune, yet it is not so that I might enjoy these things themselves. All possessions have limited inherent value. However, they can become intrinsically valuable resources through exchange. Wealth can become security, status, generosity, charity, stability, and comfort. I enjoy all the finest things in life because they represent what we all want. I am therefore the richest man in the world: not just because of my wealth, but because of the joys I find in my community, my family, my loyal friends, my security, my comfortable home, and my well-nourished

body. Like the heat of the flames that consume their fuel, I transmute lead into gold, I carry the offerings of the people to the gods as a sacrifice in the smoke as it rises to heaven, and I see the highest use of all things. If you wish, you are welcome at my table, where you will find the finest foods and the finest drink, all the best things in life. A warm fire, companionship, laughter, and welcome are all yours in my home. What good is all this wealth if it cannot be shared amongst friends? If it doesn't bring you joy? If it doesn't add beauty to your life? I am the Master of the World, and I do not weep when I survey my kingdom."

Fiery part of earth / Taurus

Illumination

The suit of pentacles is associated with earth, and therefore is the suit that is closest to our everyday experience. Although some consider them to be the "lowest" cards of the pack, this also means that they are perhaps some of the most important cards for us, because they teach us about our daily lives in the world of sensation and experience, and the resources at our fingertips. The kings, on the other hand, are all associated with the element of fire, the highest of the four elements and the one closest to spirit. Through the burning flames, mundane matter is consumed and transformed into spirit—and this is why many cultures offer sacrifices to the gods by burning them. As such, the King of Pentacles combines both the "lowest" and the "highest" of the elements, showing us the pinnacle of the everyday world. As a king, he is the ruler of his realm, the leader of his suit, and the mastery of everything pentacles represents: money, resources, health, the environment, family, home, and the everyday world. Thus, our King of Pentacles is the proverbial "king of the castle," the master of all that he surveys, the big company boss, the patriarch of his family, and the business investor. As a combination of fire and earth, he is the flames that consume fuel (compare to the Princess of Wands, the fuel for the flames) and therefore also the means by which the base metal of lead is transmuted into gold—or the Philosopher's Stone—in alchemy. We might go so far as to say that the King of Pentacles is the Alchemist, now holding in his possession the golden Philosopher's Stone itself, ready to use it to transform his own life, and the lives of others, into pure gold as well.

In the card image, we see an older man dressed in rich silk robes with wide sleeves, his head covered with an ornate and opulent headdress. His silk robes are topped at his shoulders with golden pauldrons, and his golden headdress is topped by large, gold-tipped bull's horns. We know immediately from looking at him that he is rich beyond compare, and that he enjoys demonstrating his wealth through his appearance to others. His wide sleeves show us that he currently does not have to work for a living, since such sleeves would traditionally only be worn by those who did not have to undertake any manual labour. This does not make our King of Pentacles lazy, however, but instead it shows that he is a self-made man, at the height of his financial power, who has amassed such a fortune that he no longer needs to work to support himself. All of his past efforts and achievements provide the support for his current lifestyle, and thus he could be seen as the self-made businessman who has the opportunity of taking early retirement—and since he has worked hard all of his life to get to this position, he deserves it! In fact, the King of Pentacles could be any of us in our later years, having worked to save up the finances necessary to no longer need to work. The King of Pentacles is the so-called "American Dream" made real: financial security, happy and comfortable home and family life, freedom to do with your resources as you see fit, and to retire at the top of your chosen career. The gold-tipped bull's horns on his head tell us that he has turned the most basic of resources into his dream; one pair of horns points downward, indicating the everyday, mundane world, whilst a second pair point upward, indicating his aspirations and highest goals.

This king is seated upon a stone pediment that bears his golden throne, showing us that he is a manifestation of the stable, ruling Emperor of the major arcana. The throne also demonstrates his stability, his security, his stalwart values, and the fact that he can be trusted to take responsibility. His foundations are firmly laid, and thus everything that is built upon them will remain sturdy for a long time to come. Behind him are three different constructs: a blossoming cherry tree, a white mountain, and a large stately home. These represent three different ways in which solidity and resources are gained or used. The tree is the natural resources that are available to us, as well as the natural way in which our finances can grow or blossom. The mountain is the riches of the earth, all the minerals and precious metals that we rely on for wealth, as well as the commitment and firm foundations we must have in order to allow investments and resources to grow. Finally, the house is the man-made wealth that we can obtain, such as real estate, transport, and expensive goods, as well as the ways in which we use these things to benefit our lifestyle. The King of Pentacles is the lord of the natural world, a fitting partner to the

Queen of Pentacles, Mother Earth herself, as well as the lord of the mountain from which many prophets over the centuries have pronounced laws. This makes our King of Pentacles a lawmaker, an oath-keeper, and somebody who expects intense loyalty and dedication from others. Finally, he is the lord of the hearth and home, watching over us in our daily lives, protecting and aiding those who want to create wealth for themselves.

In his two hands, cupped and outstretched toward us, is a golden pentacle, symbol of riches and wealth, as well as the everyday world. Not only does this gesture demonstrate his ownership and mastery of the material world, but he is also showing an act of generosity toward others. He is gifting the pentacle to us, offering us a part of his wealth and experience. Thus, the King of Pentacles is the rich, wealthy businessman or self-made man who enjoys the best things in life but enjoys them so much more when others can share in his joy. He'll have the finest port from the best winery, but will only open it when he's throwing a party or has the company of a good friend to share it with. He'll happily pay for the most expensive foods, but only if others will partake as well.

The bull symbolism throughout the card tells us that the King of Pentacles is associated in astrology with Taurus, the sign of possessions, wealth, luxury, and the material world. Taureans are well known for their love of the best things that money can buy; they would rather put a lot of money toward one thing of great quality, than put money toward a lot of things of inferior quality. And, like a Taurean, the King of Pentacles knows the value of things, has a great eye for quality, and knows a cheap imitation when he sees one. Yet he does not acquire quality items just as a status symbol, but as a means to an end, knowing that better quality means they are likely to last longer and work better. However, status is of some importance to the King of Pentacles, but only insofar as he is likely to be in a position to have acquired it in his community through his financial dealings, business, or career.

Revelation

As with all the court cards, the reader should be careful to assess which aspect of the King of Pentacles is appearing in a given reading, since he can represent a person in the querent's life or the querent themselves, as well as personality traits, themes in the querent's life, advice for a particular situation, or even an event. Surrounding cards, the context of the question, and the reader's intuitive response can help determine which.

As a person, the King of Pentacles is materialistic, with excellent taste in food, drink, music, fashion, and anything that can be owned. He (or she) is often in a position related to appraisal of items, such as an antiques dealer, or is a collector of expensive and interesting items. They are usually at a stage in life when luxury and comfort can be enjoyed; hard work in the past paid off long ago, so that now they might enjoy time in their home with family and friends. They place great emphasis on family and quality time with those they love, and can often be found hosting parties (though not the kind the Queen of Wands might; the King of Pentacles prefers brandy or port in the study, or wine and cheese evenings rather than tequila shots by the pool). However, they can also be stubborn, old-fashioned, and dead-set on their particular values. They might find it hard to take on new ideas, preferring to stick to traditional methods and tried and tested means. This is to be expected: the King of Pentacles is a testament to how well these methods have worked.

The King of Pentacles appearing in a reading often represents the querent's boss or employer although conversely it can also indicate retirement. Sometimes this card can point to the querent being self-employed, a "self-made man" (or woman), somebody in full control of their own finances. Occasionally the King of Pentacles shows up in a reading as a business investor, particularly if the querent is thinking about starting their own business. As an advisory card, it can suggest that the querent find wealthy people who would be interested in aiding or assisting them with a goal or plan. It can also suggest that the querent works (or will find work soon) in the financial sector.

In a reading about career or work, the King of Pentacles is certainly one of the best cards the querent can receive. It indicates a time in the querent's life when they are on course for success, financial security, and the height of their career. It also suggests that the querent has worked very hard and now this work is about to pay off, usually with a big bonus, pay rise, or promotion; this is even more certain if this card is accompanied by the Six of Wands or the Four of Wands. It might also suggest that the querent is close to paying off their mortgage or any debts that they have, or becoming reliant only upon themselves for financial security.

In romance and love, the King of Pentacles points to a well founded relationship, strong at its core, realistic and practical, with plenty of focus on the finest things that life has to offer. Strong family values are shared by the couple, yet they might be in danger of becoming too staid and cautious.

Reversed, the King of Pentacles points to investments that are taking longer to come to fruition than expected, or circumstances or an attitude in the querent's life that has led them to become "stuck in the mud," unable to move beyond their current situation. Specifically, they may be stuck in an undesirable financial situation, or they may have trouble saving money, since as soon as they obtain it, they spend it on rent, bills, and debts.

Keywords

Possessions, property, real estate, riches, wealth, generosity, businessman, self-made man, financial security, height of career, status, quality.

PART 4

Using the Tarot Illuminati

There are many ways of using a tarot deck, but the most common is for a card reading. Many people new to tarot wonder if there is a particular method for reading the cards; the answer is that there are many methods, and they are chosen by each reader based on personal preference. In order to do a reading, only three stages are required:

1. Shuffle or otherwise randomize the cards.
2. Lay out the cards in your chosen order or spread pattern.
3. Interpret the card meanings.

This simple process can be expanded upon in myriad ways, such as starting with a prayer or meditation; how many cards you use, what spread you use, whether you turn over all the cards at once or one at a time, and how you read the symbols in the images. There are many spreads to choose from, each for a different purpose, or you can just lay down a few cards and interpret them as you see fit. Here are some spreads you might find useful.

The Sun, Moon, and Stars Spread

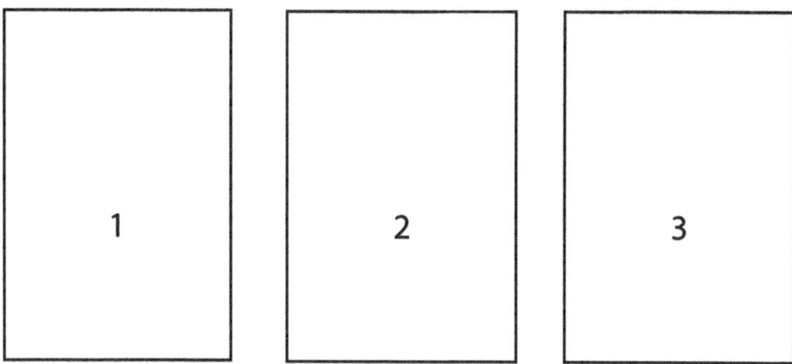

Card 1: The Sun, or the Present. Draw a card to represent the outward appearance or manifestation of the situation; how the world sees it; the actions that it causes.

Card 2: The Moon, or the Past. Draw a card to represent the inward manifestation of the situation; how it makes you (or the querent) feel; the effects it has on you (or them) as a person.

Card 3: The Stars, or the Future. Draw a card to represent the way you (or the querent) can make the situation work for you (or for them).

The Lighting the Lantern Spread

6

5

4

1   2   3

Card 1: What does this situation look like to me?

Card 2: What am I missing?

Card 3: What is keeping me in the dark?

Card 4: Where can I find the light?

Card 5: What will be illuminated?

Card 6: How will I move forward from here?

The Planetary Spread

This is a classic yet simple and adaptable spread that is perfect for the Tarot Illuminati. The planets can be seen as celestial bodies in the heavens, with the sun at the centre, each planet performing a cyclical dance around a shared source of light.

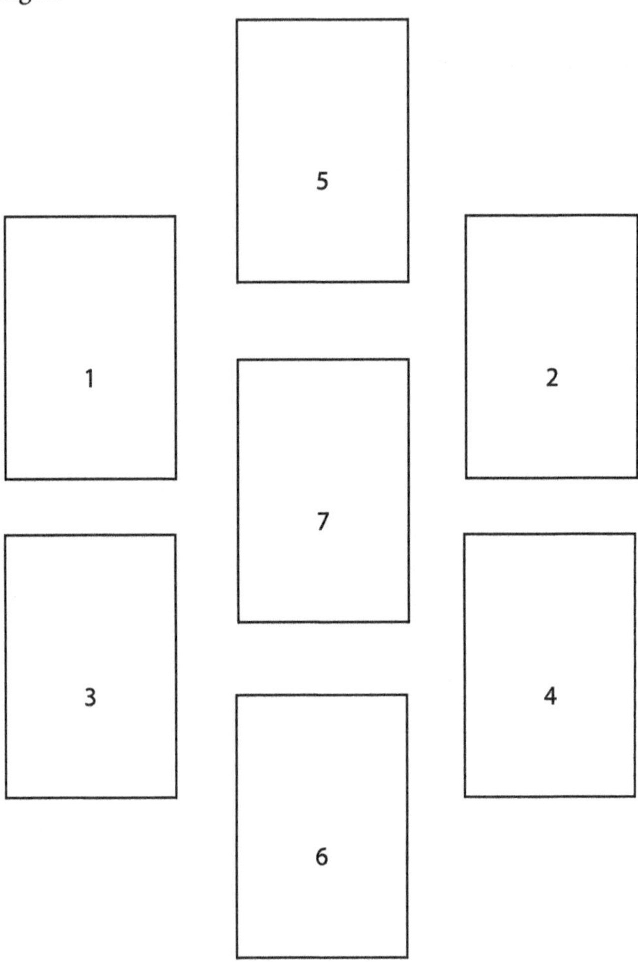

Card 1: Saturn. Karmic return, endings, and time. The issue approached from the perspective of the inevitable, big themes. (Or: What is ending in your life)

Card 2: Mars. Force and aggression, ambition and competition. The issue approached from the perspective of the ego and the self, (Or: What is in conflict or imbalanced in your life)

Card 3: Venus. Love and beauty, harmony and union. The issue approached from the perspective of bringing about peace, harmony, or inspiration. (Or: Your emotional world and relationships)

Card 4: Mercury. The mind and intellect, words and wit. The issue approached from the perspective of reason. (Or: Your intellectual world and thoughts)

Card 5: Jupiter. Growth, expansion, action, and friendship. The issue approached from the perspective of the social world. (Or: Your actions and outward being, your goals)

Card 6: Moon. Receptivity and intuition, dreams, and rhythms. The issue approached from the perspective of intuition. (Or: Your inner world)

Card 7: Sun. The centre and vitality, truth and purpose. The issue approached as a synthesis of all the other cards. (Or: The main focus of your life at this time)

The Rising Sun Spread

A simple spread for when you want to see how something, such as a project, relationship, or job, will progress.

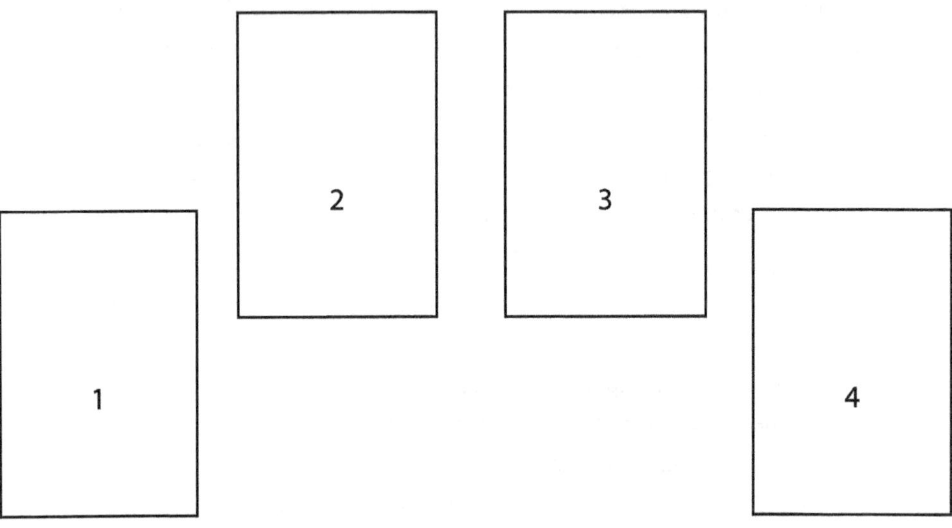

Card 1: Dawn. The beginning, what the topic is like at the start, how it starts, what inspires it.

Card 2: Midday. The halfway point, what the topic is like in the middle.

Card 3: Dusk. The ending, what the topic is like when you complete it or reach its fullest form.

Card 4: Midnight. The aftermath, what you can learn from the topic, how it changes you.

The Stream of Consciousness Reading

Not all tarot readings need to involve a layout or spread, and instead can be approached like a conversation with a friend. Simply start with the Tarot Illuminati in front of you, and think about your question or issue. Shuffle and draw one card from the top of the deck. This answers your initial question.

Now, you can continue to ask further questions about the issue, perhaps for elaboration or clarification, or because the answer you've received raises further issues, or because you need advice. Draw another card from anywhere in the deck to answer each new question, as though you and the cards are having a conversation. Keep going until you feel you've thoroughly explored the question or issue.

The Four Worlds of Your Life

It is useful to regularly sit back and assess the current state of affairs in your life, take stock, and make plans for the future. This is where tarot comes in, showing itself to be more than just a fortune-telling device. It can help you examine the present—where you are, what themes are currently playing themselves out in your life—and help you work out where you should go from here. This simple spread will give you an overview of your life, splitting it into the four realms of the four suits of the minor arcana and their associated elements.

1. Remove all the major arcana and court cards from the deck and set them aside. You won't be using them.
2. Separate the minor arcana into their four suits—pentacles, cups, swords, and wands—and set them into separate piles next to each other in that order.
3. Shuffle each pile and place the cards face down. Relax, clear your mind, and ask the cards to give you an overview of your life at this time.
4. Draw the top card from each pile and lay it face up on top of its pile.
5. Read the first card, pentacles, as the current theme or state of affairs in your everyday world of work, money, daily life, health, and home.
6. Read the second card, cups, as the current theme or state of affairs in your social or romantic life.
7. Read the third card, swords, as the current theme or state of affairs in your intellectual life, including any lessons you need to learn at this time.
8. Read the final card, wands, as the current theme or state of affairs in your inner world, your personality, ego, energy, passion, and drive.
9. Compare each card with the others: Are there any shared numbers? Did you, for instance, draw more than one card numbered five? If so, take a look back at the numerology section and see what this recurring number has to say to you at this time.

Making Light Work 8

In the Tarot Illuminati, light is an important aspect of the cards and their meanings. Examine each card, beginning with the major arcana, and ask yourself these questions for each.

1. What is the origin of the light? Is it solar? Lunar? From stars? A man-made light source? Fire? Is it coming from an object?
2. What is the strength of the light? Is it faint? Bright? Hidden?
3. Are the figures in the card turned away from the light, or toward it? Are they doing anything with the light? Do they seem to have a special relationship with it?
4. Can you see the light reflected anywhere in the card?
5. What is the focus of the light? What does it illuminate the most?

If the message you get from the card is negative or upsetting, consider how you could improve the scene by changing the light or illumination in the card image. Could you give a figure in the card a lantern? Could you give a figure in the card sunglasses? Could you simply turn a figure's head to face the other direction? What does this suggest to you about a possible solution to a problem?

Making Light Work 9

In order to become more familiar with the card images and symbols on a more personal level, and to provide you with some handy phrases that can jog your memory or inspire interpretation during a reading, try this exercise.

1. Choose a card (or let one randomly choose you!) from the deck.
2. Hold it up before you, close your eyes, and relax.
3. After a few moments, open your eyes and let them rest on two symbols.
4. For each of these symbols, create a word. This word might be the actual symbol—e.g., "the star," "the woman," "the fiery lake,"—or it might be something more abstract that the symbol reminds you of—e.g. "love," "family," "the journey," "the challenge."
5. Put these two words together to create a short key phrase for that card. For instance, if the two symbols you picked out from, say, the Ten of Cups were the house and the family, you could use the words "security" and "community," creating the phrase "the security of community" for this card.

Other examples might be:

Eight of Pentacles: "the artificer's patience" (the blacksmith as "artificer" and the careful way in which he pours molten metal into a mould, "patience")

Three of Swords: "the weathering of sorrow" (the bad weather, "weathering," and the bleeding heart, "sorrow")

The Empress: "the beauty of fertility"

Lighting the Way From Here...

The tarot journey of discovery never ends, and there are no tarot experts—only those who have more experience with it than others. Nobody can know everything about this art, and thus it offers the student a lifetime of exploration and inspiration. The Tarot Illuminati is designed with this in mind, and you will find that over the years you notice different aspects of the cards, or their voices change slightly, or another level of meaning becomes clear in the symbolism. So what can you do with the Tarot Illuminati next?

Keep a Tarot Journal

It's fun to chart your progress with the tarot, and keeping a journal allows you to do exactly that while also documenting your learning. In a journal, you can record all your readings, your studies of the cards, spreads you try out or create, the results of exercises from this book and any others you read, quotes that remind you of certain cards, brainstorms, doodles, and more. The contents of a tarot journal are unique to each individual, and it is your personalized learning tool.

Get Together with Other Tarot Enthusiasts

Having a hobby or passion is great, but it's even better when shared with others. There are plenty of online forums for tarot enthusiasts to meet and discuss all things tarot—its history, occult symbolism, spreads, meanings, newly published decks and books, and even fun games with the cards. You might be lucky enough to have a tarot study group near you, or something more informal like a tarot coffee club. If not, why not set one up yourself? This is the best way to pick up new ideas and techniques from others.

Keep Practising

It's never too early in your studies to start practising readings. You may be too nervous in the early stages of your tarot journey to give readings for others, but you can try reading for yourself, for fictional characters on TV or in books, for your cat, or for imaginary situations. The key is not necessarily to predict actual events, but to practice picking out meaning from the card images and weaving it into an interpretation. When you gain confidence, start offering readings to friends and family. You'll be surprised how much fun it can be, and how useful it is for you.

Read Widely

As with any skill or subject, the more you learn about it, the more you realize how much you don't know. With this in mind, you will soon discover a wide and diverse world of tarot, saturated with books and decks, blogs and groups, approaches and techniques, all for you to access and perhaps integrate into your own tarot practice. Read widely! Every book you pick up is like an individual with years and years of experience, sharing their approach and knowledge with you. You may not like their approach, so you don't have to use it, but there may be something you do like about it that you can use. The more you read, the more complete your picture of tarot will be, but try not to take the word of any one author as gospel.

Think Outside the Box

Try not to fall into the trap of limiting tarot through your own beliefs. It is an incredibly versatile tool that can be used or approached in any way you choose. It can relate to anything in our inner and outer worlds and everything big and small in our universe. Therefore, it contains the serious as well as the silly, the most mundane as well as the most abstract. Why not play games with the cards? Why not have conversations with them as though they were characters in a fantasy novel? Why not *write* a fantasy novel inspired by the cards? Why not use it to brainstorm a possible new business idea? The limits are only defined by you.